# THE NTL MANAGERS' HANDBOOK

Edited by Roger A. Ritvo, Ph.D.
and Alice G. Sargent, Ed.D.

D0778079

© 1983 NTL Institute.

All rights reserved. Some articles have been reprinted with permission from other sources. Each article cites the holder of the copyright for that particular work.

For information on ordering copies of this book or obtaining permission to reprint articles, write to:

Publications Department
NTL Institute
P.O. Box 9155, Rosslyn Station
Arlington, Virginia 22209

Library of Congress Catalog Card Number 83-061458
ISBN 0-9610392-0-5

# Table of Contents

## Introduction

## Section I: Laboratory Education

## Section II: Managing Interpersonal Relationships

# Introduction

In 1947, National Training Laboratories—now the NTL Institute for Applied Behavioral Science—began to apply the concepts of adult learning and social and personal change to training for educators and community leaders. "Laboratory Education" was designed to test new methods for changing human behavior and for social interaction. Eventually, many of these principles were used in management training and team development. NTL's prevailing values have been the development of the individual, collaborative problem solving, planning for change with an organization, managing conflict, encouraging diversity, and defining organization effectiveness.

Publication of the *NTL Manager's Handbook* and the development of NTL's new management track provide a forum in which managers can explore these values and the competencies necessary for managerial effectiveness. In this book we define interpersonal competence, which is part of the special contribution that NTL members and associates make to management education. We solicited manuscripts from the more than 300 NTL members and from at least 20 other colleagues with whom we work closely. The results have been rich and highly rewarding.

We think the book will encourage both NTL members and managers to look at interpersonal competence in depth. We know from Henry Mintzberg's (1974) research that managers spend up to 90% of their time interacting with other people, and 70% of that takes place in small groups and meetings. We also know that managers spend 10% of their time interacting with their bosses, 50% interacting with subordinates, and the remainder of that time interacting with people outside the chain of command. This requires entrepreneurial skills and social skills, alliance- and compliance-producing behaviors, and supportive and directive styles.

Most people have never been "taught" these skills. Most of us have learned our behavior through people in our family of origin, without much chance to understand the impact of the behavior or to have a variety of role models. Our schools had no curriculum in psychological education. Nowhere did we learn about the self-concept, an awareness of the impact of our behavior on others, how to function effectively in groups, how to manage conflict, or how to express feelings like love, fear, joy, anger, and pain. In these areas, we have been left to fend for ourselves, and few of us have the necessary repertoire of behaviors to act effectively in a wide variety of situations.

Until recently, we have been able to function in organizations by relying primarily on our technical competence. With the vast transitions occurring within organizations now, however, we must confront a new environment. This calls for a much broader range of skills. What has changed?

- The rapid shifts in technology bring with them a host of human problems.
- New organization designs demand greater feedback from the bottom up.
- Organizations have become more interdependent, from matrix to temporary task groups.
- We need to develop leaders who know how to manage and managers who know how to lead.
- We now have a new work force filled with diversity—with women and minorities who don't assimilate but who want a multicultural work environment.
- The work place must be characterized by trust if we are going to increase productivity.
- We need to learn how to stay healthy in organizations and to combat the distress we experience because of chronic and cyclical stress.
- Planning and operations need to be linked much more closely.
- Group contacts in organizations must become much more effective, and people need to be given their fair place as a critical resource.
- We now have a work force that views career transitions as options and no longer limits itself to simply climbing the organization's ladder.

In this book we discuss many of the competencies necessary for responding effectively to these changes. We take a situational or contingency approach to management and a competency-based approach to developing and evaluating managers. The competency discussed here includes interpersonal competence, entrepreneurial competence, effectiveness as a team member and team leader, self-awareness, and competence as a change agent. We have organized this book into three sections. The first section focuses on the NTL laboratory education experience. Section two deals with managing interpersonal relationships, boss-subordinate relationships, relationships with minorities and women, and situational management. The final section concerns organizational and systems change, including human resources management, the back-home application of laboratory learning, career development, performance management, quality circles, and affirmative action.

We want to express our deep appreciation to the following persons: Susan Sherman and Cathy Messina, who provided editing and stylistic suggestions to complement their organizational skills; Marilyn Swenson, who pursued this idea from its inception; and Virginia Sprecher, who assisted in the completion of the book. We are grateful to the vision of NTL that began with Lee Bradford and continues with the current Board of Directors and NTL membership. NTL has provided so many of us with developmental opportunities to pilot our dreams and to become part of a rich network of colleagues.□

**Alice G. Sargent**
**Roger A. Ritvo**

## Reference

Mintzberg, H. *The Nature of Managerial Work.* New York: Harper & Row, 1974.

# Section I: Laboratory Education

# What Is Sensitivity Training?

Charles Seashore

*"The opportunity to link up a philosophy of management with specific behaviors that are congruent with or anti-thetical to that philosophy makes the T Group particularly relevant to understanding the large organization."*

Sensitivity training is one type of experience-based learning. Participants work together in a small group over an extended period of time, learning through analysis of their own experiences, including feelings, reactions, perceptions, and behavior. The duration varies according to the specific design, but most groups meet for a total of 10 to 40 hours. This may be in a solid block, as in a marathon weekend program, or two to six hours in a day in a one- or two-week residential program, or spread out over several weekends, a semester, or a year.

The sensitivity training group may stand by itself or be a part of a larger laboratory training design which might include role playing, case studies, theory presentations, and intergroup exercises. This paper focuses mainly on the T Group (the *T* stands for *training*) as the primary setting for sensitivity training. However, many of the comments here also apply to other components of laboratory training.

## A Typical T-Group Starter

The staff member in a typical T Group, usually referred to as the trainer, might open the group in a variety of ways. The following statement is an example:

This group will meet for many hours and will serve as a kind of laboratory where each individual can increase her or his understanding of the forces which influence individual behavior and the performance of groups and organizations. The data for learning will be our own behavior, feelings, and reactions. We begin with no definite structure or organization, no agreed-upon procedures, and no specific agenda. It will be up to us to fill the vacuum created by the lack of these familiar elements and to study our group as we evolve. My role will be to help the group to learn from its own experience, but not to act as a traditional chairperson nor to suggest how we should organize, what our

concepts and theory, and as they practice new behavior and

values underlying their behavior, as they acquire appropriate

working with people is maximized as people examine the basic

5. *Skill acquisition and values.* The development of new skills in

masking their feelings.

are communicating what they are actually feeling rather than

can be open, honest, and direct with one another so that they

decrease their defensiveness. In authentic relationships persons

people and thereby increase their sense of self-esteem and

learn when they establish authentic relationships with other

4. *Authentic relationships and learning.* People are most free to

detail so that valid generalizations can be drawn.

encouraged to examine their experiences together in enough

T-Group aim is to provide a setting in which individuals are

combination of experience and conceptualization. A major

3. *Experience and conceptualization.* Most learning is a

that are facing the group.

working, the style of an individual's participation, or the issues

He or she helps participants to focus on the way the group is

examination and understanding of the experiences in the group.

2. *Staff role.* The staff person's role is to facilitate the

of the group.

readiness, and the relationship they develop with other members

own learning. What people learn depends upon their own style,

1. *Learning responsibility.* Participants are responsible for their

training from other more traditional models of learning:

the nature of the learning process that distinguish T-Group

Underlying T-Group training are the following assumptions about

## Underlying Assumptions

reactions that are the data for learning.

turn is having an impact on them. It is these perceptions and

observing and reacting to the behavior of other members and in

Whatever role a person chooses to play, he or she also is

directive role, like that of the typical chairperson.

unusual for an individual to try to get the trainer to play a more

a clearer sense of the direction the group may take. It is not

discussion. Others may withdraw and wait in silence until they get

election of a chairperson or the selection of a topic for

themselves. Some may try to organize the group by promoting an

Into this ambiguous situation members then proceed to inject

begin in whatever way you feel will be most helpful.

include. With these few comments, I think we are ready to

procedure should be, or exactly what our agenda will

obtain feedback on the degree to which their behavior produces the intended impact.

## Goals and Outcomes

Goals and outcomes of sensitivity training can be classified in terms of potential learning concerning individuals, groups, and organizations.

1. *The individual point of view.* Most T-Group participants gain a picture of the impact that they make on other group members. Participants can assess the degree to which that impact corresponds with or deviates from their conscious intentions. They can also get a picture of the *range of perceptions* of any given act. It is as important to understand that different people may see the same piece of behavior differently—for example, as supportive or antagonistic, relevant or irrelevant, clear or ambiguous—as it is to understand the impact on any given individual. In fact, very rarely do all members of a group have even the same general perceptions of a given individual or a specific event.

Some people report that they try out behavior in the T Group that they have never tried before. This experimentation can enlarge their view of their own potential and competence and provide the basis for continuing experimentation.

2. *The group point of view.* The T Group can focus on forces which affect the characteristics of the group such as the level of commitment and follow-through resulting from different methods of making decisions, the norms controlling the amount of conflict and disagreement that is permitted, and the kinds of data that are gathered. Concepts such as cohesion, power, group maturity, climate, and structure can be examined using the experiences in the group to better understand how these same forces operate in the back-home situation.

3. *The organization point of view.* Status, influence, division of labor, and styles of managing conflict are among organizational concepts that may be highlighted by analyzing the events in the small group. Subgroups that form can be viewed as analogous to units within an organization. It is then possible to look at the relationships between groups, examining such factors as competitiveness, communications, stereotyping, and understanding.

One of the more important possibilities for a participant is that of examining the kinds of assumptions and values which underlie the behavior of people as they attempt to manage the work of the group. The opportunity to link up a philosophy of management with specific behaviors that are congruent with or antithetical to that philosophy makes the T Group particularly relevant to understanding the large organization.

### Research and Impact

Research evidence on the effectiveness of sensitivity training is rather scarce and often subject to serious methodological problems. The following generalizations do seem to be supported by the available data:

- People who attend sensitivity training programs are more likely to improve their managerial skills than those who do not (as reported by their peers, superiors, and subordinates).

- Everyone does not benefit equally. Roughly two-thirds of the participants are seen as increasing their skills after attendance at laboratories. This figure represents an average across a number of studies.

- Many individuals report extremely significant changes and impacts on their lives as workers, family members, and citizens. This kind of anecdotal report should be viewed cautiously in terms of direct application to job settings, but it is consistent enough that it is clear that T-Group experiences can have a powerful and positive impact on individuals.

- The incidence of serious stress and mental disturbance during training is difficult to measure, but it is estimated to affect less than one percent of participants and in almost all cases to occur in persons with a history of prior disturbances.□

# Improving Face-to-Face Relationships*

Edgar H. Schein

*"One can hardly work out goals with others if one does not know where one's own values and goals lie."*

The challenges of management in the 1980s are enormous, but they are fairly easy to identify. The great difficulties that we face lie not in deciding what our goals should be, but in determining how to achieve them. Our problems in this area are problems of implementation: How can we reach goals that are often perfectly clear but seemingly impossible to attain?

Several explanations of these problems readily come to mind:

- Large systems have become too complex to be understood.
- "Bureaucracy" makes it impossible to get anything done.
- Intergroup hostility paralyzes all constructive effort.
- Power politics undermine and subvert rational action.
- Irrationality and human resistance to change defeat even the wisest programs.

All of these explanations are true, but they are also incomplete. Sometimes we use them only as excuses for failure rather than as constructive analyses of our management problems. On the other hand, we have learned something about implementation in the last 40 years or so, and what we have learned takes us back to one fundamental principle: societies, organizations, and families are human groups, and the face-to-face relationships among the members of these groups are a basic element of any social action. Whatever else we need in the way of systems, procedures, and mechanisms, the process of social action always starts with face-to-face relationships among people.

Think of face-to-face relationships as the glue that holds organizations together; such relationships provide the links in the implementation chain. Therefore, we should take a fresh look at these relationships to see if we can articulate some of the skills that can make them more constructive and thus enable us to move toward solving some of the pressing problems of the 1980s.

Reprinted from "Improving Face-to-Face Relationships," by Edgar H. Schein, *Sloan Management Review*, 22(2), 43–52, by permission of the publisher. © 1981 by the Sloan Management Review Association. All rights reserved.

* The author would like to acknowledge the Centre D'Etudes Industrielle, Geneva, Switzerland for its support in writing this paper. This paper is adapted from an address delivered to the 50th Anniversary Convocation of the Sloan Fellows Program, Cambridge, Massachusetts on October 3, 1980.

## The Elements of Face-to-Face Relationships

What does it take to build, maintain, improve, and, if need be, repair face-to-face relationships? I would like to discuss nine different elements that are all closely interrelated yet distinct in important ways. The following elements reflect motives and values, perceptual skills, and behavioral skills:

1. Self-insight and a sense of one's own identity;
2. Cross-cultural sensitivity—the ability to decipher other people's values;
3. Cultural/moral humility—the ability to see one's own values as not necessarily better or worse than another's values;
4. A proactive problem-solving orientation—the conviction that interpersonal and cross-cultural problems can be solved;
5. Personal flexibility—the ability to adopt different responses and approaches as needed by situational contingencies;
6. Negotiation skills—the ability to explore differences creatively, to locate some common ground, and to solve the problem;
7. Interpersonal and cross-cultural tact—the ability to solve problems with people without insulting them, demeaning them, or destroying their "face";
8. Repair strategies and skills—the ability to resurrect, to revitalize, and to rebuild damaged or broken face-to-face relationships; and
9. Patience.

I would like to discuss each of these elements in turn, putting most of the attention on those which have been insufficiently attended to in prior analyses and on those which are especially relevant to repair strategies.

### Self-Insight

One can hardly work out common goals with others if one does not know where one's values and goals lie. Leaders and managers especially must know where they are going, and they must be able to articulate their own goals. Parents and spouses must make a valiant effort to lift to the surface what is often left implicit—their own life goals and targets—so that there can be genuine negotiation among family members in the different life stages.

Self-insight is a competence—the ability to see oneself accurately and to evaluate oneself fairly. Through feedback from others and through systematic self-study, we can improve our ability to see ourselves. As we increase in self-insight, we lay the foundations for self-acceptance, which is to some extent a prerequisite for some of the other skills to be discussed.

## Cross-Cultural Sensitivity

We cannot offer leadership if we do not have a perspective on ourselves and on others, and we cannot gain such a perspective if we continue to be ethnocentric—to notice and appreciate only our own culture and values. Cross-cultural issues are not limited to the dramatic differences which can be identified in how different countries operate. Many of the most harmful cases of cultural misunderstanding occur right under our noses—with our spouses, friends, children, and subordinates—because norms, values, and behavioral codes vary widely within any country. American managers often tell tales of woe of trying to transfer people from the Deep South to Manhattan, or from an urban center to a rural plant site.

Deciphering values, motives, aspirations, and basic assumptions across occupational and social class lines is particularly difficult. The son of a successful middle-class businessman finds it hard to understand the values and career aspirations of the son of an immigrant or an unskilled worker. The general manager finds it hard to understand the values and career aspirations of the technically oriented person and vice versa. People in the different functional areas of a business find it hard to decipher each other's values and aspirations (Lawrence & Lorsch, 1967).

## Cultural Differences between Countries

When we go to countries with different languages and cultures, we do wake up to the need to sharpen our deciphering skills. But even then we have a strong tendency to look for similarities and to rationalize that "people are people" and "business is business" no matter where it is conducted. My own tendency to ignore differences was brought home to me during a visit to Australia, which is superficially and historically similar to the U. S. It took me quite a while to discover that while Australians (like Americans) are achievement oriented, they also have the "tall poppy syndrome": one must not stand out above the crowd; one must accomplish things without seeming to work too hard at them; and one must not take too much personal credit for one's accomplishments.

I kept hearing how complacent and security oriented the Australians were, even when I dealt with what seemed to be some pretty tough, aggressive managers. What one's true motives are and what is culturally acceptable as a legitimate explanation of one's motives are not, of course, necessarily the same. In comparing America and Australia, one sees a paradoxical reversal. In Australia, people claim to be mostly security oriented, though companies admitted they had many aggressive, ambitious, power-seeking managers working for them. In the U. S., the popular image holds that most people are ambitious and want to climb right to the top of the organization—though I encounter a growing number of allegedly ambitious managers who admit in private that they do not feel motivated to continue the "rat race," that they would like early retirement, or that they are considering another career altogether. Both public images reflect cultural norms, yet both to some degree misrepresent the actual state of affairs. The public selves we wear—the way we are supposed to present ourselves to others—make up a strongly ingrained set of cultural values in their own right, and tact prevents us from puncturing the illusions cultures teach us to project.

## "Face Work"

Erving Goffman (1967) has written articulately about what he calls "face work"—the behavior of people in a social situation that is designed to help everyone maintain the self they choose to project in that particular situation. Selves are forever constructed, and the audience for any given performance is culturally bound to uphold as much as possible the identities the actors claim. At the minimum, we nod and say "uh huh" when someone talks to us, or we try to laugh politely at a joke that is not really funny, or we ignore embarrassing incidents. If our boss's actions or demeanor tell us that this person believes her- or himself to be very competent in handling a given meeting, we rarely challenge this claim, even though we may privately believe that the boss will totally mismanage the meeting. The skill in this situation is our ability to compensate for his incompetence or to repair what damage may have been done. But we do not destroy the boss's face.

## The Reciprocity of Relationships

One of the most interesting features of the cultural norms of face-to-face interactions is their symmetric, reciprocal, exchange nature. We sometimes get into difficulty because we do not know how to complete an interaction. When someone in a strange country offers you an object in her or his house because you have admired it, are you supposed to take it and reciprocate at some future time when the visitor is in your home, or is it appropriate to refuse? The whole question of when and how to say yes or no is fraught with difficulty when talking across cultures or subcultures. And, as many businessmen have found out, how to interpret a yes or a no is even more difficult.

The ability to detect the subtleties of how others perceive situations and of what the values of others are requires both formal training and practical experience. Learning a new language would seem to be a prerequisite since so much of every culture becomes encoded into the language. Many people pride themselves on their extensive travel, even making lists of how many countries they have been in, without ever encountering or deciphering any of the cultures of those countries; they do not learn the languages and therefore miss the important nuances of what happens. I have heard repeatedly from multinational companies that one of the best prescriptions for success in an overseas assignment is to take time to learn the local language.

## Cultural/Moral Humility

Beyond self-insight and the ability to understand others, we need something which we might call cultural/moral humility. Can we not only sense the values of other people but, more importantly, positively appreciate them? Can we see our own culture and values only as different, not necessarily as better? Our tendency to think of things as "funny," or "odd" is a good diagnostic here. I have often been shown or told about funny things people do in other countries. An American visitor to the mainland of China found it amusing that some Chinese farmers were so proud of owning tractors that were, in fact, useless; the tractors could not turn on the tight terraces and they did not have attachable plows to pull. The fact that a Chinese farmer did not even know the function of the pin to which the plow attaches struck this American as funny and weird. It never occurred to him that his own utilitarian, pragmatic values might not be the only relevant ones in this situation.

Many American managers lack cultural humility. We are more pragmatic than other people, and if we encounter people less pragmatic, we view *them* as odd rather than wonder about the oddity of our being so pragmatic. We don't consider our own culture as funny, odd, and in need of explanation, yet it is our culture which is probably in a statistical sense the most different from all other cultures. Let me give a couple of examples.

1. Our mercantile attitude—embodied in our marketing skills and our efforts to sell anything to anybody—strikes people in other parts of the world as rather crass and superficial. I have encountered managers in other countries who have real

reservations about making products that they consider to have no intrinsic value, and who have even greater reservations about using advertising skills to create markets for such products.

2. Our attitude toward efficiency—attempting to reduce all costs for the sake of higher profit margins, even if those costs include people's jobs—falls clearly out of line with the value systems in some other countries. Yet we take the importance of efficiency for granted. We do not think of people as capital investments and we find it hard to comprehend systems of guaranteed lifetime employment.

My point is not to dissect the value system of the U. S. but rather to identify a strong tendency I have seen in managers all over the world (Americans and non-Americans alike) to be ethnocentric—to assume that one's own values are the best, and that one is excused from having to know what others think and value, or at least from having to take very seriously what others think and value. Such an absence of cultural humility can be a dangerous weakness when we attempt face-to-face negotiations or problem solving. This point is important whenever we deal with people whose values differ from our own, whether these people live within our own society or come from other countries.

## Proactive Problem-Solving Orientation

Solving face-to-face problems, especially where difficult cross-cultural understanding and humility are required, presupposes a faith that problems can be solved if one works at them and an assumption that active problem solving will produce positive results. Communication and understanding are difficult to achieve, but if one does not even try, then no possibility for achievement exists.

A proactive orientation is itself to some degree a cultural characteristic. When Americans take the "can-do" attitude, how do we determine when we are coming on too strongly, or when we are actually intruding in private lifespace in our eagerness to establish constructive face-to-face relationships in order to solve problems. The anthropologist Edward Hall (1977) has given us many excellent examples of how conducting business in different cultural contexts must be delicately handled lest we invade people's territory and unwittingly destroy the possibility of better relationships (Hall, 1977).

What I mean by a "proactive orientation" is a *motivation* to work on problems, not necessarily a high level of overt activity. We must base our actual course of action on genuine cultural understanding and not simply on a desire to act. As in the case of international diplomacy, we should always be ready to negotiate. No matter how bad the situation is between management and employees in a company or industry, each party should always be ready to sit down and try again to talk face-to-face.

## Personal Flexibility

We benefit little from sensing situations accurately if we cannot take advantage of what we perceive. I know people who can tell you exactly what is going on but who cannot alter their own behavior to adjust to what they know to be the realities. One of the reasons why experiential learning methods—such as sensitivity training or transactional analysis workshops—have been so successful is that they allow experimentation on the part of participants, thus permitting the participants to enlarge their repertory of face-to-face behavior. Role playing is perhaps the prototype of such behavioral training and is clearly a necessary component of face-to-face skill development (see Schein, 1980; Harris, 1967; Polster & Polster, 1973).

## Negotiation Skills

Much has been written about the process of negotiation and the skills needed to be an effective negotiator. To a considerable degree, what has been said reflects the same themes that I am focusing on here. Negotiation requires great sensitivity, humility, self-insight, motivation to solve the problem, and behavioral flexibility. Part of the sensitivity required is the ability to decipher others' values. Another part is the ability to elicit information from others and to judge the validity of that information. Face-to-face relationships are not always benign, not always comfortable, not always safe, and not always open, yet they are always crucial to problem solving. Especially in situations where there initially is conflict, we need the ability to maintain relationships so that negotiations can continue, to decipher messages when deliberate concealment is attempted, to convince and to persuade, to bluff when necessary, and to figure out what the other will do in response to our own moves.

As we know, negotiations can become so dangerous and threatening to one's face that we have to resort to neutral third parties as catalysts, go-betweens, message carriers, and the like. Often what is most needed is to explain the values and goals of each principal to the other. Principals often lack the skills to reveal themselves to each other without making themselves seem either too vulnerable or too threatening (Walton, 1969). One of my Australian manager friends speculated that a lack of verbal articulation skills seriously hampers negotiation in his country. He noticed that in many labor-management confrontations in Australia each side would blurt out bluntly, and with some pride at their own ability to be so open, exactly what their *final* demands were. When these demands proved to be incompatible, an impasse occurred. The situation then deteriorated to name calling and to seeing the other side as being stubborn and exploitative. This manager speculated that the educational system was partly responsible for this situation in that written English is heavily emphasized in school while spoken English is hardly attended to at all. He thought of Australians as being quite inarticulate, on the average, and therefore at a real disadvantage in face-to-face negotiations.

The important point is to recognize that openness is not an absolute value in face-to-face relationships. For some purposes, it is better not to reveal exactly where one stands. One of the ways that relationships become more intimate is through successive minimal self-revelations which constitute interpersonal tests of acceptance: If you accept this much of me, then perhaps I can run the risk of revealing a bit more of myself. Total openness may be safe and charming when total acceptance is guaranteed, but it can become highly dangerous when goals are not compatible, and acceptance is therefore not guaranteed at all (Bennis et al., 1979).

## Interpersonal and Cross-Cultural Tact

Negotiation requires great tact. The tactfulness I refer to here is the *behavioral* manifestation of the cultural humility discussed above. If we don't feel humble in the face of others' values, we will certainly offend them. On the other hand, if we feel that there is genuinely room for different values in this world, then we have the basis for showing in our speech and behavior an adequate level of respect for others.

## Repair Strategies and Skills

The repair strategies and repair skills needed to fix broken or spoiled relationships, careers, lives, negotiations, and other interpersonal or intergroup situations are probably the most important yet least understood of face-to-face skills. As the world becomes more complex and more intercultural, there will be more communication breakdowns, diplomatic disasters, losses of confidence and trust, hurt feelings between individuals and groups, hostilities, wars, and other forms of social pathology and disorder. It will not help us to resign ourselves to such situations, to lament our cruel fate, or to merely explain why something happened; what will be helpful is our attempting to repair these situations.

The concept of "repair strategies" was brought to my attention by Jacqueline Goodnow, a cognitive social psychologist who now teaches in Australia. She has been struck by the Australian tendency to "knock" things rather than to solve problems. I often heard the phrase in Australia that "we are a nation of knockers," which means that when things go wrong there is a tendency to blame government, unions, management, multinationals, OPEC, or any other handy group rather than to figure out how to repair the situation.

## The Perception of New Elements

Repair strategies presume and require not only constructive motivation but also *the ability to see new elements in the situation which one may not have noticed before.* The new elements may be *in oneself;* one may discover that one has been unfair or selfish, or lacking insight concerning the consequences of one's own behavior or concerning one's true motives. In this instance repair may begin with apology.

One may also discover new things in the other people in the situation; *they may have changed in significant ways.* One of the most damaging things we do in our face-to-face relationships is to freeze our assumptions about ourselves and others. Our stereotype of the other person can become a straitjacket or a self-fulfilling prophecy. McGregor (1960) gave us the best example of this years ago in noting that if we assume people are lazy we will begin to treat them as if they are lazy, which will eventually train them to be lazy. The energy and creativity which they might have applied to their jobs then gets channeled either into other situations or into angry attempts to defeat the organization.

We want and need predictability in our relationships, but that very need often prevents us from repairing damaged relationships. It may be psychologically easier to see the worker as lazy and hostile because we can then predict her or his behavior and can know exactly how to respond. To renegotiate the relationship, to permit some participation, or to admit that we may have been wrong in our assessment is to make ourselves psychologically vulnerable. We then enter a period in the relationship that may be less predictable.

As in the case of negotiation, we may need the help of third parties—counselors, therapists, consultants, or other helpers—to get through the period of vulnerability and instability. Often the motivation to repair is there but the skill is not—in the sense that neither party has self-insight, the capacity to hear the values or

goals of the other, the articulateness to negotiate without further
destruction of face, or the emotional strength or self-confidence
to make concessions to reach at least a common ground
of understanding.

## Taking the Other's Perspective

Sociologists taught us long ago that in childhood the very process
of becoming social is a process of learning to take the role of the
other. We could not really understand each other at all—even
though we live in the same culture and speak the same
language—without the ability to put ourselves in the other
person's shoes. We could not develop judgments, standards, and
morals without the ability to see our own behavior from the
standpoint of others, which gradually becomes abstracted into
what sociologists call all the "generalized other," or what we
sometimes label as our "reference group." Guilt and shame, the
products of one's internalized conscience, can be thought of as
the accumulated empathy of a decade of growing up. As adults
we have the capacity to see ourselves from others' perspectives
and this capacity should help us to develop repair strategies. Why
is it, then, that so often we end up in complete disagreement,
convinced that the only thing the other party really wants is to
gain a selfish advantage at our expense?

One factor certainly is our need to maintain our position and
our pride. Having suffered an affront, a loss of face, or a loss of
advantage sometime in the past, we feel the only safe thing to do
is to protect ourselves from any repetition of such an unpleasant
event. We may, in addition, recognize that our own interest and
that of the other party are genuinely in conflict. If we are in a
zero-sum game, we may not be able to afford too much
sympathy for our opponent. In such an instance, a repair strategy
would call for the ability to locate some superordinate goals,
where goal conflict is not intrinsic, and to build a new set of
interactions around such superordinate goals. Skillful diplomats,
negotiators, and statesmen build their entire careers around the
development of such repair strategies. They create one repair
strategy after another as the people they deal with destroy one
relationship after another.

Ordinary day-to-day relations within families, between
managers and subordinates, and between groups in organizations
are forever in danger of breaking down. We must be prepared to
diagnose the situation when breakdown occurs and to have the
skills to repair it if repair is needed. Let me give an example of
what is involved.

## Labor-Management Relations

My second example has to do with face-to-face skills and repair strategies in labor-management situations. I am struck by the degree to which these situations seem to turn into intergroup struggles—struggles among unions, managements, and government bodies or political parties. Once the conflicts have escalated to the intergroup level, it is easy to give up one's proactive problem-solving orientation and to resign oneself to the idea that the problem is essentially unsolvable. Yet when one looks at successful enterprises—those which have managed to maintain harmony between management and employees—one realizes that the key to this harmony is a high degree of mutual trust, active listening, appropriate levels of participation, and consistently constructive face-to-face communications.

An example will highlight what I mean. A plant manager told me that he had spent many years developing a constructive relationship with his employees, in spite of the fact that they belong to a strong national union which periodically calls for national strikes. One year his employees refused to strike. They were told by the national union that it would get all the suppliers of the plant to refuse to deliver, thus effectively shutting the plant down. Under these conditions, the manager and the employees got together and agreed that the employees should go out on strike, but everyone knew that it was not over local issues. The manager did not hold it against his subordinates that they had gone out on strike.

Intergroup trust, reinforced by open face-to-face communications on relevant issues, was strong enough to keep this plant functioning well even in a larger context that made periodic strikes inevitable. What we can learn from this is that constructive face-to-face relationships are necessary even though they may not be sufficient. Solving a problem at the national level will probably be useless if there continue to be destructive low-trust relationships within the enterprise.

## Disengaging the Critical Mind

Achieving trust in a labor-management situation that has developed into a hostile intergroup conflict over a period of decades seems like a tall order. One prerequisite to working out the problem at the group level will be, as I have argued, the reestablishment of constructive face-to-face relationships. This will only be possible if both managers and workers find a way to see each other in less stereotypic ways. There is a need here to introduce in the interpersonal arena what Zen, Gestalt training, encounter groups, and other training programs have emphasized—relaxing the active critical mind enough to let our eyes and ears see and hear what is really out there rather than what we expect to see and hear. Just as the person who is learning to draw must suspend what he or she knows intellectually about what things should look like and instead, must learn to see what is really out there, so the person concerned about repairing human relationships must first see not what he or she expects or knows should be there, but what is actually there (Edwards, 1979; Frank, 1973).

I don't think it is accidental that Americans are so preoccupied with sensitivity training, Zen meditation, inner tennis, and, most recently, right-side brain functions (Ornstein, 1972). What all of these programs and approaches have in common is a focus on learning how to perceive oneself, others, and the environment realistically, which apparently requires a certain relaxation of our active critical functions and a deliberate disengaging of our analytical selves. We cannot improve face-to-face relationships if we cannot perceive accurately. And accurate seeing and hearing is for many of us a lost skill that we must somehow regain. The place to begin practicing this skill is in our families and in our immediate superior-subordinate and peer relations.

If we cannot see ourselves and others in this relaxed, uncritical way, then we cannot develop perspective, humility, or tact, and we run the danger of acting on incorrect data. On the other hand, if we can really learn to see each other, and if we can combine more accurate perception with the ninth element in my list—patience—then we have some chance of improving and repairing face-to-face relationships.

Even though you try to put people under some control, it is impossible. You cannot do it. The best way to control people is to encourage them to be mischievous. Then they will be in control in its wider sense. To give your sheep or cow a large, spacious meadow is the way to control him. So it is with people: first let them do what they want, and watch them. This is the best policy. To ignore them is not good; that is the worst policy. The second worst is trying to control them. The best one is to watch them, just to watch them, without trying to control them. The same way works for yourself as well. (Suzuki, 1977, p. 32) □

**References**

Bennis, W., Van Maanen, J., Schein, E. H., & Steele, F. I. *Essays in Interpersonal Dynamics*. Homewood, Ill.: Dorsey, 1979.

Edwards, B. *Drawing on the Right Side of the Brain.* Los Angeles: J. P. Tarcher, 1979.

Frank, F. *The Zen of Seeing.* New York: Vintage, 1973.

Goffman, E. *Interaction Ritual.* Chicago: Aldine, 1967.

Hall, E. *Beyond Culture.* Garden City, N. Y.: Anchor, 1977.

Harris, T. A. *I'm OK--You're OK.* New York: Avon, 1967.

Lawrence, P. R., & Lorsch, J. W. *Organization and Environment.* Boston: Division of Research, Harvard Business School, 1967.

McGregor, D. *The Human Side of Enterprise.* New York: McGraw-Hill, 1960.

Ornstein, R. E. *The Psychology of Consciousness.* San Francisco: W. H. Freeman, 1972.

Polster, E., & Polster, M. *Gestalt Therapy Integrated.* New York: Bruner/Mazel, 1973.

Schein, E. H. *Organizational Psychology, 3rd Ed.* Englewood Cliffs, N. J.: Prentice-Hall, 1980.

Suzuki, S. *Zen Mind, Beginner's Mind.* New York: Weatherhill, 1977.

Walton, R. E. *Interpersonal Peacemaking: Confrontations and Third-Party Consultation.* Reading, Mass.: Addison-Wesley, 1969.

# Giving and Receiving Feedback: It Will Never Be Easy, But It Can Be Better

*"Feedback does not assume that the giver is totally right and the receiver wrong; instead, it is an invitation to in-teraction."*

We live in a world filled with feedback devices. Some are "coupled"—that is, the system *automatically responds* to feedback signals by making changes: A thermostat is one familiar example of this. However, many feedback devices merely provide us with information. It is then up to *us* to interpret that information and to decide how we want to use it.

"Uncoupled" feedback sources include such things as bathroom scales, fuel gauges, mirrors, tape recorders. Still others include ways in which people behave toward us—what they say and don't say, do and don't do, how they look, sound, etc. These "uncoupled" indicators may be either unused or misused by us—particularly when our interpretations of the data are colored by our hopes, fears, needs, and desires.

When I'm driving, for example, I have a number of devices giving me information about my car: its speed, engine temperature, oil pressure, fuel level. But I must interpret what that information "means" and make decisions as to what I want to do with it. I may, for example, note that the fuel gauge needle is low, but choose to ignore it for a while; or I may convince myself that it's broken; or I may play a game with it, to see how far I can go before I heed the information and pull into a gas station. I am not likely to cover the gauge up because it threatens or offends me; nor am I likely to wrench the needle from the "E" to the "F" (thereby "magically" filling the tank!).

Similarly, with a bathroom scale, if I think I'm not going to like what it tells me, I may not get on it at all. Or, if I'm dieting, I may weigh myself continuously and risk fretting myself out of any chance of staying with the diet. Or I may convince myself that it "weighs heavy." Mirrors? I can avoid them, except when I'm "feeling thin" or "nicely rounded." And I know full well, when I listen to myself on tape, that "that doesn't sound like me." Similarly, when we get feedback from people with whom we interact, we can play games with it, refuse to believe it,

Reprinted from NTL Reading Book for Human Relations Training © 1982 NTL Institute misinterpret it, etc. Most of us have at one time or another tried to cover up the "negative feedback" gauge ("I don't want to talk about it!"), or to wrench the pointer from "Empty" to "Full" ("You're just upset with me; it's nowhere near as bad as you say it is."), or to choose to ignore it.

Many of these behaviors can be grouped under the general heading of "defensiveness": denying, explaining, justifying, fighting, surrendering—everything but *dealing* with the feedback as information that may have great value to us if we can let it in and effectively use it.

For reasons having mostly to do with our upbringing, we want to look "good" to the world (no matter how much we may deny it), and in the interest of doing this we may try to shut out information that runs counter to that so-much-desired image. We fear information that "disconfirms" our "OKness." This fear causes us to behave in ways that cut us off from feedback (either because it causes people to stop giving it to us or because it keeps us from being able to hear it), which is a pity, because game-free feedback can have great value. It's one of the major sources of information by which we can know how we're perceived by others, develop clarity about why our relationships are what they are (for good or bad), and decide what changes, if any, we want to make in our behaviors so as to improve the quality of some relationships.

There's another problem, too. Not only are many of us afraid of feedback, but we lack skills related to sending and receiving it. Relatively few people have an opportunity to learn feedback skills. So we more or less automatically "do it the way it was done to us." And the way it was done to us is often what makes us fear it in the first place!

One way to break out of this cycle is to learn some feedback concepts. For example, what constitutes effective (i.e., helpful, non-gameplaying) feedback? And then, practice those concepts, either in a setting which validates such experimentation (such as a human relations laboratory) or with people back home with whom we can share the information and whom we can use as ongoing resources as we seek to improve our skills.

## Definition

For our purposes here, I'm defining *feedback* as information that flows between people that has to do with their interaction in the here and now.[1]

---

[1] More accurately, it is something *figural* (in the Gestalt sense)—that is, it is something *present* in their attention at the moment.

Telling someone the time or that you'd rather go to a movie than to a baseball game is not feedback in the sense that I'm using the term. It's just *information*. I define *effective feedback* as information that (1) can be heard by the receiver (as evidenced by the fact that she or he does not get defensive, etc.); (2) that keeps the relationship intact, open, and healthy (though not devoid of conflict or pain); and (3) that validates the feedback process in future interactions (rather than avoiding it because "last time it hurt so much").

Further, feedback does not assume that the giver is totally right and the receiver wrong; instead, it is an invitation to interaction, has some give-and-take to it. Also, it is a behavior that is inappropriate in interactions with people who do not have some significance in our lives (remember "Bob and Carol and Ted and Alice" and the waiter?), but all right in interactions that we know (or want) to have duration and importance.

**Criteria for Effective Feedback**

Table 1 shows 13 criteria for effective feedback. If this list sounds intimidating, keep in mind that some of them are easy to start using (once you're aware). In addition, you probably won't need to concern yourself with all of them and may find yourself focusing on a cluster of four or five which you realize (or are helped to realize) are problems for you. Also, I'm providing the "flip side" of each criterion—things we do which are not effective and which often trap us into games and other relational confusions. It may be that if you can just stop doing *some of those* you'll have made significant progress, even though you don't consciously try to do the ones listed as effective.

To repeat, that's a lot to keep track of, especially given the fact that most of us have had extensive training in how *not* to give feedback. Here are some suggestions you may find helpful:

1. Find out which ineffective feedback behaviors you most want to get rid of. You can do this by paying careful attention to what you do in significant interactions; you can also find out by asking the "challengers" (and others) in your support group if they can point out any criteria you violate frequently. (Sure! Show them the list if that will help.) Work on those—perhaps two or three. Try to *stop* doing the ineffective things, at the very least.

2. Don't expect miracles. Disconfirming feedback almost always carries some sting, no matter how skillfully given; and some people are more easily stung than others. Relationships marked by a relatively high degree of open, competent feedback are likely to be richer, more complex, more interesting than those marked by little feedback or game playing. They are, however,

Table 1.    Effective and Ineffective Feedback Behaviors

| Effective Feedback | Ineffective Feedback |
|---|---|
| 1. Describes the behavior which led to the feedback: "You are finishing my sentences for me . . ." | Uses evaluative/judgmental statements ("You're being rude") or generalized ones ("You're trying to control the conversation"). |
| 2. Comes as soon as appropriate after the behavior—immediately if possible, later if events make that necessary (something going on, you need time to "cool down," the person has other feedback to deal with, etc.). | Is delayed, saved up, and "dumped." Also known as "gunny-sacking" or ambushing. The more time that passes, the "safer" it is to give the feedback. Induces guilt and anger in the receiver, because after time has passed there's usually not much she or he can do about it. |
| 3. Is direct, from sender to receiver. | Indirect, ricochetted ("Tom, how do you feel when Jim cracks his knuckles?")—also known as "let's you and him fight." |
| 4. Is "owned" by the sender, who uses "I messages" and takes responsibility for his or her thoughts, feelings, reactions. | "Ownership" is transferred to "people," "the book," "upper management," "everybody," "we," etc. |
| 5. Includes the sender's real feelings about the behavior, insofar as they are relevant to the feedback: "I get frustrated when I'm trying to make a point and you keep finishing my sentences." | Feelings are concealed, denied, misrepresented, distorted. One way to do this is to "transfer ownership" (see number 4). Another way is to smuggle the feelings into the interaction by being sarcastic, sulking, competing to see who's "right," etc. Other indicators: speculations on the receiver's intentions, motivations, or psychological "problems": "You're trying to drive me nuts"; "You're just trying to see how much you can get away with"; "You have a need to get even with the world." |
| 6. Is checked for clarity, to ensure that the receiver fully understands what's being conveyed. "Do you understand what I mean when I say you seem to be sending me a double message?" | Not checked. Sender either assumes clarity or—fairly often—is not interested in whether receiver understands fully: "Stop interrupting me with 'Yes, buts!'" |
| 7. Asks relevant questions which seek information (has a problem-solving quality), with | Asks questions which are really statements ("Do you think I'm going to let you get away with that?") or |

Table 1. *Continued*

| Effective Feedback | Ineffective Feedback |
|---|---|
| the receiver knowing why the information is sought and having a clear sense that the sender does not know the answer. | which sound like traps ("How many times have you been late this week?") Experts at the "question game" can easily combine the two ("How do you think that makes me feel?" or "Do you behave that way at home *too*?")[1] |
| 8. Specifies consequences of the behavior—present and/or future: "When you finish my sentences I get frustrated and want to stop talking with you." "If you keep finishing my sentences I won't want to spend much time talking with you in the future." | Provides vague consequences: "That kind of behavior is going to get you into trouble." Or specifies no consequences, substituting instead other kinds of leverage, such as "shoulds" ("You shouldn't do that.") |
| 9. Is solicited or at least to some extent desired by the receiver.[2] | Is imposed on the receiver, often for her or his "own good." |
| 10. Refers to behaviors about which the receiver can *do* something ("I wish you'd stop interrupting me."), if she or he wants to. | Refers to behaviors over which the receiver has little or no control, if she or he is to remain authentic: "I wish you'd laugh at my jokes." |
| 11. Takes into account the needs of both sender and receiver; recognizes that this is a "process," that it is an interaction in which, at any moment, the sender can become the receiver. Sender: "I'm getting frustrated by the fact that often you're not ready to leave when I am." Receiver: "I know that's a problem, but I'm concerned about what seems to be your need to have me always do *what* you want *when* you want." | Is distorted by the sender's needs (usually unconscious or unconsidered) to be *safe* (not rejected): "Now, I don't want you to get angry, but . . .;" to *punish*: "You can't ever do *anything* right"; to *win*: "Ah-ha, then you admit that you *do* interrupt me"; to be *virtuous*: (Watch this one!) "I'm going to level with you, be open with you . . ."; etc. In short, most ineffective feedback behaviors come either from lack of skills or from the sender not seeing the process as an interaction in which both parties have needs that must be taken into account. |
| 12. Affirms the receiver's existence and worth by acknowledging his or her "right" to have the reactions she or he has, whatever they may be, and by being willing to work through issues in a game-free way. | Denies or discounts the receiver by using statistics, abstractions, averages; by refusing to accept his/her feelings: "Oh, you're just being paranoid." "Come on! You're over-reacting." "You're not really as angry as you say you are."[3] |

Table 1.  *Continued*

| *Effective Feedback* | *Ineffective Feedback* |
|---|---|
| **13.** Acknowledges and, where necessary, makes use of the fact that a process is going on, that it needs to be monitored and sometimes explored and improved: "I'm getting the impression that we're not listening to each other. I'd like to talk about that and try to do this more effectively." | Either does not value the concept of "process" or does not want to take time to discuss anything other than content. Consequently does not pay any attention to the process, which can result in confusion, wasted time and energy, and lots of ineffective feedback. |

[1] Most people can make significant improvements in their feedback skills by not asking *any* questions!

[2] Since this condition doesn't exist all that often, you may wonder how you can *ever* give feedback. Keep two things in mind: (1) not all the criteria have to be met all the time; and (2) if you have to *impose* it on the recipient, it's likely to be helpful to the process if you'll keep that in mind and take it into account as you interact.

[3] These may be accurate interpretations, of course, but the sender is not likely to "reach" the receiver by being "right" in these instances. In some significant human interactions there are often more important things than being "right."

---

also likely to be more prickly and intense; and they require more time and energy, at times, than do those relationships in which "disconfirmations" are withheld or masked.

3. If for one reason or another (fear of punishment, risk of losing a relationship you're not ready to lose, lack of confidence in your skills, etc.) you think you don't want to try to be more open and use more effective feedback behaviors, then *don't*. But pay attention to the choice you are making—there may be some important learning in it for you. Or you may want to test out some feedback in very small increments, to see what happens.

4. The 13 criteria are useful to you as a *receiver* of feedback as well as a giver. You may decide that you can't/won't give much feedback to another in a given relationship. OK. But do try to use what you've learned as a means of "managing" feedback you receive. If someone tells you you're being obnoxious, you may elect to be hurt or angry, or you may choose to be *curious* (perhaps *in addition* to being hurt or angry!)—to ask for descriptive information: "What am I doing that causes you to say that?" You can also try to help others "own" their feelings, rather than allowing them to shuffle them off onto others ("People are talking . . ."). You can help the sender explore his or her feelings (active listening is useful here) or clarify for you (and perhaps

himself or herself) the *consequences* of the behavior being discussed. In short, if you know something about effective feedback skills (and if you can avoid getting into a defensive posture), you may be able to be helpful to the person giving you feedback, so that the two of you are *problem solving* rather than attacking/defending. This will help you too, in that it will either get you much clearer feedback or it will indicate what "game" the sender is playing.

5. Don't become a feedback addict. Sometimes people get excited about new learnings and use them all the time and in every place. This can wear thin very quickly. Not every event needs to be worked through. Not every utterance has to be perfect. Remember to allow for some slippage in your relationships; take small risks, be willing to "approximate," and see what happens. Above all, don't use others as guinea pigs on which to practice your skills.

6. The feedback process works best when it involves people who are—at least in that interaction—equals. If one person is "up" (dominant, "right," faultless, containing all virtue) and the other "down" (passive, "wrong," the culprit or villain of the piece), it is likely to turn into one of a number of games, as the "down" person attempts (usually without realizing it) to equalize the power between them, to gain what might be called psychological parity. If you can recognize that what began as a feedback interaction between equals has moved to "helpless me" or "awful me" or "you're one, too" or "but you don't understand," or any of a variety of behaviors that might be lumped under the term "attack/defense," you may be able to alter the interaction's direction by having both you and the other person look at what's happening. Note well: both *you* and the other person. For as long as the burden is on the other, you're maintaining or increasing your "upness" and promoting an escalation of the power equalization efforts.

By now you may be muttering, "But it's so complicated; and it sounds like hard work; and it also sounds risky." Yes. And the same can be said of many of the things that are important to us. It is, I believe, a matter of *valuing*. If I value clear, open relationships, if I value the others with whom I share those relationships, and—most important, I think—if I value *myself* in those relationships, then I may find that I have no choice but to do the hard work, take the risks, suffer the losses, and be enriched by the gains.□

# Intergroup Competition and Conflict

W. Brendan Reddy

*"Only when competition and conflict are denied, badly managed, or seen as inherently bad do they become negative."*

This chapter will acquaint or re-acquaint the reader with the dynamics and behaviors of intergroup conflict and competition. Managers who observe, recognize, diagnose, and understand intergroup conflict and competition in a training conference can use those skills in the "back-home" setting. Moreover, by examining their own assumptions, feelings, and behaviors in the intergroup situation, participants can understand their own roles, contributions, and collusion, and can, therefore, be in a better position to change their behavior. The organizational setting is replete with conflicts and interdepartmental and interface situations that require knowledge of intergroup competition and conflict dynamics.

For the purposes of this chapter, I will define conflict as a consequence of competition. I will first examine conflict and competition in the workshop or conference setting and then relate that information to the "back-home" organizational setting.

## From Innocence to Intensity

Typically, conflict begins in formal or informal competition. Informally, the competition begins whenever participants belong to different groups (e.g., T Groups). As participants begin to identify with their group, one hears comments and "humor" about "the other group." Invidious comparisons and good-natured kidding take place between the T Groups. Members defend the behavior of their trainer, at least publicly, while privately they may have grave doubts about the trainer's competence. Somehow, the other group and the other group's trainer seem more attractive. The other group appears more advanced and insightful, it looks like it has moved along in its development, and, worst of all, "They always seem to have more fun!" Resentment builds toward the other group.

Then comes the *formal* competition often built into the conference. Disparaging remarks become commonplace; the humor takes on a more aggressive—and hostile—tone. Winning

© 1983 NTL Institute

the competition may become an obsession. Interpersonal and communication skills, learned early in the conference, go by the wayside. Members do not consider collaboration as an alternative strategy. Under pressure, many of the behaviors and insights learned from struggles in the T Group are, at least momentarily, swept aside by more primitive impulses. Quick decisions, conformity, stereotypic thinking, and myopia become the norm. Win/lose is the form, rarely win/win. Power and manipulation are in vogue.

When the formal competition ends, the informal competition often continues. Participants still feel conflict and resist examining the dynamics generated by the activity. The trainer conducting the exercise may become "fair game" for "shots" taken by disgruntled participants who believe they belong to a losing team. Generally, members of the group or team that has been successful in the activity have the most difficulty in examining their behavior. Somehow, success precludes struggling with understanding. "We won, so we must have done some-thing right."

In sum, participants who earlier were timid, quiet, rational, and seemingly self-aware, become, in the heat of group competition, intense, competitive, and aggressive, and resist looking at their behavior. Those who can review and examine their behavior, who can hear feedback, learn what they contributed to the situation and have taken a step toward altering some of those behaviors.

### "Is It Happening in this Workshop?"

Probably! If you see and hear the above behaviors and comments, intergroup competition and conflict are usually operating. As outlined above, we typically hear it in the humor and in the disparaging remarks members of one group make about another. Trainers need to explore the dynamics of their group's negative comments about other groups.

### Symbols, Symptoms, and Norms

We can obtain another source of clues about intergroup competition in the range of symbols group members use. For example, groups sometimes adopt group names, often with aggressive, macho, warlike, or military titles. Sometimes emblems, insignias, armbands, and signs identify the group and its members. Members refer to "our room," and "our trainer," or use other possessive descriptions. They can be seen sitting together in close configuration with their backs to other conference participants. Competitive groups frequently develop negative "pet" names for other groups, participants, and trainers.

## Fuel for the Fire

How does this get started? A number of conditions fuel the fires of intergroup competition. But first, let us look at some antecedents to competition and conflict.

Given that our American culture is competitive, feelings of competition and subsequent conflict will surface in the workshop. Many of us reactivate early feelings of sibling rivalry. Moreover, the achievement- and production-focused business culture increases that probability, as does a sports background. Thus, for many conference participants, the pilot flame is already lit. Now, add some combustible elements.

*Performance Expectations.* Some conference participants believe that they must meet certain "standards" of behavior. If an activity is designed to have one "winner," this increases the expectation for quality performance.

*Task/Goal Ambiguity.* If the path to a particular task or goal is ambiguous or the decision making involves a high degree of uncertainty, two or more groups dealing with the same task increase their competition as they strive to gain information that will give them "the edge."

*Resource Availability.* If a prize (e.g., money) is awarded for a particular accomplishment, the level of intensity of competition and conflict increases.

*Time Constraints.* Particularly given the above elements, the shorter the time available for a given task, the greater the intensity of the competition.

## Effects of Intergroup Conflict

Each group perceives the "other" group as the "bad guys" and themselves as the "good guys." That is, one sees the worst stereotypes of the other group and the best stereotypes of one's own group. Moreover, if the groups or their members interact, they do not use communication skills that may have been learned earlier. People repress basic skills like listening and paraphrasing. Conflict and hostility accelerate; humor becomes more aggressive and disparaging. Members hurl epithets, particularly about the "unfairness" of the other group or team.

## Effects of Intergroup Conflict Within Groups

Meanwhile, within each group, cohesion and loyalty become the most obvious characteristics. Conformity is demanded of group members. Members tend not to tolerate such deviance as the suggestion of collaboration. Task becomes all important, with individual members' needs secondary. Autocratic leadership is tolerated, if not encouraged, and each group becomes more organized. Members must present a strong and united public face. At this juncture, trainers find it difficult to get participants to examine their own dynamics as well as the group dynamics. The tyranny and power of the group in conflict becomes paramount.

## Winners and Losers

Schein (1965) has graphically described what happens to the winners and losers after a competitive activity. The winning team retains and intensifies its cohesion. The concern for work and task drops off and intragroup cooperation increases. Tension becomes released in the form of play and kidding. The spirit to fight is reduced. Complacency sets in. The winning team finds it difficult to examine dynamics as it confirms its positive stereotype of self and the negative stereotypes of the losing teams. This team minimizes its learning about the conflict, intergroup dynamics, or self.

Conversely, the losing teams regroup and try to work harder "for the next time." While they find it difficult to examine the dynamics, they have broken the stereotypes and have maximized their learning. An initial period of denial, however, often precedes splintering, ingroup fighting, and the surfacing of unresolved conflict among group members. Intragroup cooperation falls to its lowest. All in all, the losing team(s) more often reorganizes and becomes more cohesive, realistic about its loss, and, eventually, more effective.

## Is There a Positive Side to Intergroup Conflict?

Absolutely! If managed well, competition and conflict help create comradery, loyalty, and esprit de corps. In the struggle to manage and resolve conflicts, many creative alternatives and solutions can emerge that might not have been considered at an earlier time. Competition and conflict can produce high energy, motivation, and improved performance. Only when competition and conflict are denied, badly managed, or seen as inherently bad do they become negative. While competition and conflict can and are frequently permitted to get out of hand in many organizations, it simply does not have to be that way.

## How Does This Relate "Back Home?"

There are many groups in the back-home setting—and, therefore, much competition and conflict. Think for a moment of your own department, section, division, unit, or area. Almost any interaction offers potential conflict. It is certainly in your best interest to understand what is real and appropriate *vs.* what is unreal and inappropriate. By examining your own *feelings, assumptions,* and *behaviors* and those of others in the conference setting, you will better understand the dynamics of your own work setting. Struggle to discover what you bring to the situation. What do you contribute? How do you collude? How are your feelings of competition activated? You should strive to separate what is irrational in you from the reality of the competition and conflict.□

## Bibliography

Kidder, L. H., & Stewart, V. M. *The Psychology of Intergroup Relations: Conflict and Consciousness.* New York: McGraw-Hill, 1975.

Schein, E. H. *Organizational Psychology.* Englewood Cliffs, N.J.: Prentice-Hall, 1965.

Turney, J. C., & Giles, H. (Eds.). *Intergroup Behavior.* Chicago, Ill.: University of Chicago Press, 1981.

# "But Is This Really Me?"  Morley Segal

*"The data from management-based instruments are much more likely to have a tentative meaning than an absolute one."*

At some point during many management workshops, the facilitator walks into the room with a handful of material and says, "Good morning. Today we are going to take a self-assessment inventory." This is a chance for you to learn about your own management style and. . . ."

Reactions to the announcement vary from excitement and enthusiasm to polite—and some not-so-polite—skepticism. Participants usually have some basis for both the excitement and the skepticism because managment instruments have both considerable strengths and considerable limitations.

To make the best use of your results, you should know the general strengths and limitations of this form of learning. This article presents some of the questions and concerns managers most frequently express regarding these inventories and offers some guidelines to help you get the most from your experience.

## "What Will I and Won't I Gain from Taking This Instrument?"

You probably *won't* gain

- a definitive picture of your personality. Most management instruments are not comprehensive personality inventories.
- clear advice concerning career choices, handling your boss, your mate, or the next big decision in your life. Most management instruments highlight some of your abilities, preferences, or behavior, but they do not tell you how to use them.
- revelations of limitations in your personality or character.

Most management inventories are *not* designed to pry out your hidden flaws or weaknesses. Although most instruments report your results in numerical form, you must interpret the actual numbers in the context of your individual experience. This requires some introspection on your part.

---

© 1983 NTL Institute

By taking this instrument, you *can* gain

- a theory or framework, a new way of looking at yourself and the world;
- a tentative explanation of how you function in that framework;
- some of the likely consequences of your functioning in this way;
- some alternate ways of behaving or dealing with other people or problems; and
- an opportunity to systematically explore this explanation with your own experiences and the ways others react to you.

## "Will I Be Stereotyped or Branded with the Labels and Categories of This Instrument?"

Perhaps, someday, a Ralph Nader of instruments will appear and make every copy contain the following warning:

Not to be applied permanently. The categories in this instrument do not have fixed, permanent meanings. They are used best as a springboard for your own introspection and conversation with others. Instrument takers are cautioned not to use these results as a source of labeling for themselves or others.

The best analogy is to a rather dashing piece of clothing which you see in a store and try on "just to see how you look." Sometimes you find that the flamboyant hat or pair of boots brings out a new aspect of your appearance and at other times you decide that it's just not you. In either case, you take a new, tentative look at yourself. That is exactly what you can expect from a management inventory.

## "Why Did I Spend So Much Time Talking to Other Participants Instead of Getting an Interpretation of My Results from the Leader?"

The data from management-based instruments are much more likely to have a tentative meaning than an absolute one. The trainer or leader can provide the general theory and framework and define the terms. The trainer, however, is not necessarily the best source of information regarding *what this instrument means to you.*

One way to develop a personal understanding of the implications of your results is to use the opportunity presented by the workshop. If the workshop includes individuals with whom you work or whom you know in another setting, then you can test your results with them. Do they perceive you as your results describe you? If so, when and how? You can work to get feedback that is as specific as possible.

If you are participating in a workshop with relative strangers then the situation is most likely structured to allow you to take advantage of your contact with these people. You have the opportunity to find out how your self-management at the workshop compares with your inventory results. How do you express leadership, communicate, and respond to others in a novel situation? An additional source of information can be your own self-observation. How does your own behavior, including your enthusiasm or your skepticism for the instrument itself, confirm or deny your results?

## "Is the Instrument Valid and Reliable?"

Validity refers to whether the instrument really measures what it says it measures—i.e., is it consistent with other measurements of the same phenomena? Reliability refers to internal consistency—i.e., are the questions consistent with one another, does the instrument produce similar results when repeated, and is it free from random interference? Validity and reliability are especially important in research and clinical practice. In these situations, behavioral scientists seek to make generalizations and predictions about individuals and large populations and to base this information on numerical scales. Validity and reliability also matter in management training, but an important difference exists. When individuals fill out questionnaires in a research or clinical setting, they usually have little or no opportunity to check their results against the feelings, perceptions, and reactions of other participants or of significant persons outside of the workshop. Moreover, researchers can seldom compare their results to those of the individual participants. In these instances, the numbers speak for themselves—or at least they are supposed to.

In contrast, management training workshops usually provide ample opportunities for participants to check results with each other and with the trainer. Later they may check the results with others outside the workshop. If their results do not agree with their own or others' perceptions of themselves, they can explore these differences.

Regarding validity and reliability, you must remember that management instruments should be considered springboards or triggers for your own introspection rather than devices that provide an absolute analysis of your personality. In this context, you should actively consider what receiving a score of 35 on "cooperation" (a fictitious example) means to you at this time in your life instead of trying to find out the official meaning of this number. This cautionary advice will probably prove to be more practical to you than volumes on validity and reliability.

### "How Can I Make Additional Use of This Instrument When the Workshop Is Over?"

Management instruments vary as to their availability. Some are available to the general public while others can be obtained only through licensed or franchised facilitators. Whether or not you can obtain additional copies of the instrument, you can

• simply use the framework or theory to reflect on your own feelings and behaviors;
• share your results with others and invite feedback on what you have learned from the instrument;
• assess your own surroundings and the ways you organize your work and time to see if they build on the strengths reflected in your instrument; and
• assess your relationships with others to see if these relationships build on your strengths or your limitations.

In addition to the above, if you can obtain and score additional instruments, you can

• invite others to take the instrument, answering questions the way they believe you would answer them and thus giving you more systematic feedback;
• invite others to take the instrument and discuss their results with them; and
• with a facilitator, use the instrument as a basis for a team-building session.

### Conclusion

Management instruments provide one useful way of learning about yourself. They enable you to give yourself feedback and, most importantly, to fit that feedback into an overall theory or framework. This framework allows you to explore the meanings, possibilities, and limitations of the feedback and then to share and check out these new learnings with others.

Given these possibilities and limitations, your instrument results are not "you" in any total sense, but they offer you an opportunity to learn and discover a bit more about yourself.□

## Bibliography

Atkins, S. *The Name of Your Game*. Beverly Hills, Ca.: Ellis & Stewart, Career and Life Books Division, 1981.

Buros, O. K. (Ed.). *The Eighth Mental Measurements Yearbook*. Highland Park, N. J.: The Gryphon Press, 1978.

Guest, R., Hersey, P., & Blanchard, K. H. *Organization Change through Effective Leadership*. Englewood Cliffs, N. J.: Prentice-Hall, 1977.

Hersey, P., & Stinson, J. *Perspectives in Leader Effectiveness*. Columbus, Ohio: The Ohio State University Press, 1960.

Kiersey, D., & Bates, M. *Please Understand Me: An Essay on Temperament Styles*. Del Mar, Ca.: Prometheus, Menesis, 1978.

Myers, I. B., & Myers, P. B. *Gifts Differing*. Palo Alto, Ca.: Consulting Psychologist Press, 1980.

Pfeiffer, W. J., Jones, J. E., & Heslin, R. *Instrumentation in Human Relations Training: A Guide to 92 Instruments with Wide Applications in the Behavioral Sciences*. La Jolla, Ca.: University Associates, 1976.

# Re-Entry, or You *Can* Go Home Again— Appropriately

Kathy M. Lippert
W. Brendan Reddy

*"I can't wait to get back home; there are a couple of things I've been wanting to tell my _____ for a long time!"*

You are completing or have just completed an experiential workshop. It has been intense; you are tired, a little ragged (those three o'clock bull sessions and the booze are hell), yet you feel you are on a bit of a high. You have learned some important things about yourself, and have thought about your relationships at home and at work. There are some things you would like to change. . . .

Unusual? Not at all. Actually, the above anecdote is not atypical of participants of management work conferences, human interaction laboratories, team-building weekends, affirmative action training, or personal growth groups. The experience, as you now know, not only focuses on cognitive inputs and skill training, but on intrapersonal and interpersonal dynamics. The experiences are often emotion-arousing and defense-reducing. The value is on challenging attitudes and behavior.

Taken out of context, the experiences sometimes sound noxious, confusing, or bizarre. In context and with the psychological support of the facilitator and other members, the process helps participants "unfreeze"; it permits self-scrutiny, the learning of new interpersonal skills, and the opportunity to practice—appropriately—new and alternative behaviors. (Indeed, this is why the experiential workshops are called "laboratories." It is here that one can "experiment" with old and new behaviors and skills.) The key word is *appropriate*; that is, the use of new behaviors, thought out, and at least relatively consistent with the norms and culture of a particular setting, family, or organization so as not to be intrusive, offensive, or anxiety-arousing.

During the workshop or conference, in the context of the experiential laboratory, a wider range of behaviors is acceptable and appropriate than in the "back-home" work, family, and social setting. Participants, as noted above, share a *common culture* for the duration of the experience. But a part of that experience necessitates that you prepare yourself for re-entry to the

---

Reprinted from NTL *Reading Book for Human Relations Training* © 1982 NTL Institute "back-home" culture, particularly as you approach the end of the workshop.

This paper deals briefly with some of the feelings and issues you may be presently experiencing or which you can expect to occur when you return home. They are part of the common process at the termination of any laboratory experience and when examined can help make your experience much more complete and rewarding.

## Culture Shock

The impact on returning home will vary, depending upon your preconference expectations, your interactions with the other participants and the facilitator, your degree of active involvement and commitment to the process, the quality of the design, and the competence level of the facilitator. The greater the intensity of the laboratory experience, the greater the probability that you will experience feelings of a "high"—along with some emotional upheaval, distress, and dissatisfaction with or a basic questioning of the rightness of your current lifestyle. If you have been deeply and actively involved, it will probably require a somewhat longer period of time to adjust to the back-home situation. Certainly, the adjustment is also contingent upon already-existing factors: personality; family, marital, social, and work situation; and your adult stage of development.

## Closeness and Separation

Because of the intensity of work and play during the workshop, the encouragement and opportunity for self-disclosure in a setting of psychological safety, participants often feel, even in laboratories of short duration, that they "know" other participants at a deeper level than they know colleagues, friends, and family members. While this may be accurate to some degree, it must be remembered that the laboratory experience and culture is unique—that is, time-limited, person-focused, and without the same back-home constraints and responsibilities. It offers the opportunity to learn about one's self and to practice new skills and behaviors, monitored by feedback. It may bring about some changes and added satisfactions in one's everyday life. But because of the closeness, participants often experience sadness, a "letdown," and some separation anxiety at the end of the laboratory or shortly thereafter.

## "Let's Continue To Meet"

Frequently, group members have the fantasy that if the group could continue to meet, the feelings, openness, and intensity would continue. In reality, they probably would not. The uniqueness would be lost. Once the *system* was changed (e.g., when the group's boundaries are enlarged by the back-home realities of each member), it would become impossible to maintain the group. Moreover, the facilitator, the one who protects and helps make possible the psychological safety, would not be present.

Certainly, many participants continue friendships made during a workshop, and this is quite appropriate; but it is different from trying to relive, re-ignite, or recapture the ambience of the laboratory. A more effective strategy is to develop support pairings or groupings at work or at home, people who can share common problems, strengths, and frustrations *without creating a therapy session.* The more you can appropriately practice in everyday life the skills you learned at the laboratory, the more effective you will become in your interpersonal relations.

## "I Want To Make a Fresh Start"

You may make plans about changing your life while you are at the laboratory. *Do not* put them into effect immediately! Wait until you have gotten some distance from the experience, rethought the plans and their implications, and discussed them in collaboration with those persons whom the plans will also affect. Too many laboratory participants have returned to work or to their family and immediately announced life-changing plans— from divorce to early retirement. One *can* make a new start, but it will be most effectively done with thought, restraint, planning, continual re-examination, collaboration, and support.

Some additional words about support are in order. Evidence from research is quite conclusive: Social support not only facilitates learning, it serves as a buffer between psychological stressors and diverse forms of pathology. Indeed a primary group with whom one can closely interact may be a prime requisite for psychological and physical health. Most of us need to work on building effective support groups and relationship networks of people with whom we can interact, in whom we can confide, obtain and give nurturance, guidance, feedback, and reconfirm our self-worth.[1]

## "How Do I Describe the Experience?"

How often have you heard acquaintances or colleagues, just returned from a laboratory, describe the experience in the following ways?

[1] See Seashore, "Developing and Using a Personal Support System."

- "It was potent—so intense!"
- "I can't really tell you what it was like. You'd have to have been there."
- "We pretended a tree was growing out of our navels. . . ."
- "It was beautiful (sigh)."
- "I learned a lot—I guess."
- "This guy broke down and cried after the group jumped all over him."

The one-liners are legion. And most of them, although accurate, are taken out of context. Single statements are frequently sensational and perpetuate the myths, fears, distortions, and rumors about experiential learning. But the experience can be described (like most other experiences) in terms of the goals, methods, skills, and your personal learnings. Direct analogies to everyday life and work make the experience more understandable and meaningful to those around you—as well as to yourself.

## The Inquisition

Some participants, upon returning home, find that they are the focus, sometimes target, of many questions—some very hostile—about their experience. They feel the pressure of defending an entire movement, or worse yet, their now-suspect actions and behaviors for the past week. Clearly, it does not help to challenge the motivation and dynamics of the inquisitor. When you do find yourself in this situation and in difficulty explaining the experience, you might try describing what it "did" for you behaviorally, rather than what it was "like." It sometimes helps to share what personally important things occurred or what changes you are working on; and then, if it seems appropriate, invite the questioner to meet with you periodically to talk about the changes he or she may or may not see over time. He or she has the option of refusing, or meeting with you in a more collaborative way. Realistically, the process may go nowhere else—but it *is* good modeling!

## "How Do I Use What I Learned?"

Despite the claims of pure experience for its own sake, most participants of experiential learning need and want some cognitive connections. It takes hard work and much of your own responsibility to make those connections. After all, it *is* your experience. One method participants have found helpful is articulating their major insights, skills, and learnings acquired at the workshop, deliberately and consciously (writing it out may help) making applications to back-home (family, work, social) settings, and *planning* some concrete next steps. The most prudently made "next steps" involve built-in support and feedback from those whom you trust.

If you leave the laboratory with questions about yourself, your life, and work, and are able to make plans and take some concrete steps, the probability is that your workshop experience will continue to be a strong force. The laboratory experience is a beginning; the rest is up to you.

### Spouses, Lovers, and Attachés[2]

A few words are in order about our transactions with those closest to us. Often the "fallout" from a workshop hits these people hardest. While you have been away at a residential laboratory, quite possibly in an idyllic or posh resort setting, they have been home or at work conducting "humdrum" and routine duties. Moreover, they may have a wide range of conscious and unconscious fantasies about your behavior and about other participants at the laboratory. You may have had minimal or no telephone contact with them for a week or more, or you may have cryptically described your feelings and activities. They probably feel distant, that they are not included in this part of your life, or that their own struggles, concerns, and problems are being neglected. Reactions of hurt, anger, jealousy, and resentment are common. It is not surprising that these feelings can be exacerbated if you return on a "high," are insensitive to what they have been experiencing,[3] greet them by discussing your dissatisfaction with the relationship, and/or give immediate feedback on "old history." If you want the understanding, support, and collaboration of those closest to you, then the interface boundary between the laboratory culture and this aspect of the "back-home" culture must be understood and maintained throughout the laboratory and particularly when you return home.

### Some Repeats on Feedback

Throughout your experience you heard much about giving and receiving feedback, and the skill and practice required for its

---

[2] *Attaché*: a person with whom one has a deep emotional attachment. It may be a man or a woman, a homosexual, heterosexual, bisexual, or asexual relationship.

[3] A colleague once asked a participant—concerned about her "re-entry"—if she would like to role-play her initial conversation with her husband. In the role-play, she said to him, "Oh, we learned a lot about how to be sensitive to people . . . *but you wouldn't understand.*"

optimal impact. Feedback is indeed a powerful tool, but its effectiveness is contingent on its presentation. When it is used as a club, motivated only by the needs of the giver who disregards the needs and psychological state of the receiver, feedback will not only be ineffective, it may generate a negative, painful, or disruptive reaction. It may also evoke in the receiver withdrawal, distrust, or a verbal attack.[4]

In the "back-home" situation, a technique which seems to have a high rate of success is the collaborative establishment of contracts and effective feedback "rules," mutually agreed upon, and which all parties involved feel they can live with. These can include decisions on when, how, where, and under what circumstances. We have found that in time, when participants have become more comfortable with giving and receiving feedback, and the level of trust has risen, they often re-examine the contracts and conditions they set, and increase the opportunity for feedback.

### "Go Therefore and Teach All Nations . . ."

There is a tendency on the part of many participants, particularly those who have had an experiential "high," to convert others. Probably you have heard the group devotee preaching and proselytizing. But you are equally aware of the "snickers," hostility, or flight it evoked. Perhaps most important, no one was converted and the speaker was seen as a spokesperson for a cult or a fad. People who have not shared the experience do have an interest, questions, and, often, a healthy skepticism. Enthusiasm is refreshing, and nondefensive intellectual discussions are valuable and contribute to one's growth. If you wish to share your feeling and perceptions and encourage people to participate in a similar experience, the more effective strategy is to determine what are the information and curiosity needs of your listener and to *model* behaviorally important learnings you gleaned from your own experience.

### Some Guidelines

To sum up our thoughts, experiences, and concerns about the re-entry process in experiential learning laboratories of all kinds, we offer the following guidelines:

1. The workshop, conference, or group experience was just a beginning; cognitive *connections* and everyday applications must be made by you.

---

[4] For more information on feedback, see Porter, "Giving and Receiving Feedback."

2. If your experience was intense, you might have some brief period of mild to moderate distress, such as the "blues," physical and mental fatigue, a "high," feelings of anxiety, or dissatisfaction with the status quo.

3. If your experience was not intense, it does not mean that you are a failure or that you did not learn anything. Conversely, intensity does not guarantee success or learning.

4. Do not be surprised if you have an increase in dreams or if you dream about the experience itself.

5. Do not make major decisions—family, work, or social—as soon as you arrive home. Give yourself some time and distance from the experience.

6. Changes should be made with planning, collaboration, and support.

7. Remember what you have learned about giving feedback—appropriateness, timing, and the other person's needs and readiness in the situation.

8. The culture of the laboratory is not the culture of your world back home—nor should it be necessarily.

9. Describe the laboratory experience to others in concrete terms: its objectives, methodology, skills, and learnings.

10. If you are tempted to focus on the unusual, remember that anecdotes out of context only misrepresent the laboratory. They add to the myths regarding experiential training.

11. Proselytizing or preaching turns people off and converts few.

12. Practice, practice, practice what you have learned! It is the major factor that will make a difference in the long run.

13. When you return home, if any distress, anxiety, or symptoms you experience seem to increase or persist, consult a qualified professional! If possible, contact one who is familiar with laboratory learning and has likewise been a participant.

14. Experiential learning in a laboratory setting is an exciting, powerful, and important methodology. But it is temporary and a beginning. To apply the learnings to the "back-home" setting of work, marriage, family, and society, requires commitment, planning, work, and practice.□

# Developing and Using a
# Personal Support System

Charles Seashore

*"[Support systems] should function in such a way as to maintain and develop the integrity of the individual, which may include changing the organization, creating conflict, or leaving a particular setting."*

One method of acquiring, maintaining, and demonstrating one's interpersonal competence is to have a network of supportive relationships which can be drawn on as needed to help one achieve one's particular objectives.

There are many roles that other people can play which provide support to the individual. A well-developed support system therefore includes a variety of types of individuals and is not limited to people who are, say, close or good at listening or giving advice.

It is a skill to be able to establish, maintain, and effectively utilize a support system. As with all relationships, support systems can be difficult to establish, counterproductive and disappointing at times, and somewhat unpredictable; and they take energy to maintain. They can also be used as crutches which make an individual more dependent rather than more resourceful.

Keeping one's support system up-to-date and relevant to one's goals requires ongoing assessment of the kinds of people who are currently available, letting go of those who are not relevant or who in fact are sabotaging one's efforts, and bringing in new persons who could be of assistance.

Supportive people may or may not be aware that they are a part of your system, and they may or may not be aware of the other persons who are important in your life. Relationships with them may be close and personal or quite distant and impersonal. But it is important that they be useful and that the relationships be equitable and fair.

It is not necessary that support systems be reciprocal. However, most of us do function as parts of other persons' support systems. It is an equally important skill to know how to *provide* support in a variety of ways. Analyzing how one becomes part of another's support system and how one leaves that relationship can provide a basis for increasing one's own interpersonal competence.

---

Reprinted from NTL *Reading Book for Human Relations Training* © 1982 NTL Institute

## Definition of a Support System

The definition given below is broken into phrases for the purpose of emphasizing and elaborating on some of the major issues involved in building an effective support system.

*A support system is*

- a resource pool
- drawn on selectively
- to support me
- in moving in a direction of my choice
- that leaves me stronger.

*The resource pool* consists of people, things, environments, and beliefs. However, here primary emphasis will be given to the issues concerning people and relationships. The notion of a resource pool raises several questions for us. It is important for us to be *aware* of those individuals who could *potentially* be a part of our support system. This requires some skills at scanning our world and keeping an open mind about the possibility that any given person may be a relevant resource. It is helpful to be *proactive* in reaching out to locate and identify people since it is unlikely that the appropriate people will all come to us. *Size* of the resource pool is important since larger and more complicated systems require a lot of energy to sustain, while very small systems may not have the range of resources that you may need. The composition or variety of people thus becomes an important criterion in building an effective system.

*Drawing on people selectively* requires skills in choosing appropriate persons and keeping those persons who are not particularly helpful from getting in the way. It involves taking the risk of asking for support and being rejected or let down. It may also occasionally require dealing with jealousy and competition among those people in the system who would like to be asked for assistance and feel left out when you call on someone else. Willingness and availability are also obvious requirements for those people we ask for support.

It is often difficult for many of us to ask others *to support us.* It may, for example, arouse feelings of guilt—we may think we're "imposing." It may feel like an expression of weakness or an admission of failure. It may go against our values or beliefs that altruism is more important than taking for ourselves. It also opens up the fear that we may become dependent on another person rather than being self-sufficient. It does require that we be open to help, that we be willing to make demands on other people, and that we be reasonably clear about the expectations that we have of them.

*To move in a direction of my choice* requires that I be able to distinguish my goals and directions from those of other people and organizations. Then I can move toward achieving *clarity* so that I am in a position to make a *declaration* of that direction that can be understood by others. It means making a commitment, even if it is only for a short time or is somewhat tentative.

Ideally, a good support system will *leave me stronger.* It confronts me with my own ambivalence about growth and often will generate new demands as others perceive my strength. I am also confronted with letting others know I can do certain things without them, which means I may lose some relationships.

## Functions of Support Systems

Support systems can be used for several purposes, depending on the situation confronting an individual.

- *Re-Establishing Competence.* Particularly in times of high stress or major transitions, we may find ourselves functioning at a very low level of competence. This may be because of anxiety, the energy it takes to cope with a crisis, physical and emotional difficulties, or overload of demands on us by other people. A good support system can help us cope and return to our previous level of functioning.
- *Maintaining High Performance.* It can be equally important to have access to resourceful people when one is doing well in order to maintain that level of activity. Although it may be easier to use assistance when performing at a high level, many people tend to neglect their support systems at such times, finding it more difficult to ask for help.
- *Gaining New Competencies.* A somewhat different function of support systems is to assist in developing new skills. Persons should challenge, serve as teachers and models, and provide emotional support during periods when one may be feeling awkward or inept in dealing with new situations.
- *Achieving Specific Objectives.* Many of the objectives we strive for cannot be met without collaboration with and contributions from a number of persons. This often requires people who have skills and resources that we do not have or that we do not desire to develop.

These functions of support systems are focused primarily on the individual. They often can help an individual contribute to organizational goals and objectives, but it is equally important that support systems be used when individuals find themselves in conflict or opposition to the directions of other people, groups, or organizations. They should function in such a way as to maintain and develop the integrity of the individual, which may include changing the organization, creating conflict, or leaving a particular setting.

Support systems are particularly helpful in coping with the stress that accompanies transitions in relationships, roles and positions, or careers. Skills in establishing new support systems are essential for successful transitions into new environments.

## Different Types of Support System Members

Support system members can function in a number of ways. Some people fill a variety of roles, while others may offer only a single type of support. The following list illustrates some of the functions of support system members:

- *Role Models*—people who can help define goals for positions one might assume in the future. Role models not only show what is possible but are a source of valuable information about the opportunities and problems associated with a given role.
- *Common Interests*—people who share common interests or concerns can be especially important in keeping one motivated and in sorting out those problems that are primarily those of the individual from problems imposed by the larger system and that require collective activity to bring about change in that system.
- *Close Friends*—people who help provide nurturance and caring, who enjoy some of the same interests, and who keep one from becoming isolated and alienated.
- *Helpers*—people who can be depended upon in a crisis to provide assistance. These people are often experts in solving particular kinds of problems and may not be the type with whom one would choose to have a close or personal relationship.
- *Respect Competence*—individuals who respect the skills one has already developed and who value the contributions that one makes in a given situation. They are particularly helpful during times of transition when one may be feeling unsure of oneself in developing new skills.
- *Referral Agents*—people who can connect one with resources in the environment through their knowledge of people and organizations. They can refer one to those places where one can obtain needed assistance.
- *Challengers*—people who can help motivate one to explore new ways of doing things, develop new skills, and work toward

the development of latent capabilities. They often are people whom one may not care for as personal friends, but who are abrasive and demanding.

## Some Principles in Using Support Systems

• *Parsimony*. An attempt should be made to keep the system as simple as possible to minimize the energy it takes to maintain it.

• *Maintenance*. It is wise to keep relationships current and up-to-date so that when you do need to draw on people, they are informed and appreciative of your need for their assistance.

• *Equity*. It is important that the relationship be one in which both sides feel that there is a fair arrangement, whether it be accomplished by returning help, payment of money, joint sense of accomplishment, or whatever else makes sense. Guilt can easily build up when there is a sense of indebtedness that cannot be repaid.

• *External Support Base*. The primary base of support for being competent should be external to the system in which one is using one's skills. This will enable a person to maximize her or his autonomy and to engage in conflict when it becomes necessary. Leaning on people inside the system in which one is trying to be competent often leads to a sense of dependency. (Paradoxically, when one is seen as having an external support group, it is more likely that people inside the system will also turn out to be supportive.)

• *Back-up Resources*. It is wise to have several places one can turn to for particular kinds of support to reduce the sense of vulnerability one feels should an individual be unavailable or unwilling to help in a given circumstance.

• *Feedback*. It is important that feedback be given both ways to check on how each person feels about the process of giving or receiving assistance. Helping often creates resistance and/or resentment and unless there is a means of keeping track of the process, the relationship is likely to erode over time.□

# Section II: Managing Interpersonal Relationships

# Learning How To Influence Others

Marvin R. Weisbord
C. James Maselko

*"Supporting and confronting are the two basic skills required to influence others' behavior."*

While it is possible for organizations to have too many levels of management, or too many goals and objectives, we have never met a manager or supervisor who believed her or his organization suffered an excess of interpersonal skills. Indeed, the primary frustration reported by managers is finding ways to influence the behavior of people they work with or for.

Those who do this easily or naturally are said to have "good interpersonal skills." Those who don't are frequently packed off to workshops and seminars.

In this article we want to suggest a do-it-yourself approach to interpersonal skill development that any manager can experiment with on the job without announcing to the world that some changes are about to be made. Over many years and dozens of workshops we have reduced the basic skills required to just two—"supporting" and "confronting."

Supporting is something you do for the *other person.* To do it well requires that you separate your judgments about what somebody else is saying from the feelings that that person is expressing. Confronting, on the other hand, is something you do for *yourself.* It requires that you accept others' wants as legitimate *and* speak up directly for your own.

Support—the ability to hear, understand, and act upon what others are saying—shows up prominently on the list of characteristics of high-performing managers studied by Rensis Likert. At the same time, P. R. Lawrence and J. W. Lorsch in their widely quoted differentiation-integration research show that confronting differences openly is the preferred method for conflict resolution in productive organizations.

In his classic case for managerial teamwork, the late Douglas McGregor graphically described what "a really good top management team" does in meetings. "The members listen to each other!" he wrote. "Every idea is given a hearing . . . even if it seems fairly extreme." At the same time, "there is disagreement. The group is comfortable with this and shows no signs of having to avoid conflict. . . ." In short, the members support and confront one another.

© 1981 by Marvin R. Weisbord and C. James Maselko.

## Table 1.   Self-Diagnosis

(Circle the number that fits best for you right now.)

*Receiving support from others for me is*:

| Embarrassing/difficult | | | | | | Pleasant/easy |
|---|---|---|---|---|---|---|
| 1 | 2 | 3 | 4 | 5 | 6 | 7 |

*Offering support to others for me is*:

| Unnatural/rare event | | | | | | Easy/frequent event |
|---|---|---|---|---|---|---|
| 1 | 2 | 3 | 4 | 5 | 6 | 7 |

*Confronting others for me is*:

| Clumsy/awkward/usually avoided | | | | | | Natural/smooth/useful |
|---|---|---|---|---|---|---|
| 1 | 2 | 3 | 4 | 5 | 6 | 7 |

*Being confronted by others for me is*:

| Uncomfortable/scary/avoided | | | | | | Welcome chance for dialogue |
|---|---|---|---|---|---|---|
| 1 | 2 | 3 | 4 | 5 | 6 | 7 |

What have you concluded about yourself? Check below:

_____ I'm satisfied with my skills as they are.
_____ I need to support more.
_____ I need to confront more
_____ I need more of both skills.

## Self-Diagnosis

Improving supporting and confronting skills requires a bit of self-diagnosis. Some people are better at one skill than the other, and some have trouble with both. Take a minute to rate yourself on the scale in Table 1. Which skill do you use least now? That is the one to start practicing immediately. Learn to use it *together with* the skill that's better developed.

You don't need to go to workshops to practice. Instead, try the behavior we will recommend with bosses, subordinates, and peers. We're talking about using the innate abilities most people are born with: the ability to hear and be heard. Unfortunately, many of us lost these abilities on the education treadmill and must relearn them later in life as "interpersonal skills."

Think about a relationship you want to improve, a task you want to accomplish, an unsolved problem you want solved. Think about the person you must speak with, what you want her or him to do, and what your discussions with that person have been like until now. Then, consider the relationship in light of your own ability to support and confront.

## An Emphasis on Resolution

In working with managers we often ask what the word "support" conjures up in their minds. Responses are surprisingly consistent: trust, help, assistance, back-up, aid, and agreement. This list is notable in two ways. First, the words are loaded with positive feelings. Second, the words always imply that the supporter *agrees* with the person being supported.

At first, it seems contradictory to managers that it is possible (and productive) to support people they don't see eye to eye with. It seems somehow dishonest to support someone with whom we disagree. But that would be to hear only the *facts* in another's statements and to miss the *feelings* behind the facts.

Consider this recent situation, for example, where the parties could not hear the feelings for the facts. The scene was a meeting among physicians and administrators of a hospital to work out a new practice plan.

**Administrator #1:** "The plan we want you to accept is fair, reasonable, and essential to the survival of this hospital."

**Physician #1:** "I think it's a threat to our practice. We won't have control over the management of our patients."

**Administrator #1:** "No, it's not a threat. That's ridiculous. It's hardly any change at all from. . . ."

**Physician #2:** "There's no way we can buy this plan."

**Administrator #2:** "Well, if that's an example of your cooperativeness, we're in serious trouble. The government is insisting. . . ."

**Trustee:** "We *have* to have this issue resolved. I want you to sit down together and work out a plan for the survival of this hospital."

**Physician #1:** "We're sitting down now!"

**Trustee:** "Yes, but we're not getting anywhere."

**Administrator #1:** "Well, if the physicians would just cooperate and try to see this thing in its true perspective. . . ."

**Physician #1:** "Who's uncooperative? We didn't dream up this plan."

Both physicians and administrators are blaming each other and digging in their heels for a long battle. Neither side has been heard by the other. Each fuels the disagreement by treating the other's feelings as unreal or irrelevant.

So long as the antagonists hear only facts, they are stuck with judging whether the facts are "true" and whether, therefore, they can agree and still hold on to their own integrity. This confusion between the words (facts) and the music (feelings) is the single biggest stumbling block to supporting others. Supporting can happen only if agreement is treated as a secondary matter, one to be held in abeyance, while we try to hear and understand what the other person is saying. In short, what's required is the skill of *supporting* the feelings of people with whom we disagree.

Consider this "instant replay" of the physician-administrator meeting—an event incidentally that actually took place after the group had been introduced to the concepts of supporting and confronting. The dialogue, based on mutual supporting, takes a turn for the better.

**Physician #1:** "We still see the plan as a threat to our practices."

**Administrator #1:** "Well, that isn't what we intended. I recognize that it's a threat from your point of view, and that all of you are opposed to it. I think it *could* be a threat in the long run unless we work together to minimize the impact. Given the heat from the government, I don't see many choices."

**Physician #1:** "Well, we know that you need to go in this direction and that you're doing the best you can with a bad situation. However, we want a voice in this. If you're willing to take our problems into account, I think we can work out a plan to achieve what you want."

The problem is unresolved. The substantive disagreements have still to be confronted. Yet the mood of the parties to work it out has changed dramatically.

## Really Listening

Sometimes, the *intention* to support is evident from the start, yet people still end up behaving in ways exactly the opposite of what was intended. Consider this vignette, overheard in a factory:

**Supervisor:** "I'm running late. If we don't finish this job by five, we'll blow the contract. What'll I do?"

**Office manager** (who is also his friend): "Don't sweat it. Look at the job you did last time. With a record like yours they can't fire you for one mistake."

**Supervisor:** "Well, that's easy for you to say. I *am* sweating it, and with a boss like mine you never know what he'll do."

**Office manager:** "Ah, why don't you have a cup of coffee and calm down? It'll be all right."

The supervisor has asked his friend for help. *Intending* support, she fails him by denying his feelings ("Don't sweat it") and providing a rationalization for *not* solving the problem ("a record like yours"). In short he is advised, as a solution, to stop feeling what he feels.

In fact, the foreman *does* have a good record and won't lose his job. In fact, even if the job isn't finished by five, the contract will not be blown. It is also a fact, though, that he's running late and believes catastrophe will ensue. Those are the facts *he* considers important. He will not feel supported unless his friend validates *his* priorities by demonstrating that he is being taken seriously. A better response would have been the following:

**Supervisor:** "I'm running late. If we don't finish this job by five, we'll blow the contract. What'll I do?

**Office Manager:** "Yeah, I can see you're running late, and if the contract's blown that could be serious. What's the best way I can help you?"

The office manager shows that she accepts the supervisor's feelings. Instead of providing a nonsolution, she asks how to help. If the supervisor feels supported, he will be more open to influence on the one hand, and more capable of discovering his own solution on the other.

There are four things people often do, *intending* to give support, that are not at all supportive:

1. Give unsolicited advice. "If *I* were you, I would. . . ."
2. Tell people they "*shouldn't* feel that way." Who says so? They *do* feel that way.
3. Minimize the problem. "Oh, that's not so bad. You should be glad you don't have *real* troubles. Let me tell you about *my* boss."
4. Accept the obligation to solve the problem—without being asked. "Well, the first thing you should do is get on the phone and. . . ."

Most people will also see the following four actions as supportive:

1. Repeat what you've heard. "Let's see if I understand you. You're saying that. . . ."
2. Put *both* facts and feelings into a statement about what has been said. "You're annoyed (feeling) with me because (fact) I haven't made the phone call yet."
3. Empathize. "I can see why you're angry in this situation. I would be too."
4. Ask the other person what, if anything, they want from you. "How can I help you with this?"

The last point is especially important. Frequently, people just want somebody to *hear* them. Simply listening often solves the problem. Offering advice, denying feelings, or proposing courses of action without being asked tells others they have *not* been heard.

## Suppose You Don't Agree?

What happens when the other person is wrong in what he or she has said or directly contradicts a belief or course of action important to us?

## Table 2.    Tips on Confronting

1. Accept *whatever* feelings the differences generate—helplessness, anger, disappointment, elation, anticipation. Treat them as real and important for both parties.

2. Really listen to what the other persion is saying, and make sure you have been heard. Call time out if you're not sure.

3. Be responsible for your own feelings. Others don't *put* feelings into us. It's unreasonable and unhelpful to blame them for what's going on inside of us.

4. Treat confronting as an exercise in rationality. It requires clarity, calmness, and patience in the presence of often strong feelings.

5. Go for a resolution both parties can live with. Don't try to *change* the other person. Let others do what they want.

6. If the issue seems unresolvable, experiment—try it one way or the other and evaluate together after a short time.

---

Here we need a second skill that requires us to recognize differences. This was the stage toward which the physicians and administrators in our earlier example were moving, the point at which they would confront their disagreement.

When we ask managers what the word "confront" means to them, we consistently get back words loaded with negative feelings: challenge, fight, argue, defend, battle, force. These words are consistent with only *one* of several dictionary definitions, the one that means "to face in hostility and defiance." Rarely do managers provide another, equally valid connotation— to "face squarely." This is not the same thing as challenging, arguing, or fighting. (See Table 2.)

Learning to face a difference squarely is not always easy to do. Most people find they must give up the attitude ingrained since childhood that disagreement is "bad" and avoiding conflict is "good." Paradoxically, this attitude directly contradicts an equally powerful feeling that solving problems is "good" and indecisiveness "bad." This leads to two traps—avoiding conflict on the one hand and moving toward premature resolution on the other.

It might be helpful here to note that nonconfronters often fear the risks of genuine interaction—anger, rejection, tension, and so forth. They have a strong need to be "nice" all the time. Yet the risks of not confronting seem equally unappetizing—less power, reduced influence, lower performance, less likelihood of achieving goals.

The issue is not *whether* to confront, but rather *when* and *how* to confront skillfully. Conflict is inevitable, legitimate, and potentially useful in all important relationships.

To exploit fully the potential of conflict, however, we must also avoid rushing toward premature resolution. Conflict often starts

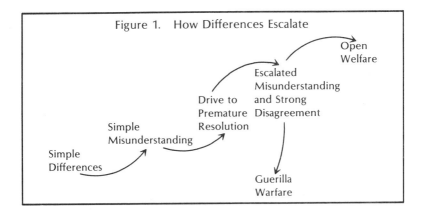

Figure 1.  How Differences Escalate

Open Welfare

Escalated Misunderstanding and Strong Disagreement

Drive to Premature Resolution

Simple Misunderstanding

Simple Differences

Guerilla Warfare

innocently, with relatively simple differences, yet the drive to premature resolution can quickly escalate the conflict. How it happens is shown in the illustration in Figure 1.

We now have an escalated misunderstanding—each party actively opposing the other's stand and refusing to accept the other's solution. One or the other party may hate conflict. In that case a guerilla action—delay or denial—will probably ensue.

## Exploring the Differences

What's called for early on is an exploration of the differences that lie between disagreement and misunderstanding. Confronting means making explicit the differences that exist between two individuals, and its success depends entirely on the ability of both parties to express their differences as strongly as possible.

There is a verbal clue that a conflict is about to escalate without sufficient exploration of differences. That clue is "but." It has no place in successful confronting.

**Sales manager:** "I'm a little behind on first-quarter results, maybe eight percent short of forecast. I know you said we need to be ahead of forecast at this point. I'm not sure how much. Anyway, that's the story."

**Vice-president–sales:** "Well, I don't like it. You may be eight percent behind, *but* you said eight weeks ago things were looking good. I'll never be able to explain this to my boss—he expects us to be ahead of forecast every quarter, and I expect you to be too."

**Sales manager:** "I didn't realize then that the new promotional displays would fall flat. Besides, marketing really let us down in sending out samples. *But* I wouldn't worry. We'll make it up in the second quarter."

**Vice-president–sales:** "I want you to be ahead of forecast, no ands, ifs, or buts."

**Sales manager:** "But I'm not ahead."

**Vice-president–sales:** "Well, you better get ahead."

Here each party moves to cancel the other's feelings. The vice-president seeks to deny the reality of the worrisome eight percent with a "but you said." The sales manager, in turn, has a "but" of his own. *He* wouldn't worry, even though the boss is obviously worried. Neither confronts the issues—the difference between goal and performance, the consequences for each party, the potential for resolution. It never develops that the sales manager sees the issue as a temporary slump easily overcome, nor that the vice-president may be in serious trouble with *his* boss unless he can make a convincing explanation. The parties have no resolution. The implied threat, "You better get ahead," suggests that warfare, open or underground, is where they're heading.

Imagine that each knew how important supporting the other person's position was to productive resolution. The conversation might go something like this:

**Sales manager:** "I'm a little behind on first-quarter results, maybe eight percent short of forecast. I know you said we need to be ahead at this point."

**Vice-president–sales:** "Well, I'm disappointed, and I guess you are too. I'm glad you let me know. How did it happen?"

**Sales manager:** "The new promotional displays bombed out; and we were slow to get the samples out. I think we can make it up in the second quarter."

**Vice-president–sales:** "Well, my boss isn't going to like it either. At the same time he has a right to know that's where we stand. I'm counting on you to catch up. Can you do it? Do you need any help?

**Sales manager:** "I think we can do it. I realize your boss keeps the heat on. I'll do my best to avoid this the next time."

Here, both parties treat the differences—in this case, of expectations—as real. The slack sales are real, so is the vice-president's disappointment, so is the pressure from above. By acknowledging all this, the parties clarify the potential misunderstanding from the beginning. Instead of escalation, they move toward resolution.

Some of us confront more naturally than we support. For others it's just the reverse. To always confront and never support is to deny the needs of others. To always support and never confront is to deny our own needs. Without both skills, working with others will be much less successful than any of us would like. As we improve these skills we will put more energy into solving the problem and less into fighting to be heard.□

# Dynamic Subordinancy          William J. Crockett

*"Our success in effectively filling our subordinancy roles is the key to our here-and-now security as well as to our future promotion and success."*

Our organizations are filled with subordinates, but few of us get much basic survival training for that role, not to mention training on how we might make those roles dynamic, synergistic, and satisfying. But we spend a lot of time helping people to learn how to be effective leaders and in learning how to fulfill their leadership roles. I believe that it's important for our organizations to start giving some attention to the development of the concept and role of "followership," because leadership is but one strand in the complex web of human relationships that holds our organizations together.

Traditionally, we have accepted the assumption that it's primarily the boss's job and responsibility to cause the work group to function well—and to take care of the people needs of subordinates so that the group is turned on and productive. Bosses have borne the chief responsibility in the past for the vitality of their relationships with their subordinates, and for the quantity and quality of their work.

But the successful and effective boss-subordinate relationship not only demands some things of bosses, it also demands some things of followers as well. Therefore, subordinates can and should be more than passive robots to be manipulated and used by bosses. They have the responsibility—as well as the opportunity—for making the situation a good one, a win/win for themselves as well as for the boss.

Another very pragmatic reason for our wishing to achieve excellence as followers is that we often get rewarded or punished as a result of our followership effectiveness. Our success in effectively filling our subordinancy roles is the key to our here-and-now security as well as to our future promotion and success. People get fired because they are ineffective subordinates. From this standpoint alone, the vitality and worth of the relationship is more important to the subordinate than it is to the boss— because it is the subordinate who has the most at stake!

There are three overlapping areas or ways for looking at the followership role and for mapping strategies for making that role more fulfilling to us, as well as more effective.

© May 1981, *Training and Development Journal*, American Society for Training and Development, pp. 155–61. Reprinted with permission. All rights reserved.

The first of these areas is the job itself. This includes how well we understand its mission and its accountabilities as well as its opportunities and the skills and attitudes this requires of us.

The second way of looking at our jobs is in terms of our relationships and, most especially, our relationships with our bosses.

The third area for review is our own feelings about our jobs, our bosses, and ourselves. Just what is our trust level and what can we do to improve it?

This article deals with each of these three areas and helps us to think through where we stand in each. It helps us to find the means of taking charge of our work lives rather than passively accepting what comes our way.

Finally, it also helps us to formulate an action plan for doing something about each of these three areas, for it is only by taking action that we can start to become more dynamic in our followership.

## The Job Itself

Being a subordinate is very much like being a steward, i.e., assuming the responsibility for the well-being of something that belongs to another. Like the biblical story of the good and bad stewards (Matthew 25: 14–30), the stewardship role is not fulfilled when it is just passively done. The good steward is dynamic and risk-taking in attending to the work that he or she has been given to do.

However, in order for us to be dynamic and risk-taking in our jobs, we must work through some things for ourselves and then with our bosses. To risk blindly is the action of a foolish person, and it courts ruin as well as success. The dynamism I am talking about is that which has a high chance of ending with success for the subordinate as well as for the boss—a win/win situation for both.

In order for us to be genuinely dynamic, we must have a strong launch pad of basic understanding about the job and our boss on which to base our actions. There are three ingredients that make up this basic launch pad.

### 1. Know What the Job Is

In a survey, a group of top-level businesspeople failed to agree upon the exact acts of subordinancy that would ensure the success of their subordinates. But they did agree upon the point that the subordinate must know precisely what it is that her or his boss expects. Doing a number of things well will not suffice if the boss doesn't care about those things. Therefore, no amount of effort in these areas will make the subordinate succeed if he or she fails to perform well in the one or two things that the boss holds dear.

Another area of potential misunderstanding about the job comes from ambiguity about the job itself. The more ambiguity there is in a job, the greater the danger in terms of the subordinate's not delivering what the boss really expects. The initiation of discussions with the boss about expectations for the tasks and responsibilities of the job is one of the first and most important responsibilities (and opportunities) of a subordinate.

It is absolutely essential that the subordinate knows and understands the critical success factors of the task, i.e., the boss's expectations. It is far too easy to overlook them in the first place, or to push them out of focus due to the multiplicity of nonessential tasks and loadings that the job (the subordinate) has acquired. It is the subordinate who has the best opportunity to know these loadings because he or she has the firsthand data. Therefore, it is the subordinate's responsibility to initiate discussions with the boss to surface expectations about the job: its accountabilities, its goals, its content, its priorities, its methodology, its standards, etc. Boss/subordinate discussions about the context and meanings of the subordinate's job, when they are initiated by the subordinate's genuine concern for the boss and her or his best interest rather than from the subordinate's dissatisfaction, can be a dynamic and exhilarating experience for a subordinate. If subordinates will take the pains to be objective in documenting their cases, and if they will present it with a genuine concern for the boss, then the subsequent discussion can be free from emotion, tension, and acrimony.

One important piece of self-research we can do is to develop the following data about the job:

a. the accountabilities . . . what end results am I account-able for?

b. the critical accountabilities . . . the ones that have the most leverage if accomplished and those that have the most risk if not accomplished.

c. the ways I now spend my time and how that relates to (a) and to (b) above.

## 2. *Know How to Do the Job*

The value that the boss places upon a subordinate is in relationship to how well the subordinate enhances the effectiveness of the boss's domain—how well the job is done. The short-sighted subordinate will conceive it to be the boss's responsibility to discover deficiencies, to train, to promote, to look after her or his career, and to help in the subordinate's success. And of course bosses do have some of these responsibilities.

One unyielding requirement for us if we are to be successful subordinates is that we must objectively look at ourselves and our skills in relation to the skills that the job requires. If we can do this, and can see our own deficiencies, then we can, through training and development, acquire the needed skills. This aggressive self-examination of one's needs and one's taking charge of one's own self-improvement is another way dynamic subordinates distinguish themselves from their more passive colleagues.

Dynamic subordinates don't wait. They soon take on that responsibility for their own professional development. They don't own their territory, for their boss can fire them at will. But the one thing that every subordinate does own, and that no one can take away, is their expertise—their professionalism. This is the most personal, most valuable, and most absolute territory a person can have. No one can hold a capable person back. Their professionalism and talents will become known, will be needed, and will be requested—if not by their boss, then by others.

The wise subordinate is the learning, developing, experience-seeking person who becomes independent because he or she is a professional! The wise subordinate never uses the maddening excuse, "That isn't my job," but will seize upon every opportunity for learning something new and having a new experience.

### 3. Do the Job

The end product that a boss expects from a subordinate is a job well done—according to what "well done" means to the boss. A subordinate succeeds, gets rewarded, and receives accolades and promotions based mostly upon successful fulfillment of her or his here-and-now duties.

Do the job! That's what the boss expects and that's what we are receiving our pay as subordinates to do. That's what will lead us to success in the future.

It is said that there are three requirements for being a successful follower, i.e., for getting the job done:

- knowing *what* the job is
- knowing *how* to do the job
- *doing* the job.

Knowing what the job is and having the required skills to do it will not get the job done *if* the person is not motivated to do it with zest. One of the most powerful drags to productivity in America is lack of motivation.

To become "demotivated" is the emotional result of all that we see happening to us in the workplace. When we are demotivated we don't care whether or not we do the job or whether we do it well or badly. Or maybe we are so turned off and angry that our hidden objective is to really punish the organization and our boss! If we are in this frame of mind, then we have but two logical choices:

a. to pull ourselves out of this pit and rekindle our positive drive, or
b. to leave.

The inevitable consequence of our staying in this negative frame of mind is to be fired sooner or later.

One plan of dynamic action that I can suggest for us if we are in this state is to make an objective (it's hard to be objective now) analysis of our entire situation:

a. search for and identify all of the negative emotional producers;
b. search for and identify the positive emotional producers (there will surely be some of these);
c. carefully analyze and examine the impact of each of these negatives and positives upon us;
d. think through ways that we can unhook ourselves from our participation in the negative producers;
e. think of ways that we can create other positive producers and enhance those that now exist; and
f. make a plan of action.

This whole analysis ideally should be shared with a trusted friend who will tell us honestly what her or his reactions are and not just what we would like to hear.

Another potential reason for our demotivation may be our feeling that we have been given little or no freedom by our bosses to get our jobs done. Freedom of action in getting one's job done has these components:

• freedom to determine the substance (the what);
• freedom to determine the timing of when things will be done (the when);
• freedom to determine how the job will be done (the how);

- freedom to determine who will be responsible for doing the job (the who);
- freedom to determine the cost of doing it (the cost).

Sometimes bosses just don't give their subordinates enough freedom to enable them to feel worthwhile, trusted, and turned on.

We can analyze each of our major accountabilities on the preceding five dimensions to get an objective evaluation of our freedom. If our analysis demonstrates to us that we aren't being given enough freedom of accountability, or on one or more of the above dimensions, we then have objective data to take to our boss for discussion. If this is the case, we need to carefully devise an action plan of how we will confront the boss as well as what we plan to confront her or him with.

The possibility exists that we subordinates can badly misread the realities about us and may thereby have actively created our own demotivation out of nothing more than our own misperceptions. If this is the case, we'll need a *personal* action plan. On the other hand, of course, the possibility also exists that our analysis and our subsequent discussions with our boss only serve to confirm our worst fears and suspicions . . . that the situation is a lost cause! If this is the case, then it will require a different kind of an action plan from us—a plan to leave.

One of the key dimensions to dynamic subordinancy is the psychological willingness and the professional capability of the subordinate to be independent of the boss and the job whenever I, the subordinate, want the end to come. When I find myself depressed and demotivated and I have done all that I could to change the conditions causing this, then it's time to think about leaving. When it becomes apparent to me that I can't respect my boss, don't approve of my boss, can't trust my boss, again, it's time to think about leaving. When I find myself wanting to punish my boss, feeling that I must compete with my boss, and am moved to "badmouth" and belittle my boss, then it's far past the time for me to move on. To stay under such conditions is to prostitute myself for money with little sense of commitment and loyalty. To stay is to lose my self-respect as a human being. To stay is eventually to fail.

Perhaps our willingness to leave a situation whenever it no longer meets our needs, fulfills our values, turns us on, or challenges our expertise is the most important single measure for ensuring that we remain dynamic as subordinates. This is the key to our own freedom and to our self-esteem.

## Boss-Subordinate Relationships

Everyone knows that there is a lot more involved in a job than just getting the job done, no matter how well we do it from a substantive point of view. One critical factor for success in any job is the quality of the relationship we have been able to create with our boss.

This relationship, like all relationships, is a mutual responsibility to develop and to nourish. But since it has so much significance for the future growth and success of the subordinate, we must go to extra lengths to try to cause the relationship to become a good one. Some of the things we can do are:

### 1. *Challenge*

We must obey the legal demands of our bosses, but in doing so we do not have to lose our self-esteem nor take on the hangdog pose of the servant. We can become the trusted adviser to whom the boss comes to get the straight dope. No one, not even our boss, can be completely infallible. Humans at all levels will make mistakes occasionally. Most managers are thinly spread over wide stretches of important and diverse activities. As a result, they can be caught in trivial errors that take on more importance than they have in real substance. Wise subordinates will be alert to ways that they can rescue their bosses from mistakes of commission and omission.

Most good bosses don't like subservience and don't trust "yes" people. Most bosses want subordinates who will challenge their ideas, differ with their decisions, give them data, put forward new ideas for doing things, and who will care to be uniquely themselves. But to get away with this kind of behavior requires that the subordinate come from a base of absolute trust and not from competitive counterdependency. To gain this preferred role, a subordinate must have done the following:

- demonstrated absolute personal respect and loyalty to the boss in other situations;
- gained the boss's admiration and respect for her or his professionalism, for the accuracy of her or his data, for the timeliness of her or his reports, and for her or his emotional maturity;
- never publicly played win/lose games at the boss's expense; and
- gotten the boss's job done to the boss's expectations when the decision was finally made.

The role of loyal opposition or devil's advocate is an important one for all subordinates to learn—if they can also learn to use it from a solid base of trust. They must learn, when practicing it, to come across as caring rather than punishing, collaborative rather than competitive, probing rather than judging.

The way this is done—how it is done—is often far more important than what the substance is.


## 2. Inform

Closely associated with the concept of subordinancy is the irksome chore of accounting for our activities. Like obedience, most of us stopped accounting to anyone when we left home. And now that we are at work, we must once more account to someone—our hierarchic superiors.

The reason for this accountability to the boss is that no subordinate, no matter if her or his title is dishwasher or president, has final accountability. We are not the full owner of the territory that we occupy. We may feel like an entrepreneur, act like a king, and be a saint. But in the final analysis, we are but a steward in the "master's vineyard."

Through the process of delegation, each subordinate is given a job to do by the boss. Some bosses tell their subordinates little, and others tell them a lot—how, when, who, where, why, how much, how often, how deep, how wide, etc. But in the end, every subordinate must account to the leader for her or his stewardship of what was done with the thing the boss assigned. It is the subordinate's duty to give and the boss's right to request this accounting.

It is the boss's territory. It is the boss's right to know. The boss must be told because he or she is also a subordinate to another boss who is also looking for that same accountability. And so it works, forever upward. The effective subordinate will fully and cheerfully perform this function of accountability. This, in reality, gives the subordinate a chance to put the boss at ease and create the first stirrings of trust.

A subordinate who, for whatever reason, elects *not* to account to the boss fully and honestly, can't win. Such actions on the part of the subordinate as withholding information, diverting data, giving half-truths, forgetting, falsely telling, etc., whatever the excuse or rationale, are examples of no-win, nonprofessional subordinancy. The system doesn't condone such subordinate behavior—no matter what kind of a boss a subordinate may have or what the private rationale may be.

The dynamic subordinate will not only fully and cheerfully perform this function of accountability, but will initiate it. The subordinate's challenge is to be able to account to the boss about the job honestly and factually and still retain the feeling of personal freedom and dignity.

### 3. Invite Her or Him In

All of us have a feeling of personal territory. My desk, my car, my coat, my home, my job, etc., are mine and are important to me. They are my territory and no one had better encroach uninvited into my domain. All of us seem to possess and exercise this "territorial imperative," this personal ownership of the things that are ours, including our jobs.

There is one area, however, where a person cannot exercise such dominion with impunity—the job that the boss has delegated. It is still the boss's territory because the boss still has accountability upward for the success of the job. The subordinate has been given only a temporary lease. The subordinate is the steward for the boss and is working to fulfill the job in the best way possible on behalf of the boss.

Some bosses, of course, for whatever reasons, will sometimes elect to respect the subordinate's area and not intrude unasked into this domain. Other bosses make no bones about their right to tell the subordinate exactly how they want the job to be done. Leaving out the psychological, motivational, and productive consequences of such dominant boss behavior, there seems to be little question of the boss's *right* to do just that. The reason for this rests upon the rule of accountability—the person who is accountable has the right. And since the subordinate's boss is accountable upward, it is her or his right to have full access to the subordinate's area of responsibility.

So the dynamic subordinates will open wide the gates of their job to the boss. They will invite her or him in to visit frequently. They will proudly show her or him the situation, explain the improvements, ask for help on problems, and seek the boss's ideas for change.

The subordinate who can share her or his area of responsibility with the boss with unlimited and uninhibited trust makes the boss her or his advocate—or partner—and gains additional trust and freedom as a result. The challenge to the subordinate is in fulfilling her or his stewardship responsibilities to the boss without falling into the trap of claiming ownership of the territory that the subordinate has so skillfully created and built.

### 4. Ask for Feedback

The job that a person does is always emotionally loaded by the subordinate's perceived behavior of the boss—and, most importantly, the subordinate's interpretation of the meaning of that behavior. Whatever the boss does or does not do in the course of a relationship, day after day, has implied (and sometimes overt) meaning for the subordinate about the boss's intentions and attitude.

For example, if the boss may seem to withhold important data that the subordinate believes is needed in order to do a job properly; if the boss doesn't invite her or him to the meetings that he or she thinks are important; if the boss looks at her or him in certain ways; if the boss appears at unusual times; and on and on, the subordinate may wonder *why*. In such cases, the subordinate supplies the reasons and the motives for the boss's behavior—and in many cases those reasons and motives, in the mind of the subordinate, may portray the boss's dissatisfaction.

This is the start of distrust, suspicion, ill will, disloyalty, and outright animosity on the part of the subordinate. Over time, these emotions can build to the point of causing the relationship to end.

The sad thing in our human relationships is that very often the subordinate's *perception* of the boss and the situation is entirely incorrect. And in such instances, subordinates again have the responsibility to act, because it is they who have the data, i.e., their perception of the boss's behavior and their inferences of the meanings of that behavior. So, it is the subordinate who has the burden of taking the matter up with the boss.

In such cases, wise subordinates will choose the time and place carefully. They will also take the responsibility for the feelings that they have and the way they express them to the boss. For example, don't start out by saying "you do so-and-so," but rather "I feel so-and-so." Usually the boss will ask "why," and then the subordinate can describe her or his perceptions of the behavior and her or his inferences of the meaning (impact) of that behavior. This can be the beginning of a very fruitful building process that may become ongoing.

This kind of dynamic behavior on the part of a subordinate will do much to keep the boss/subordinate relationship vital and unspoiled by the pollution of unfounded suspicions.


## 5. *Help Give Feedback*

The boss, also being human, will play the same game of perceptions and implied meaning that the subordinate plays.

The wise subordinate will be aware of the following two important facts:

• that the boss does indeed look at the subordinate's behavior and wonder about the implied meanings it may hold; and

• that the boss may not have the guts to openly and directly confront the subordinate about the things that the subordinate does that the boss doesn't like. It may be the boss's tendency to "store up" resentments and irritations over little things without telling subordinates. And, if this is so, this holds grave danger for the subordinate. The subordinate may be blissfully unaware of the deep resentment and irritation that some part of her or his behavior is stirring in the boss. The danger is that one little thing the subordinate may inadvertently do may wipe out the boss's perception of all the good things the subordinate has been doing. And, in fact, these irritations may result in the subordinate's dismissal. The explosion of a boss's pent-up emotions can be dangerous to all subordinates.

The dynamic subordinate will take the initiative to probe with the boss for these hidden reservoirs of resentment. One of the best ways of doing this is for the subordinate to get the boss's confidence, i.e., tell the boss of her or his hopes for success and to ask the boss for help, for coaching, for ideas, and for advice.

This may ease the situation so that the boss can feel free to express her or his feelings. And once this general base of expectations has been laid, then the subordinate should take the initiative to discuss the results of any major activity that he or she has fulfilled as to what went right, what went wrong, how the boss felt, etc. The process becomes *critique*, and not criticism.

Only the most constricted boss can fail to respond to the sincere searching of a subordinate for positive and helpful critique.

## 6. *Share Your Needs*

Subordinates also have needs, and wise bosses, realizing this, will attempt to understand and fulfill those needs. But—for whatever reasons—some bosses won't do this or are unable to start the process.

Dynamic subordinates will not elect to feel hurt when they find that the boss is not very aware of their needs. They won't sulk in their corner. They won't immediately try to find another job. Instead, they will stop waiting to be chosen and will start letting the boss know what it is that they want. In reality, there is no way for another human being to actually know our needs unless and until we make them known. Oftentimes our needs do make sense to others, do fit in with higher goals and objectives, and can indeed be met. But it's the subordinate's responsibility to take the risk of making them known. That's part of being dynamic.

## 7. Build Trust

The only relationship that is tenable for a subordinate to have is a constant, surging flow of two-way trust. Without such trust, nothing works well and the relationship is flat, unexciting, and suspicious. There can be no real professionalism without trust.

Building trust is a mutual activity and is the responsibility of both the boss and the subordinate. But the subordinate must work at it harder, take the first initiative, and avoid the depletion of trust caused by ineffective behavior because the subordinate has so much to lose if the boss's trust is lost.

When the boss loses trust, the subordinate has lost all.

Trust is built in tiny increments of positive behavior in the things that have already been mentioned: obedience with grace, accounting with absolute honesty, exercising unselfish stewardship, initiating access, and challenging and confronting. It is built by day-by-day evidence that the subordinate puts the boss's interest first, does not upstage the boss, does not let the boss look bad, saves the boss from mistakes, rescues the boss from errors, and makes the boss believe that he or she is truly happy in second place. But getting the here-and-now job done on time, fully up to its standards and fully meeting the expectations that the boss has for it, is the single most powerful producer of trust. If a subordinate will do these things, one day her or his bank will overflow with trust!

## Responsibility for Ourselves

Perhaps the greatest challenge of all for us is the opportunity we have for managing ourselves in ways that enable us to be proactive in our jobs and in our critical relationships. In my own experience, it has been neither an easy task nor a quick one. But it surely is one that is worthy of our consideration and of our effort.

Self-management is taking charge of both our emotions and our behavior so that we are not just reactive robots to every emotional stimulus that becomes activated within us. Since our emotions are, potentially, powerful motivators of our behavior, then it seems to me that we need to learn a system that puts us in charge. But the fact that I may choose self-management as an option and the actual act of fulfilling that choice (i.e., making self-management an actuality in my life) are miles apart!

There follows some ideas on how we can make a start toward self-management.

## 1. Acquire Self-Awareness

Our first challenge is to be aware of our own behavior and the feelings it may trigger in others. Do we behave in ways that arouse feelings of anger, hatred, frustration, fear, insecurity, and distrust in others toward us? To the extent that we generate these feelings in others by our own behavior—and since feelings generally cause (motivate) dysfunctional or inappropriate behavior—then we are sometimes a direct catalyst of such behavior in others. Thus, in this sense, our behavior is ineffective.

Since we each "own" our feelings and are responsible for our ways of reacting, we cannot "blame" others for our reactions. And when we hit someone's hot button (either deliberately or by accident), we are participating in and contributing to their inappropriate behavior, whatever it is. Therefore, our challenge is to become aware of the impact of our own behavior and to behave in ways that do not set in motion destructive and inappropriate chains of behavior in others—and most especially our bosses.

One important aspect of self-awareness is examination of our habit patterns of dress, of facial expression, of body language, and of speech. Have we fallen into the trap of "you know-ing" the end of every sentence? Do we interrupt? Do we listen? Are we cynical? Self-awareness requires eternal vigilance of ourselves by ourselves and, if possible, a trusted friend to insure that we are indeed fully positive.

## 2. Managing Our Feelings and Our Behavior

a. *Managing the Way I Behave.* One way we can cope with our feelings is through a process of self-disciplined control of our behavior. This requires that we remind ourselves that we are responsible for our own behavior and can shape it in a variety of ways. We can each develop a *range* of ways of reacting to different persons, in different situations, and for different results. This is to say that sometimes one deals with a bastard as a bastard deserves to be dealt with!

It is good, however, to remind ourselves that certain roles "call for" certain behavior (and control). Thus, parents have an obligation for restraint toward their children, or a boss needs to consider what responsibilities are for the well-being of her or his subordinates who have been entrusted to her or him by the organization, and subordinates must consider the boss's need for respect and loyalty. This kind of self-restraint is not a denial of the feeling; it is an optional kind of behavior that we have selected for that person in that situation. Emotionally responsive behavior is not the only choice I have for coping with the way I feel. It's just one way, and all too often it's not the best way.

I believe that it's worth the effort to manage our behavior for two reasons. First, because it does save us from many a behavioral blunder. Our perceptions aren't always accurate enough in sensing the true feelings or motives of others, despite their overt behavior, for us to risk basing all of our behavior upon them. We cannot assume that we always make the correct evaluation of their intentions and interests toward us. And second, when we do succeed, it is a great psychic reward to us because of the increased "self-esteem" that flows to us from a successful encounter with ourselves. We *can* be responsible for our own behavior.

b. *Managing the Way I Feel.* My second option of self-management is even harder than the first. This is to embrace the concept that my emotions are also my own to deal with in just the same way as my behavior.

I know and accept the fact that no one can make me "feel motivated," "feel trust," "feel love," "feel happy," and so on, unless I, too, am a willing party to that process with another person. This does not mean a denial of the feeling once it occurs, but it does mean that I don't need to have the feeling in the first place unless I bring it upon myself.

For example, if someone does something that I interpret in a way that means to me that I have been snubbed, the frequent "human" emotional response to that would be either anger or hurt—maybe some of both. A common rejoinder is that the other person made me feel these ways, and the behavioral response might be to *get even* in some way or another—to punish the person either by overt act or by withdrawal.

But my feelings (emotions) are *not necessarily an automatic reaction* to the behavior of another, unless *I myself let them be* (maybe even want them to be). It's like turning on a light bulb. There is power in the line, but the bulb won't shine unless I turn it on. There is behavior (power) in the system (the way the person acted), but my emotions (the light bulb) needn't be (won't be) activated—turned on—unless I want them to be.

c. *Our Response to Personally Painful Behavior.* If I do what others demand of me just because my boss, my subordinates, or others get angry—swear, pout, threaten, and abuse me—then I have become a participant in their process. I am partially responsible for what they are doing to me. Their behavior is effective for them because it achieves their objectives with me.

The most telling (best) response to the personally painful behavior of anyone is to deny that person the achievement of her or his objective when he or she uses painful and inappropriate behavior toward us. (Workers in business and industry all over America are in reality doing this by their uncaring attitude about the job.) We all learn from our experience, and if our behavior doesn't get the results that we want, then we will change it pretty quickly.


## 3. Our Responsibility to Confront

We subordinates are enmeshed in a web of intricate and conflicting human relationships. We often feel that we are the pawns of powerful forces that use us, direct us, and sometimes discard us, at will. Perhaps the thing that is the most important for us to learn, to accept, and to practice, is to assume full responsibility for ourselves, for our professional growth, and for our behavior. This means that we must learn to attain a high degree of self-management. We do not delude ourselves as to what we wish for any situation, and that we know what we want to have happen for ourselves as well as for our bosses. This means that we keep ourselves close to the realities of our relationships and not let ourselves be carried away by our emotional fantasies.

Finally, this means that we have the internal personal security to take whatever risks there may be for ensuring that all facets of our jobs and relationships are indeed dynamic. Perhaps the greater risk is not risking. The status quo may be the ultimate indignity.

Thus, our own self-discipline, self-management and professionalism become the underlying forces that fuel our dynamic subordinancy. We are indeed responsible for ourselves and for our own behavior. To me, this means that if I honestly have done all of the foregoing, then I take the risk of telling the boss my perceptions of the situation—my degree of psychological pain and my solutions for changing the situation. If the boss, for whatever reason, can't change either her or his own behavior or the situation, then I can exercise my final and ultimate freedom— and leave. I owe it to me to do exactly this—not as a threat and not in anger, but for my own long-run self-esteem.

Edgar Friedenberg has said, "All weakness corrupts, and impotence corrupts absolutely." The traditional state of subordinancy is powerlessness and dependency. But as we make people dependent, we increase their capacity to hate. As we make people powerless, we promote their capacity for violence.

The thing we must learn as bosses is how we can grant people freedom despite all of the demands that the work situation puts upon us.

The challenge we have as subordinates is to secure for ourselves an enhanced self-image, a sense of potency, and a feeling of significance without resorting to the ultimate power—violence. If all of us don't learn how to achieve this for ourselves, and learn how to teach others to achieve it for themselves, then our organizations are in for a continuing era of violence—not because people are bad, but because they hurt so much from the deprived condition of their human needs.□

# Situational Leadership Revisited*      Kenneth H. Blanchard

*". . . leadership style is the pattern of behaviors you use when you are trying to influence the behaviors of others as perceived by those other people."*

The acceptance of Situational Leadership as a practical, easy to understand approach to managing and motivating people has been widespread over the last decade. The concept of Situational Leadership was first described by Paul Hersey and Kenneth Blanchard as "Life Cycle, Theory of Leadership" (Hersey & Blanchard, 1969); the most extensive presentation of the concept has been the Hersey/Blanchard text, *Management of Organizational Behavior: Utilizing Human Resources* (Hersey & Blanchard, 1982), now in its fourth edition. What follows is a description of Ken Blanchard's latest thinking about Situational Leadership, which he and colleagues from Blanchard Training and Development, Inc. (BTD) are using in their work with managers throughout the world.

## Leadership and Leadership Style

Any time you try to influence the behavior of another person, you are engaging in an act of leadership. Therefore, *leadership* is an *influence process*. If you are interested in developing your staff and building motivational climates that result in high levels of productivity in the short *and* long run, then you need to be concerned about your leadership style. *Leadership style* is the pattern of behaviors you use when you are trying to influence the behavior of others as perceived by them. While *your perception* of your own behavior and its impact on others is interesting and useful, it is not very meaningful unless we compare it with the *perceptions of those you are trying to influence*.

For years, when people talked about leadership style, they identified two extremes—autocratic (directive) and democratic (supportive). Autocratic leadership was seen as based on position power and the use of authority, while democratic leadership was associated with personal power and follower participation in

---

© 1982 Blanchard Training & Development, Inc. Used with permission.
   * Situational Leadership as presented in this article has been updated and refined through discussions with practicing managers and long-term colleagues Fred Finch, Doug Forsyth, and Drea Zigarmi.

problem-solving and decision-making processes. Tannenbaum and Schmidt, in their classic article "How to Choose a Leadership Pattern" (Tannenbaum & Schmidt, 1957), argued that these two leadership styles—autocratic and democratic—were either/or styles of leadership and therefore fell along a continuum from very authoritarian leader behavior at one end to very democratic leader behavior at the other end.

## Situational Leadership

Further research (Stogdill & Coons, 1957), however, showed that leadership styles tend to vary considerably from situation to situation, and that it is not helpful to think of leadership style as an either/or continuum. While the behavior of some leaders is characterized mainly by directing activities for their followers in terms of task accomplishment (directive behavior), other leaders concentrate on providing socio-emotional support in terms of

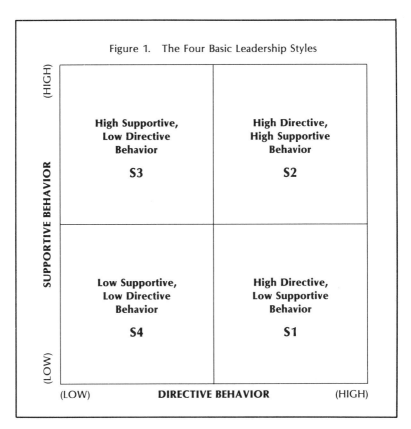

Figure 1.   The Four Basic Leadership Styles

personal relationships between themselves and their followers (supportive behavior). In other situations, various combinations of directive and supportive behavior are evident. Thus, it was determined that directive and supportive leader behaviors are not either/or leadership styles. Instead, these patterns of leader behavior can be plotted on two separate and distinct axes as shown in Figure 1.

Each of the four leadership styles depicted in Figure 1 represent different combinations of directive and supportive leader behavior.** These combinations differ on three dimensions: (1) the amount of direction the leader provides, (2) the amount of support and encouragement the leader provides, and (3) the amount of follower involvement in decision making.

## Directive and Supportive Leader Behaviors

*Directive behavior* is defined as the extent to which a leader engages in one-way communication. The manager spells out the follower(s) role and tells the follower(s) what to do, where to do it, when to do it, how to do it, and then closely supervises performance.

*Supportive behavior* is defined as the extent to which a leader engages in two-way communication, listens, provides support and encouragement, facilitates interaction, and involves the follower in decision making.

In Style 1, a leader is high on direction, low on support. He or she provides specific instructions (roles and goals) for the follower(s) and closely supervises task accomplishment. When using a Style 2, the leader is high on both direction and support. He or she explains decisions and solicits suggestions from the follower(s), but continues to direct task accomplishment. Style 3 leader behavior is characterized by high supportive and low directive behavior. The leader makes decisions together with the follower(s) and supports their efforts in task accomplishment. In Style 4, a leader provides low support and direction. He or she turns over decisions and responsibility for implementation to the follower(s).

## Leadership Behavior as Problem-Solving/Decision-Making Styles

As defined earlier, leadership style is the pattern of behaviors you use when you are trying to influence the behaviors of others *as*

** Hersey and Blanchard in *Management of Organizational Behavior* used the terms "task" and "relationship" to describe the two basic leadership style dimensions. Ken Blanchard now uses the terms "directive" and "supportive" because we have found them more descriptive and easier for practitioners to identify with.

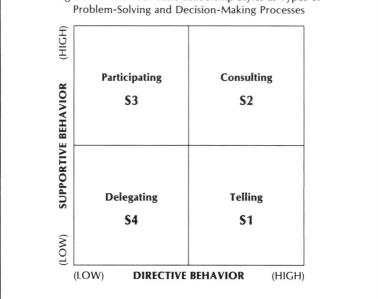

Figure 2.   The Four Basic Leadership Styles as Types of Problem-Solving and Decision-Making Processes

perceived by those other people. Since the basic behaviors that subordinates respond to in assessing your leadership style is the type of problem-solving and decision-making process you use with respect to them, each of the four leadership styles can be identified with a problem-solving and decision-making process as illustrated in Figure 2.

High-directive/low-supportive leader behavior (S1) is referred to as "Telling" because this style is characterized by one-way communication. The leader defines the roles of followers and tells them what, how, when, and where to do various tasks. Problem solving and decision making are initiated solely by the manager. Solutions and decisions are announced, and implementation is closely supervised by the leader.

High-directive/high-supportive behavior (S2) is referred to as consulting* because in using this style the manager still provides a great deal of direction and makes most of the decisions, but by

* The "Consulting" style (S2) in Management of Organizational Behavior is called "Selling." The change from "Selling" to "Consulting" was made again because practicing managers felt it better described Style 2 and eliminated some of the negative connotations of "Selling."

increasing the amount of two-way communication and supportive behavior, he or she attempts to hear the followers' feelings about decisions as well as their ideas and suggestions. While support is increased, control over decision-making remains with the manager.

High-supportive, low-directive leader behavior (S3) is called *participating* because the locus of control over problem solving and decision making shifts significantly. With the use of Style 3, the leader and follower(s) share in problem solving and decision making. Two-way communication is increased; and the manager's role is to listen actively and facilitate problem solving/decision making on the part of the follower. This is appropriate since the follower(s) have the ability and knowledge to do the task.

Low-supportive, low-directive leader behavior (S4) is labeled *delegating* because the manager discusses the problem with subordinate(s) until joint agreement is achieved on problem definition and then the decision-making process is totally delegated to the follower. Now it is the subordinate who has significant control for deciding *how* tasks are to be accomplished. The follower(s) are allowed to "run their own show" because they have both the ability and confidence to take responsibility for directing their own behavior.

*No One "Best" Leadership Style*

Once it was generally agreed that there were four basic leadership styles characterized by varying degrees of directive and supportive behavior, some writers (see Blake & Mouton, 1964; McGregor, 1960) argued that there was "one best" style—one that maximized productivity, human satisfaction, growth, and development in all situations. However, further research in the last several decades has clearly supported the contention that there is no best leadership style: *successful leaders are able to adapt their style to fit the situation* (see Fielder, 1967; Korman, 1966; Reddin, 1970).

While the need for a situational approach to leadership might make sense, it is not very helpful to practicing managers, who have to make leadership decisions every day. If "it all depends on the situation," they want to know *when* to use *which style*.

A number of situational variables influence which leadership style will be appropriate in what situation, including time, job demands, organizational climate, and superiors', associates' (peers), and subordinates' skills and expectations. While all these factors and undoubtedly others affect the effectiveness of a particular style, if practicing managers had to examine all the situational variables suggested by theorists before deciding which style to use, they would be immobilized. That is why Hersey and Blanchard based their Situational Leadership approach around the key factor that they found to have the greatest impact on which leadership styles you use in which situations—the follower(s). In particular, it was found that the amount of direction or support that a leader should provide depends on the *development level** that the follower(s) exhibits on a specific task, function, or objective that the leader is attempting to accomplish through the individual or group.

## Development Level

In this article development level is defined as the *ability* and *willingness* of follower(s) to perform a particular task without supervision. Ability is a function of knowledge or skill that can be gained from education, training, and/or experience. Willingness is a function of confidence and motivation.

It is important when thinking about someone's development level to remember that people are not "fully developed" or "underdeveloped." In other words, *development is not a global concept, it is a task-specific concept.* That is to say that people tend to be at different levels of development depending on the specific task, function, or objective that they are assigned.

For example, let's say that an engineer might be highly developed (able and willing) to handle the technical aspects of a job, but has not demonstrated the same degree of development when it comes to working with her or his budget. As a result, it may be quite appropriate for the engineer's manager to provide little direction or support (S4-delegating) on a technical problem, but provide a great deal of direction or close supervision over the engineer's budget and expense activities. Thus, Situational Leadership focuses on the appropriateness or effectiveness of leadership styles according to the task-relevant development level of the follower(s). This relationship is illustrated in Figure 3.

By dividing the development level continuum below the leadership model into four levels—low (D1), low to moderate (D2), moderate to high (D3), high (D4)—some bench marks of development level are provided. Each of these development levels suggest a different combination of ability and willingness as indicated below.

---

* "Development level" has been changed from the original use of "maturity level" for two reasons. First, the word "maturity" has negative connotations for most people. And, secondly, it was felt that the real contribution that Situational Leadership makes is that it is a dynamic developmental model that helps managers to understand not only how to manage people effectively today but how to "grow them" up so they can eventually manage themselves.

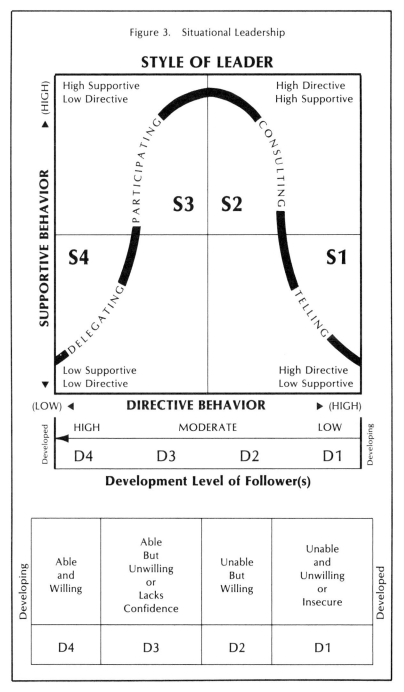

Figure 3. Situational Leadership

**STYLE OF LEADER**

(HIGH)

High Supportive
Low Directive

High Directive
High Supportive

SUPPORTIVE BEHAVIOR

PARTICIPATING

CONSULTING

**S3**    **S2**

**S4**                    **S1**

DELEGATING

TELLING

Low Supportive
Low Directive

High Directive
Low Supportive

(LOW) ◄  **DIRECTIVE BEHAVIOR**  ► (HIGH)

| Developed | HIGH | MODERATE | | LOW | Developing |
|---|---|---|---|---|---|
| | D4 | D3 | D2 | D1 | |

**Development Level of Follower(s)**

| Developing | Able and Willing | Able But Unwilling or Lacks Confidence | Unable But Willing | Unable and Unwilling or Insecure | Developed |
|---|---|---|---|---|---|
| | D4 | D3 | D2 | D1 | |

Figure 3 also attempts to portray the relationship between development level and the appropriate leadership styles to be used as the follower(s) moves from developing to developed.

*"Telling" is for low-development level.* People who are both *unable* and *unwilling* (D2) to take responsibility to do something are not competent or confident. In many cases, their unwillingness is a result of their *insecurity* or a *lack of experience* or *knowledge* regarding the necessary task. Thus, a directive style (S1) that provides clear, specific direction and close supervision has the highest probability of being effective. Again, this style is called "telling" because it is characterized by the leader defining roles and telling people what, how, when, and where to do various tasks.

*"Consulting" is for low to moderate development.* People who are *unable* but *willing* (D2) to take responsibility are confident but lack skills. Thus, a "consulting" style (S2) that provides directive behavior (because of their lack of ability) but also supportive behavior to reinforce willingness and enthusiasm appears to be most appropriate with individuals at this development level. This style is called "consulting" because most of the direction is still provided by the leader, yet, through two-way communications and explanation, the leader involves the follower by seeking suggestions and answering questions. This two-way communication helps maintain a high level of motivation on the part of the follower, while keeping responsibility for and control over decision making with the leader.

*"Participating" is for moderate- to high-development level.* People of this development level are *able* but *unwilling*, (D3) to do an assigned task. Their unwillingness is often a function of lack of *confidence* or *insecurity*. However, if they are confident but unwilling, their reluctance to perform is more of a motivational problem than a confidence problem. In either case, the leader needs to open up communication through two-way communication and active listening and to support the follower's effort to use the ability he or she already has. Thus, a supportive non-directive "participating" style (S3) has the highest probability of being effective with individuals at this development level. This style is called "participating" because the leader or follower shares in decision making, with the key roles of the leader being listening and facilitating.

*"Delegating" is for high development.* People at this development level are both *able* and *willing* or *confident* to take responsibility. Thus, a low profile "delegating" style (S4) that would provide little direction and support has the highest probability of being effective with individuals at this development level. Even though the leader may still identify the problem, the

responsibility for carrying out plans is given to those experienced followers. They are permitted to run the show and decide on the how, when, and where. At the same time, they are psychologically mature, and therefore do not need above average amounts of two-way communication or supportive behavior.

## Increasing Performance Capacity

Situational Leadership as described to this point is helpful for a practicing manager trying to determine what leadership style to use with follower(s) in a particular situation and on a particular task. Yet, suppose you are using a directive style (S1) with an inexperienced person with good results—the job is getting done. Would you want to continue to provide this direction and close supervision all the time with this person on this task? Obviously the answer is no. Style 1 is too time-consuming a style to use all the time. Therefore, your goal should be to help followers increase their willingness and ability to accomplish independently the tasks assigned to them, so that gradually you can begin to use less time-consuming styles (S3 and S4) and still get high-quality results.

As managers, we have two choices with the people that work for us. First, we can hire a winner—that is, a person who has the ability and motivation to perform at a desired level with little supervision (D4). Winners are easy to supervise: All they need to know is what are the goals, objectives, and timelines; and then they can be left on their own to do the job.

Since winners are hard to find and cost money, most managers are left with the second alternative—hire potential winners and then train them to be winners. In fact, unless managers realize and accept the training function in their jobs, they will be continually frustrated and confused about why their subordinates are not performing well. This frustration often forces managers into the most widely used leadership style, which we refer to as "leave alone—zap". They hire someone to assume certain responsibilities, tell that person what do (S1), and then "leave them alone" (an ineffective S4) and assume good performance will follow. Unless the person delegated to is a winner (D4), that assumption would prove false. When unacceptable performance occurs, or the person does something wrong or does not live up to the manager's expectations, the frustrated manager moves quickly to a punitive S1 style and demands to know why things are not getting done—the "zap." This change in leadership styles can leave managers frustrated and followers confused and often angry.

To avoid the ill effects of the "leave alone—zap" leadership style and to insure productive and satisfied employees, managers need to learn how to increase the performance capacities of their subordinates. There are five steps to training winners.

1. *Tell* the persons what you want them to do. You can't manage unless your followers understand what they are being asked to do—what their responsibilities or areas of accountability are.

2. *Show* the persons what you want them to do. Once people know what their responsibilities are, they need to know what good performance looks like. What are their performance standards?

*Show* and *tell* are both directive behaviors. Thus, training a potential (D1–D2) winner usually starts with an S1 "telling" leadership style. Since the person(s) do not know how to perform the desired task without direction and supervision, decision making and problem solving are controlled by the leader.

3. *Let them try.* Once the persons know what to do and the expected level of performance, the manager must take a risk and let them try to perform on their own. When you do that, you are essentially cutting back on directive behavior as you are turning over responsibility for doing the task to the follower. The risk here is that the follower might fail so you don't want to turn over too much responsibility too soon. Make the risk reasonable. Let the person cut her or his teeth on something where failure will not be devastating.

4. *Observe performance.* When you let a followers try to do something, do not go to a "delegating" Style 4 and leave them alone. That sets up the "leave alone—zap" leadership style. Since we know that style is not helpful in terms of productivity or satisfaction, we want to avoid it. Therefore, after you let the persons try to do what you want them to do, stick around and observe performance. A basic component of a telling S1 style is close supervision—which means frequently monitoring performance.

5. *Manage the consequences.* The main reason to supervise or monitor performance closely is to manage the consequences. A consequence is merely anything that follows behavior. There are three basic consequences.

a. A *positive* consequence or reinforcer—anything that follows performance that tends to increase the probability of that behavior occurring again, i.e., a praising or promotion
b. A *negative* consequence or punisher—anything that follows performance that tends to decrease the probability of that behavior occurring again, i.e., a reprimand or demotion
c. A *neutral* consequence or no response. Unless a person is

doing something that is intrinsically valuable (they would do it regardless of feedback from others), the lack of a response to good performance will gradually decrease the frequency of that behavior occurring again.

As you can see, the only consequence that tends to increase the probability of a behavior occurring again is a positive consequence. Thus we feel that *the key to developing people is to catch them doing something right* (Blanchard & Johnson, 1982). Most managers seem to be best at catching their people doing something wrong. You also need to remember that in the beginning with people you are training to be winners, you should try to catch them doing something *approximately right* not *exactly right*. Exactly right is made up of a whole series of approximately rights as the little steps indicate in Figure 4.

As Figure 4 suggests, when you let a person try to do something after "show and tell," you are cutting back on directive behavior. And then, when you observe that person doing something right (or in the beginning, approximately right), you should recognize that accomplishment by increasing your supportive behavior. The little steps moving up the bell-shaped curve suggest that this gradual reduction in directive behavior and increase in supportive behavior should continue until the individual or group reaches a moderate level of development (D2). As the person begins to move to higher levels of development (D3 and D4), it becomes appropriate for you to decrease not only directive behavior, but supportive behavior as well. Now the person is not only developed in terms of her or his ability to do the task, but is also able to provide her or his own reinforcement. This does not mean that the individual's work will have less structure, but the structure will now be internally imposed by the person rather than externally imposed by the manager. At this stage, individuals are positively reinforced for their own accomplishments when they are given increased responsibility and left more and more on their own. It is not that there is less mutual trust and respect—in fact, there is more—but it takes less effort on the manager's part to prove it with a fully developed person.*

More than praisings and other supportive behaviors, involvement in problem solving and decision making communicates to these people that you see them as confident, capable, responsible, trustworthy, and reliable individuals. These

* This gradual developmental process of (1) providing direction, (2) reducing the amount of direction and supervision, and (3) increasing support after adequate performance is known as "positively reinforcing successive approximations." The person most identified with this concept over the years is B. F. Skinner (1953).

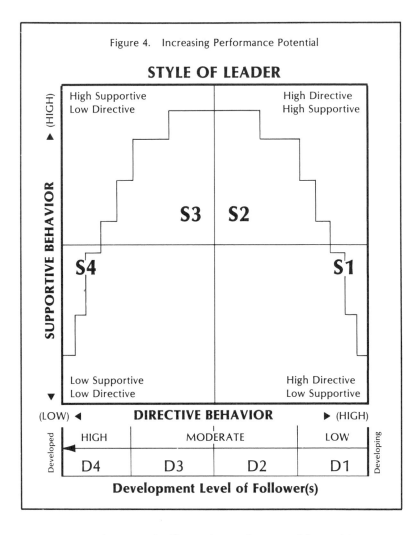

Figure 4.  Increasing Performance Potential

**STYLE OF LEADER**

| | |
|---|---|
| High Supportive<br>Low Directive | High Directive<br>High Supportive |

**S3**  **S2**

**S4**  **S1**

| | |
|---|---|
| Low Supportive<br>Low Directive | High Directive<br>Low Supportive |

(LOW) ◄  **DIRECTIVE BEHAVIOR**  ► (HIGH)

SUPPORTIVE BEHAVIOR  ▲ (HIGH)  ▼ (LOW)

| HIGH | MODERATE | | LOW |
|---|---|---|---|
| D4 | D3 | D2 | D1 |

Developed ◄  Developing

**Development Level of Follower(s)**

are messages that people like to hear; they provide positive feedback that builds confidence, motivation, and willingness.

On the other hand, if you continue to direct and supervise people closely for long periods of time, you are sending your subordinates different messages. Probably, you don't see them as confident, capable, responsible, trustworthy, or reliable. These underlying messages, in turn, affect performance. Thus, the developmental aspect of Situational Leadership and the need to gradually shift from external control of direction and support to internal control is crucial for developing and increasing the performance capacity of people.

In developing winners, the factor that triggers a change in leadership style is *performance*. Improvements in performance motivate forward shifts in leadership style along the bell-shaped curve from S1 to S2, S2 to S3, and S3 to S4. In thinking about the importance of performance you must remember one thing: High levels of performance can be obtained when any of the four leadership styles are used appropriately. That is to say, an inexperienced person can perform at as high a level as an experienced person if directed and supervised closely by a manager. The question is: at what cost? The cost is time and energy for the manager—both important management resources. Therefore, we feel that the highest performance level is achieved when followers can perform at a desired level with little or no supervision.

*Stopping Regression*

Just as improvements in performance motivate forward shifts in style along the curve, decreases in performance require a shift backward in leadership style along the bell-shaped curve from S4 to S3, S3 to S2, and S2 to S1. In other words, whenever a follower begins to perform at a lower level, for whatever reason (i.e., crisis at home, change in work, technology, etc.), it becomes appropriate and necessary for a manager to adjust her or his behavior to respond to the present development level of the person. For example, take a subordinate who is presently working well on her or his own. Suppose that suddenly a family crisis begins to affect this person's performance on the job. In this situation, it might be appropriate for the manager to increase moderately both support and even direction until the subordinate regains composure.

Take another example of a person in an individual contributor position who is highly motivated and competent (D4) and therefore can be left on her or his own. Suppose this person is promoted to a supervisory position. While it may have been appropriate to leave the person alone (S4) as an individual contributor, now that he or she is a supervisor, a task for which he or she has little experience, it is certainly appropriate for the manager to change styles by initially providing more socio-emotional support and then increasing the amount of direction and supervision provided (Style 4 to Style 3 to Style 2). This high-directive, high-supportive style should continue until the person is able to grasp all of his/her new responsibilities. At that time, movement from Style 2 to Style 3 and eventually to Style 4 would be appropriate if performance continues to improve. Using the same leadership style that was successful with this person as an individual contributor may prove devastating because it is inappropriate for her or his situation.

## Summary

Effective managers know their staff members well enough to manage flexibly ever-changing demands upon their organizations. As responsibilities and tasks are assigned to individuals or groups, developmental level must be assessed. The manager should then vary her or his leadership style in response to the individual's need for external direction and/or support. It should be remembered that over time subordinates and subordinate groups develop their own patterns of behavior and ways of operating— i.e., norms, customs, traditions and mores. While a manager may use a specific style for the work group as a group, that manager may quite often have to behave differently with individual subordinates because they are at different levels of development. Whether working with a group or an individual, changes in management style forward from S1 to S2, S3, and S4, and backward from S4 to S3, S2 and S1, must be gradual. It is this shifting forward and backward in style that makes Situational Leadership a truly developmental model for both managers and subordinates.☐

## References

Blake, R. R., & Mouton, J. S. *The Managerial Grid*. Houston, Tx.: Gulf Publishing, 1964.

Blanchard, K., & Johnson, S. *The One-Minute Manager*. New York: William Morrow & Co., 1982.

Fielder, F. E. *A Theory of Leadership Effectiveness*. New York: McGraw-Hill, 1967.

Hersey, P., & Blanchard, K. H. Life Cycle Theory of Leadership. *Training & Development Journal*, May 1969.

Hersey, P., & Blanchard, K. *Management of Organizational Behavior: Utilizing Human Resources (4th. Ed.)*. Englewood Cliffs, N. J.: Prentice-Hall, 1982.

Korman, A. K. "Consideration," "Initiating Structure," and Organizational Criteria: A Review. *Personnel Psychology: A Journal of Applied Research*, Winter 1966, *19*(4).

McGregor, D. *The Human Side of Enterprise*. New York: McGraw-Hill, 1960.

Reddin, W. J. *Managerial Effectiveness*. New York: McGraw-Hill, 1970.

Skinner, B. F. *Science and Human Behavior.* New York: The MacMillan Company, 1953.

Stogdill, R. M., & Coons, A. E., Eds. *Leader Behavior: Its Description and Measurement (Research Monograph No. 88).* Columbus, Oh.: Bureau of Business Research, The Ohio State University, 1957.

Tannenbaum, R., & Schmidt, W. H. How to Choose a Leadership Pattern. *Harvard Business Review,* March–April 1957.

# Building a Model of Managerial Effectiveness: A Competency-Based Approach

Alice G. Sargent

*"Our current management model has not only failed organizations, but has also served individuals poorly."*

In the 1980s American organizations face the challenge of learning how to manage better. The current theory of situational management, while useful, does not provide managers with the models and practices necessary to manage effectively. Organizations must upgrade the quality of management education and management systems to meet the complex problems of the decade—problems for which technology no longer provides sufficient solutions. In fact, technology now creates vast problems of its own.

To manage better, we must learn to value human resources as much as we formerly valued technology. Other countries know management practices the U. S. needs. They produce higher-quality products with fewer layers of management and with a more stable work force. While the Japanese have a better long-range financial base on which to build, they also foster human values of intimacy, subtlety, and trust in dealing with organizational problems. Because these values receive so little attention in American organizations—whether in corporations, government, or educational institutions—we now face isolation, alienation, and low productivity in the work place.

To take a step toward dealing with these issues, management must build models of managerial effectiveness at the supervisory, middle, and executive levels; a curriculum to develop managers as practitioners based on these models; and systematic methods for assessment, career development, and performance appraisal that reinforce the models.

What signs do we have that our current managerial process does not work? We have serious productivity problems and breakdowns in supervisor-subordinate communication. Many of our organizations are not "renewing," healthy places to live in eight to ten hours a day. Instead, they foster stress, which leads either to "rustout" or to burnout. Our organizations do not help many people feel efficacious or empowered. Numerous managers report that they lack a common vision to mobilize their people.

© 1983 Alice G. Sargent

To examine the issues of managerial effectiveness, we need to know what lies in store for managers in the 1980s—the issues that will confront the manager of the future. In his book *New Rules*, Daniel Yankelovich contends that we may adopt a new ethic of commitment in the 1980s. This new commitment follows a decade in which people generally focused on themselves and their own needs, rejecting the ethic of self-denial. In effect, Yankelovich says, we are now "stepping off Maslow's escalator." Many of us grew up with values that taught us to act out of guilt and responsibility. Then psychologist Abraham Maslow defined self-actualization as the principle of the individual's hierarchy of needs. Self-actualization replaced self-denial. Yankelovich, however, argues that humans cannot be wholly autonomous, solitary, contained, and "self-created." Many people are now searching seriously for something more to believe in, a workable vision that will help them to coalesce. People need a balance between the concerns for the self and for others.

Besides value shifts, the work place has experienced other highly significant changes. These include changes in the composition of the work force and changes in the nature of work. The work force no longer has a primarily homogeneous white male population. Women and minorities now bring new and different values and skills to management. Women tend to be more spontaneous, emotional, expressive, and concerned with human interaction. This contrasts with the prevailing management style, which emphasizes an analytical, rational approach that focuses on systems and tasks. Management now has the opportunity to respond to diversity, to nurture differences, and to learn from the new worker to build a multicultural work environment. If management continues to attempt to socialize the new work force into present patterns, it will forfeit the unique skills women and minorities possess.

All of these changes raise issues that concern management in the 1980s. Through interviewing managers in both the public and the private sectors, I have developed the list of contemporary management issues outlined in Figure 1.

Theorists have defined management as a concern for people and for tasks—i.e., a concern for productivity and for morale— which requires supportive and directive behaviors. Managers need the ability to deal effectively with an organization's administrative, technical, and social systems; to plan for short-, middle-, and long-term goals; to solve problems; to develop employees; and to achieve desired results. Management accomplishes tasks through people, through the relationships between executive and manager, manager and subordinates, and manager and peers.

Figure 1.    Management Issues for the 1980s

1. Transition from the industrial age to the age of communication; need to learn how to manage knowledge workers
2. Era of increasing complexity and frequency of change; high uncertainty, lack of control, everyone has a piece of the pie
3. Need for future-oriented responses; shift from tactical, short-range to strategic, long-range management
4. Decrease in hierarchical, authority-oriented managerial forms to more participative structures; productivity is increased through people, team effectiveness, consensus-building skills, and the development of networks
5. Growth of a highly diverse workforce; need to respond to diversity and to nurture differences
6. Environmental uncertainty; everything changing, especially economics, education, medicine, auditing
7. Need for leadership that builds goals and a shared vision that engenders trust; need role models and hands-on, value-oriented management
8. Labor-management partnerships characterized by trust
9. Customer-oriented/consumer-oriented styles
10. Increased methods for reward and recognition beyond salary and bonuses
11. Need for managers to experiment, take risks, continue to learn, and embrace errors as learning experiences, not as failures
12. Need for managers to deal constructively with stress to stay well; autonomy, resonance in relationships, tone, perspective, security, equity, participation, individuation
13. Need to build organizational climates that foster autonomy, colleagueship, and entrepreneurship
14. Transition from a national market to a world market

Yet business schools and public administration programs have not taught students applied management skills. An MBA is primarily a business degree; it generally requires only nine hours of management education. As Sterling Livingston (1982), president of Sterling Institute, has said, ". . . business schools teach how to problem-solve—not problem-find; how to work with money, but not with people." The new applied management skills must meet the criteria of relevance, application, and results. A competency model would provide business schools, public administration programs, and organizations with a guide for developing practitioners.

Mintzberg (1974) and others have shown that managers spend more time interacting with others than in solving problems in a more idealized, rational, objective manner. Managers spend 50%

to 90% of their time communicating; and they spend nearly 70% of that time in meetings. They use only 10% of their time communicating with supervisors and 40% to 50% of it with subordinates; the remainder is spent with people outside the chain of command. To be effective, managers need both entrepreneurial skills and interpersonal skills. In addition, organizational structures are shifting to require team effectiveness and skills in building consensus, rather than top-down authority.

Involvement and team effectiveness are crucial to building a more effective work place. Because interdependence significantly affects organization design; team leadership and team membership have become core skills. More and more matrix organizations have formed: lawyers, accountants, and health-care specialists who work in teams; quality circles; temporary task groups; and project management and program management. These forms of organizing require more collaborative and interdependent behaviors and fewer competitive, self-oriented behaviors.

Figure 2 shows the three areas of competence: technical, human, and conceptual. Boyatzis (1982) of McBer and Company has developed the more sophisticated model shown in Figure 3 for the Department of State and for the masters in management degree offered by the American Management Association. While this is one of the strongest models available, it still simply builds a management vocabulary. McBer's model does not supply behavioral descriptions. It does not describe something observable, but still relies on inferential language.

The McBer model introduces the notion of leadership—which we must differentiate from management in this decade. Leaders need to learn how to manage, to know what issues are involved

| | Executive | Mid-Level | Firstline Supervisor |
|---|---|---|---|
| Conceptual | 47% | 31% | 18% |
| Human | 35% | 42% | 35% |
| Technical | 18% | 27% | 47% |

Figure 2. Type of Skill Needed

Reprinted by permission of *Harvard Business Review,* exhibit from "Skills of an Effective Administrator" by Robert L. Katz (September–October 1974), © by the President and Fellows of Harvard College. All rights reserved.

### Figure 3.  Managerial Competencies*

*Competency: Some characteristic of a person that underlies or results in effective performance.*

    I. KNOWLEDGE COMPETENCIES—specific knowledge base
   II. EMOTIONAL MATURITY
       self-control
       spontaneity
       perceptual objectivity
       accurate self-perception
       stamina & physical energy
       adaptability
  III. ENTREPRENEURIAL ABILITIES
       efficiency orientation
       productivity—goal setting & planning
       proactivity—problem-solving & information seeking skills
       concern for unique achievement
       task efficiency
  IV. INTELLECTUAL ABILITIES
       logical thought—perceive cause/effect relationships—inductive
         thinking
       diagnostic use of concepts—deductive thinking
       memory
       conceptual ability
       political judgement
   V. INTERPERSONAL ABILITIES
       social sensitivity
       self-presentation
       counseling skills
       expressed concern with impact
       compliance producing skills
       alliance-building skills
       language skills
       non-verbal sensitivity
       respect for others
       effectiveness as team member
  VI. LEADERSHIP SKILLS
       presence
       persuasive speaking
       positive bias
       negotiating skills
       taking initiative
       management of groups—team-building skills

* This model was originally developed by Richard Boyatzis and is discussed in his book *The Competent Manager.*

in implementing their rhetoric. Managers need to learn how to lead, how to build a common vision around which people can coalesce. Leadership is an influence process. In Peter Senge's (1980) words, leadership requires the following:

- expression of a common vision that people need and want;
- communication about and alignment with that vision;
- staying the course by renewing commitment to the vision; and
- a structure to implement the vision that builds in frequent feedback.

I do not think that one organization can possibly adopt another's competency model. Rather, organizations operate more effectively by asking managers at different levels in organizations to design their own models using the language of their own cultures—models they can validate and for which they assume ownership. To accomplish this, managers must make the implicit explicit. The necessary competency exists in each organization's culture.* It can be extracted from promotion discussions or from rankings of managers, which some organizations call a "totem pole." Organizations can also ask managers to reflect on and construct such a model. A useful technique is to think of the last time someone called you about a recommendation to hire or promote someone into a management job. How did you describe the person? How did you differentiate her or him from the other candidates? What skills did you value most highly? Describe the behavior and accomplishments of a person whom you felt deserved a negative comment. Describe her or his effectiveness in the following areas: leadership; conducting meetings; level of awareness of impact on others; managing conflict; managing people; and planning.

Our current management model has not only failed organizations, but has also served individuals poorly. Those entering the new work force experience great pressure to adopt the dominant style. Organizations reward new managers for adopting a rational, analytical, problem-solving style and for giving up emotional and idiosyncratic behavior. Managers often encourage women to act highly "professional" and rational and to give up their feelings of nurturance and vulnerability. This means

---

* Organizations that use competency models include Citibank and its "managing people" program, AT&T and its assessment centers, the Department of the Navy training program, the State Department, the Overseas Private Investment Corporation and its performance appraisal system, and NASA (for more information on NASA's model, contact Professor Warner Burke at the Teachers College of Columbia University).

women must sacrifice both the strengths and the limitations of behavior labeled feminine. Some Black and Hispanic managers report that they are encouraged to give up their natural styles of problem solving and dealing with people in exchange for the more rational, analytic approach. Hence management tends to reward women, Black, Hispanic, Asian, and Native-American managers who become carbon copies of white males—the models for success in organizations.

White men, however, have paid a very high price for success. Their sacrifice has been less obvious and has come under scrutiny only recently. More and more men find that the hard-driving organizational style creates stress and inhibits close friendships. Men have had the strain of always being strong, never wrong. This style yields basically activity-oriented relationships, but not expressive, intimate friendships. It forces men to become excessively dependent emotionally on their wives—who may, at some point in their lives, become preoccupied with their own identities. Sometimes this style keeps men separate from their children.

When Fernando Bartolome, a Harvard Business School professor, surveyed American business executives, he found that most men seldom allow themselves to feel dependence or to admit to such feelings when they do experience them (1972). The executives regarded such feelings as weakness. In addition, most men acknowledged that they usually limited their expressions to tenderness to family members, especially to young children. Men said they often avoided displays of tenderness even with children, and especially boys, for fear of smothering them or making them dependent.

In a 1979 survey by Louis Harris that appeared in *Playboy Magazine*, American men ranked 11 basic values in the following order of importance: health, family life, love, friends, sex, respect from others, religion, peace of mind, work, education, and money. Yet if one compiled a behavioral instead of an attitudinal index, it would probably show that these men spend most of their time on work, television, sports, and perhaps education. The men's behavior does not support their belief in the importance of family life. Slightly fewer than half said they were "very satisfied" with their sex lives. Many men obviously do not make the development of intimate relationships a priority.

These concerns for organizational and individual well-being suggest that we must incorporate the following factors into a new definition of competence:

• Management has not been sufficiently concerned with people and relationships.

- Women and minorities who enter the workforce with interpersonal skills become socialized into the dominant style of rational, analytical problem solving and must relinquish some of their relationship-oriented style.
- Men feel dissatisfied with the dominant style because it produces great stress and inhibits intimacy.

This new model, which blends so-called masculine and feminine behaviors, is *androgynous* management. An androgynous manager can employ behaviors and capacities ascribed to both sexes—namely the more instrumental behaviors, which have been regarded as masculine, plus the more expressive behaviors, which have been regarded as feminine. For example, men would not give up their concern for power, but would learn to balance it with a concern for people. This change would require men to broaden their range of responses in the areas of affiliation, trust, openness, intuition, and the expression of feelings. Women would not abandon their concern for relationships, but would supplement it with an increased focus on outcomes. Women would become more assertive. They would depersonalize some situations and thus use more instrumental behavior. By sharing

Figure 4.   The Androgynous Manager

| Masculine | Neutral | Feminine |
|---|---|---|
| Instrumental behavior | Command of basic facts | Expressive behavior |
| Direct achievement style | Balanced learning habits | Vicarious achievement style |
| Compliance producing skills | Continuing sensitivity to political events | Alliance producing skills |
| Negotiating/Competing | Quick thinking | Accommodating/ Mediating |
| Proactive style | Creactivity | Reactive style |
| Analytical/problem- solving, & decision making skills | Social skills | Self knowledge |
| Visible impact on others | | Non-verbal sensitivity |

Reprinted, by permission of the publisher, from *The Androgynous Manager* by Alice G. Sargent, p. 42 © 1981 by AMACOM, a division of American Management Associations, New York. All rights reserved.

their competence with each other more often, women would reduce competition. Women generally need to increase their behavioral repertoire for managing conflict and dealing with power.

Figure 4 displays a competency model for an androgynous manager that includes effective masculine and feminine behaviors. This model provides only a first step in developing competencies. It does not use only behavioral descriptors; some of the terms cannot be observed. That means that further work is necessary.

One can also categorize the androgynous blend of behavior by defining instrumental and expressive behaviors (Figure 5). Instrumental behaviors have been highly valued in the marketplace and expressive behaviors in the home.

Instrumental behavior deals with ideas and tasks; expressive behavior deals with people and feelings. These behaviors become clear to us in our close relationships at home. If a couple engages in too much instrumental behavior, the relationships become stale, routine—not renewing. Instrumental discussions begin with questions like "Have you paid the insurance?" "Where shall we go Saturday night?" "Who is going to take the car to the mechanic?" If all communication is instrumental, it lacks spontaneity and self-disclosure, the precious expressive behavior that builds closeness. Some examples of expressive behavior

---

Figure 5.  Instrumental and Expressive Relationships*

|  | Instrumental | Expressive |
|---|---|---|
| Purpose: | problem-solving, avoid failure, achieve success | self-expression, be acknowledged |
| Exchange: | service, commodities, information, data | empathy, feelings |
| Based on: | data | self-disclosure |
| Needs: | control, power | let it be, here and now |
| Time: | future oriented, planning | flexible, less predictable |
| Structure: | predictable, certain | ambiguous |
| Avoid at all Cost: | surprise | boredom |

\* Developed by Peter Block of Block-Petrella-Weisbord, Plainfield, New Jersey and Neale Clapp, an organizational consultant from Little Silver, New Jersey.

---

include: "How did it go today?" "How did you feel about my being late?"

Supervisor-subordinate relationships also grow stale when they remain instrumental: "Is the assignment done?" "When are you going to take care of _____?" More open-ended communication—such as "How are things going?" "Where do you want to be five years from now?"—also matters. The absence of expressive behavior produces brief, ineffective, stilted performance-appraisal sessions and frustrating staff meetings in which what people say ten minutes after the meeting outside the room proves much more meaningful than anything said in the meeting room.

Many men fear that androgynous behavior will diminish their strength because years of socialization have taught them to develop cool, rational, stay-in-charge behavior. The opportunity to rely less on objectivity and rationality opens up the whole world of feelings, making contact, building close relationships, relaxation, and having more fun. This threatens some men who have used physical and political power to define themselves and to bend the world to their wills. Sometimes the exercise of such power is necessary and appropriate. But organizations and individuals suffer when managers use power in lieu of other more appropriate tools, such as persuasion, negotiation, concern for others, or cooperation.

For women, androgyny opens up the opportunity to become competent and to have boundaries—and to maintain close relationships. Women and minorities bring many strengths to management that should not be wasted.

Transition is the major trend in organizations for the 1980s. Everyone is questioning values, searching for new role models, learning new technologies, and seeking new forms of organizing to deal effectively with the enormous changes that are part of our lives. Our best hope for meeting this challenge successfully lies in our making explicit the issues of competencies and value differences inherent in models for managerial effectiveness so that we can continue to debate and to learn.□

## Bibliography

Bartolome, F. Executives as Human Beings. *Harvard Business Review*, November-December 1972, 62–69.

Bartolome, F., & Lee, P. A. Must Success Cost So Much? *Harvard Business Review*, 1980, *58*, 137–148.

Boyatzis, R. E. *The Competent Manager.* New York: Wiley, 1982.

Livingston, J. S. *New Trends in Applied Management Development.*

Paper presented at the ASTD National Conference, San
   Antonio, Texas, May 1982.
Mintzberg, H. *The Nature of Managerial Work*. New York: Harper
   & Row, 1974.
Naisbitt, J. *Megatrends*. New York: Warner Books, 1982.
Peters, T. J., & Waterman, R. H. *In Search of Excellence*. New York:
   Harper & Row, 1982.
Sargent, A. *The Androgynous Manager*. New York:
   AMACOM, 1981.
Senge, P. M. System Dynamics and Leadership. Presented at IEEE
   1980 International Conference on Cybernetics and Society,
   Cambridge, Massachusetts, October 1980.
Yankelovich, D. *New Rules*. New York: Random House, 1981.

# Three Models of Leadership: The Manager as Technician, Conductor, or Developer*

David L. Bradford
Allan R. Cohen

*"The Lone Ranger rides up on a white horse and overcomes great odds to solve the problem of the day."*

## "Who Was That Masked Man . . . ?"

When American managers talk about their images of managing, which idealized models do they have in their heads? They frequently mention the same few cultural heroes, who are the direct descendants of the frontiersman, long an ideal in American literature, film, mythology, and consciousness. The Lone Ranger, an imposing masked figure, rides up on a white horse and overcomes great odds to solve the problem of the day. This model of the vanquishing leader—a bit mysterious, invulnerable, generous but aloof—is one of the most common. John Wayne provides a similar model: a tough guy who never admits fear, is individualistic, and takes on the bad guys alone with only a few well-chosen words and lots of action. Our military heroes are often portrayed in this manner.

The showdown, in which everything depends on the hero's nerves of steel, complete command of the situation, quickness, and guts, dominates the fantasies of managers who grew up on cowboys and Indians, war movies, and male heroes. Even many women who have made it into middle management tend to think in these heroic terms, although the specific image may be of Wonder Woman: beautiful, strong, surrounded by admirers but still the cleverest, toughest miracle worker around. It hardly matters that these images, largely based on the development of the Western frontier, may not be historically accurate. But even inaccurate myths can persist.

Although few managers consciously or deliberately imagine themselves to be exactly like these heroes, the models provided are powerful and pervasive. It is difficult to face the constant strains of managerial life without falling back on such organizing metaphors. Recent attacks on the tough-guy, macho, hero image,

© 1981 D. L. Bradford and A. R. Cohen
* Adapted from *Managing for Excellence* by David L. Bradford and Allan R. Cohen (New York: Wiley, forthcoming).

arising out of the Vietnam War, women's movement, and other social changes, have tarnished heroism without providing an alternative model. The image of "the androgynous manager" (Sargent, 1981) offers one of the few alternate guides for managers.[1] We do not yet have widespread models for managers who might be tender *and* tough, team-minded *and* independent, development- *and* performance-oriented.

Part of the fascination with these heroes comes from their great control—of themselves and others. The frontier types face many unpredictable dangers, which they master by anticipating the villain's moves, being faster and smarter, and thereby winning. They control the villain's moves and their own emotions.

Middle managers are almost inevitably preoccupied with control, partly because by position they usually have less control than is personally comfortable or organizationally necessary to guarantee results. And the more powerless or out of control managers feel, the more they tend to exert control downward (Kanter, 1979). If they cannot control their superiors and peers, they will at least master their subordinates—or try to. That this only increases subordinate resistance is overlooked; managers just redouble their efforts to control them.

Even managers with sufficient power or control do not readily drop their obsession with it, especially in crises, since the models are so deeply ingrained in the culture. After all, the bad guys could bust out of jail any minute now, couldn't they?

The general concern about heroic control translates into the two distinct managerial models we identified in our research: *the manager as master technician* and *the manager as conductor*. These pervasive models, though effective in some situations, perpetuate the heroic ideal. After examining them, we will offer a new model, the *manager as developer*, which we find a more useful organizing principle to guide managerial behavior in many contemporary organizations where talented subordinates are engaged in complex, interdependent work. Once managers have a clear image of what to aim for, they will more easily master the skills and strategies necessary for managing high-performing systems.

The first two managerial models, manager as *master technician* and as *conductor*, share an important characteristic: each assumes that the manager is the heroic problem solver responsible for riding to the rescue with answers, wisdom, a grand vision, or the supreme effort. This can set up mechanisms that block subordinate commitment, despite the manager's good intentions.

[1] See "Building a Model of Managerial Effectiveness."

## Manager as Master Technician

Most people are promoted into management because of past performance in the technical aspect of their jobs. They have succeeded in selling products, solving technical bottlenecks, servicing accounts, or developing new programs, and have shown "managerial potential." Since they seem to "get along well with people," they become managers of those who are to do these tasks.

Many who do get promoted manage their subordinates by doing what they know best: acting as technical experts. They may give directions about what to do and the details of how to accomplish it, serve as resident experts who answer subordinate questions and solve problems, or even jump in to do the work themselves. Sometimes they explicitly carry a direct work load of clients, accounts, or complex problems. One imagines people who know what to do in every situation and have the answers to all technical problems. Saying "I don't know" or "I can't do it" is taken as a sign of failure.

The relationship between manager-technicians and subordinates tends to be personal and particularistic. It is governed less by rules and procedures and more by the particular relationship with each subordinate. The manager exerts control by informal interaction rather than by use of existing formal administrative systems.

This leadership style can be effective if the manager has much greater knowledge than the subordinates. By allowing subordinates to flounder when he or she has the answer, the manager may produce more frustration than real learning *and* waste time. This way of operating requires, however, that the manager remain on top of the technical aspects of the work, or answers will become outdated. This style also works when jobs call for little coordination and interpersonal influence, or in emergencies.

Even in situations in which this leadership approach is appropriate, managers may use it in an inappropriate manner. The superior may stress a certain technique not because it is objectively best but because it reflects what that person once learned and still favors. This approach can reduce the subordinate's growth by removing the challenge and the potential for learning how to resolve problems. It can undermine subordinate confidence and initiating skills because the leader indeed always knows better and does not hesitate to jump in and prove it!

In general, manager-technicians do not respond well to "people problems" that require flexibility, improvisation, listening, and patience. They would prefer to stick to problems that do not talk back—determining a bid price, designing a new scheduling system for loading the milling machines, smoothing out paper flow—and often do not notice when a subordinate wants support, a chance to vent feelings, or a gentle push. They love problem solving, not the messiness of people problems. They think of "work" as what they do when people leave them alone (i.e., solving challenging technical problems) and resent the time they have to spend with the difficult people who cause what they see as irrelevant problems. Their greatest pleasure comes from the equivalent of the amazed townfolk saying, "Who was that masked man who appeared in the nick of time to solve our problem?"

This style can limit organizational effectiveness and subordinate development if organizational activities are constricted to areas in which the manager feels personally competent.

## Manager as Conductor

The manager as an orchestral conductor feels responsible for controlling subordinates' efforts to be certain that they do what is right. They often see subordinates as willful and clever, needing guidance to keep them on the right track. Conductors accept the conventional notion that management is "getting work done through others," but believe that they must work very hard to stay on top of the others to prevent chaos or rebellion. Thus, conductors make themselves the central decision makers, nerve centers, and coordinators of activities. Able to see the entire picture, the conductor uses the traditional management functions to determine how the department's task is to be divided up, who is to be assigned the subfunctions, and how that work is to be integrated. Thus, the manager must coordinate (and manipulate) these parts to make sure that all members do their tasks and that everything comes together.

This second image of the leader's role more explicitly involves the followers, but still depicts the leader as the central heroic figure, one who orchestrates all the parts into one harmonious whole. The spotlight falls on the leader, who has a grand plan and keeps all followers working on their piece of it. The leader still needs technical knowledge, but only as a tool for keeping respect and for knowing how to get everyone to perform.

There are two major differences between the manager-as-technician and the manager-as-conductor. The person using the conductor style is less likely to do any of the technical tasks or to be open about intentions, methods, or personal desires. While the technician goes right after the problem and may be so focused on getting a solution that he or she pays little attention to the people involved, the conductor takes on the burden of figuring out how to maneuver subordinates into doing what is necessary. Although the conductor tries to work through others, one always assumes that, without the conductor's machinations and control, work would not be accomplished.

When dealing with subordinates, the conductor always thinks about ways to gain compliance. Even when a conductor has a preferred outcome on an issue, he or she may ask subordinates for input—to give at least the semblance of participation. If the subordinate gives the "wrong" answer, the conductor goes to great lengths to persuade the subordinate of the "better way" without having to order anything directly. If necessary, the conductor will get someone to offer counterevidence, personally refute the subordinate's logic, interpret hesitation as agreement, or, as a last resort, stall. Conductors tend to avoid displaying their authority directly; they prefer to appear reasonable and flexible as long as possible to maintain good will and cooperation.

Accordingly, the conductor is more likely than the technician to use the organization's procedures and systems to achieve planning, coordination, and control. This may allow for less personal interference, but conductors prefer to use guidelines that seem impersonal, routine, and, therefore, less susceptible to resentment and challenge than risk the appearance of pulling strings and maneuvering people into compliance. Of course, they still hold the strings, but they allow more slack. One skilled conductor pointed out that he would prefer to be the one who asks the key questions rather than the one who answers them; that way his power would be greater but less visible.

Unlike the technician who assists in getting the job done, the conductor focuses on setting up and coordinating the people and processes that get the job done. This form of management should work best in more complex situations where coordination among subordinates is needed for the department to maximize performance. Since the leader cannot be in all places at all times, procedures serve in lieu of physical presence. Furthermore, to the extent that they assist members in getting their work done, such rules and procedures can increase motivation.

Despite its advantages, the conductor approach causes several problems. The very thing that makes it effective—great coordination of subordinates—works to minimize subordinate concern about, and involvement in, the overall coordination of the unit. When subordinates know that all communication and important decisions flow through the manager, and that the conductor feels the overall responsibility, they can most freely pursue the narrow interests of their own subunits. They do not have to worry about balance or overall departmental interests; those are the conductor's problems.

This hinders development. It is hard to promote people who "only push their own area." But the conductor form of leadership style might produce such unintended consequences. When all responsibility for pulling things together lies in the hands of the conductor, the individual players are not as likely to act as though ready for overall responsibility. This, in turn, rebounds on the manager. Often, the failure to develop an adequate replacement hinders her or his advancement.

Furthermore, those who feel controlled generally invest considerable energy in regaining control for themselves, forcing conductors to work harder and harder to maintain control. Thus, the boss's objective can easily become staying on top rather than accomplishing the unit's work.

Similarly, because conductors use systems and procedures as control devices rather than as tools to help subordinates perform, they often fail to achieve the desired results. There is no system that cannot be beaten if those subject to it reject its intended use. Some people "beat" control systems by doing just the minimum necessary to get by. "Working to rules," i.e., doing only what has been explicitly required and the many variations of that form of passive resistance make almost any system impotent and often cause conductor-managers to increase the controls. Again, the conductor works harder, or becomes more rigid, and produces in subordinates the lack of overall commitment that the machinations are designed to overcome.

By discussing these problems of the conductor style, we do not mean to deny its value. It is clearly preferable to the technician style when the work requires interdependence among subordinates, and—when used well—it *does* produce at least an acceptable level of performance. But this approach, like the previous one, makes the leader totally responsible for seeing that work gets done. Although managers-as-conductors may not personally give all the answers, they feel wholly responsible for finding the answers, while the subordinates sit back. Thus, the manager-as-conductor style is appropriate when it is not worth the effort to make full use of member resources.

## Manager as Developer

A new definition of leadership frees managers from the unattractive options of too much or too little responsibility and control. The manager must create a team of key subordinates that shares responsibility with the manager for the department's success. To be effective, the manager must *simultaneously develop subordinates' feelings of responsibility for—and their ability to manage—the unit's performance.* Only when all directly reporting subordinates share in the responsibility for overall excellence will the boss cease to have sole control. And only when subordinates acquire managerial skills can shared responsibility lead to excellence. Since neither willingness nor ability to share overall responsibility is automatic, but must be developed, we call this model of leadership the *manager-as-developer.*

We created this model by observing leaders who achieve excellence. Rather than focus on heroics—having all the answers and the total responsibility—these leaders play a more developmental, collaborative, galvanizing, but subordinate-centered role.

This model demands no less effort, energy, investment, or imagination than the Lone Ranger type, since the manager needs active engagement to undertake and sustain increased subordinate learning and overall responsibility. Developer-managers must learn to be effective without total control, to be helpful without having all the answers, to be involved without centrality, to be powerful without domination, and to be responsible without excluding others.

### The Manager-as-Developer Model

The manager-as-developer must accomplish the following three major tasks:

1. work with direct subordinates as a team to collectively share responsibility for managing the unit;
2. determine and gain commitment to a common vision of the department's goals and purposes; and
3. work on the continuous development of individual subordinate skills, especially in the managerial/interpersonal areas needed to be an effective member of the shared responsibility team.

The manager-as-developer, then, seeks to develop in subordinates the willingness and ability to share the responsibility for departmental success. The manager must shape subordinates into a powerful, cooperative, hard-working, dedicated, and responsible team.

The presence on a team of strong subordinates, even when they are held responsible for overall performance, does not automatically guarantee the kind of coordination necessary for excellence. The manager must determine and use a goal for the unit that helps members transcend their own interests. But merely putting people on a team with a unifying goal and making them responsible is not enough. Subordinates may not have the skills they need to share responsibility effectively. Their technical knowledge may be too narrow, especially if they have been in highly specialized jobs. Even more likely, they may not have fully developed the necessary managerial or interpersonal skills; they may lack the ability to negotiate with and confront one another (and the boss), a full understanding of how all the parts of the organization fit together, or collective decision-making skills. The manager will need to pay continuous attention to the development of each direct subordinate's capacities.

The three elements of the manager-as-developer model are mutually reinforcing. By focusing on sharing responsibility for the overall departmental performance, a manager provides subordinates with the chance to have an impact. By emphasizing individual learning, he or she provides challenge. By teaching individuals the managerial and interpersonal skills needed to effectively share responsibility for the department, one rewards participation in running the unit with learning that both fosters further career opportunities and expands ability to reach excellence. Thus, subordinates are simultaneously made responsible, challenged, engaged, and stretched, which increases their motivation to perform well and expands their capacity to do so.

This style requires heroic effort, but not a heroic model. The developer does not drop the silver bullet and ride away into the sunset, but stays to build greater strength in the town and the townfolk.□

## References

Kanter, R. M. Power Failure in Management Circuits. *Harvard Business Review*, July–Aug., 1979.

Sargent, A. *The Androgynous Manager*. New York: AMACOM, 1981.

## Suggestions for Further Reading

Kanter, R. M. The Middle Manager as Innovator. *Harvard Business Review*, July–Aug., 1982.

Sayles, L. *Leadership: What Effective Managers Do . . . and How They Do It*. New York: McGraw-Hill, 1979.

Vroom, V., & Yetton, P. *Leadership and Decision Making*. Pittsburgh, Penn.: University of Pittsburgh Press, 1973.

# Racial Identity Development: Implications for Managing the Multiracial Work Force

Bailey W. Jackson
Rita Hardiman

*"At each stage of development, a person seems to take off one pair of glasses and put on another pair with a completely different prescription."*

The multiracial work force places new demands on the skills of managers. Managerial skills and styles that have been relatively successful with a virtually all-White* work force do not appear to function as well in a racially diverse work force. We can largely attribute the limitations or weaknesses of current management techniques to (1) their lack of consideration that any other cultural perspective other than the dominant White perspective teaches the right way to do business, (2) their lack of consideration for the impact of minorities'** racial/cultural differences on approaches to work place issues and tasks, and (3) their lack of consideration for the impact of racism on the work force, particularly in a multiracial work force. Essentially, existing management techniques fail to provide the manager with effective methods for handling many human resource-related issues because they do not offer methods for interpreting work place dynamics influenced by race and racism.

Diversifying the racial profile of an organization produces heightened concern and awareness about race; therefore, managers must have available models and techniques that will expand their understanding of race as a significant variable in human development and interaction. Managers must be able to recognize when and how race and racism affect their own perspectives and the perspectives of other members of the organization. A more comprehensive understanding of the impact of racial perspectives on workplace dynamics enables the manager to act effectively in the multiracial work environment.

© 1983 NTL Institute

* The authors use the terms "Black" and "White" to denote racial groups and therefore capitalize them.

** The term "minority" describes oppressed racial groups—Asian Americans, Blacks, Hispanics-Latinos, and Native Americans. While the authors do not concur with the popular use of the term, it will be used here for the sake of readability.

## Racial Identity Development

The field of racial identity development offers managers a perspective on some of the dynamics operating among members of a multiracial workforce. Racial identity development (RID) theory suggests that, to understand people's perspectives on race and people's reactions to racial issues, one must understand the process that people move through in formulating a perspective on racial identity.

Racial identity development theory is based on the following assumptions:

1. In any society, the society's individual members belong to one or more social groups. An individual's social group membership can either be ascribed or chosen, temporary or permanent—e.g., by race, gender, religion, age, sexual preference, class.
2. To varying degrees, an individual's social group membership influences the way one views oneself, others, and the immediate or expanded environment.
3. In a race-centered society, the process of grappling with one's racial identity is an integral part of an individual's total social identity development process.
4. Not only is this society race-centered, but it operates on judgments about the superiority/inferiority of the five racial groups. Therefore, it is racist.
5. For each racial group and its individual members, the racist social environment significantly affects the racial identity development process.

RID theory identifies each stage of development that people experience in their quest for a healthy racial identity. Each of the RID stages not only identifies a person's place in the developmental process, but also describes the consciousness that influences one's view of oneself and the surrounding world.

Trainers often use eyeglasses as a metaphor for describing the stages of RID. At each stage of development, a person seems to take off one pair of glasses and put on another pair with a completely different prescription. This new pair of glasses provides a different view of the world than did the pair that was removed. This change of glasses, or consciousness, can dramatically affect the way a person thinks, feels, and behaves.

The racial identity development theories outlined here describe the developmental stages that Blacks and Whites move through as they struggle to acquire healthy racial identities. Both

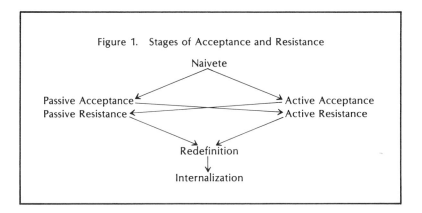

Figure 1.  Stages of Acceptance and Resistance

Naivete

Passive Acceptance — Active Acceptance
Passive Resistance — Active Resistance

Redefinition

Internalization

the Black and the White identity development theories identify
five major developmental stages: (1) naivete, (2) acceptance, (3)
resistance, (4) redefinition, and (5) internalization. The stages of
acceptance and resistance have two possible manifestations:
passive or active.

## Black Identity Development

The Black identity development (BID) theory describes Black
people's consciousness as they move through the developmental
process and the implications of their consciousness on the way
they view themselves and on the way they view and interact with
their environment. The following brief overview of BID theory
provides a description of each stage and examples of beliefs and
behaviors possibly exhibited in the work place. Because the
naivete stage occurs during childhood and, thus, is not relevant
to the work place, the description of the stages begins with the
acceptance stage.

*Acceptance*

The Black person, in the acceptance stage of consciousness,
follows the prevailing notion that "White is right." This person
attempts to gain resources—e.g., approval, sense of worth, goods,
power, money—by accepting and conforming to White social,
cultural, and institutional standards. The acceptance of these
White cultural and institutional standards requires the rejection
and devaluation of all that is Black.

A Black person who consciously (active acceptance) or
unconsciously (passive acceptance) adopts the prevailing White

view of the world weakens her or his positive self-concept or positive view of Black people. This consciousness typically causes a Black person to avoid interactions with other Blacks and to desire interaction with Whites.

In this stage, a Black employee is likely to become concerned about acceptance by White peers and superiors. The employee may manifest this through conscious attempts to adopt the prevailing White dress codes, speaking patterns, and general rules for appropriate social interaction.

*Indicators of the Acceptance Consciousness*

Beliefs:

- "People are people, and if Blacks just work hard they will be judged by their merits."
- "There is no race problem. The problem is with those Blacks who don't want to work and better themselves. They are messing it up for the rest of us."
- "Blacks can't get ahead in the organization because they are lazy—that's why they are always late to work."
- "White people are generally smarter than Black people."
- "If you want to get ahead in any organization, you have to act as much like Whites as possible."

Behaviors:

- Goes along with or excuses racist behavior on the part of fellow workers
- Views other Blacks as incompetent
- Seeks interactions with White workers
- Avoids organizational activities, events, and tasks that focus on race or racism—e.g., affirmative action committees, Black caucuses

*Resistance*

The resistance stage occurs when a Black person questions, challenges, and ultimately rejects the acceptance consciousness. An internal awareness that the acceptance consciousness contributes to the continuation of racism and poisons one's positive sense of self as a Black person stimulates the transition to this stage. Typically, a person actively engages in activities that allow her or him to broaden an understanding of the various manifestations or racism both in and outside the work place. A person actively challenges the values, beliefs, and behaviors viewed as racist and held by the organization, co-workers, and oneself.

For some Black people, the resistance stage appears to threaten all that has been acquired while viewing the world through the acceptance consciousness. These people realize that they acquired many things—e.g., job position, personal acceptance, White friendships—because they adopted an acceptance consciousness. Because they view so many of these acquisitions as necessary for survival and "happiness," they find it extremely difficult to adopt a consciousness that will threaten this position. Some will try to challenge or reject the acceptance consciousnes by "passively resisting it." They might attempt to retain the acceptance consciousness on the job and to operate from a resistance consciousness off the job.

The Black employee in this stage will typically seek out interactions with other Blacks who also view the work place from the resistance perspective. This employee's interactions with Whites are likely to be viewed as hostile and confronting.

*Indicators of the Resistance Consciousness*

Beliefs:

- "Most, if not all, White people are inherently racist."
- "Black people must confront White people about their racism."
- "White people have no respect or understanding of the Black experience."
- "White organizations will only reward those Blacks who are 'Uncle Toms' [i.e., acceptance Blacks]."
- "Black people must have their own organizations that can protect Black people and ensure that they will be dealt with equitably on the job."

Behaviors:

- Openly challenges racist behavior committed by White people and the White organization
- Actively engages in work projects concerned with racial issues
- Views and reacts to White people suspiciously. Expects that any and all White actions are in some way influenced by racist attitudes
- Distances oneself from any Blacks that manifest an acceptance consciousness

## Redefinition

The redefinition stage occurs when a Black person begins to define or redefine "Blackness" in terms independent of the perceived strengths and/or weaknesses of White people and White culture. Significantly, at the redefinition stage, Black people shift their attentions and energies away from a concern for the nature of their interactions with Whites toward a concern for primary contact and interaction with other Blacks.

Black people at this stage of development focus on the perspectives of other Blacks and, as a consequence, tend to limit their interactions with Whites. In multiracial organizations, members generally view this behavior negatively. They often label Blacks engaged in redefinition as "separatist" or "Black Nationalist"; those who view desegregation as the answer to society's racial ills see this behavior as counterproductive. Organizations that have put considerable energy into allowing Blacks into the White-dominated work place often feel confused and/or put off by this apparent "segregating" behavior. Many of the people around someone at this stage find it difficult to understand that the Black person feels primarily concerned with engaging in relationships and activities that will further and nurture this person's sense of Black identity and Black pride.

The Black employee at the redefinition stage generally avoids interactions with White employees. This person may seem socially distant from everyone else in the work force, except possibly, other Blacks in this stage.

### Indicators of the Redefinition Stage

Beliefs:

- "Black people are creative, sensitive, strong, intelligent, and nurturing."
- "Black people need to pay more attention to their own culture and heritage."
- "Focusing on White people and educating them about racism is a distraction from Black people and Black agendas."
- "Black energy and resources should serve Black people."

Behaviors:

- Tends to socialize almost exclusively with Blacks
- Interacts with Whites in business situations in a distant but professional manner
- Focuses on one's own career development and the extent to which it enhances one's redefined agenda
- Exhibits assertive and self-confident behavior

*Internalization*

Using one's redefined sense of "Blackness" marks the Black person's entry into the final stage—internalization. At this stage, Black people actively integrate and internalize the new consciousness they developed in the prior stage into their many social roles and identities. This stage often begins with the realization that while the redefinition process has been useful and nurturing, one should apply this new sense of Black identity beyond the supportive Black referent group. The Black person needs to determine how this new consciousness will affect the way one perceives and interacts in situations with people who are not Black.

Black people who work in predominantly White organizations typically begin their analysis of the implications of their new sense of Black identity with a series of questions.

• Do their jobs or careers nurture or stifle their Black identity?
• Is their sense of Black identity enhanced or hindered by the workplace environment and their interactions with colleagues?
• Are the values, customs, and philosophical assumptions of the Black culture seen as limitations in the organization, or are they respected and integrated into the culture of the organization along with other racial perspectives?
• Do their organizations nurture and support the broader Black community?

As Black people begin to fully adopt the consciousness of the internalization stage, they become more comfortable with their new sense of being Black. Even in situations where their Black perspective is not valued, they find that they have the necessary sustenance to prevail.

*Indicators of the Internalization Stage*

Beliefs:

• "Racism is a sickness in American society that infects all of its members and institutions/organizations."
• "I believe in the strength of the truly multiracial organization."
• "I value those people and activities that enhance the racial identity development of others."

Behaviors:

• Is able to interact with Blacks and Whites regardless of their stage of consciousness without being compromised or violated

- Actively participates in work place and community efforts designed to address any and all forms of oppression
- Contributes to work place projects from the strengths of a Black perspective

## White Identity Development

The White identity development theory (WID) describes the process by which Whites develop a healthy sense of racial identity. This developmental process involves two related issues— awareness of an identity as a member of the White race, and awareness of racism as part of the dominant White culture.

As with the BID theory, the description of the WID stages begins with the acceptance stage.

*Acceptance*

At this stage, the White person believes that minorities possess genetic and biological traits inferior to Whites and that these traits determine their social, moral, and intellectual qualities. Active-acceptance Whites are more commonly referred to as White bigots. Aware of their White identity, they admit (sometimes with pride) to being White racists.

In contrast to persons who actively accept White superiority, White people who passively accept the superiority of "Whiteness" may not see themselves as racists or see that they hold themselves above minorities. At the passive acceptance stage, White people do not recognize their part in the problem that affects racial minorities; they deny or are unaware that they judge minorities according to White values. They also fail to recognize the reality of racism and rationalize the plight of racially oppressed people by "blaming the victim." Passive acceptance of White racism involves blindness to racism as a systemic American problem and blaming racial problems on the "prejudice" of some Whites and/or the inability of minorities to assimilate. White managers at this stage may claim to treat everyone alike, or they may declare themselves "color blind" and indifferent to a subordinate's race.

*Indicators of the Acceptance Consciousness*

Beliefs:

- "Affirmative action is reverse discrimination; it gives unfair advantages to minorities that Whites never had."
- "Minorities need special training so that they can fit into the way the organization does business."

- "Everyone has an equal chance to succeed if they just work hard and don't rock the boat."

Behaviors:

- Avoids contacts with minorities, or else treats them deferentially or in a patronizing manner
- Hires minorities for support positions but doesn't trust them in leadership roles
- Accepts or actively supports racist jokes, language, rumors, and assumptions

*Resistance*

As in the acceptance stage, White people can experience the resistance stage in either a passive or an active mode. In both cases, however, the resistance stage begins when White people question the racial "truths" taught to them. In the resistance stage, one sees the pervasiveness of White racism for the first time; instead of passive (unknowing) acceptance of Whiteness, at this point individuals become very aware of their racial identity. Feelings of guilt, anger, and shame at being White can arise from this awareness. The manner in which White people act on this early questioning/challenging process differentiates the passive and active components of the resistance stage.

White people who *passively resist* White racism lapse into a false consciousness about racism and their own participation in racist society. At this stage, they begin to recognize the reality of racism but allow themselves to become immobilized by the magnitude of the problem. They feel that because racism is so systemic, one person can do little or nothing to stop it.

White people who *actively resist* White racism begin this stage by questioning and challenging the racist beliefs and values that whites internalize unconsciously while growing up in America. Unlike Whites who experience passive resistance, these people "own" their Whiteness and become aware of how they perpetuate racism by their inaction as well as their action.

Once White people actively begin this questioning and challenging process, they begin to see racism in its many overt and subtle forms throughout the work environment and broader social environment. Confrontation with other Whites regarding racism becomes important, and individuals may alienate or anger White co-workers in the acceptance stage of consciousness. White managers at this stage may actively support a minority employee who has been treated unfairly by the organization, or they may require that White subordinates attend race relations seminars to "straighten up" or adopt the right perspective vis á vis racist behavior and attitudes.

*Indicators of the Resistance Consciousness*

Beliefs:

- "Racism is a pervasive force in American society."
- "Minorities have the deck stacked against them in organizations, despite affirmative action."
- "Whites are responsible for maintaining and supporting racism."

Behaviors:

- Challenges racist jokes and comments by White co-workers
- Tries to learn more about personal racism and systemic racism
- Becomes active in organizational committees that focus on EEO and affirmative action or interracial projects

*Redefinition*

At this stage, White people begin to redefine Whiteness independently of the existence of perceived deficiencies in other groups. At this stage, they recognize that their racial identity has been defined in opposition to people labelled inferior—that they have based their racial identity on the crutch of White supremacy (racism).

Prior-to this stage, Whites have not been concerned with their racial identity. Up to this point, they have focused on minority groups and their "problems" (acceptance stage) or they have reacted to the social issue of racism (resistance stage). Passing through the resistance stage has left these individuals feeling negative about their White identity, confused about their role in dealing with racism, and isolated from much of their social group. Therefore, as a necessary part of this stage, White people must develop a more in-depth understanding of the meaning of being White (in addition to its connection to racism) and the aspects of White culture, society, and people that affirm their needs as individual members of that race.

At this stage, White people can see how the business world is fashioned upon such White cultural norms as linear thinking; an either/or, win/lose orientation to problems; and low tolerance for expressive behavior. They understand more clearly the strengths and limitations of the White perspective in the work place and in society at large. They also become aware that White people will benefit by eliminating racism and White bias in society and that all racial groups have something to contribute to the business world and to society as a whole. White managers at this stage will try to foster a work environment that admits the unique racial perspectives of minority and White employees and does not require people to assimilate into a White norm. Some White individuals may find they are redefining themselves in ways that create conflict between their personal values and goals and the values and goals of the organization they work in.

### Indicators of the Redefinition Consciousness

Beliefs:

- "Whites are responsible for working with other Whites on eradicating racism."
- "Organizations must continually grapple with the integration of multicultural perspectives for their own success and effectiveness."
- "Organizations' norms, policies, and structures benefit White employees and alienate minority employees."

Behaviors:

- Tries to help White co-workers become more sensitive to racism and to their racial identity
- Works more with Whites on addressing their racism and less on giving "help" to minorities
- Examines the White culture and develops an awareness of the strengths and limitations of White culture

### Internalization Stage

Whites at this stage, aware of their past and concerned about creating the future, apply and integrate their new sense of being White into all other facets of their identities. Since a person's total identity consists of personal and social aspects, change in one sector of identity affects all other sectors. Therefore, when one's racial identity undergoes change, this affects other aspects of her or his social and personal identity. At this stage, White people work to mediate these changes so that the new White identity becomes internalized into one's total identity in a healthy manner. By using the term "internalization," we assume that the new aspects become such a natural part of behavior that people act spontaneously, without external controls or without having to think about what they are doing.

At this stage, White people can acknowledge other issues of oppression, such as prejudice on the basis of sex, age, or handicap. As internalization takes place, these issues arise because individuals realize that their identity consists of many other facets and social groups, and these facets involve other issues of oppression.

*Indicators of Internalization Consciousness*

Beliefs:

• "Organizations can benefit from the diversity of perspectives of different racial groups."
• I recognize, appreciate, and affirm my own race and other races without idealizing or deprecating."
• "I see the connection between racism and other forms of oppression."

Behaviors:

• Interacts authentically with members of all racial groups, regardless of their stage of consciousness
• Attempts to integrate all cultural perspectives into the organization's operations
• Continues to work on confronting racism in the organization from a redefined White perspective

## Discussion

One should understand that while each of these theories presents identity stages as if Blacks and Whites perceive the world through one stage of consciousness at a time in all situations, this does not generally occur. Most people tend to view the world through more than one stage of consciousness in different situations. Furthermore, an individual may express a position on one issue that would suggest one stage of consciousness, while on another issue that same person may express an opinion that typifies a different stage of consciousness.

For the manager, these theories do not provide rigid labelling devices. These theories do, however, shed light on the underlying racial perspective of an individual at a given point in time, thus expanding the manager's understanding of the racial dynamics operating in the workplace.

## Implications for Managing the Multiracial Work Force

As mentioned in the introduction to this chapter, the current multiracial profile of the American work force has presented managers with new kinds of human resource management issues and problems. We have found that those managers who (1) are aware of their own place in the process of racial identity development, (2) understand and appreciate the process as manifested in subordinates' behavior, and (3) can support their subordinates' racial identity development are more able to achieve the type of organizational climate in the multiracial work force that will improve the quantity and quality of the organization's product or service.

Therefore, as a first step, we offer the following suggestions for managers:

1. Consider the stages of consciousness when interacting with subordinates. Consideration of the subordinate's world view when making work assignments, providing performance feedback, and developing career plans will enhance communication, problem solving, decision making, and planning. Managers should also consider RID theory when designing their own career development plans. Managers who can plot their own place in the racial identity development process can better identify those learning goals most appropriate for their own stage of consciousness.

2. Understand that no one affirmative action strategy, technique, or training program will be positively received by all members of the work force. For example, a Black/White encounter group might be useful for Whites at the Passive Acceptance stage and for some Blacks at the Active Resistance stage, but it will not likely assist Blacks or Whites in other stages of consciousness.☐

## Bibliography

Atkinson, D. R., Morton, G., & Sue, D. W. *Counseling American Minorities.* Dubuque, Iowa: William C. Brown, 1979.

Dickens, F., & Dickens, J. B. *Black Managers—Making It in the Corporate World.* New York: AMACOM, 1982.

Fernandez, J. P. *Black Managers in White Corporations.* New York: Wiley, 1975.

Fernandez, J. P. *Racism and Sexism in Corporate Life.* Lexington, Mass.: Lexington Books, 1981.

# Dilemmas of Black
# Females in Leadership

Rhetaugh Graves Dumas

*"Because of the myths about the strength and courage of their predecessors, black women today are also expected to have unlimited internal resources to cope with any problem that conceivably might confront them."*

From the time they first set foot in the New World, black females have struggled courageously to contribute to a better quality of life in black communities and in society at large. Their struggles have been waged from the lowest position among black and white Americans, and they have labored under the hardest conditions. While their contributions have been significant in the development of this nation and in the continuing fight against the oppression of its black citizenry, black females have yet to enjoy the full benefits of their suffering and arduous labors. Obstructed by the dynamics of racism and sexism in the groups in which they live and work, the full leadership potential of black females throughout their history in this country has remained an untapped—or at best, underutilized—resource, not only in predominantly white institutions and organizations, but also in black communities.

During slavery, organizations often were not permitted among the slaves. Free black women had limited opportunities, if any, to head the significant organizations that existed in the North during slavery or those that developed around the country after the Civil War. Organizations that included black and white males and females were headed by white males. Women's groups that were racially mixed were headed by white women. Outside the family, which was headed by males, the black church was the first major social institution fully controlled by blacks. The vast majority of black leaders, including the postwar politicians, got their start in the church. Despite the fact that women constituted 62.5% of the membership and their dues provided the bulk of the financial support, their roles were facilitative and supportive (Woodson, 1921). Men held the top posts and the power. In 1979, for the first time in history, two black women were appointed to high posts in a black church organization. Whatever access the black community had to the powerful leaders in the

© 1978 A. K. Rice Institute, adapted from the *Journal of Personality and Social Systems*, 2(1), April 1979. Used with permission.

larger community was achieved through the church. Black preachers were able to exercise more influence than others in the black community. Prior to emancipation and for some four decades to follow, black men had greater access to education. The first college degrees in the black community were earned by males. In higher education, the first black woman earned a Ph.D. degree 45 years after the first such degree was awarded to a black male in the United States. That woman was Sadie T. Mossell (Alexander) who earned her degree in Economics at the University of Pennsylvania in 1921. Edward A. Bouchet was awarded the doctorate from Yale in 1876.

Historically, because of their executive positions and training in the church and their access to formal educational institutions, men have been the most powerful and the most celebrated leaders in black communities. During Reconstruction in the South, there was a great emergence of black men who provided political leadership. Men held the franchise for their communities; 20 served in the U. S. House of Representatives and two in the Senate. Others served as lieutenant governor, sheriff, prosecuting attorney, recorder of deeds in their localities. One woman served as postmistress in Indianola, Mississippi. The vast majority of black women leaders were limited to projects for the social uplift of the community, and their main followers were other black women and youths. It was only during periods of extreme stress that the value of the black woman's leadership outside of her women's groups could be realized. Even then the women had not only to struggle on the boundary between blacks and whites, but they also had to find ways to endure the frustration and hardships posed by the lack of support from black males.

Existing circumstances and prior experiences made it difficult, if not impossible, to transcend what I call the hydraulic system principle of male–female relationships. That principle stipulates that black males can rise only to the degree that black women are held down. Black females were unable to submit to their dissatisfactions when survival in a hostile and increasingly violent environment and a sense of community and togetherness seemed so essential. Therefore, women with leadership abilities concentrated their efforts on relieving the suffering imposed by illiteracy, poverty, and disease. This situation was still very apparent as late as the 1960s. Earlier black female leaders realized the need for the strength and mutual support that would come from group effort and they began in 1892 to organize local black women's clubs and thus planted the seeds that ultimately grew into a national movement still existing today. Under the motto

"Lifting as we climb," the National Association of Colored Women provided the model for what became the most significant resource available to black women, not only for mutual support and social uplift, but also as a training ground for black female leadership. During the sixties, many young females rejected many of the traditional organizations for ambitious black women as being too middle class. Although black women found meaning in the black protest and civil rights movements, they did not occupy prominent leadership positions. They were often caught up with black men in that hydraulic principle that forced them to take only those roles that would enable their men to go forward. Many black women with outstanding leadership abilities held their skills in abeyance lest they might undermine the security and threaten the masculinity of the black men. Bound by the fear of the strong, castrating black woman, the full range of the black female's leadership was never exploited. There were, of course, exceptions. A small number of black women did not permit themselves to be bound by these dynamics.

It is significant to repeat that white males were being trained for leadership of both sexes, and some few black males were sometimes provided opportunities for leadership in racially mixed groups; black females were limited to the leadership of other black females. Furthermore, when they dared to turn their attention from service-oriented programs to the political arena, they had to struggle against strong opposition in both the white and black communities. Despite these obstacles, many black women have cleverly combined political, civic, social goals and strategies, and some gains have been made in each generation. But there is still a long way to go. Despite the outstanding achievements of some black women in many fields of endeavor, the mass of black women in America are still at the bottom of the heap. Although increasing numbers of black women are beginning to occupy important positions of authority and prestige in organizations within and outside black communities, there are forces at·work today, as in the past, that tax the physical and emotional stamina of these women. Their authority is undermined, their competence is compromised, and the power they might conceivably exercise is compromised, thus limiting their opportunities for rewards and mobility in the organization. I contend that this problem has its roots in myths about the privileged position and role of black women in slavery. The mythical image of the powerful, castrating black matriarch pervades contemporary organizations and poses a critical dilemma for black females that makes competition for, and competent performance in, leadership positions a costly endeavor. There are increasing efforts to resurrect the black mammy in today's ambitious black women. There are negative consequences for those who succumb as well as for those who dare to resist. The remainder of this paper is devoted to an elaboration of this thesis. In preparing the following section, I have utilized data compiled for a more extensive study of this topic.

Very little psychology of administration addresses the problems of black women leaders, or to those of women in general. Therefore, I have used my own experiences as an appointed city official, an associate professor and department head of a professional training program in a prestigious Ivy League university, a federal executive, and a member of a consultant staff for group relations training in the Tavistock tradition. I have relied more heavily upon the experiences of other black women leaders around the country. Some of them described their dilemmas during informal discussions at social gatherings or during professional meetings; others (totaling over 500 during the period of data gathering) while participating in institutes, workshops, or group relations training conferences. I have supplemented these sources with descriptions in the literature, particularly biographies and autobiographies of black women. These were valuable although sparse resources. The most telling autobiographies were those of Ida B. Wells Barnett (Dusier, 1970) and Mary Church Terrell (1940).

The presence of black women in leadership positions takes on highly significant meanings in organizational life. Myths of the superiority of black women over white women and black men emphasize their tremendous power and strength, and their unique capacity for warm, soothing interpersonal relationships. These myths prompt others to press black women into symbolic roles that circumscribe the nature and scope of their functions and limit their options and power in the organizations in which they live and work.

The black woman leader is often torn between the expectations and demands born of her mythical image and those that are inherent in her official status and tasks in the formal organization. The pressures to conform to the roles of her earlier predecessors are often irresistible. Whether she likes it or not, the black woman has come to represent the kind of person, a style of life, a set of attitudes and behaviors through which individuals and groups seek to fulfill their own socio-emotional needs in organizations. It is not surprising, therefore, that there is a great deal more interest in the *personal* qualities of black women administrators than in their skill and competence for formal leadership roles.

There is general resistance to having black women perform competently in formal, high-status positions. Rather, the preference is to have the black woman assume a variety of functions that resemble those described for the black mammy during the plantation era. In performing these functions, however, the power of the black woman leader is as illusory as was mammy's. It is derived from her relationships in the *informal* system, her willingness to put her *person* at the disposal of those around her. It can be maintained only as long as she is willing or able to provide what is demanded of her.

The demands very often go beyond the responsibilities of her formal position. For example, the black woman in leadership is expected to comfort the weary and oppressed, intercede on behalf of those who feel abused, champion the cause for equality and justice—often as a lone crusader. She is expected to compensate for the deficits of other members of her group, speaking up for those who are unable or unwilling to speak for themselves, making demands on behalf of the weak or frightened, doing more than her share of the work to make up for people who fail to complete their assigned tasks. Expected to be mother confessor, she counsels and advises her superiors and peers as well as her subordinates, often on matters unrelated to the tasks at hand. She is called upon to fill in for her boss in dealing with problems of sex and race, to mediate in situations of conflict, quiet the "natives," curb the aggression of black males, dampen the impact of other aggressive black women, and to maintain stability or restore order in the organization or one of its sectors.

Black women who are pressed into such positions are faced with problems that challenge their own identity and threaten their inner security. For example, they are often caught in the struggles between the boss and subordinates, blacks and whites, men and women, between units in the organization, and between the organization and the community in which it is located. Sometimes they are unclear who or what they are representing and find themselves trying to manage certain organizational boundaries without adequate authority and hence without appropriate backing and support. They are subject to high levels of tension as they become the repository of the problems, conflicts, and secrets of individuals and groups on both sides of the boundary.

Because of the myths about the strength and courage of their predecessors, black women today are also expected to have unlimited internal resources to cope with any problem that conceivably might confront them. Consequently, people around them are likely to be insensitive to their needs for socio-psychological support, reassurance, or some relief from the heavy demands on their time and energy.

Many of them work long hours in activities related to these symbolic roles, leaving less time and energy available for task performance. Consequently, doubts may be raised as to their competence for the positions they hold. Some black women in this predicament come to doubt their own ability and are disillusioned with their newly acquired status and prestige. Unfortunately, efforts to alter these situations are met with strong resistance from people who value their performance in the informal network of relationships. Such people are likely to subvert the leader's attempts to effect a more realistic distribution of time and effort between the informal and formal roles. If they persist, such situations not only undermine the upward mobility of the black woman, but also have important implications for her physical and emotional health. She takes the risk of being "used up" or "burnt out" rapidly. The trouble with symbolic leaders is that they often cannot tell where their personal lives end and where their organizational roles begin. They are treated as if they belong to the people around them, and they feel as though they do. Black women who succumb to these symbolic roles do not actually lead; they offer themselves to be used. Hence the danger of overcommitment to activities of this nature.

Realizing this vulnerability, some black women refuse to assume symbolic roles. They try hard to focus exclusively on formal tasks and become rigid in their avoidance of personal involvement with their colleagues. They are likely to interpret invitations to participate in informal relationships as bids to behave according to stereotypes of earlier black women. Intent on avoiding that image, they isolate themselves, which makes them unavailable for those informal contacts that might well enhance their executive effectiveness. The more impersonal they are, the more curious people are to know them better, and the more they will challenge the boundary that leaders endeavor to maintain between their persons and their roles. Of course, the more this boundary is challenged the more rigid it becomes, which unfortunately leads to the image of a cold, inflexible authority. Thus, in the effort to avoid becoming the symbol of the good and willing resource for the satisfaction of the needs of people in the organization, these leaders develop an image that can be equally destructive. By their aloofness they are distinguished from the symbolic benevolent black mammy, but they become instead the wicked malevolent mammy. The negative consequences of this image are no less injurious than those endured by the executives who assume the caring, nurturing, protective roles.

Although males in authority may be symbolized as good or bad mothers, the implications are more severe for females. Feminine authority cast against a black background thus becomes the most haunting of all symbolic mothers. Bad mothers who are white seem to be more easily tolerated than bad mothers who are black; bad mothers who are black and female border on the intolerable. When the black woman leader fails to give people what they believe they need, she is perceived to be deliberately depriving and rejecting, and therefore, hostile and potentially destructive. Just as she is believed to be capable of providing generative, nourishing, protective femininity of the most powerful order, she is also imagined to have the capacity to withhold or destroy resources necessary to life and safety in the organization's symbolic world. The forceful exercise of her authority thus arouses intense irrationality and creates one crisis after another with which she must deal.

The black woman leader who is perceived as a bad mother must deal with the dependency, fear, and rage that often are expressed covertly and undermine the effectiveness of all involved. Stubborn resistance to work is a frequent manifestation of anger in such situations. The leader finds herself deluged by requests for clarification of procedures or special instructions for the most simple tasks. Indeed, those who feel deprived by her will frequently relinquish their authority and behave as if only she has the knowledge and skill required for a particular task. This type of dependency leads many executives to take on themselves the responsibilities that should be delegated or shared by others.

Sometimes the anger and hostility find as targets people who are close to or supportive of the black woman in question. In these and other ways, the black woman in such situations is kept busy mediating staff conflicts, dealing with hostile confrontations, having to rush to meet deadlines for work that should have been completed long before, and having to persist against covert resistance to get information she needs to do her job well.

The black woman executive, perceived to be either good or bad, becomes a kind of superstar in the organization. People love her when she gives what is desired and hate her when she fails to perform as expected. In either case people are moved by an image they have constructed of the black person in the leadership role—how they imagine her lifestyle, attitudes, and values.

The leader who objects to being mammy may not be subject to all the honors bestowed on her benevolent counterpart. Nevertheless, she does not suffer from want of attention from the people around her who seem to enjoy the experience of hating her. They want their friends and family to witness the bad person, especially in situations where she will be embarrassed, made into a fool, symbolically "killed off." So she is given invitations that set the stage for the kill. If she is not careful she may even do the job for them. Other blacks are often recruited for the dirty work in predominantly white organizations, or other women in predominantly male-oriented situations.

For example, I refused to recommend reappointment of a member of the faculty in a program I administered. My decision alone did not determine the action; the committee voted unanimously to deny reappointment. I was challenged by the woman in question and several individuals and groups advocated that I change my recommendation, which they felt would lead the committee to reverse the decision. I refused to change my recommendation. The committee, however, was persuaded to review the decision, and a second vote was taken because some members felt that I had exerted an overwhelming influence on their votes. The decision of the committee again was to deny reappointment, although the vote was not unanimous. The aggrieved applicant elicited the support of blacks in the community who led several angry protest marches into the school and the clinical agency where she and I held joint appointments. I found myself on the boundary between the school and the angry black leaders who yelled obscenities at me for allowing myself to be taken in by "the system" that was "kicking out" the only member of the faculty who cared anything about the black community. The one other black faculty member was on leave of absence; therefore, I was the only black faculty member around at that time, and I felt totally alone. I became the target for a great deal of hostility over a period of several months. I discovered in retrospect how much I had participated in my election to the post of "flak-catcher." People had treated me as if I were so powerful that I single-handedly forced the committee to deny reappointment; as if even those who might have protected the unfortunate woman's job were helpless against my wishes. I felt confident in my reasons for refusing to recommend her appointment. However, I came to believe that in exercising my responsibility to maintain the level of quality in the program that the faculty and I had agreed upon, I had pushed the school into a terrible crisis. While I was not willing to change my vote, I did feel unusually responsible for the disturbance. Unwittingly, I was behaving as if I really did have all that power. And no one in the school objected to my taking the front line between them and the malcontents from outside. The dean was relieved to have me perform that role for her and for the school. The director of the clinical agency refused to have me assume that position in his organization. One might speculate about his reasons: being a white male and a good administrator, he was not about to relinquish his authority to me. Being a colleague and a friend, he wanted to protect me. Regardless of the real motivations at the time, I have come to appreciate the soundness of the organizational principles that he later espoused as the major determinants for his position during that series of tense and stressful episodes.

Indeed, these types of incidents are not limited to black women leaders. Nevertheless, blacks are particularly vulnerable, and black males are spared more often than black females.

I know firsthand the tremendous hardships and anguish inherent in attempts to live up to this unrealistic model in the symbolism of contemporary organizations. I have felt the pangs of guilt evoked by those who would lead me to believe that to protect myself and promote my general welfare is to let my people down. I am now beginning to see that it is possible to let my people down by *failing* to protect myself and my interests and to seek fulfillment of my own needs. Indeed in modern organizations, racism and sexism dictate that I AM MY PEOPLE. I AM BLACK. I AM WOMAN.

Numerous other black women executives know the pain and anguish to which I refer. Some of them are discovering, as I am, when and how *not* to be Mammy, Miss Truth, and still survive. This does not mean that they will be able to avoid becoming symbols in the organizations. It does mean that they are trying to have some part in the development of their symbolic images. It means that they are finding ways to balance the caring, nurturing, protective functions and those that are task-directed. There is at least one writer who argues that it is not possible for the same persons to fulfill the socio-emotional and task needs in organizations simultaneously. Perhaps the success of black women executives lies in their ability to move back and forth between socio-emotional and task-directed functions. The pendulum rarely stays in the center, and when it moves too far to either extreme there is trouble. But even the most successful black woman executive finds her life hectic at best and pays a high price for competent performance. Yet, her struggles yield greater and more lasting achievements and satisfaction than those of her black sisters who are locked into symbolic roles most of the time.

It is often difficult to separate the influence of race from that of sex; there is no doubt in my mind that the *combination* levies a heavy toll on the black woman who exercises authority and responsibility in groups and organizations. Herein lies the most significant challenge to black women executives, to those who claim an interest in promoting the upward social mobility of minority groups and women in America, and to all who are concerned with the development of social and psychological theories of organizational leadership.□

## References

Dusier, Elfreda (Ed.) *Crusade for Freedom: Autobiography of Ida B. Wells.* Chicago: University of Chicago Prem. 1970.

Neumann, Erich. *The Great Mother.* Princeton: 1972. Pp. 148–49.

Terrell, Mary Church. *A Colored Woman in a White World.* Washington, D. C.: Ransdell Publishers, 1940.

Woodson, Carter. *History of the Negro Church.* Washington, D. C.: 1921. Pp. 278–79.

# Black Professionals and Organizational Stress

David L. Ford, Jr.

*"Black professionals in major organizations often experience increased performance pressures or the underuse of their skills and abilities."*

A multitude of newspaper articles (see the *Wall Street Journal* and the *New York Times Magazine*), books (e.g., the Addison-Wesley Series on Occupational Stress), and training films deal with managerial and executive stress. Few of these works, however, address the stress-related experiences unique to black professionals. Even major works on blacks in industry (e.g., America & Anderson, 1978; Fernandez, 1975; Dickens & Dickens, 1982) do not deal directly with the topic of stress. Available data, however, indicate that stress among black professionals in major white organizations is a serious problem (Campbell, 1982).

Behavioral science research documents that minority status is, at best, a source of extra tension for an employee and is, at worst, intrinsically stressful. Minority professionals suffer from more job-related stress than white male professionals (Friday, 1981); white female professionals feel about as much job-related stress as white male professionals (Ramos, 1975). In a recent survey by *Black Enterprise* magazine (Dreyfuss, 1982), nearly 75% of the black respondents earning more than $35,000 per year reported that they experience discrimination on the job. These findings corroborate those of my own research studies, which determined that black and Mexican-American professionals with white supervisors felt significantly less satisfied with certain aspects of their jobs and felt significantly greater stress than did blacks who worked for black supervisors (Ford, 1980).

These studies do not attempt to go beyond the mere identification of a difference in the amounts of job stress experienced by black and white professionals. If, however, we wish to increase our understanding of this phenomenon and manage it better, we must do the following: examine some of the issues and actions that often confront the "different" person in a work setting; identify and describe the organizational processes that lead to the unique experiences of blacks, and develop strategies to minimize the dysfunctional consequences of stress for all employees and make use of their skills and talents.

© 1983 NTL Institute

Some authors have suggested that minorities—females and members of various ethnic groups—don't "fit" into the organizational mold and, as a result, experience undesirable work outcomes (Taylor, 1972; Kanter & Stein, 1980). A black person becomes what Rosabeth Moss Kanter (1977) has termed an "O" in a predominantly "X"—or white—setting. This is also true for a female who works in a predominantly male setting. Kanter describes an "O" as someone who differs from the majority—the "Xs"—because of some socially relevant characteristic such as age, race, gender, or culture.

Several norms of the business world have, because of the homogeneity of the group that created them, systematically discriminated against blacks and other minorities by limiting these persons' access to the organizations and by treating them differently when they do make it inside those organizations (Terborg & Ilgren, 1975; Brown & Ford, 1977). For example, black applicants are more likely to receive harsh, less positive evaluations than white applicants with identical qualifications. "Old boy" networks and traditional selections procedures that use recruiters and employment interviews generally use one role model—the white male. Additionally, whites often make untested assumptions about blacks' competencies and their ability to "fit in." Chester Barnard and other early management theorists espoused the notion that for organizations to function smoothly, especially at upper-management levels, they should maintain a culturally homogeneous group of people who "fit in" with the team (Barnard, 1948). This philosophy has often meant a team composed of white males. Recent evidence has documented the prevailing notion among whites that blacks lack the necessary motivation, drive, ambition, and initiative to succeed in the business world (Fernandez, 1975; Alderfer, et. al., 1980).

If we compare the qualifications and work histories of black professionals and managers to those of their white counterparts, however, we note that a large percentage of blacks can be characterized as "overqualified" or "superstars." Indeed, Price Cobbs has noted that blacks' credentials rarely affect their organizational experiences (1981). To survive and succeed in a major white corporation, many blacks have had to do the following: (1) learn skills different from the skills learned by whites; (2) demonstrate their skills in other work experiences before receiving consideration for the same positions for which "untested" whites have been considered (which shows that many blacks lack an "equal opportunity to fail"); (3) acquire more education than many of their white peers and supervisors; and (4) demonstrate repeatedly their competence under close scrutiny before gaining acceptance as team members. Thus, blacks experience much greater performance pressure and stress than whites do, and, as such, find it difficult to remain motivated and committed to organizational goals (Faunt, 1980).

Recent work has theorized that job-related stress results from the relationship between the person and the environment. When the environmental demand exceeds a person's ability to respond—producing overload—or the person's capabilities exceed this demand—producing "underload"—the resulting "misfit" creates stress (French, 1975; Coburn, 1975; Blau, 1981). Black professionals in major organizations often experience increased performance pressures or the underuse of their skills and abilities. Black executives may thus undergo varying degrees of culture shock, isolation, alienation, and loss of identity (Campbell, 1982).

## Complex Organizations and the Individual Member

Large, complex organizations in the United States have been characterized as "white male clubs"—or WMCs (Terry, 1974). As such, they act as purveyors of "inauthenticity" in our society—according to the definition of an authentic society as one characterized by (a) equitable distribution of resources, (b) shared power, (c) cultural pluralism, and (d) flexible and responsive institutions (Gibb & Terry, 1979). Not everyone will agree with these requirements for an authentic society. One may reasonably assume, however, that the denial of authenticity creates alienation and/or inauthenticity. Alienation occurs when people are unaware—or only vaguely aware—that a hostile system excludes them, manipulates them, makes them dependent, and keeps them from participating in that system. Inauthenticity exists when a society appears authentic but has an alienating underlying reality. Today, organizations have become increasingly inauthentic, so we have more difficulty uncovering the underlying alienating forces at play.

The WMC image captures many alienating and inauthentic dimensions of large organizations today. Organizations distribute *resources* disproportionately to white males; white males hold *power*; the organizational *climate* and *ethos* legitimizes selected white male values and behaviors; and *institutional policies, practices*, and *programs* support and reinforce white male ascendency. To protect themselves, club members draw on old traditions and rationalize their behavior with rhetoric about equal opportunity and "victim help" programs. The club itself escapes challenge. Indeed, at least one author has carried the notion of the WMC to a broader extreme by discussing a "white male system" that controls almost every aspect of our lives (Scharf, 1981).

Brown (1977) calls the manifestation of the alienating forces that work against black victims the "black tax." This tax consists of (a) the conspicuous powerlessness of black organizational members, or the "spook-who-sat-by-the-door" syndrome, (b) a mutual distrust between black executives and their peers that places black executives in paranoid isolation, (c) the double bind of being labeled a racial militant by whites and an "Uncle Tom" by other blacks, and (d) participating in and rationalizing organizational policies that do not serve the interests of blacks.

We can reasonably conclude that most large, complex organizations that employ minorities and/or women contain potential sources of stress for these groups, especially the organizations that fit the image of the white male club. Anyone who is not white and male will encounter difficulty in such a work environment. Indeed, accounts exist of organizations that relegate "non-club" members to positions that lack upward mobility or opportunity for advancement (Taylor, 1973) or who shunt people into sex-segregated positions with noticeable wage differentials (England & McLaughlin, 1979). These findings suggest that women and minorities often find themselves holding an "out-group" status.

In the absence of other pertinent information, demographic data often play a key role in determining the in-group and out-group status of organization members. Race, sex, age, and other factors become critical variables, especially in terms of the similarity of these characteristics among supervisors and subordinates. Very often, blacks who have white supervisors (or females who have male supervisors) find themselves relegated to the out-group subgroup and, once there, have an exceedingly difficult time making the transition to the in-group. Additionally, when blacks *do* obtain a "quasi" in-group status because of the positions they hold (e.g., as managers or supervisors), their WMC subordinates may behave in ways that impede the supervisory effectiveness of the black managers. These trends, however, can be changed through corrective action by individuals and organizations. I offer the following suggestions as tools to aid in the corrective process.

## Recommendations for Managers and Organizations

1. White managers and black managers who have been "on-board" for a while should formulate steps to speed up the integration process for blacks and help to eliminate the institutional racism and barriers that cause dysfunctional behavior.

2. Organizations need to establish policies that focus on human resource development. Managers should have as one of their

primary responsibilities the development of their subordinates, who should be rewarded when they accomplish this objective. The development programs must also be designed to teach multicultural management techniques.

3. Organizations must incorporate fast-track development for sharp, creative blacks—just as they do for whites under similar circumstances. Through varied experiences and job enrichment programs, blacks will transcend functional and hierarchical boundaries in the organization with greater ease and have greater opportunities to reach their potential.

4. Organizations should create mechanisms to educate managers in the requisite skills needed for managing a diverse work force. White managers should develop both an increased awareness of issues important to blacks and skill in coaching, counseling, or giving feedback to subordinates with dissimilar social characteristics.

5. Managers should scrutinize their own behavior toward persons with dissimilar social characteristics—and particularly examine the kinds of attention they give to different people, the assumptions they make about persons' skills and roles, and whom they consider for certain types of job assignments.

### Recommendations for Black Professionals

1. Blacks should present their ideas in terms of whites' self-interest so that whites can feel they have a stake in the black employees' concerns.

2. Blacks should enlist the aid of white peers and learn to manage through others. Sometimes whites listen better to other whites than to blacks.

3. Blacks should tell whites how to behave appropriately toward blacks.

4. Blacks should search for and secure organizational sponsors or mentors—people higher in the organizational hierarchy who will help make subordinates and their expertise known to the right people in the organization.

These recommendations provide a starting point for making organizations become more responsive to the needs of a diverse work force. As I said earlier, an organization improves its effectiveness when it improves the congruence—or fit—among *all* of its components.□

### Reference Notes

Cobbs, P. *Challenge of the 80s: Corporations, Credentials, and Race.* Invitational address presented to the Black Alumni Conference,

Harvard Graduate School of Business, Boston, Massachusetts, February 27–28, 1981.

Friday, E. *A Comparative Analysis of Job-Related Psychological Stress Experienced by Black and White Nonacademic Administrators in a State University System.* Paper presented at the 46th Annual Meeting of the Association of Social and Behavioral Scientists, Atlanta, Georgia, March 1981.

Gibb, B., & Terry, R. *Advocating Change in the White Male Club.* Unpublished manuscript, Neely, Campbell, Gibb, Terry, & Associates, Ann Arbor, Michigan, 1979.

## References

Alderfer, C. P., Alderfer, C. J., Tucker, L., & Tucker, R. Diagnosing Race Relations in Management. *Journal of Applied Behavioral Science*, 1980, *16*, 135–166.

America, R. F., & Anderson, B. E. *Moving Ahead: Black Managers in American Business.* New York: McGraw-Hill, 1978.

Barnard, C. I. *The Functions of the Executive.* Cambridge, Mass.: Harvard University Press, 1948.

Blau, G. An Empirical Investigation of Job Stress, Social Support, Service Length, and Job Strain. *Organizational Behavior and Human Performance*, 1981, *27*, 279–302.

Brown, H. A., & Ford, D. L. An Exploratory Analysis of Discrimination in the Employment of Black MBA Graduates. *Journal of Applied Psychology*, 1977, *62*, 50–56.

Brown, R. W. The Black Tax: Stresses Confronting Black Federal Executives. *Journal of Afro-American Issues*, 1975, *3*, 207–218.

Campbell, B. M. Black Executives and Corporate Stress. *New York Times Magazine*, December 12, 1982, 36.

Coburn, D. Job-Worker Incongruence: Consequences for Health. *Journal of Health and Social Behavior*, 1975, *16*, 198–212.

Dickens, F., & Dickens, J. B. *The Black Manager: Making It in the Corporate World.* New York: AMACOM, 1982.

Dreyfuss, J. Speaking Out about Work. *Black Enterprise*, August 1982, *13*(1), 51–53.

England, P., & McLaughlin, S. Sex Segregation of Jobs and Male-Female Income Differentials. In R. Alvarez, K. Lutterman, et al. (Eds.), *Discrimination in Organizations.* San Francisco: Jossey-Bass, 1979. Pp. 189–213.

Faunt, O. *Color Your World: The Implications of Racial Diversity in Corporations.* Cambridge, Mass.: Goodmeasure, Inc., 1980.

Fernandez, J. P. *Racism and Sexism in Corporate Life.* Lexington, Mass.: D. C. Heath, 1981.

Fernandez, J. P. *Black Managers in White Corporations.* New York: John Wiley & Sons, 1975.

Ford, D. L. Work, Job Satisfaction, and Employee Well Being: An Exploratory Study of Minority Professionals. *Journal of Social and Behavioral Sciences*, 1980, *26*(3), 70–75.

French, J. R. P. Person-Role Fit. In A. McLean (Ed.), *Occupational Stress*. Springfield, Ill.: Thomas, 1974.

Kanter, R. M. *Men and Women of the Corporation*. New York: Basic Books, 1977.

Kanter, R. M., & Stein, B. A. *A Tale of "O": On Being Different in an Organization*. New York: Harper and Row, 1980.

Ramos, A. A. The Relationship of Sex and Ethnic Background to Job Related Stress of Research and Development Professionals. *Dissertation Abstracts International*, 1975, *9*, 1862A.

Scharf, A. W. *Women's Reality: An Emerging Female System in the White Male Society*. Minneapolis, Minn.: Winston Press, 1981.

Taylor, S. A. The Black Executive and the Corporation: A Difficult Fit. *MBA Magazine*, 1971, *8*, 91–102.

Taylor, S. A. Room at the Top? Not for Blacks. *New York Times*, January 14, 1973, Section F, 14.

Terborg, J. R., & Ilgen, D. R. A Theoretical Approach to Sex Discrimination in Traditionally Masculine Occupations. *Organizational Behavior and Human Performance*, 1975, *13*, 352–376.

Terry, Y. White Male Club: Biology and Power. *Civil Rights Digest*, 1974, *6*, 66–77.

# Staying Well During— and After—Stressful Periods

John D. Adams

*"When most people experience high levels of stress, they compound their problems by giving up their best defenses against the effects of stress."*

Those experiencing high personal stress will find three pieces of information useful. *First*, stress clearly is a risk factor associated with most adverse health changes. The more stress you experience during a given period of time, the more likely you are to become ill during the succeeding months. *Second*, during periods of high stress, most people do a *poorer* job of taking care of themselves than they do during periods of low stress. *Third*, over 50% of the risks associated with the leading causes of serious illness, including stress, involve lifestyle choices. This chapter explores these three points in detail and focuses on ways to respond to increased stress.

## Stress and Illness

Most illnesses do not have a single cause. Rather, they are caused by a multitude of factors that interact with each other in complex ways. Think of any given illness as an abstract puzzle in which each piece connects to every other piece.

Stress requires the body to make internal adjustments that are commonly called the "flight or fight" response. This response evolved during our very early history to help people handle the stressors of the day, which were usually challenges to survival. The modern problem of stress arises because most of the stressors we experience today (like marriage or divorce, being laid off or reassigned) do *not* create problems of survival. Our bodies have not kept pace with "civilization" and, thus, they still respond to stress as they did many centuries ago. The problem arises when we have no ways of using up this fight-or-flight preparedness. Obviously, punching the boss or running out of the office screaming are not suitable responses to stressful work situations. Therefore, the energy (adrenalin) available for that sort of response becomes bottled up inside. This can cause considerable tension within your body, commonly referred to as "strain."

© 1983 NTL Institute

Carrying around too much strain for a period of time increases one's risk of becoming ill. The illness one contracts depends on genetic makeup, personality, past health history, lifestyle habits, the environment, and even the nature and quality of past medical care. Some people develop headaches easily, while others develop high blood pressure, ulcers, colitis, or pain in the lower back.

Why do some people seem to become ill while others, who are apparently experiencing just as much stress in life, seem unaffected? We do not yet know all the answers. Some people *do* have stronger constitutions than others. Many people protect themselves with good health habits; these are discussed later in this chapter. We have some indication that a good network of supportive relationships can protect your health during stressful periods. Also, it appears that you can withstand more stress without adverse effects if your work (and your life in general) contains sufficient *challenge*, allows you to *control* how you do things, and includes major activities to which you feel strongly *committed*.

Given this background, how do you know if you are a candidate for developing a stress-related illness? How can you tell how much stress is "getting to you"? While we have no precise way of knowing this, the following list of conditions will give you an indication of your present stress-related health risks. If you experience several of the conditions listed below, you may assume that stress presents a risk to your health. The more items you check off, the greater the risk.

- Feeling slow, sluggish, weak
- Tiring frequently and easily
- Rapid weight gain or loss
- Changes in eating patterns or amount eaten
- Constipation or diarrhea
- Withdrawal from sex or overuse of sex
- Difficulty in concentrating, short attention span
- Smoking or drinking more than usual
- Sleep disruption
- Headaches
- Feeling nervous, apprehensive, anxious
- Feeling depressed, listless
- Being irritable and displaying misdirected anger
- Being cynical and displaying inappropriate humor
- Withdrawal from supportive relationships

You can usually recognize some of these conditions as being particularly characteristic of you from time to time. These are your "red flags." As a basic step in effective stress management you should become sensitive to the occurrence of your red-flag conditions. Their presence indicates that your stress levels are getting too high and that you either need to avoid some of the stress, cope with it more effectively, or build up your health to withstand it.

## Natural Stress-Response Tendencies

Unfortunately, when most people experience high levels of stress, they compound their problems by giving up their best defenses against the effects of stress. The strain conditions listed above become self-reinforcing and extend themselves even further in a self-destructive way, increasing the amount of stress.

For example, many people withdraw from their friends during periods'of high stress. When the stress is alleviated, they "resurface" and speak, often to their friends' surprise, about what a rough period *they have just completed*! It is as if they feel they have to handle "it" themselves and not bother others, even if they know that effective use of supportive relationships makes one of the best stress management techniques.

Many people allow their best nutritional habits to lapse and eat foods high in fat, sugar, and salt (i.e., highly refined or "junk" foods). At the same time, they drink and smoke more than they usually do (perhaps seeking an instant gratification to assuage their feelings of strain). These behaviors, of course, constitute additional risk factors on top of the risks associated with the stress itself.

## Lifestyle Choices

An investigation of the risks associated with the most frequent major illnesses reveals that an average of 20% of the risk is biological, 20% environmental, and 10% attributable to health care services (drug interactions, etc.). This leaves 50% of the risk factors in the category called "lifestyle choices." Put another way, you can avoid or eliminate fully half of the risks to your health by making responsible lifestyle choices. The "last word" in long-term stress and health management is to control that which is controllable.

The following list contains most of the controllable risk factors that constitute lifestyle choices:

- Nutritional habits (the average American diet contains far too much fat, sugar, salt, chemicals, white flour, white rice, and caffeine)
- Alcohol use

- Tobacco use
- Drug use (including prescription drugs)
- Amount of rest
- Relaxation
- Exercise (aerobic, stretching, and recreational)
- Body weight (percentage fat composition)
- Psychological outlook (optimistic *vs.* pessimistic)
- Quality of relationships
- Driving habits (speed, seatbelt use, attitude)
- Strain as a reflection of excessive stress
- Blood pressure
- Cholesterol and triglycerides

The inclusion of few, if any, of these items should surprise you. Yet most people do not score very well when they assess their own practices of these habits. A recent study in California of seven of these habits (no smoking, moderate drinking, sufficient sleep, recommended weight, balanced diet, regular breakfast, and regular exercise) found that 45-year-old men who practiced six or seven of the habits could expect to live 11.5 years longer than men of the same age who practiced fewer than four of these habits. The same comparison for 45-year-old women yielded a difference in life expectancy of 7.2 years. And for everyone, at all ages, the more of these seven habits practiced, the better one's day-to-day, overall health.

Take a few moments to assess the healthfulness of your present lifestyle choices. If you are currently away from home, perhaps attending a training program, are you maintaining your habits as well as you do at home? If you are a regular traveller, do you carry your lifestyle with you on the road, or do you use travel as an excuse to stop making healthy lifestyle choices?

### Personal Planning

If the preceding sections indicated that you have room for improvement in your present stress management and/or lifestyle habits, the following questions will help you get started on a more health-protective course:

1.  How well am I avoiding unnecessary stressors (e.g., do I plan my time well? Do I try to stay away from certain people who seem to be stress carriers?)?
2.  How well am I coping with the unavoidable stressors in my life (e.g., do I have needed conflict, influence, assertiveness, problem-solving skills?)?

3. How well am I protecting and building my health (e.g., do I have healthful, nutritional, exercise, relaxation, and relationship habits, and do I take an hour a day for myself?)?
4. What do I need to *stop* doing?
5. What do I need to *start* doing?
6. What do I need to *continue* doing?
7. Have I let my support network know what is going on with me? Are there specific ways in which those people can support me right now?□

## Bibliography

Adams, J. D. *Understanding and Managing Stress Readings.* San Diego, Calif.: University Associates, 1980.
Goldberg, P. *Executive Health.* New York: McGraw-Hill, 1978.

# Man/Woman Dynamics: Some Typical Communication Patterns

Carol Pierce
Janice Eddy
David Wagner

*"Women, men, and organizations suffer from stereotypical communication styles."*

The examination of communication patterns between men and women holds the seeds of a revolution in human behavior. With the exception of sexual dynamics, we have largely overlooked the interactions between men and women. In our culture, discussion of these patterns has focused on sexual issues. This chapter addresses wider areas of interaction to develop new perspectives on male/female communication. Since World War II, human relations experts have developed knowledge and skills to help people relate to one another more satisfactorily. Now we must refocus assumptions and concerns about how men and women interact. Past efforts failed to achieve their anticipated success because they stopped short of addressing the basic pattern of relationships between men and women—patterns that affect both personal and organizational life.

The basic pattern of a one-up, one-down relationship between men and women stems from the following four long-accepted notions:

• Traditionally male qualities such as rationality are desirable for people generally, but not expected to be a part of women's behavior.
• Traditionally female qualities such as intuitiveness and nurturing are signs of weakness rather than strength and are not expected to be a part of men's behavior.
• Men should develop only their "male" qualities, and women should develop only their "female" qualities.
• The "opposition of these two opposites,"—i.e., male and female—is the "natural" state of affairs (Broverman et al., 1970; Daly, 1973).

To understand the convulsions of our times and to provide a foundation for change, we must analyze these ideas:

• The male-female polarity is not a "natural" state.
• A *whole* person develops both male and female qualities, harmonizing them rather than treating them as irreconcilable

© 1983 New Dynamics Associates, Laconia, New Hampshire.

opposites to be suppressed, overcome, or complemented only by another half-person.

• Androgyny is a "natural" state of affairs because it acknowledges all parts of a person, including those psychological characteristics traditionally defined as male and female* (Pierce, 1983).

To work toward the wholeness of androgyny requires changes in thought patterns and behavior. Many women and some men do this individually. A few explore jointly how stereotyped conditioning affects our interactions. Here one should see how "one-upness" and "one-downness" get expressed in communication patterns and influence other behaviors.

We can see one basic dynamic consistently in female/male interactions. Women use this survival mechanism because of feelings of powerlessness. It seems to predetermine and underlie other patterns of behavior. We will refer to this process as "psyching-out."

## The Psyching-Out Process

"Psyching-out," a constant—often subconscious—process, exists in the thought and behavior of women and is so pervasive that we can consider it a part of the feminine lifestyle.

Girls do not experience as active a childhood as boys—i.e., girls are conditioned to more sedentary play, while boys play in a more rough-and-tumble fashion. As a result, girls learn to control the world around them indirectly, while boys do so more directly. Girls rely on feelings and internal thought processes, while boys rely on physical actions.

Women are programmed from childhood to feel that a man's approval is better than a woman's. As a result, women compete for male approval. They do not learn to value other women's judgment.

Women are socialized to feel they have less power than men. As a result, women tend to react rather than to take action.

We expect women to take on the role of selfless helper. As a result, women live for and through others. This moves them to define themselves in terms of others, especially men and children.

With this focus on others, women begin to assume the burden and responsibility for communication in personal and social situations. Women unconsciously expect that many personal needs will be fulfilled by helping others rather than by acting

* See "Affirmative Action: A Guide to Systems Change for Managers."

directly on their own needs. This role of selfless helper denies, and frequently buries, such basic needs as

- the need to be alone,
- the need to be listened to,
- the need to be nurtured,
- the need to be respected for intellectual activity, and
- the need to be seen as a distinct individual.

Because women learn early in life to fulfill their needs through other people (mostly men), they have developed mental processes and behavior styles characterized by continual forethought on how to "use" another person. Women become schemers. They gear their thoughts to making men feel comfortable, to finding the best way to make men appear pleasing and smart to others, to learning the problems men want to talk about, and to making men feel fascinating and powerful. These thinking and behavior styles often operate in women independently of whether men actually need them or not.

Thus, "psyching-out" is a type of behavior in which a person (usually a woman) continually takes on the responsibility of figuring out what most helps and pleases another person (usually a man). She hopes that, in return, she will receive attention, be liked, and be appreciated. A major male/female issue is that the man seldom initiates or returns this form of attention. He may not appreciate or even notice the woman.

The following stereotypical communication models show graphically this collusive process of communicating between women and men.

### Typical Communication Patterns

The interactions portrayed fit cultural stereotypes. The degree to which particular individuals will find these patterns indicative of their lives depends on various life experiences and the variety of socialization.

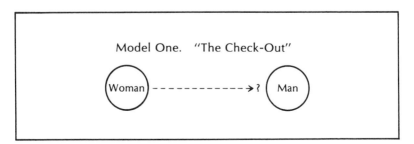

Model One. "The Check-Out"

Woman - - - - - - - - - - → ? Man

In the "check-out," the responsibility falls on the woman to initiate personal communication of a friendly, non-sexual nature. A woman has learned, often unconsciously, that if any "hello-how-are-you" pleasantries are to occur she must initiate them. In this model she sizes up the situation and decides for various reasons that she isn't interested in making the effort. She may fear seeming too aggressive, unless she is the hostess or the boss, and her role is clear. She loses possible friendships in social situations; she loses opportunities for gathering and sharing information—and for networking—in work situations.

Because of the man's socialization patterns, he has usually developed "blinders" to making contact. Many potential friendships, both on and off the job, become lost at the level of "the check-out."

A woman, for various reasons, may initiate exploratory contact by asking the man about himself, complimenting him on a job well done, or asking how he feels about a certain issue. He typically responds to her questions, discussing his interests and concerns. One needs to realize that, for the woman, the *topic* is the man's attitudes and feelings expressed through the *vehicle* of the subject matter.

The arrows in this model, as in the other models, represent the flow of energy used to focus and guide conversation, not who is doing the most talking. In Model Two, the arrows go from the woman to the man. With seemingly little effort, a woman keeps a man talking for a long time with just a few phrases, such as "Oh, really?" "Is that right?" "I never knew that!" "That's fascinating!" Her voice often takes on smoothness, showing care and total interest. The man feels listened to, affirmed, and acknowledged as a person. This conversation lacks any reciprocity. If the man does ask questions, he often has difficulty listening with interest for more than a sentence or two.

In the office, men do not seek the woman who questions and responds when they need ideas and information. She has not shown that she has any. Her questioning and responding can

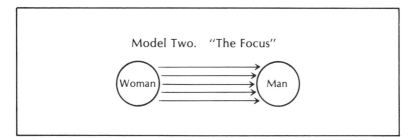

Model Two.   "The Focus"

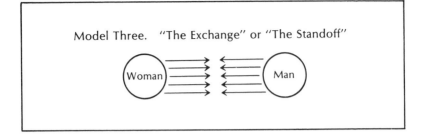

Model Three. "The Exchange" or "The Standoff"

Woman — Man

cause others to perceive her as a perpetual learner. A man can easily keep such a woman peer in a supporting role. This situation supports the woman's feeling that her needs are unimportant and invalid; and, therefore, she does not build self-confidence.

In "the exchange" or "the standoff," the energy meets equally in the middle. The information sharing in this transaction is basic to a productive work style. Such factual exchanges are appropriate in most business transactions and are delightful for passing acquaintances. Each takes initiative to ask questions as well as share ideas and thoughts.

The mode of dialogue changes from the "exchange" to the "standoff" in personal relationships. When the basic style of conversation in intimate relationships is only the sharing of information, it interferes with closeness and intimacy. Describing the mode of interacting as "the standoff" is appropriate since the two people avoid dealing with each other personally. Many relationships, including some marriages, become stuck at this level. Examples of "stand-off" conversations between couples are: "How were things at the office?" "What did you do all day?" "Were you able to get the car inspected?" Neither asks about the other's feelings. Women often initiate such conversations as "openers," hoping to get to a deeper level by this route. Sooner or later, if someone wishes communication to do something other than confirm "what is," that person must risk contact by asking or sharing feelings.

Often, people bring to the workplace the feeling that only factual conversations are appropriate and that any warmth or caring implies sexual interest. This is because the unfulfilled desire for dialogue that touches each of us more intimately within a personal relationship makes any warm or caring conversation on the job sexual. An "exchange" dialogue between two men or two women may feel comfortable. When a man and a woman guard against letting an "exchange" conversation go too far, however, they often interfere with the information flow and the building of support systems and networks.

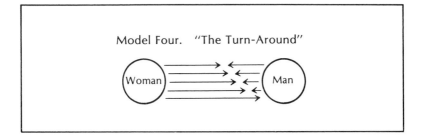

Model Four. "The Turn-Around"

Sometimes, a man and a woman have a friendly, casual conversation of "the exchange" variety. Each shares information. Then the woman, for reasons of her own, starts making slightly more caring comments and offers fewer informational ones. She may often interpret the silence that naturally occurs in conversations as a lack of interest in her, so she fills it with a series of questions about the man. As a result, the conversation changes from one in which each asks questions of the other and both respond to one in which the woman asks questions and the man makes statements about himself and his ideas. As the intense feeling of interest in the man becomes the backdrop of the conversation, the man feels no need to be interested in the woman as a person. She has started psyching him out.

The man and woman started in Model Three, "the exchange," but have ended in Model Two, "the focus." "The exhange" has progressed through "the turn-around" to the "the focus." This usually occurs because the woman feels responsible for the man. Model Four diagrams this frequent progression. The man cannot speak from "the exchange" if the woman speaks from "the focus." "The focus" will prevail.

"The dialogue" shows a mutual "psyching-out" process in which each partner takes time for the concerns and interests of the other. This is an attribute of an independent relationship, and is characterized by an interactive flow whereby persons share the

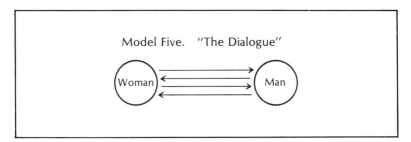

Model Five. "The Dialogue"

psyching-out function, help each other expand ideas, support each other's endeavors, and share feelings and resources—i.e., each tries to understand the other.

Some people have relationships that use "the dialogue." Many relationships of "the focus" variety, however, claim "the dialogue" status because the partners profess happiness and contentment with the woman focused on the man. Often, the woman starts in "the dialogue" and the man responds from "the exchange." The woman shares her feelings, saying, for example, "I'm feeling low today." The man responds either with advice ("Why don't you go out to lunch with your friends today?") or with an evaluation ("I don't see why you should feel like that"). He treats the conversation as though it existed in an information and problem-solving mode. Instead of trying to find out what's bothering her ("How did that happen?"), he responds to the facts rather than to her feeling.

Information based only on facts is one-sided. Often, understanding how someone feels about the facts changes a decision drastically and makes the difference between a team effort and two people just working together.

In those workplaces that women are just entering, a man's need to constantly solve problems often causes him to do parts of a woman's job for her. This may cause coworkers to resent her for not doing her own work. It also prevents her from learning to take responsibility and initiative in her job.

Women may psych men out to satisfy excessive male approval needs, to compete with a woman for a man's attention, and to keep men from encroaching on their physical space. Such uses block intimacy and sharing, and psyching-out becomes negative. Positive reasons for psyching-out are to show caring and mutual support, to give and receive thoughtful feedback, and to build networks.

Speaking still in stereotypical terms, the following three models show how men sometimes focus their energy on women.

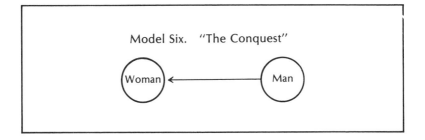

Model Six. "The Conquest"

Woman ← Man

"The conquest" shows a line of energy going from the man to the woman. Getting a date, scoring, courtship, and marriage fall within this approach.

In "the conquest," the man would like to connect with a woman. He wants to know her, perhaps sexually, and possibly marry her. He is the initiator, the one to propose. He focuses his energy on her by asking: "What would you like to talk about?" "What would you like to do?" "Where would you like to go?" He intends to find out what pleases her, or what he can do to get her to like him, to want him, to love him. He gives her flowers or surprises her with something he knows she will like.

In "the conquest," the man often intends to establish a long-term relationship, such as marriage. Once he achieves that objective, he feels he can direct his energy elsewhere. One of his life's tasks has been accomplished and he can get on with other parts of his life. He loves the woman he married and enjoys being with her. He needs her support, her love, her caring. He may help her with her work in the house and extend himself in caring ways. He does not, however, look at their relationship as growing, changing, and needing nurturing. He spends little time finding out her fears, her aspirations, and her joys. It is her role to nurture, and he expects her to do it. Men often treat relationships with women as projects to be carefully and thoughtfully developed, put in place, and left to function.

In Model Seven, the man focuses his energy on the woman in response to changes she is making. He observes that she is doing something different, such as returning to school, getting a job, or joining a women's consciousness-raising group. As a result, she directs less attention toward him. As she changes, she often becomes excited about things he does not share or control. He may feel he lacks something in his life and that he is not a part of the change. He decides that he needs to find out what is going on, so he becomes willing to question, listen, and show interest.

When he feels left out or out of control, a man will often step in to set things right, thinking of this as a task to be accomplished

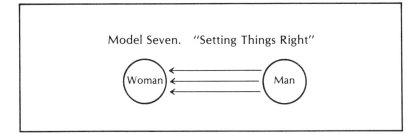

Model Seven.   "Setting Things Right"

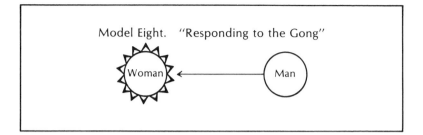

Model Eight. "Responding to the Gong"

Woman ← Man

rather than an ongoing process of interaction. We have drawn this picture in extreme terms to emphasize how this approach keeps men and women from getting what they want and need from a relationship.

In Model Eight, the woman has learned that to be heard she needs to increase the intensity of her interactions. For instance, a husband who has been insensitive arrives home from work expecting his usual greeting from his wife. Today, however, she is standing at the door, her coat on, her bags in hand. Instead of "hello," she says, "It's over. I can't take your insensitivity to me. You've not said 'thank you' or listened to me in five years. I'm leaving you. . . ." Now she has his attention! He listens and probably will do what she wants, if he still has an investment in the relationship. He is in his "setting-things-right" mode. She has learned that he hears her only when she creates a crisis.

Some men and women relate this way repeatedly. Over time, she has to raise the ante for him to hear her. If the woman throws a tantrum, the man will listen. Because women do not traditionally feel listened to, many have become conditioned to use pressure and increased pitch in their voices to be heard. Some women use this selectively, others in all parts of their lives. A supervisor may push subordinates and bosses alike by talking at the top of her voice when she wants to be heard. Unfortunately, people usually avoid her. Some women are unaware of their behavior and therefore see no other ways in which to be heard. Some men can be reached through no other means, an extreme example of this communication model.

## Costs of Stereotypical Communication Patterns

Women, men, and organizations suffer when they communicate in the styles portrayed here. These communication patterns create significant costs to organizations because

- they inhibit the flow of information between women and men,
- women act more as listeners than doers,
- support systems and networks operate without the diversity and richness that women bring,
- women supervisors and managers become unable to act powerfully on behalf of their subordinates,
- men act on inadequate information for competent decision making,
- communication often becomes inappropriately sexualized, and
- women and men receive more support for conforming than for growing as productive workers.

This behavioral setup often causes women to live without support systems in their families or jobs that affirm them as worthwhile human beings—and to lack encouragement for their personal growth. Many men have support systems of parents, wives, secretaries, colleagues, teachers, and others who "cheer" them on.

The costs to men are also clear. The obligation and responsibilities of this behavioral setup for men only make up the tip of the iceberg. It also affects men's abilities to make behavioral changes. Men are taught to be self-sufficient, intact, closed systems, and not to acknowledge their needs for interdependence. All of this limits personal growth and behavioral change.

Men eventually begin to deny their emotional needs. They lose touch with their feelings, become overly task-oriented, compartmentalized, mechanical, and/or rational. Along with this, men become dependent on women to fulfill their needs for nurturing and caring for themselves and others. Women also become responsible for establishing and maintaining interactions with others (e.g., women facilitate relationships between fathers and children, adult sons and fathers, men and friends, and male co-workers). Men are ripe for women to "psych them out," to control or manipulate them.

Men feel positively affirmed when women constantly psych them out. This continuous affirmation at an emotional level screens out other messages from men and women about the need for change. Men miss out on potent data that could help them develop.

Traditional personal relationships carrying heavy emotional involvement lock men into the patterns outlined in this model. We must have greater flexibility in communicating; we need other relationships to facilitate the growth necessary to move beyond these stereotypical interactions.□

## References

Ben, S. L. The Measurement of Psychological Androgyny. *Journal of Consulting and Clinical Psychology*, 1974, *42*(2).

Broverman, I. K., Broverman, D. M., Clarkson, F. E., Rosenkrantz, P. S., & Vogel, S. R. Sex Role Stereotypes and Clinical Judgments of Mental Health. *Journal of Consulting and Clinical Psychology*, 1970, *34*(1), 1–8.

Daly, M. *Beyond God the Father*. Beacon Press: Boston, 1973.

Pierce, C. *Women and Victim Behavior*. (2nd. ed.) Laconia, N. H.: New Dynamics Associates, 1983.

# Issues for Women Managers

Linda L. Moore

*". . . new insights into the problems encountered by women in management keep the majority motivated. The key is to have a balanced analysis of the self and the system."*

Thousands of women seek answers to questions about survival and success in the male-dominated world of work. Business and professional women find in trendy magazines and books a profusion of suggestions on the *right* pathway to power, the *key* to success, and the female characteristics to *avoid* or to *cultivate*. And many women feel confused by the conflicting points of view of the "experts." How does one establish a solid foundation of understanding and competence on which to build a rewarding career in management?

This article will explore some of the issues for women managers in the context of both individual and system analysis. I will emphasize a *balanced* analysis, for historically women have been all too willing to look inward for the source of their difficulty. And even though female socialization often leaves us ill-equipped for male-dominated power structures, system phenomena are equally critical to our success or failure.

Women in management create new relationships for both women and men. We ask a great deal of ourselves, of other women, and of men. At one level, we ask for freedom, flexibility, and a chance for *choice points* in our lives rather than for a traditional tunnel of development and movement. At another level, we ask for role shifts, role changes, and redistribution of the work responsibilities and maintenance tasks of daily life. At a still deeper level, we ask ourselves and others for a change in the psychological frame of reference we have for one another—a change needed particularly in the area of leadership roles. In this context, what typical problems do women face on a day-to-day basis? And how do we understand and deal with them?

## Visibility

First, we are highly visible. High visibility may create for some an aura of being special, but it primarily makes women vulnerable to

Adapted from "Women as Managers" by Linda L. Moore, which appeared on pp. 67–78 of *Women in Community Colleges: New Directions for Community Colleges* by Judith Eaton (Ed.). © 1981, Jossey-Bass, Inc. Used with permission.

to emotional and physical distress. When we become more noticeable, everything takes on an importance out of perspective: what we wear and say, where and with whom we sit, promotions we do or do not receive, and relationships we do or do not cultivate. Women who are in the minority are open to difficulties ranging from criticism of decisions to sexual harassment. Kanter (1977) suggests that these problems will not be solved until more women join the workforce at all levels.

Because we are few, we have little experience with one another as peers. How many female peers do you have right now? And, if you have not worked with many women on a peer basis, how do you feel about other women as they move into managerial roles? Women unaccustomed to having other women as resources often do not know how to use them and perhaps feel afraid to do so. Being the only one causes a woman to develop attitudes and defenses that she sometimes finds hard to break through, but in reality we need one another for validation, support, information, and the increase in numbers required to add a female perspective to the system.

The difficulty of working with one another (the women-against-women problem) is exaggerated and diminishing. Yet men believe we do not work well together, and such beliefs affect their behavior and decisions negatively. Although individualism and competition are inherent in male-dominated organizations, one must also demonstrate that one can be a "team player" and participate in the give and take.

### The Use and Misuse of Power

A common theme underlying women's professional problems is the use and misuse of power. Growing up female almost guarantees a misuse of power. Early in life—probably by the age of four—women are taught three negative uses of power: viewing power as a means to get what they want from those who have it, little girls learn to manipulate men by mothering them, by seducing them, and by acting childlike and helpless. Although these nurturing, sexual, and child-like behaviors are valued aspects of a fully developed personality, they become negative when used as a means to some other end. Most women recognize these behaviors in themselves. And as adults we fall back on these techniques in times of crisis—when we do not know what else to do because we have not learned positive uses of power. Mothering, seduction, and helplessness are survival tools taught to those who are assumed to need a safe place in relationships with a dominant male group.

These same tools or techniques, when carried into the office, can destroy relationships with other women and with men. Women who know this behavior will mistrust each other when power is the name of the game. And men who have been manipulated by women fear having it happen again. Finally, when old techniques don't work, women feel helpless and again forced into a victim role. Our deeply held attitudes, beliefs, and feelings contribute to our ability or inability to exercise power positively.

## Sex

People view sex as something women have that men want. Thus, it can become a subtle tool for power. Historically, it has been the basis of a bargain struck between females and males—the male provides security, and the woman provides sexual access. In fact, many of our foremothers may have viewed sex as the only real source of power available to them. Modern women may see sex in the same way, although we hope that they have more equality in relationships. Regardless of the prevalent attitude, sex still exists as a bargaining tool, and the number of sexual harassment cases in the courts demonstrates the problems that occur when sex becomes associated with power.

We regularly avoid sexual issues in work, primarily because we feel confused about appropriate boundaries. When power in relationships was clear—"men have it and women don't"—boundaries were understandable, if unfair. As women seek and obtain more personal and positional power, boundaries shift and cause incredible emotional confusion. Women and men frequently don't have the experience or the models for relating on equal levels at work. Consequently, we must heighten both individual and system-level awareness. One way to begin is by talking about this confusion with peers.

## Competition

As women, our experiences with competition and its attendant feelings are confusing. The history of our competition with one another has a negative impact on our behavior and attitudes about power. As children, we compete with one another for attention. We may have to compete with mother for father's attention; we compete with each other for the attention of boys; and we compete with each other for the limited recognition available to girls. As adults, we pretend that we do *not* compete with one another. We learned this, too, in childhood because the competition we felt and engaged in was deemed "not nice" for little girls. Consequently, we learned to smile and say nice things while we conspired behind the scenes to accomplish our goals.

As adults, we keep competition "under the table" just in case some disapproving eye catches us competing again.

Our competition with men is vaguely legitimate until adolescence. Then the messages begin: girls should not be smarter than boys; girls should not win when they play with boys. The reason why is often a mystery, but the message of potential rejection and other disaster is strong. The well-socialized female carries these old messages into work and relationships and sometimes gets hooked into diffusing her power to keep from looking aggressive and competitive.

Competition exists among girls and women because society is structured in a way that limits the total amount of attention, recognition, rewards, and opportunities available. Historically, boys and men come first. Negative attitudes toward competition exist because girls were never allowed to compete in an open and constructive manner. This is particularly true for girls and women who never played any competitive sports. The point is not necessarily to encourage competition, but to recognize it, to understand it, and to move beyond it when it becomes inappropriate. The potential among women to share power—to collaborate effectively—and to, in fact, redefine positive uses of power in organizations becomes delayed and diluted by our denial of our competitive feelings and behaviors.

**Anger**

Anger is perhaps the most confusing of feelings. For women, anger is the feeling we fail to recognize, the feeling we have least permission to express, the feeling we fear expressing, and the feeling we most need to express. Anger puts the greatest possible distance between us and the relationships we place so much value on. Thus, at the time we feel the most anger, we may also feel the most pain, fear, and insecurity. Being angry feels dangerous—it connotes possible rejection and loss. Consequently, we push it away and out of our awareness. In this process, feelings that are more familiar and at least less threatening surface: pain, frustration, resentment.

Often intertwined with other emotional sensations, anger is complex, confusing, and, ultimately, seldom dealt with. As children, unless we were in unusual families, we rarely received permission to express anger or aggression. Studies of early childhood patterns indicate that parents punish girls for aggressive behavior while they reward boys. Aggressive, angry feelings do not evaporate if left unexpressed—as we would sometimes like to believe—so girls must find some other outlet. Usually, girls become verbally agressive toward one another—they become "tattletales." And, as with competition, our early experiences with anger are hurtful ones. When boys argue, they scuffle or fight it out; when girls argue, they say bad things about one another to a mutual friend, hoping to damage intimacy. We rarely express pure, straightforward anger.

Anger toward boys also changes in adolescence. While girls may express anger in their early years, a shift occurs when boys become identified as sources of affirmation, identity anchors, and *essential* relationships. As girls and women become more and more dependent on boys and men, the ability to be angry with them—to even recognize anger—diminishes. It is self-defeating to be angry with those on whom you are dependent.

Acknowledging anger is a step in one's development and creates a sense of integrity. In the world of work and power, one needs to recognize and understand anger. Some people must deal with built-up anger in therapy, but for the majority of us, the recognition that being very angry does not mean you are crazy matters most. The development of skills for dealing with angry, aggressive feelings becomes essential to mental health. The best beginning is to take a long-term course in assertiveness training or to read about the subject.

The relationships among gender competition, anger, and power are complex and intertwined. Our gender predetermines early learnings and attitudes toward power, and our sexuality becomes a part of a barter system in the balance of power. The sanctions against expressing feelings of competition and anger handicap us in our relationships with other women and with men. Survival tools emerge as techniques for getting what we want and need, regardless of the hurt we encounter. Somehow, in spite of all these negative learnings, women possess an ability to relate to themselves and to others in ways that build unique levels of intimacy, understanding, support, and trust. When we are clear about our sometimes-negative history with one another, we can often share ourselves, our skills, our resources, and our power in ways that male socialization does not allow.

We are socialized to focus on interpersonal relationships. Because of this we have higher needs than men have for affiliation and bonding. We learn to "psych out" others[1] and then generally become more attentive to sensing, gearing, and understanding. These traits and behaviors can be translated into the following positive power tools for the woman manager:

1. the ability to build a supportive work climate;
2. the ability to collaborate on and create teamwork;

---

[1] See "Man/Woman Dynamics: Some Typical Communication Patterns."

3.  the ability to delegate and share power;
4.  the ability to facilitate the work of others; and
5.  the ability to build morale and higher levels of motivation.

These abilities are clouded by old and mysterious teachings about power, sex, competition, and anger.

## Stress—The Physical and Emotional Effects

Women who cope with the problems thus far identified often experience considerable stress. Typically, we hear phrases like "burnout" or "the system takes too much energy." Less often do we hear the secret thoughts, the fears that "I'm crazy," "I can't measure up because I don't know what's really going on," "I'll never make it," "If people knew what anger and pain I really feel, I would never be respected professionally."

Job stress has increased for all individuals. In addition to this, women must also handle the stress that comes from efforts to manage relationships and family. What happens to us as a result of recognized stressors? What physical and emotional impacts do they create? Most women recognize stress through such physical symptoms as extreme fatigue, lightheadedness, or dizziness; muscle spasms; knots in the neck, shoulders, or stomach; or tightness in the chest and difficulty in breathing. Emotionally, we may become aware of irritability, of a sensation of fragility, of crying easily, of anxiety or agitation that seems relentless, or of an ongoing state of worry and depression. Behavioral signs include the inability to get started on a task, difficulty in making decisions, thinking dozens of thoughts at the same time, missing work, and avoiding contact with others. Unfortunately, these symptoms may mount, multiply, and move along a continuum of seriousness until a person becomes physically or emotionally incapacitated. Stress that develops in this way can be understood with the metaphor of the "female trash compactor."

In general, women have far less permission to deal with feelings than we have been led to believe. In the office, the female employee, particularly the manager, has no room for emotional responses if she hopes to maintain any credibility. In this case, and in many others, the statement that women have more permission to express feelings no longer applies in the working world. Where do unexpressed feelings of anger, disappointment, hurt, disagreement, and conflict go, since they simply do not disappear or evaporate? First, visualize a trash compactor that fills the trunk of your body; the base rests on your pelvic bone, the top reaches your throat. Most of us spend our lives dumping unexpressed feelings into this large container. Our socialization teaches us to be understanding, to be receptive to the feelings and needs of others, and to put those feelings and needs of others first. Coming second in life—and sometimes third or fourth—creates hundreds of incidents in which we are forced to sit on our feelings, beliefs, and needs to understand or help someone else feel okay.

When we become managers and learn what people believe about the emotionality of women, an additional pressure to exert control is born. But the trash compactor is large. As incident after incident piles up, women experience emotional rushes of anxiety or tension in situations of conflict, feelings that "something" of intensity is rising in their bodies and threatening to emerge. Many of us become aware of such sensations in the stomach, the solar plexus, and the chest. At this time we do something to compact the trash—we hold our breath, swallow hard, count, and push our minds into a rational gear. Eventually, however, the trash compactor fills up. It simply has no more room, and the results include the following:

• an angry, emotional outburst—far out of proportion to the event—that reinforces the image of the irrational female who can't control her feelings at work;
• having an outburst or crying easily at almost any time, especially when someone says something caring;
• ongoing irritability in which everything bothers you;
• physical symptoms of some severity—e.g., ulcers, gastritis, colitis; and
• frequent physical illness—e.g., colds or flu that require bed rest and medication.

These five kinds of responses allow the average woman to temporarily clean out about two-thirds of her trash compactor. With new space, she can return to her routine behavior until, once again, the compactor begins to feel full. A vicious cycle results in that she appears to have no legitimate outlet for the negative feelings and no means of intervention in a system that encourages a woman to see herself as a victim.

## Solutions

As women continue to move into leadership and managerial roles and to encounter problems in both the private and public sectors, we must seek ways to exchange information and ideas for personal support and institutional change. Again, the way to begin is through a balance of attention to individual and system issues.

## Self-Nurturing

Women must learn more about self-nurturing. Taking care of ourselves involves paying attention to all the suggestions provided in the stress management literature, including putting emotional and physical well-being first. All too frequently we "mother ourselves" in the same way we were mothered as little girls. If we didn't get enough nurturing (and most girls don't), we continue the pattern by not giving enough to ourselves as adults.

To take care of yourself, you must do the following:

1. Focus on your total system; regard physical symptoms as "early warning signals"; understand what your body needs.
2. Maintain a healthy, balanced diet.
3. Reduce and, when possible, eliminate your intake of caffeine, nicotine, sugar, and salt.
4. Get regular, rigorous exercise. Begin by walking for 30 minutes each day.
5. Do daily meditation and/or relaxation exercises.
6. Get consistent amounts of sleep.
7. Reduce or limit your alcohol intake to an average of one ounce per day.
8. Identify the things that make you feel good about yourself—then do them.
9. Analyze your support system and, when necessary, rebuild it to include at least five people with whom you can share feelings.

## Networking

Networks created by women provide a temporary substitute for the lack of institutional recognition for women's changing roles. When our institutions cannot or will not support—through recognition—the dramatic shifts in the goals and lives of growing numbers of women, we must find alternative systems of support. Networks hold the promise of such an alternative. They provide a bridge, a transition as we struggle with new definitions. Mary Scott Welch sees networking as an integral and necessary part of one's professional day. The specific suggestions, techniques, and strategies outlined in her book Networking (1980) are "a must" for the woman new to the concept. These include: 31 things to do and not to do while networking; basic steps for starting an in-house or community-wide network; and names of existing networks in every state.

Make contacts across private- and public-sector lines. Call women for lunch or drinks, or arrange small discussion groups. Ask questions. Give and get ideas, and explore the similarities and differences. The "climate" is ripe for initiating such activities because networking is happening all over the country. Women have gradually begun to expect requests for information, support, and help from other women.

## Your Individual Analysis

Beyond the strategies of self-nurturing and networking, we must re-examine our uniqueness as women. Recognizing and nurturing the *differences* between women and men will help us name these differences. If we can exchange self-negation for celebration, we can create ways of relating that we know are possible and that will make systems healthy places. This will only happen when we stop denying who we are as a result of our gender. To begin this process, each of us must engage in both the self- and system analysis referred to throughout this chapter.

Consider your current situation and the way you feel in relation to the seven points below. Write detailed responses to each question. When you finish, you will have a more complete picture to work with. Then make some action steps for yourself. Identify at least five things you need to work on.

1. *Self.* Take a long, hard look at who you are today—personally and professionally. What do you value the most? What are your strengths and weaknesses? What are your goals and priorities? How do you feel about yourself? What needs to be changed?
2. *Attitudes and Beliefs.* What do you believe about the world of work and what it takes to "make it?" Have you "bought" the notion that "female characteristics" are the major source of problems for women? Do you feel like a victim, or do you believe you have something unique to contribute *because* you are a woman?
3. *Behavior.* Is your behavior congruent with your values, goals, priorities, attitudes, and beliefs? Do you seek contacts and work opportunities with or for other women?
4. *Feedback.* How do others perceive you? Is feedback positive, negative, inconsistent, or perhaps altogether absent? Do you know people whom you trust to ask for information on how you are regarded, both professionally and personally? Are you willing to ask for such data, to listen to it, to evaluate it, and to use it?
5. *Situation.* What specific situations do you find problematic? Who are the people involved? What is the nature of the work to be done, the interaction? When does the conflict or difficulty emerge? What resources do you have for confronting the problems?
6. *Environment.* What is the immediate work environment like? How would you describe the "climate?" Do you perhaps find it a

really crazy place? Again, who are the people involved? What is the nature of the work? How does the work get done? Do you feel valued as a person? As a professional?

7.   *System.* How well do you understand the entire system? Where are the sources of formal and informal power? What is the organization's value system? What is its true attitude toward women? How many women work at the top, on the bottom, on significant committees and task forces? And what resources do you have access to? Are you using an existing network? Could you start one?

## Conclusions

Women's problems are large, and the resulting stress on individuals, families, and organizations is significant. At times, many of us feel like giving up—but new insights into the problems encountered by women in management keep the majority motivated. The key is to have a balanced analysis of *the self* and *the system*. Such a balance assures learning in multiple directions.□

## References

Kanter, R. M. *Men and Women of the Corporation.* New York: Basic Books, 1977.
Welch, M. S. *Networking.* New York: Warner Books, 1980.

# Competing with Peers— for Fun and Productivity*

Kaleel Jamison

*"Organizational trainers can help both male and female employees develop and use the productive aspects of their differing competitive styles—to the benefit of both employee and organization."*

Although *competition* is not exactly a dirty word today—it *is* soiled. For generations, competition was *the* behavioral mode in U.S. business. In fact, most people credited it with producing the excellence and efficiency that were everywhere the hallmarks of U.S. business and industry.

But sometime during the 1950s emphasis shifted. With the emergence of the human potential movement, organizational development people embraced the collaboration model wholeheartedly. On observing organizations, they commented, "The competitive mode includes hidden agendas, the undercutting of colleagues, the withholding of information, and other devious practices. It's a kill-off game in which the only possibilities are win/lose. That's no good! Or lose/lose, which is worse. Collaboration permits win/win. That's good!"

Most of us agreed that this was all to the good. The new collaborative mode, we all thought, was not only more humane, it was also liberating and productive. But Americans in pursuit of a new idea are nothing if not extremists. And probably, quite without meaning to, we ended up denying that there are other good models and that there may be natural energy to be tapped from the correct use of the competitive mode. The pendulum had swung so far toward the new emphasis that we forgot that the old mode—the competitive one—also had merit.

How can that aspect of competitive behavior that is natural and useful and productive be developed by organizations and/or by organizational members for the benefit of both? This article spells out the differences between the competitive styles of women and men and shows both sexes how to develop the useful attributes of their own competitive style for their own enrichment and for the organization's benefit. Organizational trainers, too, can apply these principles to help employees use their full potential.

---

© 1981 Kaleel Jamison. All rights reserved.

* The author is greatly indebted to Nancy Brown for discussions, experience, and experiments in a long personal and professional relationship in which competition has proved constructive and infinitely rewarding.

For a woman, competition and the ability to manage it in herself is absolutely vital to successful and effective functioning in an organization. And for a man, learning how to use it in new, nondestructive ways instead of the old ways can lead to a productive tapping both of his traditional acculturation and of the newer collaborative techniques.

## The Uses of Adversity and Competition

The advent of women in the workforce has caused us to notice many valuable things about behaviors that we might otherwise have continued to take for granted. For as women, with their vastly different acculturation and their different approaches to problem solving, came into contact with the highly developed organizational behaviors of men, strange things came to light.

As a general rule, women had a hard time making the kinds of adjustments necessary, *either* to compete or to collaborate. Things got in the way. Women had trouble with things men had never thought about. Women's attitudes were by and large perfectly professional, but they still had trouble *either* competing with a man or collaborating with him. It was as if they were playing in a game in which somebody had neglected to tell them all the rules. And when men convened in the informal groups where so much business is conducted, women were still excluded.

An occasional successful woman would receive the "complimentary" remark that "she thinks like a man." That kind of attitude both annoyed and intrigued most women: It was intriguing because it raised the questions of why it happened and what it meant. Those who had observed the male business game for years could readily see the rules. Why were women having such a tough time learning to play?

## The Role of Basic Conditioning

Gradually, from observation of the struggles of women, patterns began to emerge—patterns created so far back in the development of both women and men that they had not been immediately noticeable. And these patterns shed important new light on competition as practiced by both sexes.

It seems clear that little girls are conditioned by our society from their earliest years to use competition in one way and that little boys are conditioned to use it in a different way. How competition is used is at the very center of traditional sex roles. So, naturally enough, when a woman tries to use her competitive behaviors in a society traditionally dominated by men, she is confused when they don't work. And the man is confused when he encounters female behaviors that conflict with his accustomed way of doing things. To all appearances, the male society "wins." The traditional mode in business prevails. That the organization "loses"—the talents, energies, and unique contributions of women—is not so readily apparent, but it is nonetheless so.

More specifically, women tell us curious things about their feelings about interacting with men in business. They find themselves inexplicably taking a subordinate role, even in a business situation in which they are working with a man of lesser rank or ability. They find their competence questioned or their suggestions largely ignored, and they are subjected to almost daily evidence of second-class status. They find their assignments dictated by traditional concepts of "what women are interested in." They find themselves excluded from line assignments and largely grouped into staff positions—that is, jobs that traditionally have only advisory status.

Men seem equally puzzled by these somewhat automatic developments. They complain that women could do anything they want to do in the organization if only they would just "take hold" and "do it." But women cannot move into the competition so matter of factly. They feel confused by what they read as mixed signals. So, in their confusion, both women and men are caught without appropriate behaviors to fall back on. A curious thing happens.

Men have business rituals to use with other men in organizations. But men do not have customary business rituals to use with women. So when they deal with women, they fall back on *social* rituals for which they have some experience with women rather than on male business rituals. They begin to employ all the social rituals they know to make themselves more comfortable—that is, opening doors, lighting cigarettes, picking up the lunch check, and so forth. But this sort of behavior confuses the situation because it's not possible, for instance, for the woman to go head-to-head with a man in a business discussion and then revert to the kinds of unequal power situations that still pertain in a social setting.

In a social setting, women and men are taught to be ladylike and gentlemanly. But the truth is that the social rituals are also based on unequal power or on the chivalric ideal that a man protects a woman, who is his inferior in strength or power. What the social rituals do for the woman *and* the man is call up the conditions of inequality and of polite behavior.

A business situation, on the other hand, usually requires very straight communication and should be, in fact, an encounter of ideas between equals. What actually happens, however, is this: Although the man has usually initiated the social context, both the woman and the man lose the clarity of the exchange. What could have been a productive exchange becomes clouded, and neither is as fully competent and honestly competitive as might have been possible.

## Why it Happens

If we look at the kinds of organizational activities that occur in groups of little boys at play and then at the activities of little girls, it is easy to see the source of some of their adult behavior.

Little boys on a playground form groups, and alliances within those groups, on the basis of proved or expected competence. You don't have to like another boy to agree to play with him on the team. His competence wins him his acceptance, and the degree of his competence wins him his rank.

A group of little girls operates differently. Little girls may compete, but their truly functional relationships are formed on the basis of liking and trust. And once alliances are formed, they by and large exclude considerations other than congeniality as an organizing principle.

Men continue the "rules" of their early groups in their business activities. Women, relatively new to business as full-fledged team members, bring along the "rules" they remember from *their* preparatory childhood organizations.

## How Differences Affect Competition

What has this all got to do with competition? Everything. For competition too is seen differently by men and women and employed differently by men and women when they are boys and girls. Because of their early conditioning, neither women nor men use competition as well as they could.

For men, a competent *team* competes with an outside opponent. There may be ranking *inside* the team, but primarily there is competition as a *team*. Certainly men do compete one-to-one. But the point is that they resort to one or the other kind of competition more readily than women do. Girls *as a group* do not compete with an outside opponent, and for girls and women, competition usually takes place between members of the same group. Thus, women find themselves competing with other women in their organization, rather than with the men in their "peer" group.

Beyond this, however, it would be useful to look at the character of the games being played by boys and by girls.

Girls play house. Boys play games of combat. As children, girls practice the competition they will probably enter into later for a mate. For a girl, the game of "house" generally represents the fabric of her existence from birth to death. So the competition she enters into represents a struggle for life—the mate and all of the attendant nurturing and nesting activities she must fulfill continuously throughout her entire life. If she loses, she loses the long-term, ongoing functions that her social conditioning tell her are hers. Although it isn't true, a loss for a girl appears cataclysmic—a one-time, ruinous event. A loss for a woman later on takes on a similar cast. For a boy, whose play involves a series of "battles," a loss is the loss of one battle. Even if his team loses the game, there is the satisfaction of having made several good plays during the game (for example, that 80-yard run for a touchdown that made the final score 7 to 21 instead of an ignominious 0 to 21). He will live to fight another day. He can lose the battle and still win the war.

These widely different games affect the ways in which women and men deal with competition and with losses in competition later on in life. In her adult life, a woman takes losses harder than a man. Women in business often marvel that a man can take a loss, swallow the defeat, and go back into the fray without apparent permanent harm to his sense of self. For a woman, a loss feels more serious and may affect her performance and her perception of her own competence adversely in the long term. The result of low self-perception is likely to be subsequent poor performance and a perception by others of incompetence.

## Constructive Competition

How does one deal with these interesting insights? My theory is that both women and men can learn to use competition productively in their business lives by doing the following:

1. Recognizing the patterns imposed upon them by early sex-role socialization rituals.
2. Acknowledging the competitive forces in themselves as legitimate, respectable opportunities to excel.
3. Learning techniques for harnessing and managing competition to render it a useful tool—for creativity, productivity, and personal renewal.

The techniques for using competition constructively are the same for women and men. It is somewhat ironic to think that what has come to be an almost unmentionable subject in organizations could be the means of untangling at least some of the perplexities that have arisen as women and men have tried to adjust to working together effectively in business. But that is exactly what I think the constructive use of competition can do.

There are two ways to approach competition. One has a personal-development focus. It consists of bringing competitive feelings into awareness and putting yourself into competitive situations, then learning how to observe your own reactions and modify them. The other involves activity with another person or with a group in the presence of a facilitator, such as an organizational trainer. The two techniques are mutually adaptable and equally useful.

## Personal Development through Competition

The first order of business is to acknowledge competitive impulses to yourself and to legitimize them. People compete for a variety of reasons. Sometimes the competition is intentional—the result of conscious thought. Sometimes competition springs from unconscious processes, old habits, old concerns.

Knowing why we compete can help with acknowledgment. Here is a list of the payoffs (not mutually exclusive) that are sometimes the legitimate motives behind competition.

• *Rewards.* Competing brings rewards: money, power, recognition, prestige, approval.
• *Energy.* Competing energizes and enables the competitors to find new sources of stamina and creativity that can only be realized in relation to others.
• *Fun.* Competing can bring exhilaration and enjoyment of the process.
• *Learning.* In competing you can discover more about yourself through behaviors and feelings.
• *Measurement.* Competing is one way to measure personal excellence.
• *Comfort.* Competing should feel natural, comfortable—as if to do otherwise would feel inhibiting or would close off a vital part of the self.
• *Closeness or distance.* Competing can draw you closer to or drive you farther away from a competitor. (Which will be the case depends finally on how we as competitors handle our feelings about the competition.)

There are also fears and costs attached to competing. Sometimes we don't compete—and this too may be a conscious or an unconscious decision. Whether conscious or unconscious, however, the decision is usually based on avoiding one or more of the following:

• Losing.
• Winning.

- Feeling uncomfortable.
- Looking foolish to others.
- Feeling embarrassed.
- Distancing ourselves from the competitor—that is, losing her or his approval or affection.
- Getting close to the competitor. This is often a subconscious concern, especially where sexual attraction is present. (But, on the other hand, competing can become a way to handle such feelings of attraction.)
- Losing a competitor's respect.
- Drawing ourselves into additional competition with this competitor or with others.
- Entering a competition that might be endless.
- Entering a competition that would have uncertain measurability because of its subjective nature.

## A Method for Competing Constructively

The competitive process can be examined and an appropriate approach can be developed in an organizational development workshop or a personally conducted activity. Beforehand, however, it must be recognized that many people's fears of competition stem from the belief that there can only be one winner or that there's only a limited portion to be won. At times, this is clearly accurate, as in some sports. But most of the time, it isn't true unless we make it so.

Usually, when we are competing in a business environment, there is an opportunity for each competitor to win in some dimensions. (Trainers who are leading workshops should emphasize this point.) For instance, in a contest in which one is the loser and one is the winner, obviously one competitor experiences defeat. But if a situation is set up in which both are competing in a number of dimensions, both can then clearly discern in which specific dimensions each is winning.

The following conscious process seems to work well for purposes of analyzing competition between either same-sex or different-sex pairs. It is not necessary to make the process known to the competition partner. In certain relationships, in fact, it is advisable to take these steps silently, either indefinitely or until a deeper relationship has been established.

Whether this exercise is done on one's own, with a partner, or in a more formal setting such as a workshop, tension will evaporate if its techniques are applied honestly, and people will end up feeling that they've improved themselves and are more comfortable with competition.

*The Competition Process*

The process involves nine steps.

1. Select or acknowledge a competition partner.
2. Make a list of areas in which you feel competitive with the partner.
3. Evaluate both yourself and your partner in each dimension—who is first, who is second.
4. Pause—take a break and allow your thoughts to settle.
5. Review the listing. Test the items on the list against reality as you see it. Be sensitive to your own internal dialogue and body messages. A tense feeling is often a signal that you are feeling "second" in a specific dimension.
6. Ask yourself, "Have I overrated or underrated myself?"
7. Ask, "What strengths of mine did I omit and/or take for granted?" Add to the list. Do the same for your competitor.
8. Use another person as a consultant to review your list. (This step is optional.)
9. Compete!

Here are other useful thoughts that individuals can keep in mind during competitive situations and that trainers can point out. As a competitor, you should do the following:

• Acknowledge competitive feelings to yourself (including fears about losing *or* winning).
• Acknowledge competitive feelings to your competitors, when that is practical. This may include fears about competition.
• Accept the fact that during competition you will have a range of feelings—such as excitement, exhilaration, fear, embarrassment, vulnerability, anger, or hurt—and that at times you will simply get tired of competing.
• Use each competitive situation as an opportunity to explore yourself more fully, as a way to develop "flat sides" (those personal dimensions that are least realized) and to continue to grow in your strength areas.
• Allow yourself a variety of settings for competition—for example, board games, athletics, knowledge areas, personal appearance, hobbies, professions.
• View being chosen as a competitor as a compliment and enjoy being regarded as a worthy opponent.
• Tell your competitor about the parts you value in her or him. Ask for the same from your competitor.
• Focus on what you know and what you can do rather than on what you don't know and what you can't do. This positive, self-

affirming focus allows you to enter into competition in areas of high risk.

Keep in mind as you explore that the process is meant to be a positive one and that the goal of the competition is enhancement for both participants.

It is unfailingly positive and energizing to realize that the ultimate judge of how well you have done in any given contest is you, yourself. This focus on self-evaluation emphasizes self-awareness and helps individuals maintain private goals and learning milestones—a necessary step because much of the process is carried on as an internal dialogue.

Recording your experiences is important in order to reflect on the process more extensively. Keep a journal, simply list your reactions, or discuss your experiences with your partner.

Remember that competing will be most difficult when you are competing with someone whom you value as a friend and whom you respect as competent. In such circumstances, you of course want to be valued and respected in turn. If you carry such wishes without verbalizing them, you will feel a stressful physical response. But when you *have* verbalized such feelings, either to your competitor or to a third party, you will at first feel vulnerable.

After a short while, however, these vulnerable feelings subside, and you learn from the experience. Moreover, your entire energy system will be unlocked to perform or compete more effectively because the very act of hiding your true feelings diverts productive energy.

When you are able to be open with your competitor, and when you have found an opponent who has a variety of dimensions against which you can test your own excellence, you are likely to feel exhilarated and pushed to new levels of experience. Eventually, laughing and celebration may become part of the experience.

The truth is that you compete in some way with every person with whom you come into contact. You are apt to be most aware of the competition when your competencies are closely comparable or when your competitor's skills are significantly better than yours. When you are far ahead of your competitor, you are likely to dismiss quickly or ignore the competition. But it is necessary to remain sensitive to nuance because in this last situation it is easy to be unaware of the origins of the behavior when somebody else feels competitive with you, but you don't feel competitive in return.

While men, as a rule, may have fewer anxieties about competing than women have, even men have fallen into all sorts of dysfunctional behavior in competitive situations and need to examine their fears.

## Group Activities

A similar procedure can be adapted for group activities. A group's self-examination process is similar to an individual's. Workshops can incorporate a series of activities designed to move from less stressful to more intense at a rate that depends on the environment, the sophistication of the participants, and other objectives.

Experienced group leaders, such as organizational trainers, can design effective workshops using favorite techniques as long as they keep in mind the following points:

- The focus of this approach is the positive use of competition.
- Feelings about competition must be allowed to surface so that they can be acknowledged and explored. The surfacing can be accomplished by each individual privately—using, for example, journal writing, or it can be accomplished through group sharing.

The kind of self-knowledge gained from an examination of the competitive process goes far toward dispelling the fear of competing. But it also does much more. It unleashes energies and exposes talents for use in developing competencies along a whole spectrum of new skills. It improves physical health by relieving tension and stress in risky encounters with people. It's fun. It's self-enhancing. People really feel better when they can compete along many dimensions and stretch themselves even though they may not come out first in all dimensions. People end up with a more positive attitude about themselves and the people around them. And finally, other bright, able people are perceived not as adversaries but as worthy opponents in a contest for excellence.□

# Managerial Responses to Transitions in Adult Development*

Robert T. Golembiewski

*"The several rhythms of the life cycle must be acknowledged and responded to, both in individual behavior as well as in organization policies and procedures."*

Adult life is neither unpredictable nor of a single piece but, by and large, organizations have only slowly and incompletely responded to the issues of adult development. This chapter seeks both to support this summary statement and to move beyond it.

The salience of transitions and phases in adult life has become more generally appreciated in the last few years. (See, for example, Bridges, 1980; Gould, 1978; Levinson, 1978; Sheehy, 1976; and Vaillant, 1977.) Managers and organizations, however, have responded erratically to the challenges of adult developmental transitions. I will note only three points from the fuller catalogue of evidence. By and large, organizations have not used aggressive approaches to adult development, such as managerial coaching or career development. In part, this record indicates that prominent approaches to adult development—e.g., as chronological stages—provide inadequate models for organizational use. Consciousness-raising on the following five specific points still seems necessary before any concerted problem solving in organizations occurs:

- greater awareness of, and consciousness about, transitions or adult phases;
- a more precise cost/benefit analysis concerning the impact of a broad range of transitions;
- more effective concern with matching career and individual needs;
- greater acuteness in recognizing human rhythms and responding to them; and
- more attention to developing humane systems and policies.

The focus described below often will be on the mid-life transition, which occurs roughly in the decade of life beginning

© 1983 NTL Institute

* This article constitutes an elaboration and updating of the closing pages of "Mid-Life Transition and Mid-Career Crisis: A Special Case for Individual Development," *Public Administration Review*, May 1978, *38*, pp. 215–222.

in the mid-30s, but attention also will be given to other transitions.

## Greater Awareness of Transitions

We still lack firm conceptual foundations for recognizing and dealing with adult transitions in organizations. Recent literature stresses the impact of such chronological stages as the "mid-life crisis," but less attention goes to the far broader range of transitions—moving to a new location, the death of a parent, or the birth of a child, which often may be followed by a spouse returning to work or school.

For evidence of this lack of awareness, one may note that few organizations have programs devoted to transitions, including specific informational or experiential programs on mid-life transition. Some have paid useful attention to career planning (Hanson & Allen, 1980), but this represents only a small advance. Many organizations reflect a concern for some specific transitions, but that concern falls short in several dimensions. Thus, many large organizations provide some kind of retirement planning (Bradford, 1982), but it tends to be too late, too brief, and preoccupied with important, but limited, financial arrangements. Perhaps personnel programs are most explicit when it comes to tragic transitions. A prestigious Eastern university, for example, waives term examination requirements for all students whose roommates die or commit suicide. And a multinational firm in effect puts transition values on death in the following differential bereavement leave policies:

- immediate family—spouse, children, or parents—"up to five days";
- in-laws—"one day."

This lack of organizational awareness of, and policy responses to, adult transitions proves both costly and troublesome for at least four reasons. First, *transitional episodes can affect the performance of adults in organizations*—such episodes include beginning a new job, reductions-in-force, becoming a parent, or introducing a new product. So we cannot dismiss this as unfortunate but practical.

Second, *much is known about facilitating transitions for individuals, and thus about cushioning their impact on organizations.* A few organizations have usefully sought to aid in such difficult transitions as plant closings (Taber, Walsh & Cooke, 1979), terminations (Connelly, 1980), and demotions (Golembiewski, Carrigan, Mead, Munzenrider & Blumberg, 1972), for example.

Such transitions can cause formidable or even frightening effects (Slote, 1977).

More generally, useful models are available for easing transitions. For example, Bridges (1980, pp. 9–10) describes such adult phases as mid-life transition as significant, but states that they constitute only a subset of "a lifetime of transitions." Moreover, Bridges views major commonalities in life changes quite broadly, while he recognizes individual differences in how specific people respond. All life changes

- begin with an ending, which typically includes disengagement, disidentification, disenchantment, and disorientation;
- include a fallow period, often characterized by confusion and distress;
- may terminate in a new beginning.

Bridges provides ample evidence that shows how such commonalities can be engaged and brought to closure in a broad range of transitions, such as getting a promotion, taking on a new job, becoming a parent, and experiencing a divorce.

Third, *emerging personnel policies place a growing premium on the effective management of transitions.* The upward adjustment of the mandatory retirement age—which all but certainly will be further increased—has such an effect, for example. And some American firms give major signs of adapting Japanese practices, which often include emphasis on security of employment and de-emphasis on rapid promotion and employee mobility (Sasaki, 1981). Moreover, major labor unions have recently emphasized employment security over higher pay and fringe benefits. Such tendencies severely heighten the need for organizations to work through transitions quickly and effectively.

Fourth, *individual transitions need not be random.* Indeed, the opposite may be more nearly true. The explosive birth rates following World War II sent segments of a very large generation cascading through life together, affecting social institutions in profound ways. In three decades or so, this baby boom will strain our retirement systems and policies. Now these "babies" are in their 30s and they represent a major wave of employment in some industries, perhaps especially in postsecondary education, with significant effects on people and schools. In colleges and universities that added numerous young and highly trained teacher/scholars, large proportions of many faculties are coming into the mid-life transition together. Organizationally sponsored attention to transitions matters not only to faculty, but also to their employing organizations, students, and families.

## More Precise Costs/Benefits of Attending to Transitions

Organizations need to develop a more acute ethical and economic sense of the costs/benefits of aiding their members through transitions. Reliable data imply fearsome costs when a plant closes its doors without seeking psychological closure for its employees (Slote, 1977). The data do not exist on a broader scale, but there seem to be enormous costs—both psychic and economic—in awkward mid-life transitions. Blue-collar workers seem especially prone to the "blahs" during this period, with both attitudes and productivity subject to substantial declines (Smith, 1955). Similarly, organizational folklore has long recounted the ravages common among salespeople who have been on the road 10–15 years. It seems no accident that the now-common mid-career crisis for professionals and managers tends to hit in the mid-30s (Cox, 1975). Personal transitions are reasonably linked to changes in career.

Career-long attention to aiding transitions seems justified. For example, longitudinal studies indicate that even in the December of life people grow psychologically (Britton & Britton, 1972). Moreover, the common notion that psychological functioning greatly deteriorates in those past, say, age 70 gets no support from newly available studies (Maas & Kuypers, 1974). In addition, many specific skills or attributes seem to have their own unique decay rates. Some steadily decline, beginning with the teen years! Others hold steady or increase till the mid-40s or later (Geist, 1968).

Because mid-life transition may mean radical career change, it may seem perverse that an organization should apply its resources to create non-members, humanitarian motives aside. But consider the costs—personal and organizational—of keeping an individual in a job or profession that has lost its allure but which the individual cannot leave without help. A few organizations have begun to subsidize career changes for some of their employees, with multiple motives. Thus, early, insistent attention to matching individual needs with career development signals the mutual concern about personal development that is the bedrock of personnel management. Moreover, unavoidable reductions-in-force or reorganizations can be facilitated by career-switches—whether they are part of an out-placement effort for internal reassignment or even for demotion, options we will be seeing more frequently (Golembiewski et al., 1972). Finally, each subsidization acknowledges past employee contributions while it may solve the dilemma of senior officials for whom the "go-go" has largely gone—but who nonetheless provide (unfortunately) role models for lower-ranking personnel—and eliminate the spiritual and legal complications of purges through overt dismissals or "early retirement."

Most importantly, subsidization of career change—especially when it occurs higher in the hierarchy—can contribute to the sense of a dynamic organization. That is, one career change might permit a chain of promotions or reassignments. Dollars spent on career change consequently can create positive motivational effects, especially when organizations stabilize or decline after growth spurts (or during a recession) and when older members who have lost their zest for creative and energetic management become objects of derision by their younger colleagues.

## Matching Career and Individual Needs

To provide a third perspective on enhancing an organization's sense of human transitions, one should continually check career progress against individual needs, making early diagnoses and taking action about growing mismatches. Active reflection may be crucial to a successful mid-life transition—isolating what is important and attainable for the individual, assessing whether he or she is working toward these goals, and doing something when things go wrong. Such active reflection does not just occur when needed. It must be encouraged and nourished over the long run, until it becomes part of an individual's attitudes about self.

The emphasis on what should be done points out the deficiencies of what is currently being done. Since the prevailing bias in most organizations is more "go-go" than "look-see," it is difficult to meet this challenge. The emphasis on career planning in some organizations provides a major ray of hope. Organizations need full-cycle systems of performance appraisal plus career planning, with "full-scale" meaning that career development emphasizes feedback about *potential* while performance appraisal highlights data about *current effectiveness*. The two perspectives must be linked, with feedback about work supported by a climate and resources appropriate for making improvements and adjustments.

## Recognizing the Several Human Rhythms

The three previous themes commonly imply that the several rhythms of the life cycle must be acknowledged and responded to, both in individual behavior as well as in organization policies and procedures. "By recognizing the patterns," Gould notes, "we may gain some control over the forces by smoothing the transitions and muting the peaks and valleys of adult life phases." Without knowledge of the cycle, people are obliged to be its unknowing pawns. But there is hope. "While children mark the passing years by their changing bodies," Gould observes (1975, p. 78), "adults change their minds."

Perhaps "uneven but hopeful" best describes the state of organization response to human rhythms. In small but still significant matters, the tuning of organizations to human rhythms has improved substantially in the last decade, as shown by the rapid extension of flexible-work-hours programs, which allow individuals greater flexibility in responding to the "little rhythms"—the body's circadian rhythm, or the variable cadence of family need or personal whim—with freedom to choose hours of work. The consequences for individuals and organizations have been largely positive (Nollen, 1982), at least over the first several years of application (Golembiewski, 1982).

The record concerning the "big rhythms" is less clear, but major opportunities in adult development seem obvious. All approaches to human development suggest that at different life periods individuals have different needs and expectations. Sensitivity to these life-period differences—differences shift over time from a need for mastery, to a stress on identity for self, and then to generativity through aiding others in their quests for mastery and identity—should underlie career planning. Illustratively, the search for a "mentor" seems quite appropriate in early adulthood. Later in life, a career pattern should emphasize humane and efficient ways for unbuckling from mentors, a delicate process whereby one meets development needs without rejecting the mentor's previous contributions and present needs. Still later, the unbuckled person might well become a mentor for others, thus completing the cycle.

**Toward Humane Systems and Policies**

Employing organizations also need to strive for a better fit between systems or policies and human cycles or needs. This tailoring could be both generic and specific. Organizations can generically permit easier responses to human cycles and needs at all life stages in these ways:

• by providing a cafeteria approach to benefits and "fringes," an assortment from which employees can pick and choose specific packages (up to some common dollar value) responsive to their individual situations (Tavernier, 1980); and
• by sponsoring activities—ranging from full-fledged sabbaticals to episodic "life-planning experiences"—that provide individuals with time and support to clarify their own needs/aspirations/abilities, and to do something with such clarifications to improve their work life and home life (Kirschenbaum, 1977).

Organizations can also develop systems and policies for specific life-stages. For example, human cycles and needs during the child-rearing years can be responded to in the following ways:

• by hiring matched pairs of employees, as in the case of individuals with similar skills and young children, who each work every second day and care for all the children on alternate days (so-called "job sharing") (Nollen, 1982);
• by hiring husband-and-wife teams—often scientists or technicians with the same skills and training, no longer a rare occurrence—who share duties at work and at home, as when each works half-time; and
• by carefully monitoring transfers, relocations, and time on the road when employees' children are adolescents and seem especially vulnerable to trauma.[1]

Finally, systems and policies could also be developed for those in the mid-life transition, or just coming out of it. Illustratively, the mid-life years often enlarge the individual's focus from acquisition to integration, from a narrow emphasis on "making it"—acquiring or achieving one's key goals—to an emphasis on fulfillment of broader social and psychological needs. These subtle dynamics might be facilitated in several ways:

• by recognizing mid-life transitional phenomena and by providing resources to help employees cope and understand, as via training programs;
• by subsidizing mid-career changes, with benefits being most apparent when individuals at senior levels of responsibility depart, requiring a chain of promotions or reassignments;
• by negotiating contracts with "permanent part-timers" at all levels of organization who seek some better balance between "making it" and satisfying broader needs or interests (Nollen, 1982);
• by helping employees cope with realities that severely complicate mid-life transition, such as by subsidizing career changes for individuals who have been passed over for promotion (Cole, 1981);
• by establishing procedures and traditions by which those in mid-life transition can devote greater attention to integrative and supportive activities that develop others, as by serving as a

[1] The traditional ideal seems to have been based on a quick-strike strategy. "Clean out your desk by five o'clock" seems to have been a favored tactic for dismissals on a Friday, when the weekend buffers the organization from adverse effects of its action. Many organizations also use rapid transfers to inhibit those "going native" and to increase central control.

mentor, replacing the emphasis on competition and self-development characteristic of earlier life stages;[2]
• by establishing policies and traditions that enable full-time employees to accept lesser job responsibilities at reduced compensation, as opposed to "up-or-out" systems.[3]

These suggestions are easier made than accomplished, of course. Each would require appropriate policies and procedures, and the support of accepted values and traditions.

Prescribing that those facing mid-career transitions begin to serve as mentors is easier said than done. The prescription is sensitive to the "stage of generativity" of the mid-life years, when there is a growing emphasis on the development of others as well as on the important role of mediating between the requirements of younger personnel and the demands of their organization (Levinson, 1978). Most likely, job requirements may have to be changed to aid people in transition in acting on their new urges. In addition, one may feel severe cross-pressures when developing her or his own replacement, especially if organization norms and practices fixate only on personal achievement and advancement. Organizational norms and work pressures, along with one's earlier experiences and reputation, may inhibit required expressions of emotional support and affection. Finally, a person's own unbuckling from mentors may have been incomplete or traumatic, and any residual guilt or anger will probably contaminate her or his future service as a mentor.

## Conclusion

This article provides a first step, and hence is both limited and tentative. But this constitutes no disclaimer about what needs to be done. We begin where we are. Like other aspects of our world, this part will not stop moving because it would be convenient for us to get off.□

## References

Bradford, L. *Preparing for Retirement.* La Jolla, Calif.: University Associates, 1982.
Bridges, W. *Transitions.* Reading, Mass.: Addison-Wesley, 1980.

[2] Witness the city manager profession, which has developed a "circuit-rider" role that legitimates the availability of help to junior professionals from a travelling senior, who gets to multiply her or his expertise and get relief from the burdens of a specific constituency.
[3] In business organizations, seasoned managers can become "internal consultants" to younger persons who occupy the kinds of jobs they once held. Often, these roles involve reduced workloads.

Britton, J. H., & Britton, J. O. *Personality Changes in Aging.* New York: Springer, 1972. Pp. 169–70.

Cole, D. W. *Professional suicide.* New York: McGraw-Hill, 1981. Pp. 26–39.

Connelly, S. *Welcome to the Titanic.* Paper presented at the Fall Meeting of the Organization Development Network, San Francisco, October 1980.

Cox, A. J. How to love your job—and yourself, too. *Advertising Age,* June 23, 1975, *46,* 39.

Geist, H. *The psychological aspects of the aging process with sociological implications.* St. Louis, Mo.: Warren H. Green, 1968. Pp. 36–37.

Golembiewski, R. Do flexible workhour effects decay over time? *Public Productivity Review,* 1982, *2,* 112–120.

Golembiewski, R., Carrigan, S. B., Mead, W. R., Munzenrider, R., & Blumberg, A. Toward building new work relationships. *Journal of Applied Behavioral Science,* 1972, *8*(2), 135–148.

Gould, R. Adult life stages: Growth toward self-tolerance. *Psychology Today,* February 1975, *9,* 78.

Gould, R. *Transformations.* New York: Simon & Schuster, 1978.

Hanson, M., & Allen, L. *Career planning for adults.* Livermore, Calif.: Lawrence Livermore Laboratory, UCRL 77109, 1980.

Kirschenbaum, H. *Advanced value clarification.* La Jolla, Calif.: University Associates, 1977.

Levinson, D. J. *The seasons of a man's life.* New York: Knopf, 1978.

Maas, H. S., & Kuypers, J. A. *From thirty to seventy.* San Francisco: Jossey-Bass, 1974.

Nollen, S. D. *Alternative work schedules.* New York: Van Nostrand Reinhold, 1982. Pp. 23–52.

Sasaki, N. *Management and industrial structure in Japan.* Elmsford, N.Y.: Pergamon Press, 1981.

Sheehy, G. *Passages.* New York: Dutton, 1976.

Slote, A. *Termination: The closing at Baker Plant.* Indianapolis, Ind.: Bobbs-Merrill, 1977.

Smith, P. C. The prediction of individual differences in susceptibility to industrial monotony. *Journal of Applied Psychology,* October 1955, *39,* 322–330.

Taber, T. D., Walsh, J. T., & Cooke, R. A. Developing a community-based program for reducing the social impact of a plant closing. *Journal of Applied Behavioral Science,* 1979, *15*(2), 133–135.

Tavernier, G. How America can manage its flexible benefits program. *Management Review,* August 1980, 8–13.

Vaillant, G. E. *Adaptation to life.* Boston: Little, Brown, 1977.

# A Model of Influence Strategy

Bonnie R. Kasten

*"All of us have the ability to improve our personal power and influence."*

Managers who behave in ways that make a difference feel personally powerful in a positive sense. They know how to assess situations and how to choose appropriate behavior to achieve desired results.

Different behaviors *do* produce different results. Being personally powerful essentially means being able to do the following:

1.  assess which situational variables indicate which behavior or behaviors to use;
2.  listen to and understand others so that you may assess which behaviors will have positive results;
3.  execute those ascertained behaviors clearly, with skill, so that what is *intended* matches the *impact.*

*Influence strategy* (Figure 1) is similar to the concept of force-field analysis: to understand those forces impeding an action, one analyzes the forces within her- or himself, the forces in others, and the forces in the environment. When applying this concept to influence strategy, you must be able to choose and execute effectively the behavior appropriate to the situation, regardless of whether that behavior or set of behaviors fits other situations.

Effective managers exhibit behavioral flexibility in the situations they encounter daily. Dr. David Berlew of Situation Management Systems, Inc. and Dr. Roger Harrison of Harrison-Kouzes Associates have identified five basic styles that reflect the ways individuals exercise personal power. These behavioral styles, although separate and distinct, can be used in combination and become a pool of energy that the influencer can draw from to make a difference. A brief sketch of each style appears below. Imagine yourself using each of these styles.

1. *Persuading.* I produce detailed and comprehensive proposals for dealing with problems. I am persistent and energetic in finding and presenting the logic behind my ideas and in

---

© 1982 by Situation Management Systems, Inc., Plymouth, Massachusetts. Used with permission.

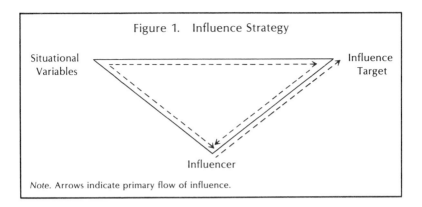

Figure 1.   Influence Strategy

Situational Variables

Influence Target

Influencer

Note. Arrows indicate primary flow of influence.

marshalling facts, arguments, and opinions that support my position. I am quick to grasp the strengths and weaknesses in an argument and to see and articulate the logical connections among various aspects of a complex situation. I am a vigorous and determined seller of ideas.

2. *Asserting.* I am direct and positive in asserting my own wishes and requirements. I let others know what I want from them, and am quick to tell others when I am pleased or displeased with their performance. I am willing to use my influence and authority to get others to do what I want. I skillfully use a combination of pressures and incentives to get others to agree with my plans and proposals and I follow up to make sure they carry out agreements and commitments. I readily engage in bargaining and negotiation to achieve my objectives, using both tough and conciliatory styles according to the realities of power and position in each situation.

3. *Bridging.* I am open and nondefensive, and am quick to admit when I do not have the answer, or when I have made a mistake. I listen attentively to others' ideas and feelings, actively communicating my interest in their points of view. I am willing to be influenced by others. I give credit to others' ideas and accomplishments. I make sure that everyone has a chance to be heard before making decisions, even when I do not agree with their positions. I show trust in others and I help them to bring out and develop their strengths and abilities.

4. *Attracting.* I appeal to others' emotions and ideals through my use of forceful and colorful words and images. My enthusiasm is contagious and carries others along with me. I help others to believe in their abilities to accomplish and succeed by working together. I see and can communicate my vision of the exciting possibilities in an idea or situation. I get others to see the values,

hopes, and aspirations they have in common and I build these common values into a shared sense of group loyalty and commitment.

5. *Moving away.* I am skillful at molding consensus out of diverse opinions. I prefer to look for a compromise position that all can accept and support. In group meetings and one-on-one situations, I can discover others' needs and find ways to meet them. Through the use of well-timed jokes, stories, breaks, or calls for a vote, I manage differences of opinion and conflict. I prefer a decision that is generally acceptable to one that must be imposed. I am good at diffusing tense situations and maintaining a calm, peaceful working climate.

## Summary

All of us have the ability to improve our personal power and influence. Systematic practice to (1) assess consciously situational variables; (2) listen to the approaches the influence target responds to; and (3) increase your ability to execute the influence styles will increase the effectiveness of your influencing attempts. It will also bring you a greater sense of personal confidence and power, and a sense of achieving results in your organization. You will realize that you *do* make the difference.□

## Bibliography

Berlew, D., & Rubin, I. M. *Positive Power and Influence, Trainer Manual* (2nd. Ed.). Plymouth, Mass.: Situation Management Systems, 1981.

# Section III: Organizational and Systems Change

# Strategic Planning for Managers*

Peter B. Vaill

*"Strategic planning is not bloodless and dispassionate analysis and decision making, but is rather as thoroughly pervaded by human quirks and idiosyncracies as any other kind of action in the organization."*

## Introduction

"Strategic Planning" is planning for the fulfillment of the organization's fundamental purposes. It includes establishing and clarifying purposes, deciding on the objectives whose attainment will help fulfill purposes, and determining the major means and "pathways," i.e., strategies, to pursuing these objectives.

This introduction makes a few distinctions that experience has shown to be important. The article then takes up the following topics in turn:

1.   the nature of an organization's purposes and their relation to the present and future world the organization lives in;
2.   the nature of the organization's environment;
3.   techniques to start a strategic planning process; and
4.   the impact of strategic planning on organizational behavior and managerial leadership.

## Further Remark on Definition

The definition with which this article begins is quite carefully phrased. Planning enables an organization to determine its purposes and how to pursue them. This use of the term "planning" differs somewhat from the usual connotation. For many people, planning means laying out a detailed schedule of actions and events that are supposed to occur in a particular sequence over a defined period of time. There is nothing wrong with this way of thinking about planning; such activity is essential. But this conventional meaning of the word "planning" is not

© 1983 NTL Institute

    * Many of the ideas contained in this paper have been developed in connection with the NTL workshop, "Strategic Planning: A New Focus for Organization Development." I am grateful to the approximately 150 participants in these workshops during the period 1978 to 1982 for their enthusiastic and creative participation. In particular, I am grateful to my colleague Irv Robinson, who has co-conducted several of the workshops with me and has been a continuing source of support and new ideas.

*strategic* planning. Strategic planning must be performed before the organization can make the more detailed scheduling of activities usually called planning. Strategic planning defines a desired character and identity that the organization will seek to develop and maintain, and broadly determines the kinds of activities the organization will pursue in service of that character and identity.

People find it a bit difficult to think of strategic planning concretely because for most of human history it has been done intuitively by organizational leaders and has remained implicit, i.e., "between the lines" of what organizations do. Two things have happened since World War II, however, that force people to conduct strategic planning as a deliberate organizational process. First, the world has become an extremely complex and uncertain place in which the intuitions of a single person are frequently insufficient to determine what an organization ought to do. Second, organizations have become larger and more interconnected with their environments. Furthermore, most large organizations in both the public and private sectors have moved from being focused on just one or two major objectives (e.g., "profit") to a system of interrelated purposes and objectives. These two characteristics of organizations, together with the increased complexity and turbulence of the surrounding world, make strategic planning both more important and enormously more difficult. It is paradoxical but true that strategic planning becomes more important as it becomes more difficult.

**The Role of Models**

Considering the complexity and unfamiliarity of strategic planning, one should naturally want as specific a methodology as possible. The literature contains many step-by-step models of how to perform strategic planning, "wiring diagrams" as it were. I believe, however, that casting strategic planning in a wiring diagram mode is inappropriate. My experience with managers trying to determine broad purposes and strategies shows that the nature of the problems defeats any simplistic application of a step-by-step model. Fundamentally, strategic planning consists of the ongoing interrelating of data so diverse and diffuse that no single step-by-step method is adequate.

**What is the Strategic Unit?**

Strategic planning was originally formulated as a description of what the *top* management of an organization should do. However, this need not be the case. Each subunit of an organization has a basic purpose and has some latitude in choosing the more specific objectives and means of reaching it (strategies). Thus, managers at all organizational levels can apply ideas from strategic planning to their units. Indeed, strategic planning for organizations as a whole might be better performed if managers have learned to think strategically about the various subunits they managed as they rose through the ranks.

Once having chosen the unit to consider "strategically," managers must adhere to this focus because the consideration of strategy depends on the nature of the environment in which the unit exists. If the unit of focus shifts, the environment changes correspondingly, and confusion may develop. The term "organization" will be used in the remainder of this article to mean "any given strategic unit."

## Public-Sector Connections

Finally, strategic planning evolved in the for-profit, private sector out of many years of experience with product, market, and financial planning. The corporation, unlike most public agencies, experiences a relative similarity of values and objectives between the managers at the very top levels of the organization and the managers at the middle levels who implement daily the various strategies that have been formulated. This similarity of outlook between levels makes it possible for the top executives to determine new strategies based on operational experience with current ones. From the middle level managers' perspectives, the people at the top want the same things for the organization as do those concerned with daily operations.

Of course, the different levels in the private sector do not have a perfect similarity of outlook. This similarity, however, exceeds that found in the typical public agency in which top executives are political appointees with political objectives and the middle managers are "careerists" whose appointments and performance reviews depend to a much lesser extent on political criteria. Thus, in public agencies the middle- and top-level executives frequently disagree sharply about the agency's basic purposes and about which programs will best fulfill those purposes. These divisions are accompanied by feelings of impotence: the top people feel they can't "move the bureaucracy"; the middle people feel they "can't convince the top people of the real needs and opportunities of the agency." As a result, public-sector managers are skeptical of strategic planning's assertions that the organization can indeed be consciously shaped and guided. They have seen too many ambitious strategic plans go into the bottom drawer.

Strategic planning in the public sector is a frontier problem that cannot be resolved here. Public-sector managers, however, can learn much from current ideas about strategic planning, even though their political context requires some adjustment in applying these ideas.

## Purposes and Environment: The Fundamentals

An organization's purposes continually answer the question "Why should this organization exist at all?" Richard Beckhard, an important contributor to the theory and practice of strategic management, describes an organization's purposes as "its reason to be."

Purposes are *not* objectives. One either attains or fails to attain objectives, whereas purposes, being broader, more philosophical, and perhaps idealistic, cannot be "attained" in the same sense. Objectives are reached in the future, whereas purposes act as real and abiding influences in the present. Objectives usually result in some observable change in the world, whereas the relative fulfillment of purposes results more in changes in the *meaning* people attach to the world. Purposes constitute fundamental images people hold about the organization and the world in which it lives. These images or ideals transcend the mechanical performance of daily tasks. Purposes *justify* activity and, by extension, existence.

No aspect of strategic planning is more difficult or more important than attending to the organization's purposes. Many action-oriented managers feel impatient with what they perceive as a rather abstract and impractical discussion. They become tempted to write something general and philosophical and then get on with the "real" discussion of "what we're going to *do* and *how* we're going to do it." A variation on this tendency occurs when one asserts that "we've already done it; we all agree; we don't need to do it again." This may be true and can be easily determined. But in today's rapidly changing world in which a continuing stream of new issues and opportunities couples with turnover in personnel, managers should always ask: "Does the organization mean to us what we want it to mean?"

Some people who are happy to talk about purposes have no interest in anything more specific. They appear at the other extreme from those discussed above, but their style can also harm any effective formulation and reformulation of purposes. Ultimately, purposes are expressed in action; purposes that cannot be expressed in action are Utopian dreams.

The strategic planning discussion begins with purposes, but then moves iteratively among the following four sets of relationships:

1. the relation of purpose to the aspirations and values of the organization's leadership;
2. the relation of purpose to the demands, opportunities, and constraints of the present and future environment;
3. the relation of purpose to specific objectives the organization pursues and programs it conducts; and
4. the relation of purpose to the organization's ways of structuring itself.

When a management group performs strategic planning, it discusses four relationships. (1) Is the discussion of what we want for the organization and to what we can commit ourselves a valid expression of our values and our sense of responsibility? This dimension frequently becomes underplayed, and a manager feels expected instead to do whatever the organization needs. The psychology of leadership, however, requires that the leader believe in the organization's initiatives. Those activities that are right for the organization and that feel right to the leader/manager will gain commitment.

Relation (2) asserts that the organization's purposes are situated in a constantly changing world. What role will the organization play in this present and future world? Is there a need for the role? Does it constitute a "contribution?" Can the organization find an identity that endures through time instead of having to "reinvent" itself every few months or years?

Relation (3) is especially important because, unless the organization is absolutely brand-new, it is already pursuing many objectives, the consideration of purposes occurs in the context of the organization's current work. Often the organization has acquired a variety of objectives and programs that bear little relation to each other and, together, do not point toward any clear purpose.

Relation (4) is not often seen as having a role in strategic planning. How an organization structures itself, however, can be of crucial importance to formulating and maintaining clear purposes and to conducting more specific programs that cumulatively contribute to the fulfillment of purposes. How "tall" is the hierarchy? Is the basic divisional structure a functional one, a product-line one, a matrix, or something else? How are geographical divisions determined?

As noted above, the organization's statement of purpose defines the role it intends to play in its environment. The organization's structure determines, to some extent, what it can "see" in its environment. With a functional structure, an organization tends to be primarily aware of the state of those same functions in the environment, e.g., accounting, finance, manufacturing, personnel. With a product-line structure, the organization tends to be more aware of the sources of input to the product, the product preferences of consumers, clients, and users, and the actions of competitors.

Depending on the kinds of subunits the organization structure contains, various kinds of "boundary roles" will exist. A boundary role is defined as a job in the organization that requires the ability to understand and interrelate the points of view of members of the organization and the entities in the environment. Thus, a salesperson must understand how the customer looks to the organization *and* how the organization looks to the customer. A recruiter must understand how recruits look to the organization *and* how the organization looks to potential recruits. Persons in boundary roles are the primary means through which the organization learns about its environment and takes action in relation to it. The extent to which a boundary-role player acts as an "informed scout" of the environment affects how the organization pursues its purposes effectively. Without effective performances in various boundary roles, the organization becomes relatively "blind."

In summary, an organization's purposes become meaningful and relevant in relation to various environmental factors and trends. Therefore, these factors and trends must be understood. The notion of the boundary role suggests a means by which organizations can keep track of their environments.

## A Way of Thinking about the Environment

One typically describes the "environment" of an organization in terms of "factors," "forces," "trends," and "dimensions." Although these terms may be commonly used to describe the environment, they become very misleading *when one is trying to perform strategic planning*. One cannot inquire of factors, forces, trends, or dimensions because these are abstractions. One can only inquire of people. A management group trying to perform strategic planning will want to talk to someone about its environment. This is why the boundary-role players described in the previous section are so important.

Beyond boundary-role players, however, there exists in every organization's environment another category of persons and groups who constitute a vital source of information about the environment. These are the organization's "stakeholders." A stakeholder is a person, group, or organization in an organization's environment that defines itself as having a stake in the way the organization conducts itself. Notice that the organization does not define who its stakeholders are, though some management groups might wish they had such control. The stakeholders themselves make these definitions. In various ways, they are dependent on the organization. They express their dependence by communicating to the organization what they think it should and should not do.

Stakeholders may be of many kinds because they define themselves. In general, however, the following categories will include most of an organization's most important stakeholders:

1.  those who supply the organization with the resources it needs (personnel, materials, money) to do whatever it does;
2.  those who receive all the outputs of the organization, including outputs like pollution, which may not be part of the organization's primary purpose;
3.  those who compete with the organization for access to input-stakeholders and output-stakeholders;
4.  those who regulate the organization;
5.  those who own or charter the organization; and
6.  stakeholders of all these stakeholders.

In general, organizations are very familiar with the expectations of some of their stakeholders but may not be aware of the existence of others. Stakeholders who feel ignored can be expected to take some action to change their situation. They may seek to bind themselves more closely to the organization—for example, through contracts—or they may seek to reduce their dependence on the organization. In the extreme cases, they may find ways of terminating all contact with the organization, sometimes to the severe detriment of the organization.

Strategic planning goes on in relation to a continuing attempt to manage relationships with stakeholders. To some extent, the ways in which an organization defines its purposes and key objectives can be interpreted as a decision to involve itself with some particular set of stakeholders and avoid involvement with others.

The ideal situation is to have good working relationships with stakeholders, with stable sets of expectations and behaviors on both sides. In the dynamic world we live in, however, such stability is always problematic. One never knows when some change in government regulations or prices or interest rates will render the organization unable to meet stakeholder expectations and/or cause a stakeholder to place new demands on the organization.

Thus, the nature of the relationships between the organization and its stakeholders is critical, for it is through these relationships that problems will be worked out. In my experience, few managers have thought of the range of actions that are open to them in relation to stakeholders. This does not refer to the action's content, but to its *mode*. For instance, some organizations use relatively formal modes: official letters of intent, meetings with lawyers present, contracts, or covenants. Other organizations are much more informal, keeping things on a handshake basis as much as possible. Some organizations rarely see their stakeholders face to face; others prefer not to do business any other way. With some stakeholders, organizations rely on casual, unplanned encounters—for example, at annual conventions. Some organizations positively avoid some of their stakeholders, which is why in litigation we have the summons and the subpoena.

Organizations use a variety of methods in working with stakeholders, some traditional and some even illegal (e.g., bribes and kickbacks). In general, all managers must be more aware of the variety of methods available so that they may consider whether their methods are the most effective.

In summary, it is not useful to think of the "environment" as a set of blind, impersonal forces. The manager's real environment is composed primarily of stakeholders—individuals, groups, and organizations.

As both the labor, the anti-war, and the civil rights movements showed, groups that are ignored for too long find ways of forcibly making their needs known. By the time things reach this point, the organization cannot often do anything to compensate stakeholders for the years of frustration they have felt. Therefore, it behooves every manager to notice any early-warning signals that indicate that a group or organization in the environment wishes the organization would conduct itself somewhat differently. This does *not* mean that the organization should always try to be all things to all stakeholders. It does mean that when an organization becomes unaware of the existence of a stakeholder and/or unable to understand what the stakeholder wants, it is in no position to *decide* what its posture should be.

## Techniques for Getting Started

Those getting started with strategic planning face two tasks: (1) clarifying purposes and objectives; and (2) analyzing the environment. Because what the organization is trying to be and do and the world in which it lives are so closely intertwined, strategic planning can start in either place, depending on the organization's particular circumstances and the preferences of the management.

## Clarifying Purposes and Objectives

De facto *Purposes and Objectives*

Completing the following sentence provides a simple and effective method for starting discussions: "We manage now *as if* our specific objectives and broader purposes were. . . ." The method is especially effective in organizations that produce a great deal of activity but lack consensus on what it all means, what it all adds up to. A variation on the task is to ask, "If a Martian were to try to figure out *why* we are doing what we are doing, what conclusions might it develop?" Yet another variation is to ask, "What do our stakeholders probably think our objectives are, based on the way we deal with them?"

This exercise produces a list of objectives and broader purposes embedded in daily activity. Some of the items on the list will not be flattering, not exactly what organization members feel comfortable owning up to. But the point is to develop an agenda for rethinking the basic objectives and purposes.

*Means-Ends Analysis*

Closely related to the "*de facto* objectives" technique is means-end analysis. Once again, one starts with daily activities, but then answers the question: "What is the broader end to which this activity is aimed?" One names a slightly broader end and then asks, "To what broader end is this end in turn a means?" And so forth. One develops a hierarchical chain going from the most concrete activities and events to very broad and abstract values and ideals. In performing this analysis, one looks for "breaks," i.e., places in the chain where no broader end can be discerned. Means-ends analysis helps to identify those programs and activities that "hang in space" and that have little to do with the main thrust of the organization. Means-ends analysis becomes especially useful when the strategic task is to prune the organization of superfluous activities.

*Force-Field Analysis*

Force-field analysis is a very old and useful technique. One usually uses it to explain past or present events; in the context of strategic planning, it can be an effective forecasting tool. As one considers various strategic alternatives, the force-field question is: "If we choose this alternative, what future driving forces will tend to bring about what we intend, and what future restraining forces will tend to prevent what we intend?"

## Strategic-Adequacy Analysis

This is the 20/20 hindsight method. Here the strategic planning group asks itself, "What have been the real, operative grounds for strategic decisions we have made in the recent past? How well have we understood our problem in the past? To the extent that we can see *now* what we could not see at that time, how can we incorporate this learning into strategic decisions facing us now?"

This method works best in a strategic planning group that has a relatively high level of mutual trust and openness. A tremendous amount can be learned from past strategic decision-making processes if the group is willing to look.

## Learning from the environment

We have already suggested that an intensive analysis of who the stakeholders are and what they want provides a powerful method. The idea of "boundary-role analysis" has also been discussed. It is worth repeating that members of the organization in boundary roles can be informed scouts of various sectors of the environment. Beyond these two approaches, there exist some other methods that aid understanding of the organization-environment interface and development of a strategic agenda.

## The Output Congruity Matrix

This is a powerful device for seeking mismatches between what the organization thinks of its output and what one or more stakeholders think of it.

In Figure 1, we are primarily interested in cells two and three, although the happy circumstance of cell one should not just be ignored, but rather understood. We assume that in cell four the organization is ready to do something. But this readiness may not exist in cells two and three.

The value of this matrix lies in the discussion of where some particular output belongs. The strategic planning group often discovers that it needs more information about stakeholders and/ or about its own organization, and this results in a quite focused research effort.

| | | Stakeholders' point of view | |
|---|---|---|---|
| Figure 1. Output Congruity Matrix | | | |
| | | Relatively satisfied with output | Relatively dissatisfied with output |
| Organization's point of view | Relatively satisfied with output | Cell 1 | Cell 2 |
| | Relatively dissatisfied with output | Cell 3 | Cell 4 |

An alternative use of the matrix is to array all of the organization's outputs on it as a means of assessing the general pattern of relations the organization has with its stakeholders. However it is used, the matrix's value comes from developing an agenda for the action the organization must take to improve its relationships with various stakeholders in the environment.

## Metaphorical Images

Sometimes, when the relationships between an organization and its environment are extremely complex, managers find it easier to get started by working with symbols and metaphors rather than by addressing the data directly. Here the strategic planning group creates a guiding image or metaphor, then discusses the organization and its environment at considerable length in terms of this metaphor before returning to the "facts." For instance, suppose the group chooses this metaphor: "Our organization is a newborn fawn in the forest." Bearing in mind that such an image is not chosen casually, and that it is very meaningful to the group employing it, they would then move on to discuss the "fawn" and the "forest" as thoroughly as they could, seeking insights that can be transferred back to their real situation.

Like all holistic methods, the creation of metaphorical images tends to be a bit "all or none" in its results: It either produces very little or a great deal.

## Scenarios, Weak Signals, and Delphi

The next decade will see a proliferation of new methods for understanding the environment. This is one of the most lively topics in management. These three methods all attempt to evoke insight out of initially meaningless data. The scenario method involves telling stories about the world the organization lives in or may soon be living in and then trying to decide which scenarios are most likely to occur and what the organization's posture in the various scenarios should be. This method takes a while to learn because story telling is not a widely distributed skill, but when it works, it works very well.

Weak signals are present events, trends, activities, persons, and issues that somehow embody and portend the face of the future—if we could only know it. The Beatles' appearance on the Ed Sullivan Show in 1964 was such a weak signal. In any given moment, however, millions of weak signals exist, most of which never result in trends or events that organizations need to take account of. How to separate those that count from those that do not requires judgment and experience. The first step, however, calls for management groups to ask themselves more consistently, "What weak signals can we perceive? What are they signals of? Should we 'track' them over the coming months and years?"

Delphi is one of a growing number of methods that involve pooling perceptions in unusual ways. Delphi tries to filter out the "group process" aspects from the "expertise" aspects. It helps in making judgments about the future environment, but, by itself, does not foster commitment to those judgments made by members of the Delphi panel. Therefore, strategic planning groups who use the method will have to do additional work if they want action and commitment from organization members in relation to results of a Delphi study.

## Reconstructing the Present

Finally, I have been working on a method that by itself does not help an organization understand its present or future environment, but rather increases an organization's understanding of the nature of the issues and of methods that might help. The idea is simple: pick a point in time at some distance in the past— say, five years. Restricting oneself to the data available five years ago, ask, "How much of today's world could we have foreseen with those data? What could we not have possibly foreseen? How might we have misled ourselves?" By repeatedly doing this type of analysis, we assume that one builds up a sensitivity to the kinds of variables that make the most difference. One then hopes to be able to look five years into the future and make valid predictions by using these variables.

But, in closing this section on peering into the environment, Herbert Simon's remark from *The Sciences of the Artificial* (1981, p. 178) must always be borne in mind:

> Each of us sits in a long, dark hall within a circle of light cast by a small lamp. The lamplight penetrates a few feet up and down the hall, then rapidly attenuates, diluted by the vast darkness of future and past that surrounds it.

## Strategic Planning as Organizational Behavior

The strategic planning literature has only now begun to reflect the awareness that strategic planning is not bloodless and dispassionate analysis and decision making, but is rather as thoroughly pervaded by human quirks and idiosyncracies as any other kind of action in the organization. In general, we have little systematic knowledge of what top managers really do, and this applies to strategic planning in particular. Thus, those who are doing it, learning to do it, or watching others do it need to be aware that we are talking about forms of organizational action that are only beginning to be understood.

Some men and women do seem to have a knack for strategic planning, though. Here is a list of attitudes and skills that they seem to possess:

1.  Effective strategic thinkers are eclectic in their interests and are not bound by stereotypes and categorical assumptions.
2.  They are good at holistic thinking, in addition to having good analytical skills; they can both break down and build up issues and interpretations.
3.  They are future-oriented and, in particular, they realize the reality of the future—it is more "present" for them than for others. They realize what needs to be done now to accrue benefits in the future.
4.  They are both whole-headed and wholehearted. They use both sides of the brain, and they bring a certain passion and intensity to the task of strategic thinking and decision making.
5.  They think big; their vision reflects ambition for the organization. They are not interested in the status quo or in short-range, expedient strategies.
6.  They realize that strategic thinking can no longer be the solitary enterprise of one wise person, that it cannot be made in a closet or on a mountaintop, but rather that it is a social,

interactive process in which the task is to learn to use the diverse talents and experiences available in the organization.

7.    For all their vision and ambition, effective strategic thinkers have their projects grounded in the operational problems and opportunities of some particular organization. In this sense they are practical as well as visionary.

8.    Finally, effective strategic thinkers have combined the relatively passive, comtemplative modes of thinking with active "can-do" modes. They accept responsibility for shaping the organization and the world around it, but they know also that with shaping goes understanding and insight.

More and more men and women possessing these and other qualities find "strategic planning" to be one of the most challenging tasks one can imagine. All of the signs suggest that strategic planning is fast becoming the leading mode of action for the top manager.

In summary, one must not lose sight of the fundamental question: "Why should our organization exist at all in the world it now lives in and in the world that is unfolding before it?"□

## Bibliography

Ackoff, R. Redesigning the Future. New York: Wiley, 1974.

Beckhard, R., & Harris, R. Organizational Transitions: Managing Complex Change. Reading, Mass.: Addison-Wesley, 1977.

Cribbin, J. J. Leadership: Strategies for Organizational Effectiveness. New York: AMACOM, 1981.

De Jouvenal, B. On Power (2nd. ed.). Boston: Beacon Press, 1962 (originally published 1945).

Drucker, P. Managing in Turbulent Times. New York: Harper & Row, 1980.

The Journal of Business Strategy, a quarterly published by Warren, Gorham, & Lamont, Inc., 210 South Street, Boston, Mass. 02111.

Maccoby, M. The Leader: A New Face for American Management. New York: Simon & Schuster, 1981.

Miles, R. H. (Ed.). Resourcebook in Macro Organizational Behavior. Santa Monica, Calif.: Goodyear Publishing, 1980.

Musashi, M. A Book of Five Rings. New York: Overlook Press, 1974.

Quinn, J. B. Strategies for Change: Logical Incrementalism. Homewood, Ill.: Richard D. Irwin, 1980.

Schendel, C., & Hofer, C. W. (Eds.). Strategic Management. Boston, Mass.: Little, Brown, 1980.

Selznick, P. *Leadership in Administration*. New York: Harper & Row, 1957.

Simon, H. A. *The Sciences of the Artificial* (2nd. ed.). Cambridge, Mass.: MIT Press, 1981.

Siu, R. G. H. *The Craft of Power*. New York: Wiley, 1974.

Vickers, G. *Value Systems and Social Process*. New York: Basic Books, 1968.

Vickers, G. *Making Institutions Work*. New York: Basic Books, 1973.

West Publishing Company Series in Business Policy and Planning, 1978: Schendel, D., & Hofer, C. W. *Strategy Formulation: Analytical Concepts*. Richards, M. *Organizational Goal Structures*. Galbraith, J., & Nathanson, D. *Strategy Implementation: The Role of Structure and Process*. MacMillan, I. *Strategy Formulation: Political Concepts*.

# An Introduction to Organization Development*

John J. Sherwood

*"In an effective OD effort, each member of the organization begins to act as a resource to others and becomes willing to help others when asked to do so."*

Organization development is an educational process by which human resources are continuously identified, allocated, and expanded in ways that make these resources more available to the organization, and, therefore, improve the organization's problem-solving capabilities.

The most general objective of organizational development—OD—is to develop self-renewing, self-correcting systems of people who learn to organize themselves in a variety of ways according to the nature of their tasks, and who continue to expand the choices available to the organization as it copes with the changing demands of a changing environment. OD stands for a new way of looking at the human side of organizational life.

What is OD?

(a)   A long-range effort to introduce planned change based on a diagnosis that is shared by the members of an organization.

(b)   An OD program involves an entire organization, or a coherent "system" or part thereof.

(c)   Its goal is to increase organizational effectiveness and enhance organizational choice and self-renewal.

(d)   The major strategy of OD is to intervene in the ongoing activities of the organization to facilitate learning and to make choices about alternative ways to proceed.

© 1971 John J. Sherwood
* This statement liberally uses material from "What is OD?" *News and Reports from the NTL Institute for Applied Behavioral Science*, Vol. 2 (June), 1968; Wendell L. French, "Organization Development Objectives, Assumptions, and Strategies," *California Management Review*, Vol. XII (Winter), 1969; Richard Beckhard, *Organization Development: Strategies and Models*, Reading, Mass.: Addison-Wesley, 1969; John W. Gardner, "How to Prevent Organizational Dry Rot," *Harper's*, October, 1965; Thomas A. Wickes, "Organizational Development Technology," unpublished manuscript, TRW Systems, October, 1968; Warren G. Bennis, *Organization Development: Its Nature, Origins, and Prospects*, Reading, Mass.: Addison-Wesley, 1969; and Douglas McGregor, The Human Side of Enterprise, New York: McGraw-Hill, 1960.
I appreciate the comments by Richard E. Byrd, Donald C. King, Philip J. Runkel, and William J. Underwood on an earlier version of this paper.

## Objectives of Typical OD Programs

Although the specific objectives of an OD effort vary according to the diagnosis of organizational problems, a number of objectives typically emerge. The following objectives reflect problems that are common in organizations and that prevent the creative release of human potential within organizations:

(1)  to build trust among individuals and groups throughout the organization and up and down the hierarchy;
(2)  to create an open, problem-solving climate throughout the organization in which problems are confronted and differences are clarified, both within groups and between groups, in contrast to "sweeping problems under the rug" or "smoothing things over";
(3)  to locate decision-making and problem-solving responsibilities as close to the information sources and the relevant resources as possible rather than in a particular role or level of the hierarchy;
(4)  to increase the sense of "ownership" of organizational goals and objectives throughout the membership of the organization;
(5)  to move toward more collaboration between interdependent persons and interdependent groups within the organization because when relationships are clearly competitive, it becomes important that competition is open and managed so the organization might benefit from the advantages of open competition and avoid suffering from the destructive consequences of subversive rivalry; and
(6)  to increase awareness of group "process" and its consequences for performance—that is, to help persons become aware of what is happening between and to group members while the group is working on the task, e.g., communication, influence, feelings, leadership styles and struggles, relationships between groups, how conflict is managed, and so forth.

The objectives of organizational development efforts are achieved through planned interventions based on research findings and theoretical hypotheses of the behavioral sciences. The organization examines its present ways of work, its norms and values, and generates and evaluates alternative ways of working, or relating, or rewarding members of the system.

## Some Assumptions Underlying the Concept of OD

Using knowledge and techniques from the behavioral sciences, organization development attempts to integrate organizational goals with the needs for growth of individual members to design a more effective and fully functioning organization, in which the potential of members is more fully realized. Some of the basic assumptions underlying the concept of OD are as follows:

(1)   The attitudes most members of organizations hold toward work and their resultant work habits are usually more *reactions to* their work environment and how they are treated by the organization than they are intrinsic characteristics of an individual's personality. Therefore, efforts to change attitudes toward work and toward the organization should be directed more toward changing how the person is treated than toward attempting to change the person.

(2)   Work that is organized to meet people's needs as well as to achieve organizational requirements tends to produce the highest productivity and quality of production.

(3)   Most members of organizations are not motivated primarily by an avoidance of work—for which tight controls and threats of punishment are necessary—but rather, most individuals seek challenging work and desire responsibility for accomplishing organizational objectives to which they are committed.

(4)   The basic building blocks of organizations are groups of people; therefore, the basic units of change are also groups, not simply individuals.

(5)   The culture of most organizations tends to suppress the open expression of feelings that people have about each other and about where they and their organization are heading. The suppression of feelings adversely affects problem solving, personal growth, and satisfaction with one's work. The expression of feelings is an important part of becoming committed to a decision or a task.

(6)   Groups that learn to work in a constructively open way by providing feedback for members become more able to profit from their own experience and become more able to fully use their resources on the task. Furthermore, the growth of individual members is facilitated by relationships which are open, supportive, and trusting.

(7)   An important difference exists between *agreement* and *commitment*. People are committed to and care about that which they help create. When change is introduced, it will be most effectively implemented if the groups and individuals involved have a sense of ownership in the process. Commitment is most assuredly attained when people participate actively in the planning and conduct the change. Agreement is simpler to achieve and results in a simpler outcome—people do what they are told, or something sufficient or similar.

(8)    The basic value underlying all OD theory and practice is that of *choice*. Through the collection and feedback of relevant data—made available by trust, openness, and risk—more choice becomes available to the organization, and to the individual, and hence better decisions can be made.

## Organization Development Technology

Basic to all OD efforts is an attempt to make the human resources of the organization optimally available. Outside consultants often share the responsibility for this process, but they also work toward increasing the organization's own capacity to understand and manage its own growth.

In contrast to management development that focuses on the individual manager, OD focuses on groups and changing relations between people. The system—whether it is a unit of the organization or the entire organization—is the object of an OD effort.

A frequent strategy in OD programs is the use of an *action-research* model of intervention. An action-research approach has three processes, all of which involve extensive collaboration between a consultant and the organization: data gathering from individuals and groups, feedback to key client or client group in the organization, and joint action planning based on the feedback. Action-research is designed to make data available from the entire system and then to use that information to make plans about the future of that system.

Some OD interventions or building blocks of an OD program are the following:

(1)    *Team building.* In team building the focus is on early identification and solution of the work group's problems, particularly interpersonal and organizational roadblocks that stand in the way of the team's collaborative, cooperative, creative, competent functioning.

A group's work procedures can be made more effective by using different decision-making procedures for different tasks and by learning to treat leadership as a function to be performed by members of the group, not just as a role or as a characteristic of an individual's personality.

The interpersonal relationships within a team can be improved by working on the following: communication skills and patterns; skills in openness and expression of what one thinks and feels; the degree of understanding and acceptance among team members; authority and hierarchical problems; trust and respect; and skills in conflict management.

(2) *Intergroup problem solving.* Groups are brought together for the purpose of reducing unhealthy competitiveness between the groups or to resolve intergroup conflicts over such things as overlapping responsibilities or confused lines of authority, and to enhance interdependence when it appropriately exists.

Intergroup problems sometimes exist between different functional groups that must work together—e.g., sales and engineering—or between line and staff, labor and management, or separate organizations involved in a merger.

(3) *Confrontation meeting.* This is a problem-solving mechanism when problems are known to exist. An action-research format is used. The entire management group of an organization comes together to collect problems and share attitudes, set priorities, and establish and make commitments to action through setting targets and assigning task forces.

(4) *Goal-setting and planning.* Supervisor-subordinate pairs and teams throughout the organization engage in systematic performance improvements and target setting with mutual commitment and review. Goal setting becomes a way of life for the organization.

(5) *Third party facilitation.* This involves the use of a skilled third person to help in the diagnosis, understanding, and resolution of difficult human problems—e.g., difficult one-to-one relationships between two persons or two groups.

(6) *Consulting pairs.* Often a manager can benefit from a close and continuing relationship with someone outside her or his own organization (a consultant, either internal or external to the organization), with whom he or she can share problems early.

In an effective OD effort, each member of the organization begins to act as a resource to others and becomes willing to help others when asked to do so. Such attitudes develop into norms or shared expectations. Once such a norm is established, members of the organization become potential consultants for one another, and the dependence of the organization on outside resources lessens considerably.

A major characteristic of organization development is that it relies heavily on an educational strategy emphasizing *experience-based learning* and on the skills such a procedure develops. Thus, the data feedback of the action-research model and the confrontation meeting provide examples of how the experiences people have with each other and with the organization are shared and become the basis upon which learning occurs and upon which planning and action proceed. To be sure, OD is not simply human relations training—nor is it sensitivity training. Openness about one's own experiences, however—including feelings, reactions, and perceptions—represents a cornerstone of many organizational development efforts. Furthermore, laboratory training experiences often help members of the organization develop more interpersonal competence, including communication skills, the ability to manage conflict better, and insights into oneself and into groups and how they form and function. Laboratory training programs, therefore, provide a good preliminary step to an organization development effort.□

# A Manager's Guide to Evaluation

Dale G. Lake
Roger A. Ritvo

*"If you see that evaluation exists to serve decision makers, you will be more likely to use it as a management tool."*

## Why Don't We Evaluate?

If you are like many managers, consultants, trainers, and change agents, the word "evaluate" probably conjures up images of esoteric research designs, t-tests, and analyses of variance. You may have also found yourself in the position of trying to convince others to start a new program of team building or human resource development, only to be stopped short when asked, "But how will we evaluate it?"

At the same time, in being honest with yourself, you have probably wondered, "Just what will a team-building effort do for my organization? Will quality circles really result in improved productivity and quality of work life? Is there a way to start up our new plant that could substantially reduce costs and shorten the time it takes to operate at a profit? Would the new dental program really improve morale? Does our succession-planning system select high performers?"

## A Change in Perspective

If you have hesitated or avoided evaluating important change efforts in your work because it seemed too esoteric or too costly—or because you simply did not know how to begin—the following material will provide helpful guidance. We wrote this article as a conversation among colleagues—not evaluation experts or researchers, but managers and consultants who must determine the relative worth of one or more programs. While we agree with the experts that evaluation is the use of systematic data collection methods to make informed judgments about programs and performance, we view evaluation as a process whereby one asks the right questions for the right audiences and then takes reasonable precautions to ensure that the information collected to answer those questions is credible.

This questioning approach—or "Socratic" method, as we prefer to call it—makes evaluation an integral part of the program development and planning process. For example, let's put ourselves in the position of a staff member, manager, consultant,

© 1983 NTL Institute

or other program developer who has just accepted an assignment to try out team building in a plant, regional office, or hospital to see whether it works. First, we must begin with a set of questions.

- What are the goals of a team-building effort?
- In what settings might they work best?
- Do particular plants or regional offices need team building more than others?
- Do we need to accommodate certain company politics when deciding where to try team building?
- What evidence will the corporation or headquarters need to "prove" that the team-building was worthwhile?

When you try to answer these questions before installing a team-building effort, *you are evaluating.* In the jargon of evaluators, when you try to answer these questions, you conduct *contextual evaluation* by defining the environment where change is to occur, specifying the unmet needs, and noting the problems underlying those needs.

Suppose this time you plan to install quality circles, not team building. Again, you wish to see if they will work. You have answered your questions about the program's location, its settings, and your basic objectives. Now you begin to ask how to build the program.

- What procedures do we need to develop to train persons to operate quality circles?
- Who do we use to do the training?
- How much will it cost?

When you begin to raise these questions, you move from contextual evaluation to *input evaluation*—i.e., you determine how to use resources to meet program goals and objectives. The end product of input evaluation is an analysis of alternative procedural designs that determines potential costs and benefits.

For both of the illustrations above, two major problems remain. First, you will have to raise questions on how to make midcourse corrections as the program develops. These *process* evaluation questions help to continuously monitor the implementation of the program, for they provide periodic feedback for control and refinement of plans and procedures. Finally, you will want to consider *product* evaluation questions that relate outcomes to objectives and to context, input, and process information.

- Did it really work?
- Have things really improved?

- Have we identified cost savings, reduced error rates, improved quality, increased motivation, or noted other appropriate factors?

This approach views evaluation as a continuous activity used by program developers and implementors to guide their efforts, to provide information for decision making, and to demonstrate that the results achieved were worth the effort. If you see that evaluation exists to serve decision makers, you will be more likely to use it as a management tool.

## Evaluation Planning

In the introduction, we stated that evaluation involves asking the right questions of the right audiences and then taking reasonable precautions to ensure that the information collected to answer those questions is credible. This same logic applies to the development of an evaluation design and program. We have examined reviews of over 600 evaluation studies and have served as evaluators and as program managers on numerous evaluation projects. This experience has taught us that evaluators must face three major areas of concern at the beginning of an evaluation effort: policy making, human relationships, and technical aspects.

In the area of policy making, we will consider how much the evaluation effort may influence decisions made about the project being evaluated. The answer to this question may dictate the kind of evaluation model used. Human concerns center on the problems related to the building and maintenance of productive relationships between program implementors and evaluators. In particular, management must choose whether to use "inside" or "outside" evaluators. In the technical area, we discuss the traditional methods for ensuring the validity of the data collected. Finally, the utility of any evaluation must be known in advance; this provides the framework for the effort.

## Policy Making

The basic reason for evaluation is to provide information for decision making. For example, a large U. S. electronics company now has more than 200 quality circles operating in its plants. Several findings led to this situation. First, the CEO and other top managers became inundated with the information that Japanese firms were dramatically out-performing their U. S. counterparts. Management attributed this difference to the Japanese use of quality circles. When the top executives visited Japan to examine quality circles firsthand, they sat in on several quality circle meetings, saw productivity charts, and decided that quality circles could work in their own plants—a policy decision. Rather than try to install quality circles throughout the company immediately, they tested their decision with a trial effort and a planned evaluation. Before the organization completed its evaluation, it received such encouraging process information from the experiment that management made another policy decision to expand the experiment throughout the company. Thus, we see that evaluation efforts may influence policy decisions at any point during the evaluation.

The program implementor must consider that the evaluation data will likely influence policy decisions. If so, this will affect the choice of evaluation model. We present the four essential models below.

1. *Evaluation as decision making.* This model examines questions and the decisions they relate to throughout the stages of project development. The decision-making approach provides the advantage of involving the evaluator in a symbiotic relationship with the program manager. Thus, it ensures that the manager will use the data throughout the life of the project. The model's major drawbacks include its costs and a constant demand for quick turnaround of data for decision making.

2. *Evaluation of discrepancies.* The discrepancy approach designs evaluation according to project-defined criteria. In its simplest form, a discrepancy study involves periodic measurement during a project to determine if it conforms to stated goals. This model is useful for making midcourse corrections as the project unfolds. It also requires high interaction between the evaluator and the program manager.

3. *Goal-free evaluation.* This model proceeds from a unique set of assumptions. Some managers have argued that any involvement by the evaluator in the planning or development of the program "contaminates" or biases the evaluator in favor of the program's purposes. Therefore, this option allows organizations to bring in evaluators after program completion and to tell them to use their own perspectives to examine the plant, hospital, or school in which a new program has been installed. The organization tells the evaluators nothing about the program, and may assign them to evaluate a comparison plant, hospital, or school without telling the evaluators which ones participated in the change effort and which did not. This model's major requirement is that evaluators must be experts in the program area. The advantages of this approach are that organizations evaluate programs after completion and that positive findings that favor the experimental location over the control location have high face validity because of the lack of contamination. The model's major problem

concerns its lack of clarity about the meaning of any negative findings. This method of evaluation usually costs less than other methods and does not require high interdependence between the evaluator and the program administrator.

4. *Ethnographic evaluation.* With this model the evaluator "lives" in the program setting and uses the tools of anthropology for observation and unobtrusive measurement. The evaluator attempts to discover how program interventions affect program participants within the subculture of the program. A skillful, trained ethnographer can provide valuable feedback to program managers throughout the project. This model's major problem lies in finding the right ethnographer.

## Human Concerns in Evaluation

The foremost problem related to the human side of evaluation is the identification of audiences for the evaluation. Evaluations have several audiences that vary over the life of the project.

- *The stakeholders.* These are managers, budget officers, personnel directors, and project team members who have direct responsibility for the creation and implementation of the project itself.
- *The clients or program participants.* These people are the targets of the program intervention. This audience needs to know what the program involves them in and its probable risks and benefits.
- *The field.* These people constitute a network of similar professionals. An experiment in team building has an audience consisting of other organization development specialists who want to know about the utility of team building in general.

Each audience has different information needs. Planning for evaluation proceeds best when the program manager and the evaluator clearly understand which audiences they serve.

A second human issue in evaluation concerns resistance. People naturally resist new programs. The program manager and evaluator must plan for several types of resistance. One type arises—particularly in service organizations—from the belief that "you can't quantify it." Many medical clinicians, educators, and welfare workers view the evaluation process and evaluators as numerical "whizzes" who lack the requisite understanding of the population groups in need. Resistance also develops from unclear goals. Evaluators who studied an educational reform designed to provide principals with more autonomy in decision making, labeled "school-based management," found that several persons who thought they opposed this reform had already begun to make the change—but under a different label. Third, resistance can arise from a fear of how the data will be used. To overcome such resistance, evaluators must make assurances of anonymity.

The most important human relationship we will discuss—and, potentially, the most problematic—occurs between the program manager and the evaluator. First, management must determine whether the evaluator should work "inside" the system and become employed by the company on a full-time basis or work "outside" the system as a contractor. The primary advantages of an inside evaluation study are that evaluators can design the study to fill the information needs of the program implementors and that persons knowledgeable about the program will conduct it. In contrast, outside evaluation studies benefit from objectivity and autonomy. Such studies may ask more difficult questions and collect data in a more rigorous, perhaps more useful form.

Management should also consider the interaction of evaluators and program participants. In several cases, organizations terminated evaluation studies after evaluators "turned off" participants simply by collecting data. Sometimes, evaluators use young graduate students to collect sensitive data in interviews, only to find that respondents have been reluctant to reveal information. Participants in experimental programs want to know that the evaluators are not just technicians, but that they are sensitive to the participants' concerns of anonymity and confidentiality. Participants also have concerns about feedback, and they wonder, "What did the evaluators learn about us?" Prompt and concise feedback usually facilitates the collection of subsequent data.

A third issue concerns the relationships among program managers and their staff. Such relationships matter as much to the successful implementation of the program as the substantive content of the program itself. Program managers and evaluators need to know clearly at the outset of the program just how much these relationships can be investigated.

The final set of relationships occur among the program staff and the person they report to in the hierarchy of the company or agency. Once, while serving as evaluators, we found a chief administrator in a hospital who had assumed that the project would close in the fall and had budgeted the project staff back into the line organization. This administrator made this assumption because the project staff had not really reported any progress on the project during the previous six months. In fact, the project had been re-funded and would continue for two more years. This discrepancy emerged during our context evaluation.

These relationship issues can be incorporated into the basic evaluation design. Project or program managers who work with evaluators must determine which of the above relationships to monitor during the course of the evaluation.

## Technical Issues

You will usually find it best to hire a professional to help you with technical matters. Managers, trainers, or change agents, however, must understand how to adapt to an evaluation if necessary. They need to make judgments about the quality of the evaluation and its credibility.

Cook and Campbell (1976) have provided a most useful conceptual scheme for analyzing the adequacy of evaluation studies. They extend the well-known validity criteria developed by Campbell and Stanley (1966; see also Weiss, 1972) and propose four criteria to assess evaluative studies.

- We review *internal validity* when variables other than those we are trying to test cause the results. This occurs, for example, when we test for the effects of quality circles and discover an increase in morale, only to find out later that a new incentive program really caused the change.
- *External validity* checks our ability to generalize across times, settings, and persons (e.g., will the program that worked in the Erie plant work in Phoenix?).
- *Statistical conclusion validity* refers to the appropriateness of the statistical test used.
- *Construct validity* refers to the problem of labeling (e.g., were the changes in the rating scales really an attitude change?).

Evaluators must also consider *face validity*. In its simplest form, this is the criterion of whether the results presented are believable to those who have to make decisions. One strategy for ensuring face validity calls for evaluators to make early interviews with those likely to use the evaluation for decision making to ask them specifically, "What kind of evidence do you need from this evaluation to make a decision to expand the program or close it?" If the decision maker says that all the morale data in the world will not help, that the only valuable information concerns cost savings, quality improvement, and better services, then the evaluation design should include such data.

## Linkage to Planned Change

A central thesis of this article, and of most managerial work, holds that change will occur whether it is planned or not. When change occurs unplanned, most managers respond well, fighting

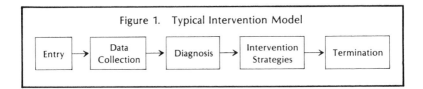

Figure 1. Typical Intervention Model

Entry → Data Collection → Diagnosis → Intervention Strategies → Termination

the crisis of the moment. Lost contracts, layoffs, retirements, accidents, and illness illustrate these uncontrolled events. But planning for change can also include an evaluation component. In this section, emphasis shifts to integrating evaluation into the planned change effort.

The flow of activities in Figure 1 represents the typical change intervention process from entry to termination. We believe that evaluation can be coupled to this process, as illustrated in Figure 2. In the initial phase of organization development (OD), entry, data collection, and diagnosis, the same data required by the OD specialist also serves the evaluator. Additional questions for evaluation may arise, but these usually relate to what the OD specialist needs.

Similarly, we noted previously that the input evaluation helps define the nature of the intervention, the process evaluation helps to build in short feedback loops that inform the program implementors while the program unfolds, and the product evaluation defines the work accomplished.

Because the four stages of evaluation parallel the planned change or OD so closely, this might deceive people into believing that the evaluation can be planned in parallel, too. This is not so. Planning for evaluation must begin at the entry stage. The evaluator must always operate at least a step ahead of the actual change process. We indicated in the previous example that the context evaluation helped us to understand what is at stake in introducing quality circles. When the entry process begins, we must ask such evaluation questions as "What outcomes can we expect?" and "What will be different?" Alternatively, if we were to install a quality circle into an operation in which management considers waste to be higher than it should be, for the purposes of our product evaluation we would need to determine a pre-intervention level of waste associated with production. The first measures we must take include the baseline assessment of what we expect to change over the course of the planned change activities.

Whether or not any manager supervises a change program matters less than the awareness of the uses of evaluation. Such knowledge can increase a manager's ability to work with

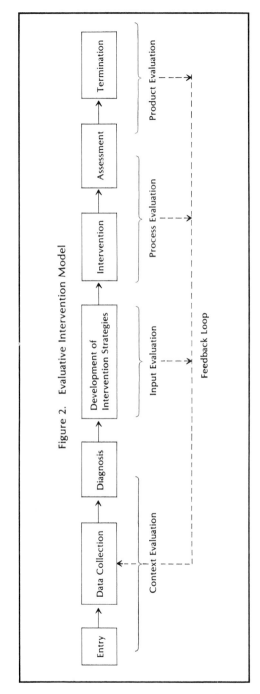

Figure 2. Evaluative Intervention Model

consultants, trainers, and other managers. Most organizations consider increasing accountability to be a positive value.

## Putting It All Together

The following illustration demonstrates how a project team can proceed in its evaluation planning.

Let's assume that preliminary discussion among the program staff and evaluators has already led to a contract sensitive to the technical, human, policy, and utility issues raised earlier. Discussions next focus on which questions the change agents will use in their entry and diagnosis. Management questions will focus on the nature of the intervention(s) to be used, the process data the change agents will need, and, finally, what they expect the overall program to achieve. For each goal, the evaluators will want to develop an evaluation program to give management and the change agents both information about progress made toward the objectives and outcome data on the objectives. Some managers may resist having to spell out their hoped-for outcomes in terms that can be assessed.

The following steps will complete the evaluation design:

1.   Formulate questions for each phase of the evaluation/ change process.
2.   Specify who will receive data related to each question.
3.   Specify the unit of organization from which data are to be collected for each question—i.e., the individual, team, division, department, or organization.
4.   Specify the type of measure to be used for each indicator related to each question—i.e., descriptive statements, mean, median, mode.
5.   Determine for each question whether everyone involved will be assessed or whether sampling will be used. If sampling is to be used, specify the statistical treatment.
6.   Determine the information cycle—e.g., how often and to whom the information must be provided.
7.   List program and evaluation questions, assessment periods, and feedback deadlines into a Gantt or PERT chart.

The process is launched!

## Conclusion

We designed this discussion to help you "demythologize" the world of evaluation. We hope that if you consider these issues in the development of an evaluation plan and then follow the steps as outlined, you can easily build evaluation into your planned change efforts.☐

## References

Campbell, D. T., & Stanley, J. C. *Experimental and Quasi-Experimental Designs for Research.* Chicago: Rand McNally, 1963.

Cook, T. D., & Campbell, D. T. The Design and Conduct of Quasi-Experiments and True Experiments in Field Settings. In M. D. Dunnette (Ed.), *Handbook of Industrial and Organizational Psychology.* Chicago: Rand McNally, 1976.

Weiss, C. H. *Evaluation Research.* Englewood Cliffs, N. J.: Prentice-Hall, 1972.

# Human Factors in Planning and Budgeting

James R. Cleaveland

*"Designers of an organization's planning process need to work with three dimensions—the right people, the right topics, and the right timing."*

The budget is one of the most underused tools of management—yet it lies at the heart of managing any large business. Its importance goes unrecognized because most managers know the budget only as a financial drill. The thesis of this article is that the budget can and ought to be used not only to foster financial control, but to strengthen management. In the pages that follow, I will discuss some of the approaches managers can use to get more out of budgeting than just a column of numbers that satisfies the company's controller.

As a financial drill, budgeting amounts to preparing a set of spending estimates. Unit managers make initial estimates, then submit them directly to department managers who review and summarize them for the controller. Financial analysts may then question the numbers in an effort to "squeeze the water out."

## Financial Control

In its simplest form, the budget is a spread sheet or list of expenditure categories (salaries, space, travel, equipment rental, contractual expenses, and so forth) with columns of numbers on the right. Column headings usually include Expenditure—Prior Year, Budget—Current Year, and Projected Budget. The last column is empty. On that column lies the focus of budgeting. The manager fills it with her or his budget estimates for the next year.

The Projected Budget column becomes the unit's financial plan: targets for the unit's expected spending. The plan is the basis for financial control. As the unit spends money during the operating year, the amounts for staff travel, supplies, and so forth are entered into the appropriate expenditure categories. The unit manager and her or his superiors receive a computer printout—usually on a monthly basis—that compares actual spending to projected spending: the budget.

The monthly report allows financial monitoring by the controller and department manager. They can decide whether

© 1983 NTL Institute

each manager is under, at, or above any targets (variance analysis). To aid variance analysis or financial control, managers may be required to "break out" their annual budget into monthly or quarterly amounts. Armed with variance analysis, higher levels of managers can exercise financial control by questioning the reasons for over- or underspending and asking unit managers to take any necessary corrective action.

## Budgeting and Planning

The mechanistic aspects of budgeting, while important, can overwhelm management uses. The need to fill in the "Projected Budget" column encourages arithmetical extrapolation of trends: one adds a few percentage points (for inflation) to the current budget.

One extremely important way managers can use the budget is to enhance planning. A planning process calls for developing goals, objectives, or expected results and a description (plan) of how to achieve those results. When the planning process is done well, budgeting is merely putting price tags on plans.

The planning process should begin well in advance of the budget to ensure time for careful and systematic thinking. The subordinate manager should also leave time for discussion with her or his superiors. Ideally, the "plan" should evolve from a series of discussions held over a period of weeks.

The planning process culminates when the manager describes what he or she expects to accomplish during a year and how to produce those accomplishments. Rather than "shoot from the hip," the manager should go through a logical progression of thought. That progression should have the following elements:

- *Goals.* These statements explain why the unit exists—its *raison d'etre.* Goal statements should allude to problems that would arise if the unit did not exist. This forces the manager to think about and justify how her or his unit contributes to the company's profitability and its long-term plan.
- *Objectives.* Within the context of these goals, each manager should know what mid-term and annual objectives or results he or she expects to achieve. If successful in achieving short-term results, the manager will attain middle-range objectives and justify the unit's existence. The superior can use discussion of goals and objectives to establish realistic levels of performance that stretch the manager's effort and force improvement in performance. Improvements listed may include both the increased results delivered or the strengthened management abilities—including

the adoption of better methods, improved personal development, or restructuring of responsibilities.

- *Plan.* The plan itself describes how the manager and her or his unit will achieve expected performance. Part of this process should include questioning current methods of operation and procedures and searching for improved productivity. The manager may also question current staffing levels, analyzing what would happen with a significant reduction or increase in budgeted resources. The plan allows superiors to question the manager's current operation and current staffing levels.

## Planning and Management

Too often, we equate planning merely with completing forms and/or producing a document. Document-driven planning tends to be as sterile, in terms of management, as numbers-driven budgeting. It provides information for superiors—department heads, the controller—but does little for unit *managers* or their subordinates.

With a little imagination, planning can reinforce several management needs. The planning process can help

- *communication* by structuring discussion between subordinates and superiors about business problems;
- *teamwork* by helping managers develop an appreciation of how different individuals or groups must work together to ensure the success of a unit or department;
- *change orientation* by preparing responses to new directions, new ways of doing things, or cutbacks in operations; and
- *management or organizational development* by helping instill new skills or improved attitudes and behavior among managers and subordinates.

Specialists in organization development use group process techniques built around management or team exercises to accomplish many of these same goals. A real-life management problem—a plan and budget—can achieve these same ends. It creates not only plans or budgets, but also organizational growth.

To achieve these nonfinancial results from planning, designers of an organization's planning process need to work with three dimensions of the planning process—the right people (who is involved), the right topics (what they do), and the right timing (when they are involved). No particular magic is required, but the general principle is one of top-down communication of strategies and plans. The planning should result in the connection of

| Figure 1. | Elements of Planning Process For Calendar Year | |
| Who | What | When |
| --- | --- | --- |
| Executives | Set growth profit objectives<br>Formulate strategies for competition, markets, technology, raw materials, acquisition, labor policies, and so forth | Spring |
| Managers | Participate with executives in planning strategies<br>Assess and plan for new requirements of changes in objectives and strategies<br>Coordinate planned actions to improve sales, reduce costs, and strengthen operations and management<br>Indicate resource needs (budgets) | Summer to Fall |
| Middle Management/ Supervisors | Assist managers in their planning/ budgeting<br>Prepare action plans for improvement<br>Set standards of performance for subordinates | Fall |
| Employees | Draft and discuss performance plans for middle managers/supervisors<br>Prepare and discuss personal development plans with superiors | Early Winter |

corporate or company-wide strategies—one link at a time—to successively lower levels in the organization. In this way, the individual employee's daily work, if done well, will help further corporate goals.

Figure 1 attempts to summarize one set of answers to the who, what, and when of the planning process. The method of communication matters less than the substance of planning. As I indicated above, these processes make better management tools when communication between levels in the management hierarchy takes place in face-to-face group meetings rather than by a purely mechanical, forms-driven process. This group discussion not only helps clarify needs and expectations between levels vertically, but improves communication and teamwork horizontally. The message, to paraphrase John Wayne, is to talk first and fill out forms later.□

## Bibliography

Giegold, W. C. *Management by Objectives: A Self-Instructional Approach.* New York: McGraw-Hill, 1978.

Vancil, R. F., & Lorange, P. Strategic Planning in Diversified Companies. *Harvard Business Review,* 1975.

Vancil, R. F., & Lorange, P. How to Design a Strategic Planning System. *Harvard Business Review*, September-October 1976, pp. 75–81.

# Affirmative Action: A Guide to Systems Change for Managers

Alice G. Sargent

*"Social and psychological research indicates that behavior changes precede attitude changes."*

Organizations currently take a piecemeal approach to affirmative action. A more effective approach would seek to integrate affirmative action across all organizational planning and management systems. Affirmative action can succeed only if management links it to the following: human resources management, which deals with having the right people at the right place at the right time; an effective performance management system, which includes both career development and appraisal; and the quality of work life, which concerns managing diversity and developing a multicultural work environment. Another approach, characterized by Juanita Kreps, former Secretary of Commerce, calls for "the second bottom line to be corporate social responsibility." The first line is profit; the second is a concern for such social factors as the effective use of human and environmental resources. At their roots, these approaches seek to generate awareness and then change the processes that have systematically failed to use fully our most important resource—people.

Affirmative action is a management problem, and as such proves the effectiveness or lack of it of most management practices within the organization. It spotlights the extent to which organizations make managment of human resources a priority. It raises intense interdepartmental issues and evokes turf protection when no highly effective collaboration exists. Hence, affirmative action programs work best when handled by a top management task force working in conjunction with an Equal Employment Opportunity (EEO) staff member. Without the management group, this staff member can only cajole, threaten, and beg to persuade managers to do their part.

Affirmative action covers all personnel management functions, including hiring, recruitment, training, firing, and awards. Organizations must assess and alter management practices in all of these areas to remove discriminatory practices. As Diane Herrmann, the Director of Office of Equal Opportunity Programs at the Department of the Treasury, told me recently,

---

© 1983 Alice G. Sargent

It is critical each year to analyze and target priorities and to focus resources. We are talking about changes in management practices that will take years. Each year we work at moving toward parity. One year the priority may be shortening the time frame from the current two to three years it may take to process discrimination complaints in the federal government. The next year, it may be emphasizing training which could include an upward mobility program, awareness training for managers and information on sexual harassment.

The following issues are central to developing a total systems affirmative action program:

• To what extent does the organization now value management of human resources?
• What is the current organizational culture for women, minorities, and white males? What would improve the climate for the employees and the organization?
• What sort of management resources does the organization need to make affirmative action work in recruiting, hiring, training, mentoring, monitoring the progress of women and minorities, and increasing the effectiveness of supervisors?

To deal with these questions, organizations need a total systems change model for affirmative action. I developed this approach when I worked for over four years with a large manufacturing company and have used segments of it in government agencies and several other manufacturing companies (see Figure 1).

### The Model for Total Systems Change

1. The best situation occurs when the organization appoints a *top management task force* to set goals and objectives for affirmative action, to develop a plan, and to ensure enforcement. Provide this team with the following: data on employee utilization; a workforce analysis by gender, race, and job classification to determine status of women and minorities; an availability study for each job group; and statistical information on selection, training programs attended, and promotion.

2. Conduct a *climate survey* to collect data on the quality of work life for women and minorities. Use group-sensing sessions to collect data so that group discussions occur in both homogeneous and heterogeneous groups.

3. Design an effective *recruiting and hiring* program that employs women and minority recruiters. Identify areas of underuse and analyze barriers.

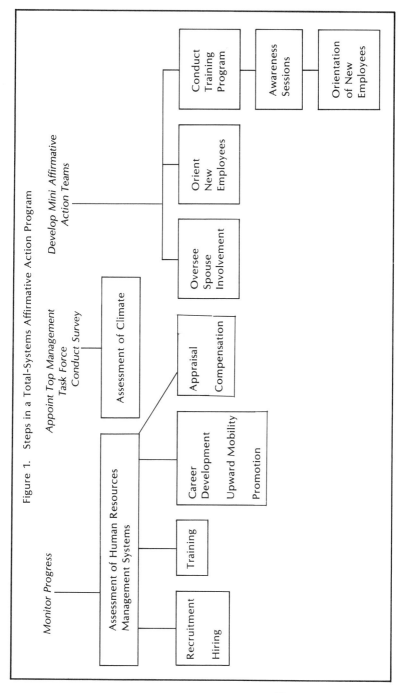

Figure 1. Steps in a Total-Systems Affirmative Action Program

4. Assess *management systems* for their effectiveness in the affirmative action effort, particularly the performance appraisal process that monitors equal employment opportunity and the career development system.

5. Provide *training* programs that include women and minority managers. Offer supervisor/woman manager pairs training, supervisor/minority manager pairs training, and supervisor/secretary workshops. Mandate team building for groups that include women and minorities. Conduct awareness sessions on racism, sexism, and antidiscrimination. Include training modules in ongoing management education programs.

6. Promote *supervisory* relationships that fulfill such human resource management functions as managerial coaching, career development, performance management, and development of high-potential but poor-performing employees.

7. Assess *upward-mobility* programs to evaluate the effectiveness of placement and targeting for jobs.

8. Provide such *alternative work schedules* arrangements as flexitime, job sharing, part-time work, and child care.

9. Encourage *network building* among women and minorities, such as minority managers' work groups.

10. Establish a *spouse-involvement program* to explain affirmative action and to deal with such issues as health benefits, financial planning, and men and women working and traveling together.

11. Create *affirmative action teams* to identify problems and carry out programs.

## 1. Top Management Task Force

The task force needs a key decision maker who can assure organizational commitment to affirmative action efforts. Neither personnel nor the Equal Employment Opportunity office should direct the task force, but they should help staff it. The task force's basic goals are to change the climate, structures, policies, practices, and interpersonal relationships within the organization to eliminate discrimination and to build a multicultural work environment.

Affirmative action task forces commonly begin work with off-site team building. For several days, team members work with external resources to increase their awareness of the issues and to build a better understanding among themselves. In one instance, an all-male task force recognized that they could not commit themselves to the effort until they discovered their own reasons for joining the affirmative action group. These men were asked to list 10 ways affirmative action would benefit them. For several men, the only obvious answer was that their helping promote women and minorities provided one measure of managerial effectiveness on their performance appraisal. Several managers wanted to understand the issues because women in their families had become deeply involved in consciousness-raising groups or had returned to work or to school. No one could suggest more than two reasons.

A reading list helped task force members learn about issues and, particularly, to identify male sex-role expectations. Some men in manufacturing doubted that women could perform the required physical work. The men had a lingering concern that women possessed less strength and energy. Therefore, task force members talked about the implications of such sex-linked characteristics as the physiological effects of testosterone and estrogen. The men thought that physical education programs and sex-role stereotypes in the educational system helped perpetuate the physical differences between the sexes. The most compelling logic presented was that the bona fide occupational requirement in most states for lifting ranges from 35–50 pounds; women routinely lift children or grocery bags that exceed 35 pounds.

The task force developed an action plan that established affirmative action goals for the next several years. The goal included the following: data collection on the climate for women and minorities; recruitment, with women helping recruit for the first time; hiring objectives; and an upward-mobility program that considered educational backgrounds other than engineering. The task force also planned training, supervisor/secretary workshops, family awareness groups in the plant, work groups for women managers, and "mini" affirmative action teams composed of male-female pairs and minority-white pairs for each manufacturing module that comprised approximately 75 employees.

## 2. Climate Survey

A team of women and men should interview white women and male managers and minority women and men—both individually and in groups—to identify the factors that contribute to an effective or ineffective work climate for women and minorities. A paper-and-pencil questionnaire does not help nearly as much as an interview, for it usually measures only the level of awareness, not the nature of the climate.

## 3. Recruitment Programs

When recruiting women and minorities, a central need is the identification of new networks and new contact persons. Networks that can lead organizations to minorities and to women exist in all areas. Organizations must also build credible relationships with women and minority faculty in universities who can refer their students to employers. These approaches suggest the depth and significance of affirmative action. It frequently requires a sizeable change in organizational attitudes and practices, because organizations generally lack the institutional mechanisms to draw on these resources and to radically shift old hiring patterns. If business continues to function the way it always has, it will not yield new patterns. Adopting affirmative action requires major restructuring.

## 4. Assess Management Systems: Performance Appraisal

Performance appraisal is the critical management system for effecting the changes sought in an affirmative action effort. If organizations do not evaluate and reward or punish managers for their behavior in implementing affirmative action, the system will lack accountability. Therefore, each manager must have a management by objectives (MBO) plan that emphasizes clear performance criteria for hiring, developing, promoting, and supervising women and minorities. Craig Schneier, professor of personnel and organizational behavior at the University of Maryland, told me (in 1976),

> In order to implement an effective affirmative action program, a manager's effort must be anchored to the reward system. The evaluation tool for this performance appraisal system makes explicit the degree to which the manager's behavior is responsive to the affirmative action plan.

## 5. Training Programs

Few white male managers have had much contact with women or minority professionals. Awareness workshops that address such issues as dealing with differences, style versus competence, dependency, control, and sexuality can help these managers. Furthermore, coalitions or support systems between women and minorities can increase these persons' awareness, skill, and effectiveness in communicating their feelings.

People in organizations have only begun to learn to work with a heterogeneous population; their social lives, however, have experienced little integration at all. Awareness provides the first step toward collaborative behavior across racial and gender differences. People do not yet understand differences in style, dress, language patterns, topics of conversations, and laughter— and this lack of familiarity keeps them apart.

*Issues To Be Covered in Awareness Workshops*

*Competence.* Since competent men and women may not have the same styles, they must be able to differentiate between style and competence. Significant gender differences occur in verbal and non-verbal behavior, namely in the areas of touch, interpersonal space, gaze, and body movement (Mayo & Henley, 1981). All of these elements have power and warmth and dimensions, but people interpret them differently, depending upon whether they are displayed by women or by men. Studies document that women can more skillfully decode non-verbal cues than men can. Therefore, since women are more partner-oriented, non-verbal behavior more likely affects women's responses than those of men. Eileen Morley (1976) of the Harvard Business School has pointed out that women tend to feel/think and men tend to think/feel. In other words, when you ask a woman what she is thinking, she may report her feelings; when you ask a man what he is feeling, he may report his thoughts. In a world dominated by male values, managers need to be able to recognize competent behavior in different styles.

*Dependency.* Under present practices of socialization, dependency typically is encouraged in girls and discouraged in boys. This has led to what has been labelled the "Cinderella Complex" in women and to "learned helplessness" in both genders when they face certain tasks. Men may experience learned helplessness in the work place, for example, when they must get coffee or deal with tears, whereas women may experience it when dealing with numbers and statistics. In terms used in transactional analysis, this leads to parent-child interactions rather than adult-adult behavior. Some examples of the types of communication follow.

- *Father-son.* Rather than acknowledge vulnerability, male managers adopt a can-do approach until they make themselves physically sick.
- *Mother-boy.* Men use women managers as mothers by telling them personal information instead of treating them as real colleagues with whom they also solve problems and perform tasks.
- *Father-girl.* Male managers become angry at women employees but also protect them.
- *Mother-boy.* Male managers defer to female managers in emotional situations in which pain is being expressed. The woman comforts an employee who cries, while the man steps aside.
- *Father-girl.* Women managers defer to male managers during policy making or budget appropriations.

*Control.* Men are used to being in control in mixed groups and women are not. Habitual patterns of responding to control become critical when men and women managers work together—and when women manage men.

To achieve communication among equals in work interactions, managers must eliminate the following behaviors:

• *Girl-girl or mother-girl.* Women managers fail to share their competence with one another.
• *Father-girl and mother-boy.* Men and women managers use sex for power and control.

A parent-child interaction may feel more comfortable because it is familiar and because it helps people deny that sexual attraction exists. Managers must explore these dimensions in awareness programs and use skill building to re-educate both men and women so that they can interact as adults.

*Sexuality.* Both actual incidents of sexual relationships that develop through work and fantasies and anxieties about it make sexuality a more pervasive issue in the work place than many anticipated. Sexuality always exists in male-female interactions, whether it takes the form of attraction or discounting. Rarely, indeed, do men and women not appraise one another sexually.

Without discussion, men and women may not understand why they are attracted to one another. Their fantasies may escalate, and they may feel that the pressure of feelings denies them a sense of choice. Yet we know that the reasons for this attraction may include curiosity, the desire for power or control, boredom, joy, and love. Talking about their motivation may defuse fantasies—or at least clarify the terms of the relationship. When people feel attracted to one another sexually in a way that interferes with work, the situation must be discussed for the sake of the people involved and of the organization.

### Differentiated Competency Based Training Modules

Sex-role stereotyping and differential socialization have caused some men and women to acquire different abilities. Business, government, and academe have valued masculine competence highly. Men and women, therefore, need training to recognize each other's skills, and organizations need to learn to value the "feminine" skills that men can learn to benefit from. We describe men and women who display skills associated with both masculine and feminine styles as *androgynous.*

To be androgynous, some women may need to learn to do the following:

- be powerful and forthright and have a direct, visible impact on others rather than function behind the scenes;
- initiate and take risks, despite their visibility and vulnerability;
- state their own needs and not back down, even if these needs are not immediately accepted;
- focus on a task and regard it as at least as important as the relationships of the people performing it;
- build support systems with other women and share knowledge with women rather than competing with them;
- analyze and generalize from experience;
- behave "impersonally" more often rather than always personalizing experiences;
- stop turning anger, blame, and pain inward, which causes them to reject feelings of suffering and victimization;
- reject feedback when it is inappropriate;
- respond directly with "I" statements rather than with blaming "you" statements;
- become effective problem solvers who are analytical, systematic, and directive rather than fearful or dependent; and
- stop such self-limiting behaviors as allowing oneself to be interrupted or laughing after making a serious statement.

To be androgynous, some men may need to learn to do the following:

- become aware of feelings rather than avoiding or suppressing them;
- regard feelings as basic and essential to life, rather than as impediments to achievement;
- accept a share of responsibility for "providing," but refuse total responsibility;
- assert the right to work for self-fulfillment rather than as a mere "provider";
- value an identity that is not defined totally by work;
- learn to accept failure at tasks without feeling they have failed as men;
- accept and express the need to be nurtured when feeling hurt, afraid, vulnerable, or helpless, rather than hiding those feelings behind a mask of strength and rationality;
- be close to both men and women;
- listen actively and be empathic without feeling responsible for problem solving;
- build support systems and friendships with other men, sharing competence without competition;
- personalize experience, rather than assuming that the only valid approach to life and interpersonal contact is "objective";

- accept the emotional, spontaneous, and irrational as valid parts of themselves to be explored and expressed as needed and to openly express their feelings of love, anger, pain, joy, loneliness, and dependency;
- understand how men value women as "validators of masculinity," havens from the competitive male world, the expressive partners;
- understand the impact that being male has on shaping their lives and their responses; and
- nurture and actively support men and women in their efforts to change (Sargent, 1977).

## 6. Supervisory Relationships

The most critical component for women's and minorities' success is their relationships with their supervisors. This comes as no surprise given what we know about the importance of "expectation effects" in teacher-pupil relationships and intimate relationships. Expectation effects critically affect success or failure on the job, in school, and in marriage. As Robert Rosenthal (1969) reported on IQ scores, the children who received higher numbers—although the scores were false—improved more quickly because of teacher expectations. The so-called "bright" rats learned mazes more quickly because of researcher expectations. Behavioral scientists regard the supervisory relationship as a major factor in women's or minorities' success.

Research on personnel interviewers by Rosen and Jerdee (1974) underscores how interview bias can determine whether women or men enter a system. Furthermore, supervisors may hold the same stereotypes as the interviewers. For example, interviewers in industry expect men to be effective because they believe men understand financial matters, analyze situations, like science and math, know how to set long-range goals, and want to get ahead. Characteristics attributed to women include enjoyment of routine, sensitivity to criticism, timidity, jealousy, overemotionalism, sensitivity to the feelings of others, a tendency to quit more frequently than men, and a propensity to put family matters ahead of the job. In fact, women do not have more job instability than men, and they do not necessarily enjoy routine more than men. Managers who hold such stereotypes generally act upon them. Male supervisors report that they feel more sympathetic when home life interferes with a man's work. The manager helps male employees by suggesting such solutions to the problem as different kinds of services or counseling. The supervisor probably thinks, "After all, he's the primary breadwinner." But supervisors commonly hold an "I knew it was going to happen" attitude when a woman's home life interferes with her work.

To illustrate the sex-linked differences in expectations of supervisors, Kathryn Bartol and Anthony Butterfield (1976) reversed the names of men and women in a number of case studies. They found sex-linked differences regarding assumed effectiveness on two components of managerial behavior: (a) initiating structure (considered masculine) and (b) showing concern for others (considered feminine). In the initiating structure exercise (a), participants were asked to rate managers for effectiveness based on the three weeks they spent in a new office finding out what was happening and then developing a reorganization plan. Only the names of the managers were changed; the behaviors remained the same. The participants rated the men as more effective than the women, whom they described as autocratic, taking too much initiative, and undemocratic. Sexual prejudice cuts both ways. In contrast, regarding concern for others (b), the participants rated the women managers as effective when they sought the opinions and feelings of others and became involved with employees who had problems. But participants described a male manager who used the same approach as wishy-washy and as becoming overly involved.

The solution is not for men to give up their proactive organizing style or for women to become directive at the expense of feelings and concern for others. Both sexes would enhance their effectiveness by learning the attitudes and behaviors generally attributed to the other sex and by developing a blend. Compensatory training can help both men and women develop qualities of so-called "masculine" independence and "feminine" nurturance.

Similar issues exist in building a multicultural environment across races. The values learned from the experience could also change the nature of organizational life. The majority group of white people subconsciously develops an arrogance that could be tempered by humility. White people also tend to rely too much on rationality—which could be mediated by the "common sense," more natural approach of many minorities.

## 7. Upward Mobility Programs: Career Development

When management seeks the effective promotion of women and minorities, it will find unclear career paths and a lack of long-range human resource planning. For effectiveness and for morale to improve, all employees must have a sense of where they are going in the organization and what it takes to get there. This comes from specific information about career paths, targeted jobs, and developmental assignments that lead to specific positions.

## 8. Alternative Work Schedules

While women have widely supported alternative work opportunities, men now find them valuable, too. The specific alternative work schedules that organizations have tried and found successful include flexible working hours, the compressed work week, permanent part-time work, and job sharing. The organization benefits from these options through increased productivity; higher morale; retaining highly competent employees who only want part-time work because of other demands in their life; reduced absenteeism, tardiness, and turnover; and a progressive image that may attract other employees. Individuals benefit from the opportunity to be at home when children arrive from school; the opportunity for two-career couples to share child care; more leisure time for education, home life, and developing other sides of one's identity; commuting at different hours; the opportunity to work during the hours of the day when one feels most effective; and opportunities for additional work.

## 9. Coalition Building Among Women and Minorities

Networks for women and minority managers help both new and old employees. Such groups also help the organization to recruit, orient, and retain employees. Groups of minority or women managers can identify key concerns, ranging from promotion to maternity leave to part-time work.

Over a period of time, coalitions can alter the typical pattern of entry into the system for minorities and women. New female employees often try to succeed in the white male-dominated workplace without first turning to other women or minorities for friendship and support. In this process of proving themselves, many women take on necessary so-called "masculine" characteristics when dealing with power and conflict and shed some of their valuable "feminine" behaviors of nurturance and spontaneity. This causes them to suffer a great deal from a sense of frustration and failure.

Many women report that they avoid being branded as too seductive or nurturing by reducing their emotional responses when they are the only women in a group. One corporate affirmative action program dealt with the problem of the lone woman by focusing on a natural work group—such as a mechanical engineering department. When a woman prepared to join the group, members talked about the issues involved both before and after she joined. The group held follow-up sessions because instances of isolation developed quite quickly even when they were temporarily solved. She just wasn't "one of the boys" and thus part of the informal communication network.

Women's networks offer an important way to deal with the problems of isolation, loneliness, and pressure to conform to male norms. They provide a sanctuary where women can express feelings of frustration, anger, or loneliness in a concerned environment. Because they participated in these coalitions, a number of women indicated that they felt better able to hold on to their own style and sense of self-worth rather than merely adopting the dominant male patterns.

Affirmative action efforts highlight tension and the lack of communication between women and minorities. Often, style differences create barriers. Sometimes black men and white women fear that they will be used by each other. The relationship becomes complicated by fantasies about power and sexual attraction. Women think black men can have power because they are men; black men think white women have access to power by asking their men for it. Both groups would benefit from joining forces and acknowledging that neither group has had much access to information or power.

## 10. Spouse Involvement

Organizations often like to keep the personal lives of their employees quite separate from their work lives, but women's entrance into the workforce necessarily combines the two. The greatest concern develops when men and women travel together on business trips and experience more relaxed norms and opportunities for closer contact. Instead of pretending that sexual attraction and sexual harassment could never arise, organizations that have dealt directly with such issues have been able to defuse some of the fantasies and problems. Spouse involvement in affirmative action programs has altered the traditional split between work and home life and has improved morale and cooperation. In affirmative action programs, spouses have also discussed mobility policy, which can help them prepare for a move. Other significant topics include child-care policies, cafeteria benefits, flexitime for two-career couples, and health benefits.

## 11. Affirmative Action Teams

One organization established male-female and black-white pairs for each department. The teams informed new employees about affirmative action activities. The teams also identified the development of occupational stereotyping by noting what became women's work in the plant. For example, quality control jobs quickly became women's work. The teams also monitored the progress of women and minorities and served as troubleshooters.

When possible, each team included the technical training director. In a manufacturing environment, one training director obtained additional technical training for women. The program was so successful that men also sought the training. Affirmative action provided everyone with an opportunity to improve themselves and altered ineffective management training practices.

## Summary

In the total systems approach, affirmative action becomes a management problem. The organization views women and minorities as the experts who can solve this problem with important assistance from the human resources office. The goal is for key decision makers to take on the problem and to use their analytical and interpersonal competence to solve it. All decision makers become involved so that no one feels her or his territory has been invaded.

Social and psychological research indicates that behavior changes precede attitude changes. Action may elicit a different kind of response from the habitual one. Changes in the reward system can produce further changes in both behavior and attitudes. The first phase of change is to increase awareness of and responsibility for problems. Organizations maintain momentum through such incentives as performance appraisal, coalitions among women and minorities, and temporary structures within the system—e.g., a mini affirmative action team. Organizations need at least three to five years to produce initial changes.

This approach benefits the white male who now holds power in the organization by increasing his life options and his work options. It also helps women and minorities who seek equal power and influence in the workplace. The total systems approach offers people the chance to change organizational patterns of majority dominance and minority dependence and frustration.

A reallocation of power and influence occurs along with the development of new networks across more heterogeneous segments of the American population. A shifting of the organizational norms to encompass members of the new workforce also occurs. America appears to be experiencing a value shift: The U. S. is no longer a melting pot, but is actually developing a multicultural environment.□

## References

Bartol, K. M., & Butterfield, D. Sex Effects in Evaluating Leaders. *Journal of Applied Psychology*, 1976, 61(4).

Mayo, C., & Henley, N. M. *Gender and Nonverbal Behavior*. New York: Springer-Verlag, 1981.

Morley, E. Women's Thinking and Talking. *Harvard Business School, Case No. 9-477-055*. Boston, Mass.: Harvard Case Clearing House, 1976.

Rosen, B., & Jerdee, T. H. Effects of Applicant's Sex and Difficulty of Job on Evaluations of Candidates for Managerial Positions. *Journal of Applied Psychology*, 1974, 59(4), 511.

Rosenthal, R., & Jacobson, L. *Pygmalion in the Classroom*. New York: Holt, Rinehart & Winston, 1969.

Sargent, A. G. *Beyond Sex Roles*. St. Paul, Minn.: West Publishing, 1977.

## For Further Reading

Aries, E. Male-Female Interpersonal Styles in All-Male, All-Female and Mixed Groups. In A. G. Sargent (Ed.), *Beyond Sex Roles*. St. Paul, Minn.: West Publishing, 1977.

Bartolome, F., & Evans, P. A. L. Must Success Cost So Much? *Harvard Business Review*, March–April 1980.

Jackson, B., & Hardiman, R. Racial Identity Development: Implications for Managing the Multiracial Work Force. *The NTL Managers' Handbook*. Arlington, Va.: NTL Institute, 1983.

Leavitt, H. J., & Lipman-Blumen. A Case for the Relational Manager. *Organizational Dynamics*, 1980, 27–41.

Sargent, A. G. *The Androgynous Manager*. New York: AMACOM, 1981.

Wilkins, R. *A Man's Life: An Autobiography*. New York: Simon & Schuster, 1982.

# The Clonal Effect in Organizations

Natasha Josefowitz

*"When employers must hire someone with whom they will work, they tend to look for someone with whom they will have a fair chance of getting along, of communicating well, and of sharing basic values. . . ."*

It's all around us. We are the consistent perpetrators of it—we are its constant victims. And yet we do not see it. When it's first pointed out to us, we rationalize it away. When confronted with it repeatedly, we eventually admit it and then have no options left but to become aware, conscious of our unconscious, and to act—to do the uncomfortable, the foreign, the difficult thing.

What is the clonal effect? It is the tendency of individuals, groups, and organizations to replicate themselves or others close to them whenever the opportunity to do so presents itself. The *American Heritage Dictionary* defines a clone as a "group of organisms descended asexually from a single common ancestor." A cell that reproduces itself clones.

Let us start this discussion with the most evident form of cloning in organizations. Every time a manager must hire or promote someone from a pool of available candidates, two criteria enter into the decision. One is the competence to do the required job, which can include supplementary competence or skills not provided by the rest of the staff or team. The other is the fit between the person hired and the rest of the organization. This fit depends upon how comfortable the employer feels with the person hired or promoted. Fit is in the eye of the beholder— how can a person measure fitness except by intuition? And on what is that intuition based? I do not argue with the legitimacy of using intuition—far from it, because for me feelings are valid signals from unconscious that we must examine and understand to make a decision—and then act on them or not.

In other words, we can only control our actions to the extent that we become aware of our unconscious motivations. Forces unrecognized by us dictate much of our behavior. When we have concrete evidence of our unconscious behavior, we have the opportunity to control outcomes instead of being controlled by our unidentified motivations.

Recent research findings show that people are hired according to gender—not in terms of pure discrimination against one sex or

© 1979 Natasha Josefowitz

another, but in terms of "fit." Male managers are hired more often if they will have male subordinates, and women if they will have female subordinates (Rose & Andiappan, 1978). The fit relates to the unconsciously perceived comfort levels of the subordinates and their ability to communicate better with someone of their own gender. I do not say that this perception is erroneous, but we must note that it means that females will seldom be hired as managers in male-dominated organizations—and that this will produce unconscious discrimination.

When employers must hire someone with whom they will work, they tend to look for someone with whom they will have a fair chance of getting along, of communicating well, and of sharing basic values such as work ethics, standards of quality, imagination, precision, punctuality, dress, humor, politics, leisure activities, and so forth—the list is endless, and so are the possible prejudices. Whom do we trust? Those whom we can understand, those who are most predictable. Who are these people? Those most like ourselves (Kanter, 1977). Stop a moment and think of your closest friends. What do you base your comfort and trust on? Differences exist, but you share similarities that make your friends known to you in a way that some people can never be known—so these others must remain strangers to you. You will not hire these "strangers," nor will you be hired or promoted if you do not fit the comfort level of your employer. The discrimination known to women, to blacks, to minorities is not necessarily based on sex or color alone, but is frequently based unconsciously on "otherness" or "differentness."

"I would not work for a woman." "I would not hire a black." "I would not go out with a Jew." These are statements of discomfort with the unfamiliar upon whom we project a different value system that we believe precludes our understanding each other.

Now think of your team, group, or organization. What similarities exist? What differences? Who is friendly with whom? Who is the last person hired—and by whom? Do you see the clonal effect operating between these two people—one of whom may be yourself?

The joke about bankers says that if you don't already look like one, they won't hire you. We talk about the "Madison Avenue" type, the cloak-and-suiter, the salesman, the social worker, and we all know what we mean by these stereotypes. Stereotypes perpetuate the species, for each will keep cloning itself until stopped by its own awareness of that behavior.

Is it by chance that many of the Kennedy men came from Harvard and played touch football and that many of the Carter men came from Georgia and played softball? Is it sheer coincidence that in some companies golf is the game, while in others it's tennis, or bowling, or drinking beer after work?

When hiring a new assistant professor at my university, I realized that our most dynamic professor felt the candidates were too quiet and wondered if they were depressed, while our most quietly thoughtful colleague worried about their hyperactivity. The one I liked best just happened to be short and freckled like me.

The clonal effect does not stop at reproducing oneself; we also tend to clone those who were or are close to us. In choosing a mate we unconsciously select people with a physical and/or psychological resemblance to a parent or sibling. Frequently, the youngest boy of a family will tend to select a woman who has a younger brother and she in turn will look for someone who has an older sister. Family positions tend to become replicated in our marital relationships because of the familiarity—and comfort—we recreate for ourselves. We clone the sibling into the spouse.

Just as individuals and families tend to replicate themselves, so do groups and organizations. They tend to replace lost members with people who have similar characteristics or to add people who would not change the dynamics of the usual patterns of communications too much. Even when organizations seek to add people with complementary skills or knowledge to work units, a certain comfort level of predicted interactions is maintained.

We often talk of race, gender, and ethnic origin as bases for discrimination; we do not discuss class as frequently. Yet class is as much a factor in our selecting mates, friends, and colleagues— and in hiring and promotion practices—as the more publicly evident characteristics of race, gender, and ethnic origin. Because we have more difficulty defining class, the cues are subtler and discrimination becomes based on the identification of often subtle clues as giveaways of class. A walk, a choice of words, a piece of clothing, a look, a joke, a mannerism, the way one enters a restaurant, orders, eats, pays the check, talks to the waiter— most of us will recognize class.* *The prejudice does not lie in the acknowledgement of the difference, but in the preference of one over the other—discrimination results from acting upon this preference.*

Again, people tend to find comfort with a person who comes from a similar background. We mostly trust people from the same class as our own. In hiring and promotion, classes will tend to clone themselves, too.

People feel comfortable with others of their own age, yet this does not seem to be as pervasive a cloning need as the others,

* Here the term "class" means belonging to a specific socioeconomic segment of society.

perhaps because all of us have been younger and hope to be older. We attach less stigma to age. Youth connotes high energy and potential; age connotes maturity and wisdom. We all have come in frequent contact with people of all ages, and this in itself makes age not quite as different and foreign a factor as race, sex, class, or ethnic origin. Although—as many of us know—the generation gap can be a painful reality, and we often feel little in common with "different generations," discrimination against "age" results from stereotypes about "the old," not from cloning.

Although the clonal effect reduces diversity and therefore reduces the resources for creativity, concious cloning might be appropriate at the following times:

- when communication is poor, and people need to understand each other easily;
- when language barriers exist;
- when the culture of the organization or the country it is located in differs greatly from one's own;
- when one feels a great deal of uncertainty;
- when the margin of error for decision making is small;
- when the time span for decision making is short;
- when interdependence is substantial; and
- when no need for diversity or creativity exists.

In multinational companies, unless the situation is prohibited by law, top management will often be of the same nationality as the national origin of the company. People in organizations need a "predictable other," and, as we have seen, that "other" can only be someone familiar. Even with several of the above factors at work, however, we must take great care not to violate affirmative action, local politics, and one's own and others' value systems.

We must make the clonal effect a thing of the past—when we were unconscious. Let us look for the discomfort of diversity, the challenge of the different, for the potential for disagreement. Only then will women, blacks, Hispanics, native Americans, Asians, people of different religions, the handicapped, the young, the old, the skinny, the fat, the oddly dressed, and the foreign have a chance to "be"—a chance to "do" so that all of us can contribute our differences and become enriched by them.☐

### References

Berscheid, E., & Walster, E. *Interpersonal Attraction*. Reading, Mass.: Addison-Wesley, 1969.

Kanter, R. M. *Men and Women of the Corporation*. New York: Basic Books, 1977. Pp. 48, 63, 68.

Rose, G. L., & Andiappan, P. Sex Effects on Managerial Decisions. *Academy of Management Journal*, 1978, 2, 104–112.

# The New Work Force: Strategies for the 1980s

Elsie Y. Cross

*"When the transition proceeds from homogeneity to pluralism in the work place, managers must develop new approaches to integrate different kinds of people."*

Early on a gray Monday morning the Chief Executive Officer (CEO) of a major Fortune 500 corporation sat at his desk, frowning as he read the list of recommended promotions before him. Summoning the responsible department manager, he demanded an explanation of the list.

"Why is it, out of a group of 20 managers, that there is only one white woman and only one non-white person recommended for promotion?"

The department manager shifted from foot to foot, uncertain how to respond.

"Well, sir, it seems that we don't have any other qualified white women or black men and women or other people of color who are eligible. These men have . . ."

The CEO interrupted impatiently. "Not eligible? After all we've spent on affirmative action and equal employment opportunity programs, and all the training we've invested in bringing these women and black men along—you tell me there are none eligible for promotion." He waved the list indignantly. "I want to know why Lorna Jones's name isn't on here. And Bill Miller—I think he's one of the best young managers we've got. Black or white."

The department manager was nervous. "Uh, well, it seems Lorna accepted another offer recently, right before the review. She told somebody in her section that if she got promoted she'd have to report to Hinkson. And you know Hinkson," he said with a nervous laugh. "He does like the ladies, sir."

The CEO didn't laugh. "You mean we lost a top-flight manager because some old fool can't keep his hands off women? Is that stuff still going on down there? Haven't I made it clear we won't tolerate it here? We can't afford to pour money into training new people and have them leave because our white male managers can't adjust. What about Miller?"

"Miller's going over to Acme Corporation. His supervisor said he didn't seem to fit into the work group—dressed a little too flashy, for one thing, and his way of speaking—well, the other guys in the group just didn't feel comfortable with him, sir. He

© 1983 NTL Institute

was bringing in some new ideas they hadn't heard about too. He's a good manager, that's for sure. It's a shame to lose him."

The CEO was on his feet. "Damn it, Smith, we're throwing good money after bad around here. I won't have it—you've got to figure out what's wrong and fix it. Somebody's got to do something and do it fast."

"Yes sir. I've got another problem that doesn't look as apparent as the other two. It involves Martin Green, the engineer who insists on flexitime and who took six months off when his wife—I mean they, ha, ha—had a baby."

"Well what's the problem with him? He seems to be the kind of person we need around here."

"Well, he's smart enough, but he's as committed to the nuclear freeze and to environmental issues as he is to the work he's doing for us. I want 200% out of him, not 125%. Next he'll be organizing a day-care center. Oh, for the good old days when we didn't have this to worry about!"

So Smith went back to the division with an order to "do something." He tried this and he tried that. A training program here, a sensitivity workshop there, Theory X, Theory Y, and finally Theory Z. And still good people left, and the jokes around the water cooler stayed off-color, and the "old boys" kept on networking. And worst of all, the company did not take seriously the competent and exciting people who differ from the white male norm. And the CEO got angrier and angrier, and the Fortune 500 company kept slipping in productivity and creativity.

This scenario is being played out in American business across the country, as white women and people of color—black men and women, Hispanics, Asian-Americans, Pacific Islanders—enter the work force in ever increasing numbers, especially at the lower levels of supervision. The reverberations of change have just begun to affect the ranks. These different people have changed the face of the American industrial/business community. They have clearly indicated that we have a new work force that differs in many important ways from the old work force—which was primarily white and male and socialized with a homogeneous set of norms. The interaction between the new work force and the older work force generates stress and tension and creates a new set of problems for managers. The new work force also creates new opportunites, which are barely recognized and then only by a few forward-thinking managers and executives.

I can describe the new work force more easily by stating what it is *not* than by stating what it is. It is not predominantly or exclusively made up of middle-class and working-class white men. The new work force includes representatives of many races, of both sexes, of various ethnic groups—some whose native language is not American English—and of a variety of socio-economic and class backgrounds. Some of this new breed have physical disabilities and some are white men and young people who grew up during the 70s with a different set of values than the traditional white male manager. They have refused or have been unable to "melt" into the work force. If management ignores them, it will lose valuable resources and face potential conflict. If management accepts their presence, it must find new ways to use human resources creatively. Members of the new work force retain their own individuality, with all the discrete characteristics of individuals. And they have begun to call on their own particular experience—of being female, of being black, of being younger or older, of being from a different culture—to enrich the life and vitality of American corporations.

Managers whose training and experience came from a more homogeneous work force do not always know how to work effectively with new colleagues, subordinates, and bosses. They often feel confused because they receive hostile reactions to what seem like innocent jokes or to the subtle behaviors that "put down" or discount white women and men and women of color. These managers sometimes feel threatened by the new work force and may also feel that these very different people are not competent to do the job. They also know that white men now compete with these different kinds of people and may sometimes lose to them. These managers have old biases and prejudices that have often been built into the organization norms and therefore seem "normal." Their confusion is compounded by different styles of solving problems or by different sets of values, which challenge cherished assumptions about success, relationships, and style.

Because of this, the managerial climate in American business is often highly charged. An energy level, a tension exists that, if not channelled and controlled, becomes debilitating and therefore unproductive. In the past, organizations masked this tension with apparent uniformity and homogeneity—white men only competed with other white men—and with what seemed like endless resources and the ability of business to hide errors and deficits by pouring in more resources. Management can, however, effectively use this tension through carefully planned methods to enhance the competence and productivity of those within the organization. This effort requires the involvement of the total organization in the implementation of an effective management program to develop harmonious and productive relationships among all the factions of the work force—and it cannot be aimed at one group alone. This total organizational effort must have commitment and involvement at the top and throughout the organization. The change program must aim to change the culture and normative structure of the organization and to help managers and workers see that "difference" is positive, exciting, challenging, and creative.

## The Buck Stops Here—At the Top

Organizations need to use diversity to help managers and workers deal effectively with change. With the need for a radical restructuring of our industrial base, managers' ability to handle change as reflected in a diverse work force can lead to more flexible and technologically sophisticated organizations.

An effective program to enable an organization to develop smoothly functioning, productive relationships hinges on the belief that attention to differences results in an increased ability to handle conflict constructively, in reduced negative energy, in the ability of managers to mobilize workers more productively, and in the ability of the organization to handle a variety of stress-induced issues. It can also result in white women and people of color feeling greater job satisfaction and believing that the upper levels of management and responsibility respond to them. Studies have demonstrated that significant and lasting organizational change occurs *only* when sanctioned and monitored by those in the organization who have the *authority* to reward change and the *prestige* to demonstrate the desired, appropriate behaviors in their own work lives (Dalton, 1976).

A change effort that focuses on managing the new work force, therefore, begins when top managers envision what the new organizational values and structures would be like. For example, women and people of color would occupy supervisory and management positions throughout the organization. Their work assignments would be creditable and highly visible and risk would be distributed equally. The reward system would recognize skills and abilities that differ from the norm. Managers should explore their own attitudes about race, gender, class, and age—and other differences.

The overwhelming majority of those who hold the top positions in U. S. corporations are white men. They have not had to examine their assumptions and attitudes about working with people who differ from themselves, especially as peers or as bosses.

Many of these top managers—and employees at every level in the organization—experience varying degrees of cognitive dissonance: They think or believe one thing, but feel another. Most people, including most managers, *think* that all people are equal, but *feel* that "some of us are more equal than others." Many white men believe that white women and men and women of color are hired and promoted to fill quotas and therefore cannot also possess competence and ambition. Managers commonly believe that people who come from different cultures are "passive" and therefore not competent enough to manage. Most people tend to evaluate those "different" from themselves as "inferior," especially when the persons making these judgments hold "superior" positions.

These assumptions and values need explication and exploration. Organizations must debunk old myths. When people see others who differ from the norm holding positions of power and authority, they experience initial discomfort in competing on equal terms with those formerly considered incompetent—and this provides a significant experience for learning about and appreciating differences.

## We're All in This Together

Even as top management explores the issues outlined above, change efforts must provide activities that involve all levels of the organization. A variety of formats serves this purpose: workshops, individual interviews, same race/gender groups, and such follow-up activities as seminars, discussion groups, support groups, and ad hoc task groups. Whatever the context, the purpose remains the same: to provide participants with a *personal* awareness of difference, to equip them with skills to cope effectively with both their own attitudes and behaviors and those of the people around them, and to devise ways of altering the environmental climate of their work settings so that the organization can more effectively use the talents and resources of all members of the work group.

When the program takes hold, white males will communicate more openly with women and with people of color and all employees will gain an increased ability to address problems of race and gender. This behavior develops trust. Women and people of color begin to hear more candid information about their performance and can consequently become more direct and open with their feelings and ideas. They feel more relaxed, for they no longer need to guard against insults and thoughtless comments, and, therefore, they have more energy to manage and to work. As white men become aware of and sensitive to different people's needs and styles, they will likely see white women and men and women of color as serious contributors and valuable resources.

When the change process moves from the top managers who set generalized goals to all employees who turn these goals into specific objectives, a number of things will happen. First, social ties within the organization shift (Dalton, 1976). Old relationships that supported old patterns of behavior give way to new relationships that support the new behaviors. For example, managers report that lunch groups become more integrated after several months of work on diversity; subgroups formed to work on specific tasks become diverse; work pairings (male/female) work more smoothly. If top management demonstrates that the organization will clearly reward non-sexist, non-racist, non-classist attitudes and behaviors, those individuals who can adopt these new attitudes and behaviors will seek out one another. These non-oppressive behaviors include dropping demeaning language, giving support to women and others in meetings, challenging inappropriate jokes and language, using nonsexist language in written communication. This "seeking out" enables employees to reinforce the new behaviors, to practice new ways of working and relating, and to form new social groups that reward the new behaviors.

Characteristic of this process is a period in which the organization experiences an upsurge of self-doubt and lowered self-esteem. As people become more sensitive to demeaning behavior, or to ways in which the organization continues to reward old habits, they may feel a sense of hopelessness, a sense that things will never change. When managers begin to realize that old behaviors and attitudes are no longer valued, they may lose their confidence in their own abilities. Top management may not give clear reasons for demanding new behaviors, and even when it does, some individuals may be unwilling or unable to change their habitual mode of thinking and acting. Successful change programs must include structured groups that allow the participants to practice new behaviors—such as small work groups and task forces—and also to form new support groups that can serve to reassure, encourage, and affirm the desired behaviors.

While the total change effort progresses, the organization must begin to institutionalize the values and skills and new behaviors identified throughout the program. Managers and their subordinates can develop a variety of mechanisms, including a "mix" group responsible for identifying problems and making recommendations for change, work teams that can serve as models for other teams using new skills, one-on-one consultation with managers and supervisors in the use of new reward mechanisms, and other methods internal people can use to develop responsibility for the change process.

This change program is based on organization dynamics theory and practice, and has been modified to heighten the following basic issues:

- The authority dynamics—power, influence, leadership—present in all experimental groups can combine with race, gender, and power issues to provide a powerful catalyst for examining discrimination in organizational contexts.
- The group dynamics of experimental learning both increase the white male's feeling of being threatened by those different from him and provide an arena for understanding and thereby reducing the anxiety associated with the threat.
- White women and people of color in socialized positions similar to white men's experience opportunities to test assumptions, to learn skills in being powerful and assertive, and to have successful experiences in providing leadership to task groups. They also receive support both from those like them and from those different from them.
- Coalitions of different kinds of people demonstrate productivity and facilitation in such different kinds of work as decision making, problem solving, improved climate for feedback, skill building, and so forth.
- Conflict and confrontation, no longer avoided and feared, can become creative forces for discovering different philosophies, values, and approaches.

Such a change program must be located in the management chain to support the affirmative action program. It should spur both management development and the responsible use of resources. Ultimately, this kind of change will produce an improved "bottom line" and a healthier work climate.

All of us continually influence the attitudes and behaviors of those with whom we come in contact. We can use this influence to help corporations and their managers find solutions to their management problems and simultaneously provide employees with opportunities to broaden their social horizons and to enhance their managerial effectiveness.

When the transition proceeds from homogeneity to pluralism in the work place, managers must develop new approaches to integrate different kinds of people. New and different styles of management will inevitably use fully the unique skills of all individuals. Women and men of color and white women continue to gain access to the middle and upper ranks of management and know that their skills and intelligence are valued. The acceptance of their diversity will help create a climate for improved communications, for more individual creativity, for new and different options for doing things, and for a more exciting and profitable workplace.□

## Reference

Dalton, G. W. Influence and Organization Change. In J. B. Ritchie & P. Thompson (Eds.), *Organizations and People*. New York: Est Publishing, 1976. Pp. 363–387.

## For Further Reading

*Consultations on the Affirmative Action Statement of the U. S. Commission of Civil Rights, Vol. I: Papers Presented February 10 and March 10–11, 1981*. Washington, D. C.: U. S. Government Printing Office, 1982.

Cross, E. *The Impact of Black Managers on White Organizations for Creative Change—Or Re-Defining Corporate Strategies for Organization Equality*. Unpublished paper, copyright 1979.

Harrison, R. Choosing the Depth of Organizational Intervention. *The Journal of Applied Behavioral Science*, 1970, 6(2), 181–202.

Jamison, K. Affirmative Action Program: Springboard for a Total Organizational Change Effort. *OD Practitioner*, 1978, 10(4), 1–8.

Kirkham, K. Rethinking Your "Good Guy" Image: Attempts to Achieve Racial Equality Must Recognize that the Actions of both Whites and Minorities Should Be Examined. *Exchange*, Fall/Winter 1977, 20–23.

# Managing Diversity: What's in It for You?*

Nancy Brown

*". . . learning about issues of racism and sexism involves learning about* all *managing processes, as they relate to* all *employees."*

I want to be clear at the outset that my position is one of *advocating* the inclusion of racism and sexism as topics in the development of ourselves as managers. The more I read the literature, scan the research, listen to others, and reflect on my own èxperience as a manager and as a consultant to organizations, the more strongly I conclude that these two subjects lie close to the heart of becoming an effective manager in any segment of the economy.

## Background

For years, U. S. managers have been predominantly white and male, and they have managed, in many cases, people like themselves—other white males. In the last 10–20 years, the people being managed have become significantly more diverse. Blacks, Hispanics, Asian-Americans, and other people of color have come to constitute a higher percentage of the work force. Women of color and white women are entering the economy in greater numbers than before and often in traditionally male jobs. Now organizations must *manage diversity* rather than homogeneity.

Not only the people being managed but also managers are becoming a more diverse group—albeit at a much slower rate of change. Despite these changes, the vast majority of management development programs today do not cover the management of diversity, nor do they include any mention of racism and sexism in organizations. This is true of publicly offered programs, in-house programs given by internal or external resource people, and university-sponsored programs. While the last five years have witnessed a trend toward more coverage of these topics, it is clearly a trickle—not a river—and the majority of programs remain an untouched desert.

---

Adapted from "The Management of Diversity: Or Why Include Sexism and Racism as Topics in Executive Development Programs" by Nancy Brown, *Exchange,* 4(4), 19–22, 1979. Used with permission.

* I wish to recognize in particular Kaleel Jamison, Chip Henderson, and Steve Fink for their significant contributions to the development of this article.

When I speak of managing diversity, I refer to the following:

- managing people, some of whom differ from the manager in race or gender (e.g., a white woman who manages a black woman); and/or
- managing a number of people who differ from one another in race or gender (e.g., a white man who manages a black man, two white women, and a Hispanic man); and/or
- managing people who differ in race or gender from their organizational context (e.g., a black woman who manages a group of black women in a mostly black male organization).

To manage diversity effectively, a manager needs, among other abilities, to understand personal and institutional racism and sexism and to behave in non-racist, non-sexist ways.

For the purposes of this article, I will focus on *race* and *gender* diversity, but many of the concepts used here can also be applied to such other kinds of diversity as age, religion, physical ability, national origin, educational level, technology, and values. Also, I will focus primarily on managers in white-male-run organizations, since these persons still constitute the largest and most influential group of employers in the U. S. We no longer question whether women and people of color will enter previously all-white and all-male organizations and jobs. The question is how rapid and how effective their entry will be. Even though this change will require both structural and educational change, this article will address only the latter aspect.

## The Impetus for Addressing the Issue

From an organizational standpoint, three general reasons exist for introducing race and gender issues into the development of managers. The number of "X's" in Figure 1 reflect what I judge

Figure 1. Importance of Diversity for Organizations

| | Context | |
| --- | --- | --- |
| | Domestic U.S. Operations | International Operations |
| (A) Productivity Issues | ×××    | ××× |
| (B) Legal Issues | ×      |     |
| (C) Ethical/Social Issues | ×      | × |

to be the relative importance of each factor as an impetus for addressing the issue.

## A. Productivity

When managers behave in less racist and sexist ways, they become better able to manage diversity. This means they make better decisions about the development and deployment of human resources. When organizations use human resources more wisely, productivity increases. From my work in organizations, I see two trends in particular that require better use of human resources.

1. In response to an increasingly complex world, many systems have come to rely more heavily on temporary work units for problem exploration and problem solving. Task forces, committees, and project teams are multiplying. These temporary teams require skills in rapid engaging and conflict management. Racist and sexist behaviors inhibit the efficacy of such teams.

2. More systems are experimenting with "matrixed" or "semimatrixed" methods of operations, which use lines of reporting both to a project boss and to a discipline/technology boss. These operating structures require more sophisticated human skills than traditional ways of managing do. Therefore, in these systems racism and sexism tend to block the attainment of system goals.

Given the priorities of most organizations, the most cogent reason, then, to teach managers about racism and sexism is increased productivity. I have observed, however, that social responsibility, personal ethics, or legal considerations are mentioned much more often.

## B. Legal Responsibility

Legal reasons for educating managers about racism and sexism apply mainly in the U. S. since few other nations use the court systems and/or the withdrawal of government contracts to penalize erring organizations. Even in the U. S. the legal enforcement of anti-discrimination laws has been so sporadic that the laws have become ineffective. In fact, few organizations seriously fear such enforcement.

## C. Ethical and Social Responsibility

Ethical and social reasons for educating managers about racism and sexism cannot reasonably be expected to provide any significant thrust for such effort. You must understand that the unconscious racism and sexism of most white male managers make them blind to the implications of their own behavior. Most indeed think they are already "doing right by" women and people of color.

## Other Benefits of Educating Ourselves on Racism and Sexism

In addition to and in support of productivity increases, other benefits accrue from education about racism and sexism.

1. This education produces a more sophisticated, more highly skilled manager who

- is more alert to structural elements and dynamics and to their impact on individual performance;
- is more knowledgeable about organizational change;
- is more skillful in analyzing her or his own organization; and
- has increased skills in related areas (e.g., managing conflict, problem solving, using power).

Additionally, if the executive is a white male, this type of education usually enables him to learn from people of color and women some things he probably could not learn as well from other white men—such as how to live in two or more cultures or how to be emotionally expressive.

In short, learning about issues of racism and sexism involves learning about *all* managing processes, as they relate to *all* employees.

2. Education about racism and sexism frequently energizes the manager through an increased sense of integrity and self-esteem. When managers feel an increased ability to influence the organization, they bring newly found energy to all tasks.

3. Most managers report a raised interest in learning as a result of education on racism and sexism. I think this stems from the preceding point and from discovering that racism and sexism are complex and subtle. This education offers almost endless chances to learn new, useful things. I have watched white male managers in their 50s come alive through this process and change from being seen as "shelved" or "over the hill" to being regarded as effective and powerful.

4. In addition to the above, directly job-related benefits, I see that education on racism and sexism leads to a fuller, richer, more complete-as-a-human manager. When worked to an appropriate depth, this education can involve a reassessment of general values, which results in more conscious decisions about such matters as gender roles in the home, community involvement, and work/family balance.

5. Education on racism and sexism helps the manager act appropriately regarding anti-sexism, anti-racism efforts in her or his own system. Laurence Megson of Boston and I have identified three essential functions the manager can perform vis-á-vis these efforts. The manager can become

• a *role model for others*, behaving in non-sexist, non-racist ways and maintaining a learning posture on these issues.
• a *determiner of rewards* to ensure that the system rewards those who behave in non-racist, non-sexist ways. Without this, any educational effort would have only a short-lived effect.
• a *decision maker in high-risk and/or unprecedented areas*. Any decision is typically referred up the organizational hierarchy when it is either high-risk or unprecedented. Affirmative action decisions tend to be both.

As managers perform better in these three functions, we will see fewer wasted policy statements on affirmative action and more effective behavior. This will speed up and improve organizational change processes in this area.

6. Effective education on racism and sexism in these areas raises overtly for managers the ethical dilemmas they face daily—but not often consciously—as they manage any subordinate. Examples include the following:

• How much should I reinforce differences *vs.* similarities among my subordinates?
• What are the valid prerequisites for a certain job?
• What are the true measures of performance for a certain job? How important is style—as distinct from results?

Raising these and other ethical questions to a more conscious level results in higher quality management performance.

## Concerns about Including Issues of Racism and Sexism in Management Development Efforts

In discussing the difficulties that often accompany the inclusion of these topics, I intend to show how they may be anticipated, not that they form insuperable obstacles.

This education often generates personal and organizational stress of an unusual nature. People must re-examine themselves, and this can be disconcerting in the short term. This examination frequently extends beyond the work place as people face questions about family relationships and community involvement.

Furthermore, organizations will experience stress as they discover that some standard ways of operating have racist or sexist implications. For example, an organization that has depended solely on a vertical chain-of-command mode of communicating must now make its information flow more flexible. This must occur to allow information about racism and sexism to flow from the bottom—where most women and people of color are located—to the decision makers at the top, without being filtered (either intentionally or unintentionally) by the middle managers who are usually of the same race and gender as those at the top. At the same time, the middle managers should not be made to feel alienated or isolated, nor kept uninformed.

Another concern is that such an educational process is costly. Organizations must not only pay the fees of the competent resource people, but also the cost of the managers' time. The decision to incur the expense must often be made against the resistance of those who do not see a sufficient—or any—reason for such a program.

Moreover, these educational efforts cannot be one-shot programs, but must be sustained over a period of years to allow participants to integrate what they have learned into their work behavior. People also need time to move progressively deeper into new levels of exploration and learning. Conversely, a key danger of one-shot efforts is that those in decision-making positions may come to feel complacent, to finish the project prematurely, or to overestimate the positive movement of the system. This reduces the energy directed toward these issues. As a result, the pressure for change eases and the sytem regresses to earlier, more racist/sexist behaviors.

One final concern is the degree to which participation is voluntary. Requiring people to attend can produce heightened resistance, but, if left to themselves, many white managers and others would not attend because their own racism and sexism generates resistance.

## Conclusion

The inclusion of discussions of racism and sexism in management development is necessary to make organizations function more effectively. While the expense in energy and money is significant, the payoff is much greater than the cost.□

## Bibliography

Kanter, R. *Men and Women of the Corporation*. New York: Basic Books, 1977.
Sargent, A. *Beyond Sex Roles*. New York: West Publishing, 1977.
Terry, R. *For Whites Only*. Grand Rapids, Mich: Wm. B. Eerdman's Publishing Co., 1970.

# From Performance Appraisal (PA) to Performance *Management* (PM): The Manager's Responsibilities and Required Skills

Craig Eric Schneier

*"Of all managerial tasks, honestly and realistically evaluating or appraising subordinates and conducting face-to-face feedback discussions with them is perhaps the most difficult. . . ."*

Few would deny that a successful manager can manage human resources effectively. Effective management of financial resources, technology, or the external environment, while necessary, is not sufficient criteria for managerial competence. Human resource management (HRM) can be viewed at two levels—that of the organization and that of the individual manager.

At the organizational level, HRM involves the design, implementation, and evaluation of programs and activities that assist in meeting organizational objectives. Such programs and activities include the following: *planning and forecasting* (e.g., predicting next year's demand for new positions or updating the position descriptions in a department); *performance appraisal and review* (e.g., setting standards for an occupational group); *procurement* (e.g., recruiting strategies, screening and interviewing applicants, designing psychological tests); *development* (e.g., preparing a training course for technical workers, coaching women in career management techniques); *utilization* (e.g., redesigning jobs to enhance participation in decision making, designing a new compensation system for managers); and *managing the external environment* (e.g., formulating a promotion policy to comply with discrimination legislation, negotiating a union contract).

Most of these programs are initiated with the assistance of HRM professionals in personnel, training, employment, and/or other similarly named units, depending on organization size and type. The individual manager not only participates in the design of such programs but also assures their effective implementation. At the level of the individual manager or executive, HRM involves such activities as selecting persons for vacancies,

© 1983 NTL Institute

providing on-the-job training, assisting in managing career movement, coaching and monitoring performance, recommending rewards, and making job assignments.

Yet these HRM activities hinge on the manager's skill in evaluating subordinates' performance. Of all managerial tasks, honestly and realistically evaluating or appraising subordinates and conducting face-to-face feedback discussions with them is perhaps the most difficult, often leading to conflict and strained relationships. Managers must apply the central HRM values of equity, trust, and openness to performance appraisal, performance improvement, and performance management.

Managers' anxiety over performance appraisal increases when subordinates perform below expected levels or when performance expectations and/or measures have little meaning. Their frustration stems from the amount of time appraisal takes from what most managers regard as their "real" jobs—getting the work done.

I will examine the human resource management or personnel activity called *performance appraisal* (PA), identifying and explaining the problems it creates and providing suggestions for alleviating them. This article takes the perspective of the manager (or executive) who must use PA and make it work, not necessarily the perspective of those in human resource or personnel staff positions charged with technical and administrative responsibilities in PA systems.

After this article introduces the PA activity, it discusses common problems managers face and presents a *performance management* (PM) system as an appropriate way to view the manager's wider role in staff assessment. It also details the sequential set of tasks managers use to fulfill this PM role and the skills they need to be effective. I then discuss how to be an effective rater, the choice of an appraisal form, and legal implications of PA systems.

## Performance Appraisal (PA)

Through PA, one identifies, measures, and develops performance in organizations (see Figure 1) (Carroll & Schneier, 1982; Baird, Beatty & Schneier, 1982; Latham & Wexley, 1981). First, the manager must decide what to evaluate—what criteria to use and how to measure them. He or she then takes measurements typically on one of an innumerable variety of appraisal forms. The manager sometimes discusses the evaluation with the person being rated, praising strengths, noting deficiencies, and perhaps planning developmental activities to improve performance.

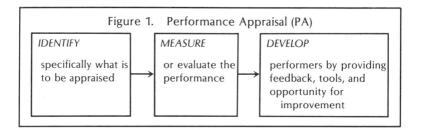

Figure 1.  Performance Appraisal (PA)

| IDENTIFY | MEASURE | DEVELOP |
|---|---|---|
| specifically what is to be appraised | or evaluate the performance | performers by providing feedback, tools, and opportunity for improvement |

While managers can appraise the performance of individuals, subunits, groups, departments, or entire organizations, I will concentrate here on PA at the individual level. The basic notions apply, however, across the levels of analysis. Performance itself refers to behavior (e.g., writing reports, making sales calls, operating a lathe, leading a meeting) that has been evaluated as to its appropriateness, utility, or desirability. Desirable performance should lead to valuable outcomes or results (e.g., a tactful sales call results in a large order).

Every organization, from the corner store to the international conglomerate, has PA. The degree of formality and what PA produces, of course, vary considerably. Just because an organization has no PA forms does not mean it has no PA. The proprietor of the corner store knows how well the high school student hired to make deliveries is doing—no form is necessary. Unfortunately, people in many organizations perceive PA solely as the form itself. People often focus their criticism of PA on the form because it is visible, contains the actual rating, and requires a manager's time to complete. Figure 1 depicts a much broader notion of PA.

Regardless of its level of formality or complexity, PA is a crucial human resource management activity because of the decisions that hinge on its results. PA results can determine who should be promoted, who should be terminated, who should receive a merit increase, or who needs training. PA results thus affect both individual careers and organizational effectiveness. A useful PA system provides valuable data for other human resource management programs (e.g., wage/salary/incentive systems, training program design, human resource planning and forecasting systems, internal selection processes).

## Problems in PA

*Deciding what to rate.* We can trace the problems in the PA process to three broad classes (see Figure 2). The first concerns

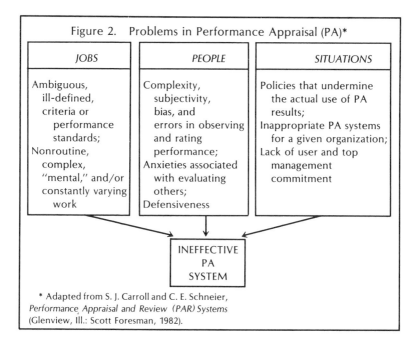

Figure 2.   Problems in Performance Appraisal (PA)*

| JOBS | PEOPLE | SITUATIONS |
|---|---|---|
| Ambiguous, ill-defined, criteria or performance standards; Nonroutine, complex, "mental," and/or constantly varying work | Complexity, subjectivity, bias, and errors in observing and rating performance; Anxieties associated with evaluating others; Defensiveness | Policies that undermine the actual use of PA results; Inappropriate PA systems for a given organization; Lack of user and top management commitment |

INEFFECTIVE
PA
SYSTEM

* Adapted from S. J. Carroll and C. E. Schneier, *Performance Appraisal and Review (PAR) Systems* (Glenview, Ill.: Scott Foresman, 1982).

aspects of the jobs or positions themselves. Should one measure personal characteristics? Should one measure the manner or process used to perform the job? Should one use overall results? They all may be important. We can evaluate the typist by looking at speed and accuracy—both are measurable, even quantifiable. But how do we evaluate a branch manager, an R&D (research and development) project director, a staff assistant, an accountant, or a construction laborer? For most jobs, particularly those closer to the top of the hierarchy and for those that have no easily obtained and measured outputs, PA can be quite difficult. Jobs with variable, unprogrammed, or complex tasks, in which one largely determines performance by mental capabilities, cause problems for PA. This includes most managerial positions. Such job characteristics often lead to ill-defined and ambiguous PA criteria. Managers may interpret standards and rating factors differently, producing inaccurate appraisals.

*Making the judgments.* The second set of PA problems comes from the raters. No matter how conscientious and well-meaning a rater may be, human judgment is complex and subjective. We understand little about observing behavior, recalling it, interpreting its causes and effects, evaluating its desirability, and finally making a rating on a form. The manner in which the raters process information about ratee behavior may affect the resultant rating more than the ratee's behavior itself. Indeed, current thinking and research evidence on PA point to this conclusion (Carroll & Schneier, 1982; Feldman, 1981). Here, one sees PA primarily as judgment and information processing, not merely completing forms.

In studying the impact of a rater's judgment, personality characteristics, and perspective, consider attribution theory (Carroll & Schneier, 1982; Feldman, 1981; Wagner & Vallacher, 1977). Attribution theory states that if we "attribute" people's performance to different sources, this affects our evaluations. One manager might observe a subordinate performing well and attribute this performance to the subordinate's high ability. Another manager who views the same subordinate might feel he or she performed well because the task was not very difficult. The first manager, attributing behavior to an *internal* cause (the subordinate's own ability) might give a high rating. The second manager, attributing behavior to a cause *external* to the subordinate (the nature of the task), might give a lower rating. The *rater's* judgment and perspective determine the rating more than the *ratee's* actual behavior does.

People use their own conditioning, perspectives, values, expectations, philosophies, experiences, biases, prejudices, and styles when making ratings. For example, one may weigh events that occur closest to the rating most heavily. (What happens to your appraisal if you come to the office late three times during the week before the appraisal? In your superior's judgment, would an almost perfect punctuality record the preceding 50 weeks outweigh your recent tardiness?) PA becomes quite difficult, with lenient and otherwise less-than-accurate ratings so common regardless of the type of form used.

*Giving the wrong signals through appraisal policies.* As Figure 2 indicates, the organizational context provides the third major source of PA problems. PA becomes ineffective when unsupported by top management, when policies governing it are ambiguous or conflicting, or when those making decisions on promotion and incentive pay do not use appraisal results. If PA produces no real consequences, why should managers take time away from the demands of their jobs and engage in the anxiety-producing tasks, such as giving subordinates negative feedback, that come with PA?

### The Manager's Perspective: Performance ''Management,'' Not Performance ''Appraisal''

Admittedly, I have not drawn an encouraging picture of PA. Yet most managers who have dealt with PA systems have experienced these problems. A manager should handle the problems inherent in most PA systems by viewing the PA role as not only an *appraiser* of performance, but also a *manager* of performance. The viewpoint thus becomes one of performance management (PM) (Carroll & Schneier, 1982; Sargent, 1981). Regardless of the specific appraisal form used (see discussion of forms below), managers must see PA as an essential and integral part of their responsibilities. Most managers consider monitoring and assessing subordinates' performance, setting expectations, assigning and delegating work, and coaching and counseling subordinates as legitimate tasks. These are the same tasks required for effective PM. An appraisal system, whether it relies on results or objectives, behaviors, personal characteristics, or any combination of approaches, is doomed to failure unless it belongs to the larger PM responsibility managers must have.

*The PM cycle.* A sequential set of managerial tasks and responsibilities forms the PM cycle (see Figure 3). These tasks become the recurring, day-to-day management process. Unlike PA, PM is not just the isolated activity of completing a rating form, which lasts a few hours (or less) and occurs once or twice a year. The PM perspective takes the view of integrated tasks; together, these tasks define day-to-day activities.

As noted in Figure 3, the PM cycle has eight steps, each one dependent on the preceding one, yet not entirely separable from the others. Step four, labeled "performance monitoring, assisting, and controlling," is, of course, a continual activity. Furthermore, one may not often complete the entire cycle in sequence; shorter "loops" are commonplace, as when one monitors performance (step four) and then requires a revision in expectations (step two). Each step is important, however, to building an effective PM process, regardless of level in the hierarchy. Organizations need subordinate participation at each step.

*How the cycle works.* The PM cycle begins with an analysis to determine important job duties or responsibilities and expected outcomes (e.g., products, services, data, and so forth). The crucial question becomes, "What is the purpose of this job?" One identifies the criteria or dimensions used to judge ratees. These can include broad work processes (e.g., leading meetings or supervising staff), work outcomes (e.g., completed reports, parts manufactured, sales volume, profit levels), specific behaviors (e.g., seeking subordinates' opinions, checking figures for errors), personal characteristics (e.g., decisiveness), or combinations. PM requires performance standards or targets that must be communicated clearly to ratees so that expectations become known and understood. Next, the manager might work with the

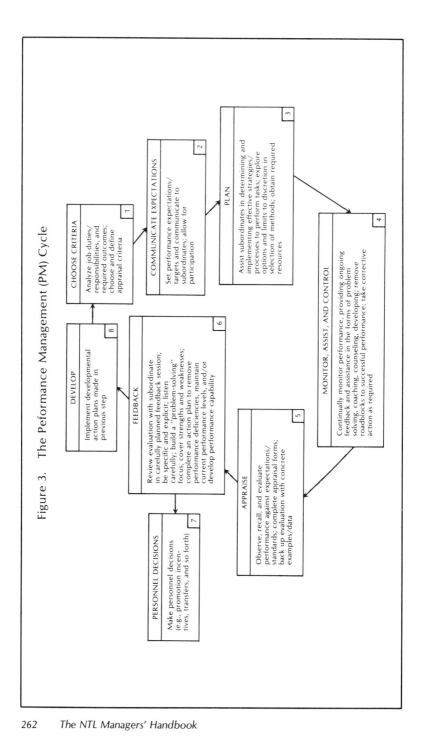

Figure 3. The Peformance Management (PM) Cycle

**CHOOSE CRITERIA** [1]

Analyze job duties/responsibilities, and required outcomes; choose and define appraisal criteria

**COMMUNICATE EXPECTATIONS** [2]

Set performance expectations/targets and communicate to subordinates; allow for participation

**PLAN** [3]

Assist subordinates in determining and implementing effective strategies/processes to perform tasks; explore options and limits to discretion in selection of methods; obtain required resources

**MONITOR, ASSIST, AND CONTROL** [4]

Continually monitor performance, providing ongoing feedback and assistance in the forms of problem solving, coaching, counseling, developing; remove roadblocks to successful performance; take corrective action as required

**APPRAISE** [5]

Observe, recall, and evaluate performance against expectations/standards; complete appraisal forms; back up evaluation with concrete examples/data

**FEEDBACK** [6]

Review evaluation with subordinate in carefully planned feedback session; be specific and explicit; listen carefully; build a "problem-solving" focus; cover strengths and weaknesses; complete an action plan to remove performance deficiencies, maintain current performance levels, and/or develop performance capability

**PERSONNEL DECISIONS** [7]

Make personnel decisions (e.g., promotion incentives, transfers, and so forth)

**DEVELOP** [8]

Implement developmental action plans made in previous step

ratee to develop plans and strategies for doing the work. The intensity depends upon such factors as the ratee's experience level, the complexity or novelty of the job, the manager's level of trust, and the manager's comfort with delegation. After establishing ground rules for performing, the manager plays two crucial roles: securing resources (i.e., materials, people, information, money) necessary to performing the job and removing roadblocks (e.g., constricting policies) to successful job performance.

The monitoring process is a primary managerial function in PM. The manager has ultimate responsibility for subordinates' work. He or she must assess performance levels and provide continual feedback to control performance. One must coach and counsel ratees and solve unanticipated problems. At some point, one makes the formal appraisal. The manager must attempt a bias-free rating, best illustrated with examples of ratee behavior that can be obtained from anecdotal records kept during the appraisal period. One must recall behavior over the entire period, weighing the typical and atypical, the positive and negative. Evaluation must use the performance expectations and standards set earlier. The rating form and system's procedures determine how the ratings are combined or indexed.

After rating, the manager reports results to the ratee in a performance review session. Here, one should detail strengths and weaknesses, provide concrete examples of performance to ratees, hear their views, and solve performance problems (most managers find this difficult when a ratee has not performed well). Those involved develop action plans to remove performance deficiencies through training, practice, or job assignments; to reward positive performance; and to accomodate preferences for additional, future responsibilities. One also makes personnel decisions, such as promotions and allocation of bonuses, on the basis of appraisal results. These decisions should, however, be separated from the performance review process, as Figure 3 indicates. Finally, one implements plans to develop ratees, and the PM cycle begins again.

*The personnel department provides tools and training.* From the managerial perspective, personnel, human resource management, training, or other staff units can *assist* in PM by providing advice, training, tools, techniques, or guidelines for a successful PM cycle. The manager must ultimately take responsibility for the setting of performance standards and evaluation of performance. Staff units can help in design phases, developing procedures and forms to be used as *tools* in the implementation of PM. The appraisal form, or its accompanying policies, can never replace managers skilled at PM. Nor can a form, no matter how sound psychometrically, how comprehensive, or how specific, remove managerial judgment. At best, forms, policies, and procedures help managers structure their judgments, reduce capricious or biased evaluation, and compare relative contributions made by other job groups. For managers to argue that they have little time for appraisal is futile. The PM process *is* managers' work!

## Skills Required of Managers for Successful PM

Recognizing that PM is integral to a manager's work does not, of course, assure PM effectiveness. Along with *willingness*, managers must develop the *ability* to perform their PM tasks. As noted above, PM skills (and tasks) largely duplicate those required for successful management in general. Many managers, perhaps promoted for technical competence, skills, knowledge, or ability, view their PM responsibilities with understandable anxiety or distaste because they lack confidence or ability in PM. Since managers take little time to develop, practice, or use their PM skills, they improve little. Using the term "skill" broadly, Figure 4 lists a sample of the more obvious ones necessary for PM (Baird, Beatty & Schneier, 1982; Bernarding & Buckley, 1981; Carroll & Schneier, 1982; Lathan & Wexley, 1981; Sashkin, 1981). The appropriate boxes represent steps in the PM cycle described in Figure 3. The lists are neither exhaustive nor mutually exclusive.

*Self-assessment of PM skills.* Managers can use Figure 4 as a diagnostic tool to assess their skills and design opportunities to improve PM through practice and training. Fortunately, managerial positions offer ample opportunity for practice at PM. Staff units can assist greatly through courses and other developmental experiences.

*Appraising managers on PM skills.* As staff assessment and development, accomplished through the PM cycle, becomes increasingly visible and important in organizations, it must eventually become a PA criteria for evaluating all managers. By understanding the PM cycle, the effective skill development programs for managers, and the availability and use of incentives, an organization can overcome the typical PA problems noted above. Of course, top management must make a serious commitment to use PA results, employing technical expertise from staff units or consultants, supportive policies and procedures, adequate appraisal forms, and incentives for managers to improve their PM skills.

## The Manager's Role as an Effective Ratee

The discussion to this point has centered around the roles and responsibilities of managers as *raters* in a PM system. Yet it is an

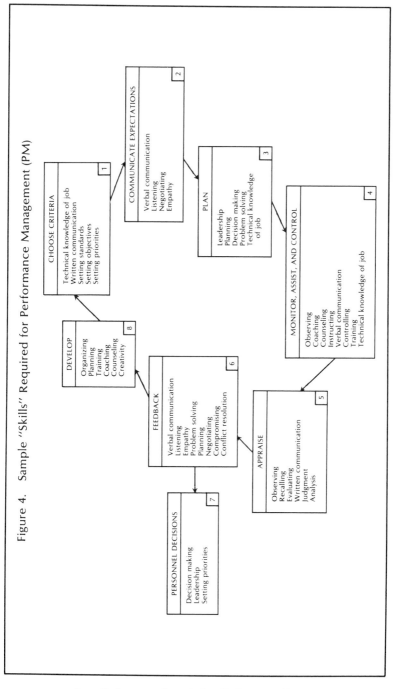

Figure 4. Sample "Skills" Required for Performance Management (PM)

**CHOOSE CRITERIA** (1)
Technical knowledge of job
Written communication
Setting standards
Setting objectives
Setting priorities

**COMMUNICATE EXPECTATIONS** (2)
Verbal communication
Listening
Negotiating
Empathy

**PLAN** (3)
Leadership
Planning
Decision making
Problem solving
Technical knowledge
of job

**MONITOR, ASSIST, AND CONTROL** (4)
Observing
Coaching
Counseling
Instructing
Verbal communication
Controlling
Training
Technical knowledge of job

**APPRAISE** (5)
Observing
Recalling
Evaluating
Written communication
Judgment
Analysis

**FEEDBACK** (6)
Verbal communication
Listening
Empathy
Problem solving
Planning
Negotiating
Compromising
Conflict resolution

**PERSONNEL DECISIONS** (7)
Decision making
Leadership
Setting priorities

**DEVELOP** (8)
Organizing
Planning
Training
Coaching
Counseling
Creativity

organizational fact of life that they are also *ratees*. The subordinate being evaluated has as much difficulty as the evaluator. Ratees and raters in a PM system have similar responsibilities and need similar skills, however. As depicted in Figures 3 and 4, ratee participation in the PM process can be crucial to its success.

The ratee's responsibilities include honesty, openness, interest and ability in self-assessment, and being proactive in one's career and job (see Figure 5). Managers can assist their supervisors by preparing for their appraisals and by reducing their defensiveness in performance review sessions. In addition, the more effective managers are as ratees, the more empathy and skill they use when they act as raters.

## Appraisal Forms and Legally Defensible Systems

This discussion has emphasized the manager's role in PM and has noted that the particular appraisal form is not as important as

---

Figure 5.   The Manager as an Effective Ratee: Some Suggestions

—Engage in a realistic, periodic self-assessment of managerial and technical strengths and weaknesses.
—Think about your performance objectives: Set your own targets and expectations, determine your own PA criteria, and compare with those set by superiors.
—Take stock of your career: its history, its progress, its current state, its future.
—Develop strategies, options, and action plans for your own future.
—Separate what you can do to realize your career objectives from what you expect of your superior and your organization.
—Take stock of your position and status in your organization: What (or who) is your power base; how secure is your position; what people or forces (inside and outside the organization) can change your status; who are your colleagues, your mentor(s), your competitors; what makes you indispensable, what makes you dispensable; how marketable are you?
—Assess how well you fit in with your organization's (or unit's) values, philosophy, and culture.
—Be open to feedback, both positive and negative; resist the temptation to be defensive.
—Carefully listen to and observe superiors, subordinates, peers, and others for clues about your performance and your position.
—Assist your superior in evaluating you by documenting your own performance where appropriate and providing data.
—Be proactive and creative in stating your preferences, in (tactfully) selling yourself, and in devising career options and paths.
—Help your superior understand the forces that facilitate and impede your performance.

---

understanding, commitment, and skill in the PM process. The form used should be designed, however, after one knows the major PM objectives and specific characteristics of the organization and job(s) to be rated. As noted above, outcomes or results, behaviors, work processes or methods, or personal characteristics can be measured, usually with a Management by Objectives (MBO) format, which sets target objectives and indications for successful attainment (e.g., "Increase sales by five percent in six months."). One can measure behaviors with a variety of rating scales that may spell out varying performance levels (e.g., "Excellent," "Proficient") for each behavior (e.g., "Meets regularly with staff to solicit ideas"). Much has been written about the variety of forms, scales, and PA measurement systems (Beatty & Schneier, 1981; Carroll & Schneier, 1982; Landy & Farr, 1980; Schneier & Beatty, 1979). Each, of course, possesses strengths and weaknesses, depending upon specific PM objectives and job types. But forms are tools that emerge from the design of the overall PM process. They cannot drive it.

One must consider legal compliance when designing and choosing appraisal forms and the characteristics of the PM system itself. Equal Employment Opportunity (EEO) laws, Executive Orders, federal, state, and municipal legislation, published federal guidelines, and court decisions have all addressed PA systems in both the public and private sectors, specifically about discrimination (Carroll & Schneier, 1982; Cascio & Bernardin, 1981; Klasson et al., 1980). While legislation, guidelines, and court decisions are exceedingly difficult to interpret, complex, and even contradictory, I can make some recommendations. Figure 6 lists characteristics of legally defensible systems, though no assurances can be given here.

---

Figure 6.    Sample Characteristics of Legally Defensible Appraisal Systems

Formal and standardized forms have written instructions for users.

Peformance standards or criteria are based on a thorough job analysis for each job type.

Performance standards or criteria are based on work actually done by those being rated and are defined specifically.

Decisions based on results do not "adversely affect" or discriminate against minorities, women, other groups.

Users are oriented and trained.

Intended uses of appraisal results are known and communicated to those affected.

Supervisors' subjective evaluations are not relied upon exclusively.

Appeal/review procedures are established.

Raters have ample opportunity to observe ratees.

---

Just as appraisal forms should not solely dictate a PM system's characteristics, neither should an organization begin PM system design by focusing solely on legal compliance. Both are obviously crucial and must not be ignored, but neither alone can assure an effective system. Ultimately, that is the manager's role and the manager's responsibility.☐

## References

Baird, L. S., Beatty, R. W., & Schneier, C. E. *The Performance Appraisal Sourcebook*. Amherst, Mass.: Human Resource Development Press, 1982.

Beatty, R. W., & Schneier, C. E. *Personnel Administration: An Experiential/Skill-Building Approach* (2nd ed.). Reading, Mass.: Addison-Wesley, 1981.

Bernardin, H. J., & Buckley, M. R. A Consideration of Strategies in Rater Training. *Academy of Management Review*, 1981, 6, 205–212.

Carroll, S. J., & Schneier, C. E. *Performance Appraisal and Review (PAR) Systems*. Glenview, Ill.: Scott Foresman, 1982.

Cascio, W. F., & Bernardin, H. J. Implications of Performance Appraisal Litigation for Personnel Decisions. *Personnel Psychology*, 1981, 34, 211–225.

Feldman, J. M. Beyond Attribution Theory: Cognitive Processes in Performance Appraisal. *Journal of Applied Psychology*, 1981, 66, 127–148.

Klasson, C. R., et al. How Defensible Is Your Performance Appraisal System? *The Personnel Administrator*, 1980, 25, 77–83.

Landy, F. J., & Farr, J. L. Performance Rating. *Psychological Bulletin*, 1980, 87, 72–197.

Latham, G. P., & Wexley, K. N. *Increasing Productivity Through Performance Appraisal*. Reading, Mass.: Addison-Wesley, 1981.

Sargent, A. G. *The Androgynous Manager*. New York: AMACOM, 1981.

Sashkin, M. *Assessing Performance Appraisal*. San Diego, Calif.: University Associates, 1981.

Schneier, C. E., & Beatty, R. W. Integrating Behaviorally-Based Effectiveness-Based Methods. Part I: Appraisal Objectives, Problems, and Formats. *The Personnel Administrator*, 1979, 24, 65–78.

Wagner, D. M., & Vallacher, R. R. *Implicit Psychology*. New York: Oxford, 1977.

# The Manager's Role in Career Development: A Link Between Employees and Organizations

Zandy B. Leibowitz
Caela Farren
Nancy Schlossberg

*". . . the four key roles that managers can play in career development [are] coach, appraiser, advisor, and referral agent."*

Managers are increasingly called upon to play a more active role in the career development of their employees. Employee requests for career assistance from their managers have multiplied as organizations increase in complexity and become affected by such factors as the recessionary economy, deregulation, increased emphasis on productivity, rapid technological changes, and decreasing size.

Requests from employees for career assistance are also mounting as organizations begin to experience the shift to "new-value" workers described by Yankelovich (1981). Yankelovich's research indicates that workers will continue to press for self-fulfillment, and that this will cause them to more actively manage their own careers. As a result, managers will be pressured to respond to the employees' increased need for managers to become more involved in their subordinates' careers.

Future trends also provide data that support the growing importance of managers' involvement in and interaction with employees' careers. Naisbitt's book *Megatrends* (1982) states that managers need to balance the growth of high technology with human response—the "high-tech/high-touch" approach. Naisbitt also discusses an organizational structure that does not resemble the traditional pyramid but instead comprises a wider band of technical specialists in the middle. This predicted change in structure—coupled with the changing demographics of the work place in which the average age in 1990 will be 40 years—will produce increased pressures for managers to be able to assist employees in considering a wide range of career options. Organizations in which managers currently help employees with their careers have realized some of the following benefits:

- increased employee effectiveness;
- better matches between employee abilities and organization needs;

© 1983 NTL Institute

- an identified pool of managerial talent;
- increased attractiveness of the organization to potential employees;
- reinforcement/improvement of existing personnel system; and
- improved long-range planning and forecasting.

Because of these pressures and benefits, many other organizations have begun to urge their managers to become effective career coaches and have tied responsibilities in this area to performance appraisal and compensation schemes.

Some managers are effective career coaches—others are not. Many report that they have not received career assistance themselves and feel uncomfortable and unskilled in this area. Thus, many organizations have instituted training programs to help managers undertake this new role more comfortably and skillfully.

The first part of this article will provide an overview of the manager's role in career development—where managers fit in the total career management system, their responsibilities in career development, and the payoffs for helping employees with their careers. The second part will present several models, skills, and behaviors that will aid career discussions with employees.

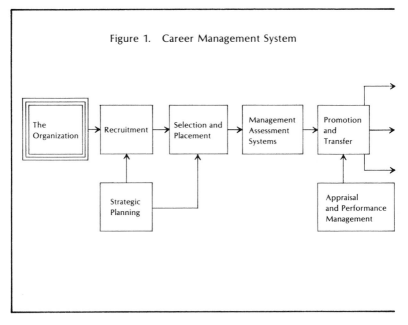

Figure 1.   Career Management System

## The Manager's Role in Career Development

*Where Do Managers Fit?*

In the total career management system, managers take on the integrative function between employees and the needs, constraints, and realities of the organization. They help employees plan their careers in concert with organization requirements.

Figure 1 illustrates the manager's role as an integrator between the organization and its employees. Managers use structures such as skills inventories and job posting systems to promote the best fit between the organization and its employees. The organization's functions—such as strategic planning and selection and placement—are often present in career management systems. For employees, the steps in designing career action plans are indicated.

*Who's Responsible for What?*

Three key players share responsibility for an employee's career development: the employee, the organization, and the manager. Primary responsibility for an employee's career lies with the employee, but managers and the organization can provide vital assistance.

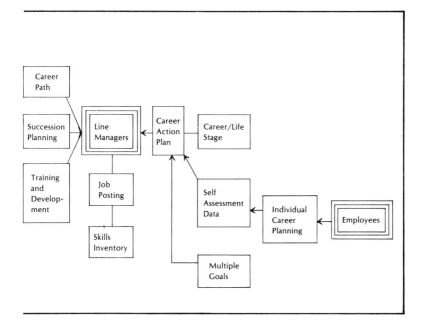

The relationship managers hold with their employees provides a vantage point for helping employees with career issues. First, managers observe employee behavior on a day-to-day basis in the work setting. As Bowen and Hall (1977) state, "The primary advantage of boss as coach or counselor is that the boss should have considerable knowledge of how the subordinate actually behaves on the job over long periods of time." A second strength managers have is being able to see the "big picture" of the organization and being able to balance employee aspirations and planning with real organizational needs.

For the key players in career development systems to play their roles successfully, each must assume a set of responsibilities.

The *organization's responsibilities* include the following:

- providing resources for self-understanding and goal setting;
- setting and communicating missions, policies, goals, and objectives;
- providing information on organization options and career paths;
- providing training, education, and mobility opportunities; and
- reinforcing and supporting the managers' role in career development.

The *manager's responsibilities* include the following:

- giving clear feedback about what employees should reasonably expect;
- providing forums for discussion;
- providing support and opportunities;
- identifying employee potential;
- providing growth opportunities consistent with employee and organization goals;
- communicating the formal and informal realities of the organization;
- providing exposure for employees; and
- linking employees to appropriate resources and people.

The *employee's responsibilities* include the following:

- self-assessment;
- setting goals and plans;
- expressing expectations; and
- making use of opportunities, education, and training.

*What Are the Payoffs?*

The payoffs and benefits for involvement with employee careers must offset the time and energy required. Managers who have assumed the responsibilities detailed in the previous section have begun to report the following outcomes:

- more focused performance discussions;
- planned development instead of random activity;
- reputations in their organizations as "people developers;" and
- increased productivity in their own work groups.

## Meeting the Manager's Responsibilities

We have described the manager's relationship to the total career management system, explained the responsibilities of the key players in the system, and presented several benefits that managers may obtain. The following sections will provide a career development model that provides a conceptual framework for managers working with employees and will suggest behaviors that managers can use at each stage of the model. We will also provide guidelines for structuring a career discussion.

### Career Development Model

Figure 2 presents a career development model. The first column lists a set of career-related questions that employees often ask. The second column lists a key role that managers can play in answering the related employee question. The third column lists a desired result for employees.

We will discuss each of the sections of the model, beginning with the development of the four manager roles.

| Figure 2. Career Development Model | | |
|---|---|---|
| Employee Question(s) | Manager Role | Result or Output for Employee |
| Who Am I? | Coach | Self-Statement |
| How Am I Seen? | Appraiser | Reality Check |
| What Are My Alternatives?<br><br>What Are My Goals? | Advisor | Goal Identification |
| How Can I Achieve My Goals? | Referral Agent | Development Plan |

*Four Critical Roles*

In a series of "critical incident" interviews, Leibowitz & Schlossberg (1981) asked employees to describe the ways their managers had helped them with their careers. Some descriptions of effective managerial behavior were

- "He introduced me to other people in the field."
- "My supervisor worked behind the scenes on ways to help me move up."
- "I wasn't sure I could do the assignment, but she encouraged me to try it."
- "She arranged for me to be seen by top management through speeches and presentations."
- "We would talk about what I would be doing in the future, not just about specific tasks."

On the basis of these interviews, the researchers identified the four key roles that managers can play in career development: coach, appraiser, advisor, and referral agent. These four roles can be placed on a continuum—as shown in Figure 3—with major emphasis on the employee at one end and major emphasis on the manager at the other. Individual managers may find their styles more consistent with the advice and action required by the advisor and referral agent roles than with the support and feedback required by the coach and appraiser roles. A good career developer, however, can use all four roles comfortably and interchange them when necessary.

Although managers use all four roles throughout a career discussion, each of the roles relates to one of the four career questions employees ask. As Figure 2 indicates, the coach responds to "Who am I?"; the appraiser to "How am I seen?";

---

Figure 3.   Emphasis of the Manager's Four Roles

Employee                                                    Manager

←——————————————————————————————————→

| Coach | Appraiser | Advisor | Referral Agent |
|---|---|---|---|
| • listens<br>• clarifies<br>• probes<br>• defines<br>  concerns | • gives feedback | • generates<br>  options<br>• helps set goals<br>• recommends/<br>  advises | • links employee to<br>  resources/people<br>• consults on<br>  action plan |

the advisor to "What are my alternatives? What are my goals?";
and the referral agent to "How can I achieve my goals?"

*Four Questions—Four Critical Roles*

The following sections will describe each of the employee
questions in depth and detail the critical behaviors for each of
the related manager roles.

*Who am I?* Self-knowledge is an important first step in career
planning. At this stage, employees need help in identifying their
values, interests, strengths, and skills. Examples of employee "Who
am I?" questions include the following:

- "What do you see as my main skills?"
- "I'm feeling 'dead-ended' in this job. What should I do?"
- "I don't seem to enjoy my work any more. What would
you suggest?"
- "I'm having extra demands at home right now that seem to
interfere with my work. Can we talk about it?"

In response to employee "Who am I?" questions, managers use
the *coach* role. The manager who acts as a coach assists
employees in identifying their strengths, weaknesses, interests,
and values by maintaining open, effective communication and by
providing ongoing encouragement. Coach behaviors include
the following:

- setting an open and trustful climate;
- encouraging two-way dialogue;
- listening attentively and demonstrating understanding; and
- probing employees' work accomplishments for skills, interests,
and values.

*How am I seen?* When employees ask this kind of question,
they are looking for feedback on their performance and
potential. After they have made a self-assessment, employees
need validation and information from their managers. Do their
managers see them in the same way that they see themselves?
Examples of employee "How am I seen?" questions include
the following:

- "I don't feel as if I'm effective in my job. What could I do to
improve my performance?"
- "Would you give me some feedback on my work?"
- "Do you think I'm ready for a promotion?"

- "What are my chances for advancement?"
- "What areas do I need to develop to improve my performance?"

Managers can respond to "How am I seen?" questions by assuming the *appraiser* role. The manager who acts as an appraiser evaluates employees' performance in an open, candid way and relates this to potential opportunities. Appraiser behaviors include the following:

- providing specific, frequent, timely feedback;
- identifying employee strengths;
- identifying employee weaknesses or development areas; and
- linking present performance to future development.

*What are my alternatives? What are my goals?* At this stage employees need information about the possibilities in the organization. Employees need to decide what makes sense in view of the information they have gathered about themselves and their options and to set realistic, obtainable goals. Examples of employee "What are my alternatives/goals?" questions include the following:

- "What other career areas or options am I suited for?"
- "What are the growing and declining areas in this organization?"
- "What are the implications of not taking a promotion?"
- "What jobs are available?"
- "What are the implications of future changes in the organization for the work in our department?"

The *advisor* role can help managers answer employees' informational and goal-setting questions. The manager who acts as an advisor provides organizational information, describes realities, and offers resources to employees in a coherent way and helps them set realistic career goals. Advisor behaviors include the following:

- sharing knowledge of the formal and informal organization;
- showing employees ways to study the organization and to gain an understanding of other departments and job requirements;
- helping employees understand the current opportunities and limitations in the organization; and
- helping employees develop realistic, attainable career goals.

*How can I achieve my goals?* To make their goals a reality, employees need to detail the specific steps required to carry out their plans. Examples of employee "How can I achieve my goals?" questions include the following:

- "How do I find out about training opportunities?"
- "How do I move from one department to another?"
- "How can I get more responsibility and more recognition in the job I have?"
- "How do I sell myself to a prospective manager?"

The *referral agent* role focuses on ways to assist employees with realizing their career goals. The manager who acts as a referral agent assists employees in meeting their goals through contacts with people and resources. Referral agent behaviors include the following:

- helping employees formulate development plans and consulting on strategies and actions;
- providing opportunities for experience and recognition;
- using personnel resources—who you know and what you know—to create opportunities;
- assisting in employee placement, either lateral or vertical; and
- identifying training and development resources both within and outside the organization.

## Career Counseling Results

One way to ensure the success of the career discussions managers have with employees is for employees to record the results of these discussions. With their managers' assistance, employees should be able to document the following in writing: a *self-statement*, which describes career strengths, achievements, values, and skills; a *reality check*, in which the manager and other colleagues validate the employee self-statement; a *goal identification*, which identifies multiple career goals—for example, moving laterally, upward, or into a new career field; and a *development plan*, which details the steps and time frame for reaching each goal.

## Assuring Success

Structuring and managing the career discussion itself is the manager's key to success. The career discussion model in Figure 4 details the four essential stages: climate setting, structuring the interview, exploring, and clarifying and defining the next steps.

## Figure 4.  Career Discussion Model

| Stage | Goal | Behaviors |
|---|---|---|
| Climate Setting | • To establish a relaxed and open environment<br><br>• To establish a collaborative problem-solving atmosphere | • Create informal "space"<br><br>• Prevent interruptions<br><br>• Create privacy |
| Structuring the Interview | • To establish purpose, goals, and time constraints | • Clarify expectations (e.g., what the employees hope to achieve during this session)<br><br>• Set time limit |
| Exploring | • To conduct an in-depth, two-way discussion that accomplishes the agreed purpose | • Draw out employees<br><br>• Encourage them<br><br>• Ask open-ended and penetrating questions<br><br>• Paraphrase |
| Clarifying and Defining Next Steps | • To gain commitment and clarification of who needs to do what next | • Summarize<br><br>• Clarify responsibilities<br><br>• Set time lines<br><br>• Specify critical steps each will take |

The model describes both the goals of each of these stages and the key behaviors associated with each one.

## Summary

Managers can play a pivotal role in the career development of their employees. The models, roles, and behaviors described in this article can help assure the success of career discussions. As managers increase their skill as career coaches, organizations will benefit from better matches between employee skills and aspirations and organizational needs.□

## References

Bowen, D., & Hall, D. T. Career Planning for Employee Development: A Primer for Managers. *California Management Review*, 1977, XX(2), 23–25.

Kaye, B. *Up Is Not the Only Way*. Englewood Cliffs, N. J.: Prentice-Hall, 1982.

Leibowitz, Z., & Schlossberg, N. Training Managers for their Role in a Career Development System. *Training and Development Journal*, July 1981, 72–79.

Naisbitt, J. *Megatrends: Ten New Directions Transforming Our Lives.* New York: Warner Books, 1982.

Yankelovich, D. *New Rules: Searching for Self-Fulfillment in a World Turned Upside Down.* New York: Random House, 1981.

# Up Is Not the Only Way          Beverly L. Kaye

*"As a manager, you can help your employees to feel better about their present jobs and their future ones if you take the time to counsel them on [their] career alternatives."*

Employees, like organizations, are facing change. In today's society, in which technological obsolescence is a reality, career development is a necessity. Managers are held accountable for helping subordinates cope with, adapt to, and plan for change. In other words, the manager now has one more function to add to the management repertoire: career development.

In the "developer" role, a manager helps subordinates with their career concerns. Talking with subordinates about career changes isn't easy. Many people fear any type of change, no matter whose idea it is. Furthermore, talking with subordinates may be difficult for managers because career development is not a judgmental process, as job supervision is. Instead, it involves interpersonal understanding and trust.

Your role as a manager is to act as a coach or catalyst to the subordinate, pointing out the choice of career goals that exists. Most employees are aware of only one kind of movement—up—although five other viable alternatives exist. These options are moving across, moving down, exploring, staying put, and moving out.

The positive psychological impact of examining alternative career options is significant. Multiple goals encourage flexibility. The employee will feel more autonomous and less at the mercy of external forces. If one desired direction becomes blocked, he or she has other options from which to choose.

## Option #1: Moving Up

Most individuals are interested in moving up—probably because they are unaware of the opportunities offered by the other options. Also, many consider upward mobility the only acceptable and rewarding way to develop a career. Upward mobility provides additional status, responsibility, compensation, and weight of title to a professional reputation. For many, movement "up" equals success; all other movement either does not count or counts against. And most literature on career development (both

Adapted from Beverly L. Kaye, *Up Is Not the Only Way*, © 1982, pp. 98–118.
Adapted by permission of Prentice-Hall, Inc., Englewood Cliffs, New Jersey.

scientific and popular) continues to tout the idea that "up" is the best and only direction in which anyone should desire to move.

You can assist your employees by discussing positions at the next higher level or by organizing resource material to help them make plans. Resource materials might include job listings by salary grade or title, reports showing job families and subfamilies, job descriptions showing entry requirements, and specially designed job content profiles. If such information cannot be provided directly, you might show employees where they can obtain this information on their own. For example, you could identify key contact people within the organization who might act as information resources. You can also encourage employees to use data available in the system, such as job-posting bulletins, so that they can determine what the job requirements are for positions in other parts of the organization.

## Option #2: Moving Across

Horizontal or lateral moves clearly demonstrate the concept of the transferability of skills, abilities, and job knowledge. An employee who has strong product knowledge from a background in production and who has also demonstrated successful sales skills by "selling" production proposals to top management may indeed be qualified to make a lateral move into a position in marketing by virtue of transferable skills and knowledge.

Moving across involves a change in function and/or title without necessarily undergoing a change in status or salary. Although such moves were once considered a way of dealing with "deadwood" employees, they are fast becoming a way of demonstrating adaptive abilities and broadening skills, learning about other areas of the organization, and developing new talents. Lateral movement is one way that organizations with limited advancement opportunities can continue to challenge their highly motivated employees. Furthermore, providing individuals with this kind of exposure is becoming a grooming mechanism for positions in higher management since it broadens an individual's base of knowledge and is an opportunity to demonstrate management skills.

Before presenting horizontal movement as an option to your employees, you should be aware of the cultural norms concerning such a move within your organization. By norms we mean biases for or against such movement.

In many companies horizontal moves occur frequently and are considered part of routine training and development. Job rotation programs are also common, ongoing processes in certain companies. Such programs are designed to prevent overspecialization and to encourage understanding of the unique demands faced by each function within the organization. In such organizations, a lateral move would not cause any problems.

Where horizontal movement is infrequent and/or seen as a sign of probable failure, the manager may be able, with the assistance of human resource professionals in the company, to determine whether and how such mobility can be legitimized. It may be as simple as pointing out that the frequency of such moves is actually greater than it is perceived to be by most employees. Based on this information, the company newsletter, for example, may be encouraged to present histories of several successful people who have benefited from making lateral moves.

More formally, managers might suggest that a job-posting or transfer system be instituted, or, if already in effect, that it be publicized as providing an opportunity both as a means of transferring skills to new work areas and learning more about other parts of the organization. Internal job rotation programs designed to rotate people on a temporary basis can also be implemented, thus encouraging employees to experiment with transferring their present skills to similar-level jobs in other departments.

An organization can use a variety of ways to show that it is open to horizontal mobility, and it is the manager's job to convey this message to her or his subordinates.

## Option #3: Moving Down

Moving down is another option that our changing value system has made more feasible during the last few years. Many people are looking toward outside interests for self-fulfillment and see the opportunity to move downward as a chance to free themselves from time-consuming positions.

Of course, employees probably will have difficulty in making this type of move because of the "failure" stigma attached. You, as a supervisor, can help make the transition easier by pointing out the positive aspects of the move. For instance, an employee may be unhappy in her or his position, and the solution may be to move back to the former job where he or she performed successfully. After all, most people will agree that it is better to do what they do well than to struggle along in a job that is not suited to them. This can be the case when the best worker is promoted as department supervisor. It is not until the new supervisor has been in the position for several months that it is discovered that the individual is just not cut out to be a supervisor. By counseling your employees on downward movement, you can help to keep the "Peter Principle" from becoming rampant in your organization.

Some workers may look to downward movement for health reasons, or to relieve job-related tension and stress. You can help them to make this decision by encouraging them to seek out information from the media about the increasing numbers of people who are choosing this option. Internal publicity in a company newsletter also might make employees feel more at ease with this alternative.

When counseling an employee who is about to make a downward move, try to prepare the individual for a negative reaction from her or his colleagues. You can help by making sure that co-workers know that the move was voluntary and that the employee is not being punished for failing. If the move was made for health reasons, co-workers may be wary of putting any burden on the employee, and he or she will have to learn to cope with their attitude. If the employee is a woman or a member of a minority group, he or she may have to deal with pressure from peers who are unhappy with the "failure" out of fear that they, also, will be thought of poorly.

## Option #4: Exploring

Exploratory goals encourage employees to consider other areas of the organization without yet committing to an actual move in another direction. Discussing exploratory goals with employees replaces fantasizing about greener pastures with planning for action. Exploratory goals do require effort, but they can be easily pursued in tandem with other goals.

Exploring involves the process of researching, interviewing, and testing out ideas and opportunities so that a decision about another field of interest eventually can be made. You might help initiate this process by suggesting that an employee select one area of slight interest and investigate possibilities associated with it. Managers can help best by coaching employees on how to write a detailed statement of areas of possible interest as well as a structured plan for researching them. From this effort, enough information should be gathered to enable the employee to make a sound decision as to whether or not a move into a specific area is feasible.

One way you might use the development discussion to stimulate exploratory goal selection is to ask, "If you were given a six-month paid sabbatical from your present job to explore any other area within this organization, what would it be?" Also, during the talk, encourage your employees to interview or talk informally with individuals in other areas of the organization about their jobs.

## Option #5: Staying Put

The fifth option—staying put—suggests that opportunity begins at home. In fact, when employees recognize the advantages open to them in their present assignments, it is not unusual for them to decide to remain in their current jobs a little longer. If the supervisor-counselor is to sell this option, he or she needs to increase the employees' job satisfaction. It also calls for taking another look with them at the present job and viewing it as a potential launching pad for future opportunities.

In essence, this option involves increasing the challenge or meaning of the job by changing either the job itself or the employee's concept of it.

Jobs can be improved by (1) increasing the number and variety of skills and talents used in performing the job; (2) having the opportunity to work on a job from beginning to end; (3) determining and understanding the type and degree of impact the particular job has on the lives and work of other people in the organization and on the organization as a whole; (4) increasing responsibility, independence, and discretion in determining one's own work procedures; and (5) seeking or establishing opportunities for feedback from the job itself as well as from co-workers and supervisors.

If you work with employees to help them realize that their present jobs represent good opportunities to learn and grow, you will find numerous payoffs. Beyond simply making the job more bearable for those who are unhappy, you will help your employees learn to turn the experience to their favor—to discover ways to turn problems into opportunities or convert the "run away and start again somewhere else" drive into a push to stay and turn the situation around. If successful, the reward is high—each of your employees will have created one psychological success upon which future successes may be based.

All employees should learn to look upon their present jobs as opportunities to showcase their present skills and to further the development of new ones. The key job of the manager in this effort is to help the individuals understand and recognize that they can modify their own jobs or their concepts of them sufficiently to better meet some of their needs. A job description covers the areas of responsibility and duties of one just starting out. No rules say that one cannot grow *within* a position.

Tips for Managers in Guiding Career Discussions

1. Ask questions that encourage thought and discussion. Questions that require only a "yes" or "no" response will not stimulate thinking.
2. Be an active listener. Try to comprehend what an employee is saying and repeat it for verification.
3. Give direct and immediate feedback. Be honest, especially in your evaluation of the employee's skills and talents necessary for a particular career move.
4. Present alternatives for consideration. Provide subordinates with a fresh perspective on their present jobs.
5. Follow your subordinate's train of thought. Be flexible enough to drop your own train of thought if it's not appropriate at that point in the conversation.
6. Schedule your career development session carefully. Meeting in a different physical setting and putting aside special times for these discussions help in role separation.
7. Maintain realistic expectations of your subordinates. Progress may not be as quick to come as you would like.
8. Be aware of the tension that is part of the career development process. Recognize that change is uncomfortable, and be patient.
9. Summarize the important points that were made during the discussion.
10. End the discussion only after you feel that you have covered all the important issues.

Managers who are interested in this option might use the career development discussion to work with an employee to compile a list of job duties. You can then discuss how each of the job duties could be modified to increase the challenge, interest, and responsibility. The employee could then rank the possibilities on the list in order of importance and ease of attainability. From there, you can decide how these changes would best be implemented.

Employees will have many suggestions on how to change the nature of their own jobs; it is just a matter of stimulating or legitimizing their ideas. The end result of this effort is high morale, and when the morale of employees is high, turnover and absenteeism are reduced and productivity can be increased.

## Option #6: Moving Out

While manager-employee career development discussions should be aimed at keeping the employee satisfied and challenged within the organization, it is naive to assume that this will always be possible. After serious introspection, some individuals may find that their present occupation, industry, profession, or firm does not meet their needs and may opt to move out. One aim of the career development discussion may be to ensure that your employee has not made this decision too hastily. Needless to say, those employees who may be better suited elsewhere should not be discouraged from leaving jobs at which they may be only marginally productive or satisfied.

A final career option, then, is moving to another position outside of the organization. This option can be suggested when layoffs are frequent, when the organization cannot continue to facilitate an individual's efforts to meet personal goals, or when personal and organizational goals are in conflict.

Managers can help employees in this area by encouraging them to think through various alternatives and to follow through on those that seem particularly interesting. The dilemma, of course, is how much help the manager can or should give. To choose to provide such assistance must be in accordance with your own values and those of the organization. Some companies believe that an employee who is mismatched with her or his present job or company will be less productive than one whose needs are being satisfied. Assisting one individual to consider moving out would create opportunities for others who might make a better match. In addition to possibly improving productivity and increasing promotion opportunities, funds that otherwise might have been spent in trying to motivate, train, or develop the former employee can be redirected to those who have identified a desire for such work and development.

## Communicate

As you can see, the options for an individual who is dissatisfied in his or her present position are varied. As a manager, you can help your employees to feel better about their present jobs and their future ones if you take the time to counsel them on these career alternatives. In a tight market, an upward move may be impossible—and if you can make your employees see that up is not the only way, you will find yourself supervising a more satisfied and productive staff.□

# Team Building: A Family Dynamics Approach

Gail Silverman

*"How one was raised, the values one cherishes, and the expectations about work and people one learned as a child form the backdrop for behavior at work."*

Are there similarities between work teams and families? How much does the way the family handles relationships determine how people communicate at work? This chapter answers these questions by describing how behavior in the workplace relates to customary behavior in one's family of origin.

A team is composed of a boss and the immediate subordinates. Several specific characteristics and dynamics that occur between members make it a team rather than a task force or a project group. These characteristics include task interdependence, accountability and reportability, and the boss's ability to reward, reprimand, and punish.

Because of these characteristics, any specific problems that arise can often be resolved at team-building meetings. The problems commonly addressed in these meetings include the following:

- boss/subordinate or member/member expectations and relations;
- unclear and/or overlapping role definitions;
- unclear or changing group goals;
- fears and feelings of incompetence created by changing technology;
- feelings of inequality between members of the team;
- differences between those who feel "in" and those who feel "out" of the group, despite the fact of being "on board";
- inadequate planning, problem-sensing, and problem-solving methods;
- uncertainty about or discontent with how decisions are made;
- inadequate or incorrect information related to the task of the group and/or the organization itself;
- inability to manage day-to-day differences between members' styles, values, and cultural backgrounds, which leads either to eruption or avoidance of conflict;
- antiquated or useless practices (i.e., from the perspective of group members) such as unnecessary procedures, meetings, and so forth;

© 1983 NTL Institute

- inability to have productive meetings;
- absence of supportive behaviors, especially between the boss and subordinates.

When team members meet for team building, the group's task is to resolve and/or understand its members' differences and to commit itself to priorities, changes, and action plans. To succeed in team building, the group needs sufficient, uninterrupted time; a high commitment to identifying and solving its problems; and a facilitator from outside the group who is skilled in dynamics.

Many organizations focus on management or personal style, frequently using instruments to label and measure different attributes of leadership and personality. Some of these attributes include the following:

- one's level of need for power, control, inclusion, affiliation, and achievement;
- the degree to which one needs and can give and receive support;
- the ability to adapt style and needs to others; and
- the ways in which one manages conflict and competitiveness in her- or himself and with others.

To be effective, a manager must know and understand how her or his own personal style affects others. We often assume that the technical knowledge of the job or the organization is of primary importance, and these personal attributes are either superfluous or secondary. In practice, however, most managers discover that personal abilities to deal with people are primary and that one can learn the technical knowledge and skills more easily.

Another assumption, increasingly challenged in recent years, is that one's work life and one's home life are separate and relatively unrelated. How one was raised, the values one cherishes, and the expectations about work and people one learned as a child form the backdrop for behavior at work. This awareness leads us to use the family as a theme or metaphor in team building.

Reflecting on the aforementioned issues listed as a possible agenda for team-building meetings, one can easily see the parallel questions and issues that families must confront—either implicitly or explicitly—as they live together. All too often, families do not discuss or resolve these critical life issues. Instead, people carry problems modeled in childhood into adulthood. Sometimes, unresolved issues become so troublesome that one seeks therapy. I must stress that contemporary families usually do *not* discuss their conflicts and their relationships. In team building, the group reverses this norm of avoidance and discusses issues openly.

Key family questions and issues that parallel team-building issues include the following:

- How do children or junior members of this family group relate to senior members?
- Which behaviors between those in authority and the children are acceptable and which are unacceptable?
- Which behaviors of older children and younger children are acceptable and which are unacceptable?
- How do children get permission to try new things (i.e., projects, experiments) or to be unconventional?
- Are girls expected to behave differently from boys and to have different privileges?
- How do these differences affect their self-concepts and their expectations for their roles in life?
- Who is the favored child, or who is more "in" with the parents?
- What are the subgroups in this family, and how do they affect who gets what they need and who does not?
- How does the family treat the "out" or deviant members?
- How does it treat the "new" members (i.e., when a child marries), and what are the rites of entry to this family?
- How does the family relate to extended family and grandparents? Is it with deference and respect, regardless of how they behave, or can differences be confronted, discussed, and resolved?
- How are crucial decisions made, especially those related to money, leisure, and access to limited resources (e.g., the family car)?
- How easily influenced are the older family members by the younger members?
- How has competition between siblings been handled?
- Who nurtures whom, and how much does the idea of "peace at all costs" prevail?
- What happens when there is a divorce?
- How are the separation and attendant feelings of grief handled?
- What happens in merged families?
- How do they handle the "merger" of two sets of norms, practices, and expectations?

Usually, management schools teach only the technical aspects of management. They overlook the degree to which we learn the art of management from our families.

When conducting team-building meetings, I frequently ask the group to become a family composed of grandparents, parents, and children. Depending on the situation, the group includes influential people, such as a best friend, a boy- or girlfriend, a housekeeper, or a cousin. The grandparents are requested to stand behind the parents (i.e., their children), and we select children of different ages. The group will then try to solve a typical, contemporary family problem, such as handling a "non-performing" teenager. They may be asked how the family should spend Dad's or Mom's bonus pay. The grandparents should not participate as members of the problem-solving meeting, but should occasionally tell their daughter or son how they feel about her or his behavior as a "good mother" or "good father" while the parent deals with the family's problem. This method demonstrates how our parents' ever-present judgments about how we "should" behave, even when they are not physically present, influence us.

Inevitably, these products of contemporary management theory start out with a very participative and receptive style. But then strange things happen. As the tension builds and the clash between what is considered acceptable role behavior for each generation surfaces, Father becomes increasingly authoritarian. Long-ingrained, anachronistic sayings surface, such as "Respect your elders," "Children should be seen and not heard," "Women/girls should ————," "Men/boys should ————," "How dare you talk like that to me?" and many other epithets that suggest the right and deferential way children should address authority figures, whether they consider them to be right or wrong, fair or unfair. One can stimulate old, unfinished anger from competition among siblings by saying, "If your sister/brother did it, you will too!" In the role play, Mother frequently becomes the peacemaker as Father becomes more authoritarian. Some of the most liberated women cannot believe themselves when they see videotapes of what looked to them like "primitive, 10-year-old me." They ask, "How could this happen to *me* with all of my assertiveness training?"

Surfacing old images and patterns of male-female dynamics in team building demonstrates how easily we all can regress to the ways of our families of origin, especially when confronted with conflict. The important point is that, unless specific replacement behaviors have been witnessed and practiced, people will inevitably use the behavior they have learned, whether they approve of it or not.

Few managers can alter their typical patterns of responding unless they witness new ways to handle old problems and make a conscious effort to change in an environment that rewards experimentation with new behavior. They may be motivated intellectually and persuaded to change, but what makes the critical difference to their success in changing is experiencing observable, describable behavior that they can try to perform and about which they can receive feedback. This explains why the T Group works so well for people who want to expand their abilities to express feelings.

We use the family as a vehicle in the team-building meeting not to solve old family business, but rather to demonstrate our vulnerability to our past and to set the climate for practicing new behaviors with a heightened commitment to change.

How does all this translate in a team-building meeting? The same group that played the family is asked to become the team they really are and to work on an identified issue. The group should handle problems related to personal style or role conflicts as a next step. In the discussion that follows, the parallels between families of origin and present behavior stimulate tremendous insights and a resolve to consciously allow the ambiguity of the unknown to occur and to flounder in it, rather than to use anachronistic or inappropriate behavior. Very significant awareness about fears of authority, rejection, failure, confrontation, and feelings of inadequacy vis-à-vis other members are shared.

As the group moves to work on concrete problems, it usually develops an almost palpable change in tone, humor, and creativity among its members. As they settle down to resolve their team issues, a sense of deepened insight and commitment transforms their struggle to change and grow.

Members learn to confront each other openly and competently with practice and feedback. They do this, fully aware of the political ramifications of differing with "the boss." They begin to recognize that they will not be fired or reprimanded (i.e., in most cases) if they have done their homework and they state their views directly and clearly. Instead, respect and comradeship increase among team members and the supervisor. This openness leads to a real dialogue on issues in which the boss feels less isolated and the team members feel they are heard and are influential in decisions affecting their lives.

People need to explore the images they carry from their early years, to study their fears in the face of people who are different or more powerful, and to witness "maskless" conversations. To learn not to use or abuse one's knowledge, skill position, sex, or color when with another human being is a challenge for a lifetime, and it can prove to be fruitful, satisfying, and appropriate in the context of organizational life.□

## Bibliography

Haley, J. *Problem-Solving Therapy*. San Francisco, Calif.: Jossey-Bass, 1976.

Minuchin, S. *Families and Family Therapy*. Cambridge, Mass.: Harvard University Press, 1974.

Napier, A., & Whitaker, C. *The Family Crucible*. New York: Harper & Row, 1978.

Suter, V. *Peoplemaking*. Palo Alto, Calif.: Science & Behavior Books, 1972.

# The Heart of Team Building

Richard E. Byrd

*"When differences affect the productivity of the team, and when the manager or team members can't discuss the differences in a way to bring about a constructive exploration and resolution, they need team building."*

Team building is a term often passed about as an answer to increasing organizational teamwork—a *must* today. Some managers think team building means doing what you've done before, only better. Others misunderstand, believing it means developing a group-think approach to management. Still others, including me, understand it and use it as an "intervention by a third party conducted in a work unit as an action to deal with a condition or conditions seen as needing improvement" (Dyer, 1977). The purpose of this paper is to describe the heart of a team-building intervention to help managers assess whether this approach matches their needs.

The heart of team building is the *surfacing, exploration,* and *resolution* of differences among people that resist ordinary management methods. It always involves a skilled process consultant and the major benefit is higher quality of individual and group (team) productivity.

Side benefits from team building generally include more effective communication among colleagues, more efficiency, and more realistic and less defensive approaches to common problems. Often it leads to more fun.

Groups often identified as needing team building include the following:

*Threesomes.* The consultant may meet with two department heads whose differences in approach, philosophy, or practices cause pain to a common customer, client, user of their services, or each other.

*New work families.* The consultant may help new work families, whose personalities are not particularly suited for each other, to work through appropriate areas of differences and forestall later team traumas.

*Old work families.* Those who fear to speak the truth because they are too close to those with whom they work to develop norms of more openness and problem solving can be helped by the consultant to disentangle dysfunctional alliances.

---

© 1981 Richard E. Byrd. All rights reserved.

*Collaborating work families.* When two teams collaborate on a given project but compete on different projects, they often get caught in a quandary of not discriminating between their self-interest and the interests of others.

*Manager and subordinate.* Sometimes a valued subordinate and the manager have a win-lose argument leading to a standoff in which both acknowledge the need for outside help.

In these and other settings, the consultant uses the threefold approach—he or she surfaces differences, explores differences, and resolves differences.

The balance of this article will examine the typical kinds of differences addressed, the means of surfacing them, and the kinds of resolutions that can be expected.

## Surfacing

### Kinds of Differences

Most groups "with a common charter and an absolute need to cooperate in order to achieve the expected output" (Byrd, 1978) are likely to deal with the following differences:

*Values.* People may differ on standards of work that should be expected, the meeting of commitments, the need to follow through, the importance of winning, getting to work on time, working on weekends, the amount of travel required, and the kinds of attitudes toward other organizations that are given tacit approval. When these and other differences seem to block working together, team building helps.

*Perceptions.* Differences in perceptions, often unspoken, may be the key blocks to productive work. They may include not knowing how one stands with the manager, while the manager thinks he or she is clear about it. There may be significant differences in how competent, cooperative, tough, or supportive each team member sees the other as, leading to a lack of mutual respect. Teams with women and minorities may have distorted stereotypes of each other's attitudes or behavior that negatively affect open communication.

*Affective style.* Different levels of emotionality may block work. In other words, great differences in how team members deal with conflict, react to aggression, need to be directed or need independence, want to be included, use overstatement, or want to be personally close to colleagues, may produce excessive counterproductive turmoil.

*Expectations.* There may be unclear or unstated differences of opinion on long- and short-term goals, or overlapping roles and responsibilities. Turf conflicts that were initially only confusions and distortions can build into subtle or open wars.

*Career goals.* Some team members may need to make an immediate splash because of past failures. Others may not feel their careers will be affected by outcomes. Some may feel slow growth will enhance their careers. Some may try to impress the manager for career purposes. The differences in career stakes can affect commitment to a goal or a schedule of accomplishment.

*Dealing with authority.* Some members of the team may show excessive deference to the manager; others may be hostile. Some may be insensitive to the person in authority. Some may still be attached to the old manager. Some may be impatient with how the manager uses or doesn't use her or his authority. Authority conflicts are always present. When the differences among team members are great, the result may be flight, fight, or simply despair.

*Business approaches.* When the team does not have a long history in the same firm, they may seriously but in unstated ways disagree on such processes as estimating, bidding, working with the customer, risk taking, or concern for return on investment. Sometimes old patterns developed in previous corporate lives are hard to surface and even harder to overcome.

*Semantics.* Again, if teams consist of people from different organization backgrounds, from different companies, from different regions, or from foreign countries, meanings of words can be different. These differences may be in the use of technical words, business words, management words, humor, different ways of talking to the opposite sex, using word pictures to express oneself, highly intellectual ideas, or talking in analogies with which others may have difficulty.

While there are other areas of differences, these seem to be the areas most likely to cause a manager to say, "Let's have a team-building session."

When differences affect the productivity of the team, and when the manager or team members can't discuss the differences in a way to bring about a constructive exploration and resolution, they need team building. The consultant is a catalyst and facilitator, helping the manager and the team deal with what they may have the will but not the way to change.

## Methods of Surfacing

Once the consultant and manager decide that there is a readiness or a perceived necessity for better teamwork, they must choose the data-gathering process that will most likely surface underlying differences so that the team can constructively explore them. The consultant will propose the method he or she prefers. The following are most successful:

- Open-ended interviews with each team member, leading to a report or data package that quotes them while protecting their identity. The interviews are open-ended, but focused on the major area of differences. One may catagorize the comments to make future exploration easier for the team.
- A second method is one suggested by Ed Schein (1969). Team members write the consultant a letter describing what they are concerned about. The consultant then categorizes the issues and again quotes the letters, protecting the source.
- A third method is that of gathering survey data dealing with the major area of differences. Sometimes the data from a recent employee attitude survey or from a Likert-type survey can be used.
- A fourth successful way is a structured interview based on prearranged questions in areas such as planning, control systems, communication, organization.
- A fifth method employs small-group interviews. The advantage of this kind of session is that participants can discuss differences on the spot. The disadvantage is that the consultant has no prior opportunity to build personal trust with the individuals and therefore may not get data that the participants feel cannot be aired in public.
- Finally, the consultant may walk in without having done prior work and without an agenda, simply depending on her or his skill to surface those differences in a meeting of the team. This is generally a high-risk approach and should be used very selectively.

## Exploration

*Exploring the Differences*

A retreat time should be set aside by the manager and team members, the amount depending on the nature and intensity of the differences to be explored. All things being equal, an overnight retreat of 24 hours or more is ideal. The consultant and manager need to understand that everything cannot be done at once. Team building takes several sessions and may focus on sets of differences over the period of a year or two. If this assumption is accepted, one does not even have to complete the exploration of all the differences surfaced in the data package at this first session. In any case, the first step when in the retreat setting is an introduction by the manager explaining why he or she has arranged this activity. The consultant explains her or his role and then may ask each person to share her or his expectations at the beginning of the session.

The data package is then handed out and used for the meeting itself, generally under the direction of the manager with the process consultant clearly remaining in the role of facilitator or catalyst.

While the meeting is in process, the consultant clarifies, "I heard him say . . ."; points up differences that are being avoided; observes and describes the open or closed quality of the team's communication; helps people say what they may be hesitant or fearful of saying; monitors communication accuracy; tries to create a climate of "owning up" so that people feel support to take more risks than they normally might; and supports the afflicted and encourages the fearful. Sometimes the consultant may give individuals who have dysfunctional communication styles feedback on their impact and give suggestions on how to increase their individual communication effectiveness. For example, a team member may have a habit of stating disclaimers before giving an opinion. The consultant may point this out if he or she thinks it causes the person and the team difficulty. If the team member never seems to have a clear meaning or a desired result in her or his statements, thus receiving only polite but not intelligent reception, the consultant might point this out or simply begin asking for a more definite statement from the person. If the manager constantly interrupts a speaker, the consultant may ask the speaker, "How do you feel when X interrupts you?" The consultant, therefore, is constantly making explicit the implicit team difficulties.

A professional consultant does not permit the following to take place in team-building sessions:

• the "scapegoating" of an individual member as the sole source of the problems;
• personal attacks on one person by people in the group;
• physical abuse;
• uncontrolled emotional level;
• the revelation of grievances and hidden feelings in a nonproductive, personal, castigating manner;
• pressure on any individual in the group to reveal her or his issues.

## Resolution

### Resolving the Differences

As each point is discussed and differences clearly examined, team members will have an inherent need to work together. Because of the consultant's behavior, they will begin to empathize more with each other's point of view. Upon discovering an apparent but not real difference, they breathe a sigh of relief and surprise. After exploring a difference, sometimes losing their tempers and then backing off to discuss the concern less heatedly, a better bond is formed through the shared anger, if neither person loses face.

Initially, the most significant (and insignificant) differences may appear to be with the manager. These have to be explored and resolved. If this is done effectively, team members will then be emboldened to do the same with each other.

Resolution, then, is defined as having the following several possible meanings:

- the discovery of agreement in apparent disagreement;
- a genuine changing of minds or the synthesis of differences;
- more empathy, if not agreement, with the other person's position, style, point of view;
- genuine acceptance of and respect for each other;
- resolution not to let future differences fester.

*Picking a Team-Building Consultant*

To choose a consultant, the manager needs to consider the following questions:

- What is the reputation of the consultant with other managers?
- Does the consultant impress you as a person of maturity, who is not naive about organizations?
- Does the consultant have a reasonable approach that avoids creating trauma for trauma's sake?
- Is the consultant certified or licensed by an appropriate professional association?
- Do you trust the consultant?

## Conclusion

Team building is a useful procedure for managers who feel that some combination of people over whom they have authority or responsibility is not as productive as it might be. After determining who the third-party consultant is to be, the manager, with the consultant, plans the best approach to surfacing the unresolved differences that seem to be blocking the team effectiveness. The consultant then gathers information from the team members and presents it in a useful form to the entire team. With the consultant's assistance, the manager and team explore and resolve differences that emerge as significant.

Team building is ideally used as one technique in developing the entire organization's capacity to use its human resources, adapt to change, and create a satisfactory quality of work life.□

## Bibliography

Argyris, C. *Intervention Theory and Method.* Reading, Mass.: Addison-Wesley, 1970.

Beckhard, R. *Organization Development: Strategies and Models.* Reading, Mass.: Addison-Wesley, 1969.

Blake, R. R., Mouton, J. S., & Blansfield, M. G. How Executive Team Training Can Help You. *Journal of the American Society of Training Directors,* 1962, *16*(1), 3–11.

Byrd, R. E. Shared Management: An Innovation. In R. T. Golembiewski (Ed.), *The Small Group in Political Science.* Athens, Ga.: University of Georgia Press, 1978.

Byrd, R. E. Do Groups Help or Hinder? *A Guide to Personal Risk Taking.* New York: AMACOM, 1978. Pp. 49–57.

Dyer, W. *Team Building: Issues and Alternatives.* Reading, Mass.: Addison-Wesley, 1977.

Harrison, R. Role Negotiations: A Tough-Minded Approach to Team Development. In W. Burke & H. Hornstein (Eds.), *The Social Technology of Organization Development.* Washington D.C.: NTL Learning Resources, 1971.

Lewis, J. W. III. Management Team Development: Will It Work for You? *Personnel,* 1975, *52,* 11–25.

Schein, E. H. *Process Consultation.* Reading, Mass.: Addison-Wesley, 1969.

Walton, R. *Interpersonal Peacemaking.* Reading, Mass.: Addison-Wesley, 1969.

# Individual vs. Group Approaches: Some Guidelines for Managers for Problem Solving and Decision Making*

John J. Sherwood
Florence M. Hoylman
Alice G. Sargent

*"Knowing when to turn to a group or to an individual for decision making can be critical to organizational effectiveness."*

Most of us are only too familiar with the phenomenon that what is said outside the room 10 minutes after a meeting may explain the silence, rigidity, and ineffectiveness of the meeting much better than anything voiced inside the room. Too often, spontaneity is frowned upon, surprises are taboo, and the roles taken by key actors are well scripted in advance. Groups frequently are used on an ad hoc basis, with widespread dissatisfaction resulting from their efforts.

In addition, managers often lack skills necessary for effective team leadership and team membership. Pelz and Andrews (1976), in their study at MIT, found that effective research and development (R&D) environments were characterized by high autonomy and high comradeship (Pelz & Andrews, 1976). Yet we rarely find an R&D manager who can manage effectively for colleagueship and autonomy.

Still, managers often lack clear and explicit criteria for assigning a problem to a group or to an individual for solution. This article discusses some criteria for determining which is likely to produce better results at a given task—a group or an individual. The following five factors need to be considered when deciding whether to assign a particular task to one person or to a group of people for their joint consideration:

1. the nature of the task itself;
2. the importance of acceptance of a decision or commitment to a solution for its implementation;

© 1983 John J. Sherwood, Florence M. Hoylman, and Alice G. Sargent.
* Portions of this article appeared in *Supervisory Management*, 1978, 23(4), 2–9. This paper relies heavily on the original contributions of Norman R. F. Maier (see especially "Assets and Liabilities in Group Problem-Solving: The Need for an Integrative Function," *Psychological Review*, 1967, 74, 239–249); L. Richard Hoffman ("Group Problem Solving," in L. Berkowitz (Ed.), *Advances in Experimental Social Psychology*, vol. 2, New York: Academic Press, 1965, pp. 99–132); and on an unpublished work by Lee Bolman ("Scientists in Organizations," Institute for Social Research, University of Michigan, Ann Arbor, 1976). We appreciate the comments on an earlier version of this paper by Conrad N. Jackson and Donald C. King.

3. the value placed on the quality of the decision;
4. the competence, investment, and role in implementation of each person involved; and
5. the anticipated operating effectiveness of the group— especially the leadership.

## The Nature of the Task

The nature of the task itself is the first and most important criterion. Research shows that individuals generate ideas and creatively solve problems more effectively than groups. (Groups can be taught to brainstorm. When brainstorming, a group becomes a collection of noninteracting individuals following an established procedure. Under these conditions, groups generate more ideas than individuals working alone.) Several categories can be examined in light of this research.

*Creative Tasks.* An individual performs better than a group on tasks that call for creative solutions, such as new alternatives or previously unconsidered options. For example, individuals do better than groups at creating or constructing original crossword puzzles, designing technical concepts, or writing computer programs. When seeking a creative solution, one would do better to find an expert in the area of concern rather than assemble a group of people.

*Convergent or Integrative Tasks.* Groups do better than individuals when the problem requires that various bits of information be brought together for a solution, such as developing a business strategy or solving a crossword puzzle. It is essential, of course, that the group of people is able to work together effectively.

*Independent Tasks.* Sometimes, in our eagerness to establish more teamwork, we encourage people to work together when for the most part their jobs require them to work independently. Frequent or occasional work together may be useful when one needs to get one's job done. Temporary teamwork may be needed because of the flow of work or the need to share information or skills. Insisting that people with independent jobs work together, however, will ensure unsatisfactory work-group meetings. Effective managers know which of their subordinates need to work together to get their jobs done and which do not.

## The Importance of Acceptance of a Decision

People who participate in the making of a decision have more stake in its successful outcome. They have more personal interest in the outcome and are likely to devote more energy to ensure a satisfactory outcome.

But when an individual solves a problem or makes a decision, two tasks still remain. First, the person must persuade others that the decision provides the best—or at least a desirable—course to follow. Second, others must agree to act on the decision or to carry it out. Participation in decision making increases ownership of the decision and reduces problems of surveillance, monitoring, and follow-up in implementation.

Not all solutions to problems depend on the support of other people for effective implementation. Therefore, a manager needs to be aware of those issues that require commitment by others for a solution to work. For these issues, the manager should convene those people essential to the effective implementation of the solution. Planning and goal setting are functions that require acceptance and commitment. A manager needs to seek group consensus about the management-by-objectives (MBO) goals for the forthcoming period.

In some cases, a manager may be willing to make a decision known to be unpopular, or to assign a problem to an individual expert for solution, with the knowledge that other people will need to invest additional resources to monitor its implementation. For example, a group would decide more effectively than an individual how to collect money for the United Way Campaign, how to cut costs or increase effectiveness, and how to schedule summer vacations. In each instance, the successful implementation of the decisions depends on acceptance and commitment. On the other hand, one person can often decide what supplies need to be ordered by reviewing past use.

### The Importance of the Quality of the Decision

The best managers know when they must make tradeoffs between producing high-quality outcomes and carrying out decisions in a timely manner. A manager may be concerned with distributing responsibilities to assure that a solution will be carried out quickly and completely. In this case, the manager may accept a solution of somewhat lower quality because it has widespread acceptance, rather than insisting on a higher-quality solution that lacks acceptance among those upon whom the manager must depend to carry it out.

Managers know what quality to expect from an expert in the field. But the quality of a group decision depends on the competencies of group members, the information available to them, and how effectively they work together.

## The Characteristics of Individual Group Members

Managers must consider the following three criteria when assembling a group of people to address an issue:

- the expertise each person brings to bear on the problem;
- the stake each party has in the outcome; and
- the role each person is likely to play in implementing any decision (that is, how dependent others will be on each individual's support of the group's solution).

Obviously, managers will not convene the same collection of individuals to address every issue. For example, in the use of quality circles, the group of employees who attend typically do similar work, have the most relevant information for surfacing problems, and can offer meaningful solutions.

## The Potential Effectiveness of the Group

When considering whether to use a group, the manager needs to ask how effective a particular collection of people will be in working together and coming up with sound solutions. It may be better to ask an individual to solve a problem or make a decision than to call several people together who have great difficulty in working with each other.

## Effective Leadership

Once the decision has been made to assign a task to a group of people, the behavior of the group's leadership becomes critical to its success. It is important, therefore, to understand *the leadership dilemma*: The more power leaders have, the more positive their contributions to the group's functioning and procedures. The more power leaders have, however, the more their own behavior can be a barrier to the free exchange of ideas. The best solutions come from *strong* leaders working with *strong* group members. In this situation, conflict and disagreement tend to be creative. All resources have a chance to be used fully when

- two-way initiative exists between leader and group members (not simply two-way communication, but two-way initiative); and
- responsibilities for leadership are shared, provided
- that the strength of subordinates coupled with their assuming leadership responsibilities does not threaten the boss. The leader

can do more than anyone else to facilitate or block effective group functioning.

Several things are required from members of a problem-solving group in which leadership is conceived of as a set of *functions* to be performed by anyone seeing the need, rather than as a *role* to be filled by the boss. These functions include encouraging broad participation by bringing others into the discussion and by protecting minority points of view; assuming responsibility for accurate communication among group members; summarizing progress by pointing out where things stand at the moment; and questioning the appropriateness or the order of agenda items. The more all members of a group share and perform the requirements of effective leadership, the more productive and creative the group will be—provided this kind of behavior does not threaten the boss. More than anyone else, the boss can provoke group members into thinking, "If I can only get through this meeting, then I can get some work done." On the other hand, the boss can also do the most to provide the conditions for effective group effort.

Awareness of stages every group goes through, as characterized by Paul Hersey and Ken Blanchard (1969), enables a manager to encourage leadership and maturity among other group members. In the introductory stage, the manager needs to exert a high-task/low-relationship style to help the group gain clarity about goals and objectives. In stage two, a high-task/high-relationship style is needed as the group organizes and seeks to become more cohesive as a team. Stage three calls for a high-relationship/low-task style as group members begin to know each other better and to gain clarity concerning mission, goals, and procedures. In this stage, the group also needs to become cohesive to get the job done. The manager needs to adopt a low-task/low relationship style in the final stage as more responsibility is delegated to the mature work group and the manager moves on to new tasks.

## Assets of Groups

*Greater Total Knowledge and Information*

Even where one person, such as a supervisor or technical expert, knows much more than anyone else, the limited and unique information possessed by others can fill gaps. A group of people draws on more information, experience, and competencies than any one of its members. Clearly, the issue of how to improve effectiveness requires the resources of the team members. The issue, therefore, becomes how to make this expanded pool available and how to use it effectively.

## Greater Variety of Approaches

Each person approaches problems from a different perspective. These different viewpoints can open avenues of consideration beyond any one person's awareness. In addition, everyone gets into ruts in her or his thinking or into patterned ways of defining problems and approaching issues. A group expands the opportunities for breaking out of these mental grooves. The three types of managers described by Virginia Satir (1972)—logical thinkers, tough battlers, and friendly helpers—all have functional and dysfunctional aspects to their styles.

## Reduced Communication Problems

Decisions probably will be implemented more smoothly and require less monitoring when people are fully aware of the goals and obstacles, of the alternatives that were considered but rejected, and the facts, opinions, and projections leading to the decision.

A group clearly has more firepower than an individual, plus greater potential for discovering new perspectives and developing integrated solutions. Why then can five or ten capable persons meet to solve a problem or make a decision and wind up frustrated, with little progress, or with results that are not accepted by many of them? Seven obstacles hamper effective group functioning.

## Liabilities of Groups

### Social Pressures to Conform

Majorities, powerful minorities, or a boss can pressure people into going along with their lower-quality decisions. People often keep disagreements to themselves in their desire to be accepted or to be considered good group members. The idea is often expressed in the aphorism "to get along, go along." Reservations are expressed in private to close associates after the meeting. And the decision lacks the necessary support for an effective outcome.

### Quick Convergence

Groups tend to want to seize quickly on a solution that seems to have support. This apparent acceptance of an idea can overshadow appropriate concerns for quality or accuracy. Agreement often is erroneously assumed to signal the correct or best solution. Ideas of higher quality that are introduced late in a discussion may have little chance of real consideration. Yet research shows that when groups are required to produce two solutions to every problem, the second solution frequently is better.

## A Dominant Individual

Sometimes an idea offered by one person prevails because of her or his status, activity level, verbal skills, or stubborn persistence, all of which may be unrelated to competence in the task facing the group. Since leaders are particularly likely to dominate a discussion, their skills or insights into the consequences of excessive control are especially important.

## Secondary Goals or Hidden Agendas

People often work on assigned tasks and on their own needs at the same time. Their personal agendas are usually covert. These agendas may include personal pride, protection of one's position or department, desires for visibility or acceptance, or personality conflicts with others who are present. These factors can lead to attempts to "win the decision" rather than to find the best solution. A drive for prominence or deference can also subvert the best interests of the group.

## Time Constraints

A group simply may not have enough time to make a good decision. An individual usually can make a decision more quickly than a group. The group also requires a lot of time to develop the skills and procedures needed to work together effectively— to capitalize on group assets and to limit liabilities.

## Problems with Disagreement

Disagreement and conflict can sharpen and clarify issues when a group is defining the problem, seeking the preferred solutions, obtaining information, or establishing perspectives. People react differently to conflict, however, and animosity among group members may block progress. Some people experience disagreement as a cue to attack; others freeze or withdraw when faced with conflict or controversy.

   Well-managed disagreement often produces new ideas and innovative solutions. Solutions tend to be more creative when differences between people are seen as sources of new information rather than as obstacles to be overcome.

## Premature Discussion of Solutions

Proposed solutions may create confusion and conflict if the group lacks sufficient agreement and clarity about the problem being addressed. Unwittingly, different solutions may be offered with different problems in mind. Both the quality and the acceptance of solutions increase when a group delays seeking solutions until goals and potential obstacles are identified.

The keys to a group's success lie in identifying and mobilizing the group's resources and overcoming obstacles to effective group functioning. The quality of a group's decision obviously depends on whether the people with the best ideas or those with the worst ideas are more influential. The declaration "Let's get all the facts on the table and then make a decision" is a naive wish, as the foregoing catalogue of the liabilities of groups indicates. Getting all relevant information and assuring that it receives an appropriate hearing is a very difficult task.

## Conclusion

Knowing when to turn to a group or to an individual for decision making can be critical to organizational effectiveness. The manager can make this key decision more productively by being aware of the advantages and disadvantages of group *vs.* individual decision making. The criteria for selecting a group or an individual to make decisions work most effectively when situational management prevails. Then the manager is free to select the appropriate managerial mode with reference to the criteria discussed in this article.□

## References

Hersey, P., & Blanchard, K. *Management of Organizational Behavior.* Englewood Cliffs, N.J.: Prentice-Hall, 1969.

Pelz, D. C., & Andrews, F. M. *Scientists in Organizations: Productive Climates for Research and Development.* Ann Arbor, Mich.: University of Michigan Institute for Social Research, 1976.

Satir, V. *Peoplemaking.* Center City, Minn.: Science & Behavior Books, 1972.

# Quality of Work Life: An Overview

Herman Gadon

*". . . QWL has two main objectives: to improve morale and to increase productivity."*

In 1973, a special task force to the Secretary of the Department of Health, Education, and Welfare issued a report that asserted that much of the work performed in the U. S. was unnecessarily brutish, impersonal, menial, unrewarding, and inefficient (Department of Health, Education, and Welfare, 1979). This report made a sweeping indictment of American institutions—including private organizations, public agencies, and trade unions—for affronting individual dignity in the work place and wasting human resources. Shortly thereafter, the select participants of the Forty-Third American Assembly on the Changing World of Work, which met at Columbia University's Arden House, concluded that "improving the place, the organization, and the nature of work can lead to better work performance and *better quality of life* in the society" (Rosow, 1974).

HEW and the American Assembly were responding to both the deepening unrest of a younger, better educated and more assertive work force than that which organizations had previously encountered and to new competitive pressures from economies that had recovered from the devastation of World War II. American businesses needed improved morale and increased productivity. The HEW and American Assembly reports were signal events that marked a turning point in American attitudes toward work force organization and management. The U. S. soon paid increasing attention to the problems these reports reflected. Organizations underwent a great variety of experiments with work arrangements, which have become known as quality-of-work-life (QWL) programs.

QWL is a loose term that includes a number of organizational interventions that may be directed toward the individual groups in an organization or the organization as a whole. It also covers methods that range from those that rely only on changing processes to those based solely on new structures. A QWL effort may also combine methods and focal points in any of many possible combinations. These include such commonly known activities as quality circles, participation teams, alternative work

© 1983 NTL Institute

schedules, union-management productivity committees, job redesign, sociotechnical systems, and, more recently, "wellness" in the workplace. A review of relevant literature and conference contents indicates that this list is hardly complete and is still growing.

Numerous centers, both public and private, have been established as projects brokers to distribute information. These include the following: the Center for the Quality of Work Life at the University of California at Los Angeles; the Work in America Institute in Scarsdale, New York; the American Productivity Center in Houston, Texas; the American Center for Quality of Work Life in Washington, D. C.; and the Quality of Work Life Councils in Maryland, Massachusetts, Michigan, and New York.

## QWL—What Is It?

QWL is first a label, an umbrella term. It is not a discipline or even a field. Some questions exist regarding the nature of the attitudes QWL represents. Interventionists do agree, however, that QWL has two main objectives: to improve *morale* and to increase *productivity*. QWL interventions thus confront two of the most pressing problems organizations face today. All QWL efforts share the premise that people at work will respond creatively, productively, and with satisfaction to conditions that confer

• personal dignity and respect, with provisions for individuals to influence events that affect them;
• some reasonable measure of self-control or autonomy;
• personal recognition for contributions made to organizational effectiveness;
• rewards commensurate with performance, including opportunities to develop, to face challenge, to experience variety, and to receive more pay, promotions, and favorable assignments;
• identification with work groups and organizations that provide sources of pride and support; and
• job security, protection from arbitrary treatment, and decent working conditions.

Because so many activities have been called QWL interventions, the term has become confusing. A program best indicates that it deserves a QWL label if it can meet the criteria mentioned above. You will also find it useful to identify the categories into which the bulk of the activities used to achieve QWL objectives fall: *personal development, work redesign, teamwork, work schedules,* and *the total organization.*

## Personal Development

Personal development activities include the following:

- MBO (management by objectives);
- career counseling;
- employee assistance programs; and
- health improvement and maintenance programs.

These activities focus on the individual. MBO and career counseling emphasize professional development by providing opportunities for individuals to participate in plans that challenge them and to acquire new skills while directly contributing to organizational goals.

Employee assistance programs deal with the mental health of employees. Health improvement and maintenance programs address physical and mental well-being and stress management. Organizations have increasingly seen that healthy minds and bodies lead to high productivity and satisfaction. The first of an intended succession of annual meetings, the "Wellness in the Workplace" Conference sponsored jointly by the ODN (Organization Development Network) and the NTL Institute (National Training Laboratories) in May 1982 recognized the emergence of national interest in this field.

## Work Redesign

Work redesign activities include the following:

- job enlargement and
- job enrichment.

These activities attack the deadening effects of boring, repetitive, controlled, and limited tasks by increasing variety, challenge, discretion, and feedback. Because work redesign alone tends to neglect interpersonal and group effects, interventionists now generally include it with other efforts to improve the quality of work life.

## Teamwork

Teamwork activities include the following:

- quality circles (QCs);
- task forces and committees;
- team building;

- joint labor-management productivity committees;
- semi-autonomous work groups; and
- socio-technical systems.

The largest of the five categories, this one treats the individual as a member of a group. Teamwork explicitly builds on such concepts of interpersonal and group dynamics as identity, pride, interdependence, trust, and support.

Teamwork acknowledges that group norms and peer pressure act as powerful sources of influence that emerge from consensus and push groups to achieve goals to which they become committed. A basic assumption of teamwork is that genuine individual differences will be valued and resolved, leading to personal satisfaction and to high individual and group productivity.

Some of these activities simply increase autonomy in decision making or provide new opportunities to advise others. These activities include QCs, task forces, committees, team building and joint labor-management productivity committees.

Semi-autonomous work groups and sociotechnical systems also manipulate organization structures, interpersonal processes, leadership roles, pay, feedback, training, and technology in various combinations.

*Work Schedules*

Work schedule arrangements can include the following:

- FWH (flexible working hours)—also called flexitime or flextime;
- staggered work hours;
- compressed work weeks;
- job sharing; and
- part-time employment.

These arrangements help give employees more control over their work schedules so that they can balance them against other demands in their lives. The schedules offer different degrees of freedom. In Europe, where flexible schedules started, employees commonly balance their time over a period of a month. In the United States, the period of flexibility rarely exceeds a week and is often confined to a single day. With flexible schedules, organizations allow employees to start and stop work when they choose—provided they work the required number of hours within the period assigned.

Whereas flexible schedules allow employees to make *continuous* choices about the allocation of their time, such arrangements as staggered work hours, compressed work weeks, job sharing, and part-time work provide the opportunities to select specific *fixed* balances between work and nonwork time.

Given the heterogeneous composition of the work force—and the changing labor requirements of organizations in turbulent environments—the variety of work schedules now available increases the potential to make a favorable match between individual and organizational needs.

*The Total Organization*

Total organization activities include the following:

- Scanlon Plan;
- Rucker Plan;
- Improshare;
- parallel organization;
- work councils; and
- codetermination.

These efforts focus on the organization as a whole. They may include elements of any of the other programs previously described. When using these concepts, interventionists view the organization as a culture which both influences and is influenced by all activities within its boundaries.

With the Scanlon, Rucker, and Improshare plans an organization's employees have the opportunities, through elected representatives, to make suggestions and to participate in making decisions intended to increase operating efficiency. These plans also feature gain sharing—and sometimes losses—based on predetermined formulas. These formulas evolve through negotiations if employees are unionized and through discussions if they are not. Though formulas tend to remain unchanged for long periods of time, they are adjusted occasionally to account for new circumstances. Managers often participate in the plans.

General Motors coined the phrase "parallel organization" to refer to a participatory system of recommending and taking action that coexists with the traditional organization. Task groups are members from many levels in the organization who are selected on the basis of their potential contributions. The task groups assemble to perform specific tasks and disband when they complete the job. During their temporary life, they report to a permanent supervisory "steering committee," which has a rotating cross-hierarchical membership of its own (Stein, 1980; Stein and Kanter, 1980).

Dale Zand refers to this form of participation as "the collateral organization." In *Information, Organization and Power* (1981), he describes the way such a structure and process works in a bank and in a research and development company. Graphic Controls calls its version of sharing power in this manner "consensus management," attributing to it high levels of satisfaction and superior organizational performance (Dowling, 1977).

To overcome what he considered the drawbacks of his formal organization, William W. George, president of the microwave cooking division of Litton Industries in the 1970's,

> developed the concept using informal *task teams* to carry out the bulk of the work. Each team has a designated leader (generally a member of middle management), representatives from several functional departments and participation by members of top management on an 'as-required' basis. (George, 1977)

George held the "task teams" directly responsible for his division's remarkable growth rate, substantial profit increases, ability to adapt quickly to changing conditions, high productivity, and buoyant moral.

Cohen, Fink and Gadon (1979) found improved moral and productivity—and more creative decision making—in service organizations that used a form of organization they called "key groups," which are remarkably similar in form and method to General Motor's "parallel organization." The service organizations they studied were a large metropolitan hospital, a hotel chain, and a small city public school system.

Works councils, required by legislation in West Germany and the Netherlands, are rare in the United States. These are representative assemblies of workers and/or union officers, and they have the right of access to considerable information about a firm's affairs, including acquisitions, divestitures, investments and plant closings. Though the councils have only limited decision-making power, their influence can be substantial.

Codetermination refers to the participation of worker representatives on Boards of Directors. In some European countries (e.g., Germany, Sweden) it is mandated by law. It first appeared in the United States when the president of the United Auto Workers was appointed to the board of directors of Chrysler and when the president of the Air Line Pilots Association served on the board of directors of Pan Am. In the United States, where labor relations have developed along adversarial lines, codetermination has historically had little appeal for either the leaders of organized labor or for industry.

## QWL: Does It Work?

Quality-of-work-life programs have two objectives: to improve productivity and to increase employees' satisfaction. Yet the effects of QWL on productivity and morale in specific activities are difficult to measure unequivocally. Therefore, evaluations of the effectiveness of QWL programs tend to reflect considerable anecdotal evidence. Since surveys seem to provide a fairly reliable index of attitudes, some companies rely on them to justify their QWL efforts. Still, behavioral scientists have little certainty that they can trace results to single factors even in this area because complex organizations are affected by many variables.

Some rigorous studies have attempted to isolate dependent and independent variables and to explain the connection among programs, satisfaction, and productivity. A research group at Case Western Reserve University for the National Science Foundation (Srivastra et. al., 1975; Cummings & Molloy, 1977) undertook such a study. Looking for productivity and attitude effects in programs of sociotechnical systems (in 16 firms), job restructuring (in 27 firms), participative management (in seven firms), and organization change (in seven firms), the investigation team reported overwhelmingly positive results. Their criteria were costs, productivity, quality, withdrawal, and attitudes. Rigorous studies of the effects of flexible schedules have reported similarly positive results (Cohen & Gadon, 1978; Nolen, 1979; Alternative Work Schedules Experimental Program: Interim Report to the President and Congress, 1981). Numerous studies of Scanlon Plans show favorable results (Driscoll, 1979).

Participants in QWL programs probably care most about the achievement of objectives that they deem important. Many measures may, therefore, become criteria of success or indicators of problems that require attention. Criteria may include output/ labor ratios, numbers of rejects, turnover, absenteeism, complaints, the ability to resolve conflicts, frequency of communications across organizational boundaries, and so forth. A consensus reached to use any particular indices will increase the likelihood of commitment and provide some guidelines to desirable behavior.

Managers in Europe, in contrast to American managers, are more likely to go ahead with plans solely because they make sense. American managers, on the other hand, seem to require considerable quantitative proof before they act (Foy & Gadon,

1976). Attention to reasonable objectives—and to ways of measuring achievement of them—can inspire confidence and generate commitment, but an insistence upon accumulating large quantities of statistical proof to remove all risk may be a thinly disguised effort to prevent anything from happening.

For managements ready to make the emotional commitment of time, energy, and resources to improving productivity and satisfaction, many choices exist in the realm of quality of work life programs. Those that seem to provide the most substantial results, that endure, and that help the organization to cope better with changing circumstances take the total organizational culture into account. Two comprehensive studies suggest strongly that companies that are better managed—and that use their human resources most effectively—reflect the characteristics associated with QWL programs in *all* their policies and practices.

This conclusion appears in a major report by McKinsey & Company, Inc. called "Findings From Excellent Companies" (1981), the culmination of a "four-year R&D effort to reexamine Management and Organization Effectiveness." In a summary statement, the report observed:

> We have surfaced perhaps hundreds of interesting devices (e.g., reviews, team structures); we think *each* is important as an example of a climate support; on the other hand *none*, or no small set, constitutes a panacea; it is to a great extent the large number of supporting devices *per se* that underpins the observed self-renewing, innovative climates. (1981)

Fred Foulkes, in his study of "Personnel Policies in Large Non-Union Companies", reaches a remarkably similar conclusion. While acknowledging the difficulty of evaluating organizational effectiveness, he concludes from his data that

> The personnel policies and practices of the companies studied seem to be, for the most part, quite effective. . . . From the experiences of the companies studied there can be no doubt about the importance of the integrity of their managements and the climate of the organizations. The critical question is not whether a climate of trust and confidence is important, but rather how such a climate is created and maintained. This field survey has shed much light on this important issue. It has suggested that the combination of certain top management attitudes, values, philosophies, and goals and certain substantive policies— including the effective management of environmental factors and company characteristics; employment security; promotion from within; an influential and proactive personnel department; satisfactory compensation and

benefit programs; effective feedback mechanisms, communication programs, and complaint procedures; and careful selection, development and evaluation of managers— will produce such a climate. (1980, p. 325)

The cluster of characteristics that McKinsey and Foulkes associate with outstanding performance has also been associated with the characteristics associated with outstanding performance of Japanese management. W. Ouchi (1981) calls this cluster "Theory Z." R. Pascale and A. G. Athos (1981) refer to it as the "art of Japanese management." I should point out that these studies emphasize that leadership—as seen in the commitment, visibility, and example of top management—has a critical effect on results.

## Why Now?

QWL is not based on new notions. Its principles have been proposed for many years as concepts that will produce more productive and more satisfying organizations. Elton Mayo, celebrated for his part in the well-known Hawthorne experiments by Western Electric in the 1930s, suggested as much. So did inheritors of his legacy, including the following: Douglas McGregor (Theory X, Theory Y); Abraham Maslow (an ascending order of needs satisfactions); the Tavistock group in London, England, including Eliot Jacques, Fred E. Emery, Eric L. Trist, and A. K. Rice (sociotechnical systems); and the M.I.T. group of Kurt Lewin, Alvin Zander, Dorwin Cartright, Douglas McGregor, Alex Bavelas, Charles Myers, Paul Pigors, Douglas Brown, and Joseph Scanlon (force-field analysis, group dynamics, and the Scanlon Plan). Numerous other behavioral scientists, like those above, have been writing about, experimenting with, and studying for over 50 years the effects of the themes that form the basis of all quality-of-work-life activities. The number of these doers, thinkers, and scholars has increased steadily since then.

During the last 10 years these ideas have finally had a substantial effect on organizational practice. Organizations throughout the world feel the competitive pressures from which the United States had been largely insulated for many years after World War II. With our capital base, infrastructure, and organizations intact, American products, managerial practices, and technology spread throughout the world. The economic bases of most of the rest of the industrialized world had been ravaged by World War II. For all practical purposes, American organizations operated with little competition for 20 years. In the middle 1960s, the first signals of potential danger were masked by the commitment of resources to the Vietnam War. The U. S. had an economy pushed by the demands for "butter and guns," and it appeared to provide both. Under these circumstances, we could not readily see the developing weaknesses in our internationally competitive position.

American industry spent less on capital improvements and organizational innovations, relatively, than organizations in other countries. Whereas other countries honed themselves to a fine competitive edge because of a need to catch up, we lulled ourselves into a false sense of security, confident in the apparently overwhelming size of our advantage. Therefore, we did not upgrade equipment in our factories or modernize technology as rapidly as our developing competitors.

The end of the Vietnam War exposed our weaknesses. The steel industry became one of the first to suffer seriously from international competition. In a defensive effort, the United Steel Workers of America, AFL-CIO, and the major steel producers agreed to suspend strikes between contracts and to submit unresolved differences to arbitration. The industry could not afford the permanent loss of customers to foreign sources that had followed previous work stoppages. The steel union and management also made tentative efforts to cooperate to increase productivity through joint productivity committees.

In 1974, the oil embargo by OPEC nations forced upon industry—and the automobile makers in particular—a critical awareness of our vulnerability to foreign competition. In responding to the threat of competition, American management has had to acknowledge the shift in values that has occurred in American society. An emphasis on equity, freedom of choice, and fulfillment have emerged as expectations of a younger and better educated work force. Since the late 1960s, Yankelovich (1981) has documented this change through surveys conducted at regular intervals. General Motor's experience in the early 1970s in Lordstown, Ohio—a plant built to produce its new line of Chevrolet Vegas at low cost—represents a classic clash of new worker values with unchanged management attitudes. Workers simply wouldn't perform as expected. Rallying around cries for consideration, dignity, humanity, and better working conditions, young workers struck and forced GM to change its perceptions of the way to treat its employees. Perhaps the Lordstown confrontation had to occur before GM could make a full-scale commitment to improving the quality of work life.

When the stakes become high enough, managers search for options. This phenomenon is not confined to the United States. For example, driven by a labor shortage and social change that stressed more democratic values throughout their societies, European countries experimented with organizational forms designed to increase both output and worker satisfaction. From this source came semi-autonomous work groups, flexible working hours, works councils, codetermination, and worker-managed enterprises. A reputation for cheap, poorly made merchandise once limited the appeal for Japanese goods in the markets of the world. The need to export so that it could live decently pushed Japan toward a compulsive attention to quality. Quality circles is one legacy; this term has entered our language as another association with the Japanese miracle. People must feel the pressures for change before change can occur. American managers must now pay attention to quality-of-work-life programs.

## Conclusion

Although the concepts that lie behind America's present interest in quality of work life have had a wide circulation for more than 40 years, U. S. industry had to experience changing circumstances in international competition and attitudes toward work before we would make a large-scale reconsideration of existing organizational practices.

Because QWL responds to environmental pressures, the efforts to cope with them that QWL represents will continue. The label may change but the momentum will not. Americans' awareness that the world's resources are limited has been heightened by the rising clamor of nations to share more of them. The good life will be pursued in the marketplaces of the world, and our access to it will depend substantially on our ability to compete successfully. Quality of work life is not, therefore, a passing fancy—or even an appeal to better, more humane values. It is a practical way of addressing our productivity and psychological needs in a harshly competitive world.□

## References

*Alternative Work Schedules Experimental Program: Interim Report to the President and Congress.* Washington, D.C.: U. S. Office of Personnel Management, September 1981. Pp. 60–79.

Cohen, A., & Gadon, H. *Alternative Work Schedules.* Reading, Mass.: Addison-Wesley, 1978.

Cohen, A., Fink, S., & Gadon, H. Key Groups—Not T-Groups—for Organization Development. In D. P. Sinha (Ed.), *Consultants and Consulting Styles.* New Delhi, India: Vision Books, 1979. Pp. 171–186.

Cummings, T. G., & Molloy, E. S. *Improving Productivity and the Quality of Work Life.* New York: Praeger, 1977.

The Department of Health, Education, and Welfare. *Work in America.* Cambridge, Mass.: MIT Press, 1979.

Driscoll, J. W. Working Creatively with a Union: Lessons from the Scanlon Plan. *Organizational Dynamics*, Summer 1979, 61–80.

Dowling, W. F. Consensus Management at Graphic Controls. *Organizational Dynamics*, Winter 1977, 23–47.

Foulkes, F. K. *Personnel Policies in Large Non-Union Companies*. Englewood Cliffs, N. J.: Prentice-Hall, 1980.

Foy, N., & Gadon, H. Worker Participation: Contrasts in Three Countries. *Harvard Business Review*, May–June 1976, *54*(3), 71–83.

George, W. W. Task Teams for Rapid Growth. *Harvard Business Review*, March–April 1977, *55*(2), 71–80.

McKinsey & Company, Inc. *Findings from the Excellent Companies*. San Francisco: McKinsey & Company, 1981.

Miller, E. C. The Parallel Organization Structure at General Motors: An Interview with Howard C. Carlson. *Personnel*, *55*(4), 1978, 64–69.

Nolen, S. D. Does Flexitime Improve Productivity? *Harvard Business Review*, September–October 1979, *57*(5), 12–22.

Ouchi, W. *Theory Z*. Reading, Mass.: Addison-Wesley, 1981.

Pascale, R. J., & Athos, A. G. *The Art of Japanese Management*. New York: Simon & Schuster, 1981.

Ronen, S. *Flexible Working Hours: An Innovation in the Quality of Working Life*. New York: McGraw-Hill, 1980.

Rosow, J. M. (Ed.). *The Worker and the Job*. New York: The American Assembly, Columbia University, 1974.

Srivastra, S., et. al. *Job Satisfaction and Productivity*. Cleveland, Oh.: Department of Organizational Behavior, Case Western Reserve University, 1975.

Stein, B. A. *Quality of Work Life in Context: What Every Practitioner Should Know*. Cambridge, Mass.: Goodmeasure, Inc., 1980.

Stein, B. A., & Kanter, R. M. Building the Parallel Organization: Creating Mechanisms for Permanent Quality of Work Life. *The Journal of Applied Behavioral Science*, 1980, *16*(3), 371–388.

Yankelovich, D. *New Rules*. New York: Random House, 1981.

Zand, D. E. *Information, Organization and Power*. New York: McGraw-Hill, 1981.

**For Further Reading**

*A Plant-Wide Productivity Plan in Action: Three Years' Experience with the Scanlon Plan*. Washington, D. C. The National Center for Productivity and Quality of Working Life, 1975.

*Reading Book of the Ecology of Work Conference*. Readings from conferences held in Boston in spring 1979; in St. Louis in spring 1980; in San Diego in spring 1981; in Baltimore in fall 1981; and in Pittsburgh in spring 1982. Arlington, Va.: NTL Institute-Organization Development Network.

# Implementing Quality-of-Work-Life Programs by Managers

Susan A. Mohrman
Thomas G. Cummings

*"Quality of work life is primarily a philosophy that an organization will enhance both individual and organizational outcomes if it stresses worker task involvement, preservation of worker dignity, and elimination of dysfunctional aspects of hierarchy."*

Efforts to increase productivity and quality of work life (QWL) constitute a growing phenomenon in American corporations and government in the 1980s ("The New Industrial Relations," 1981; "Working Smarter . . . ," 1981). Organizations in all sectors of the economy are searching for innovative ways to use employees' creative energies to solve pressing economic and productivity problems. People from all stages of corporate and bureaucratic life flock to conferences and workshops that extoll the virtues of QWL in general and of such particular techniques as quality circles, job enrichment, "gainsharing," and flexitime. Consultants declare themselves willing and equipped to "put a program in place."

QWL programs typically have the dual objectives of improving both productivity and employee fulfillment. These programs are generally multifaceted and may include simultaneous changes in work design, participation decision making, leadership style, reward systems, and organization structures. Those who implement QWL programs hope that these changes will make work more satisfying and motivating, and that consequently employee commitment and task performance will improve.

Although we would be premature to judge the overall impact of the QWL trend at this time, we can learn from the experiences of the early innovators of QWL approaches. This paper draws on experiences with a broad array of QWL programs and suggests that success depends largely upon the manner in which an organization implements a program. QWL is not an innovation that an organization can simply *adopt*, for QWL requires new behaviors and assumptions about organizations that people must strive to *learn*. Because QWL learning leads to a fundamental alteration in one's world view, its practical implications are substantially different and more far reaching than those obtained by merely adopting innovations.

© 1983 NTL Institute

## Implementing QWL: Common Misconceptions

I've read some articles about QWL, and I'm curious about it. We've got some real people problems, and a QWL program sounds like a good way to turn things around. Let's put one in place in the next few months. We can hire a consultant and get started right away. We have to get some of our people to start acting differently. Maybe set up a few of those quality circles or enrich some of the jobs. This will show our people that we care about them, and it might get us a lot of favorable visibility in the company.

With these words, another manager or administrator embarks on a QWL program. Unfortunately, the path to higher productivity and employee fulfillment contains a number of pitfalls that a manager can more easily identify than avoid. A major cause of these often unexpected difficulties is the common misconception that QWL programs resemble other innovations that organizations typically adopt, such as new pieces of equipment, accounting methods, or production techniques. The statement above demonstrates that managers often erroneously assume the following: (a) the innovation is clearly defined and understood; (b) they can implement QWL through a series of specifiable steps; and (c) the organization can readily gain the necessary knowledge and skills to use the innovation. We will assess each of these assumptions and their validity below.

### "QWL Programs Are Well-Defined and Clearly Understood Organizational Innovations"

False. The popular literature overflows with testimonials on the benefits of worker-participation groups, enriched jobs, facilitative supervision, skill-based pay, the removal of artificial status barriers between workers and managers, and other techniques. Managers who adopt such techniques identify and try to mandate QWL components that they expect will be accepted and effective in their work setting. This approach presupposes that people can predict the effects of these individual components on desired outcomes by learning how they operated in other organizations. QWL processes, however, tend to be complex and multifaceted—which makes it impossible to tell which particular components produce positive organizational outcomes. Most QWL efforts lack evaluation efforts. So, despite global testimony on their positive impact, managers cannot clearly link positive change to many of these projects (Cummings, Molloy & Glen, 1977).

Limited knowledge exists regarding QWL programs. Therefore, managers take risks when they treat QWL as a set of innovations that can be adopted through imitation. The appropriateness of a QWL design depends upon individual, technological, and organizational contingencies. The fit among various QWL components matters as much or more than the nature of any one component (Nadler & Tushman, 1977). This complexity means that managers should act cautiously and secure sound advice before they reach into the grab bag of techniques.

If QWL is not an innovation, then what is it? Quality of work life is primarily a philosophy, a set of beliefs that an organization will enhance both individual and organizational outcomes if it stresses worker task involvement, the preservation of worker dignity, and the elimination of dysfunctional aspects of hierarchy. QWL also holds that people who become involved in day-to-day decision making will use their knowledge and skills to make decisions that enhance both satisfaction and performance. When managers treat QWL programs as the implementation of prespecified innovations, they violate these very principles of employee involvement and participation.

A manager cannot *mandate* design to promote worker input and involvement. Each QWL effort must have its unique properties, which will unfold under the guidance and direction of those who know and have a stake in the local setting. What emerges cannot be specified in advance.

*QWL Programs Can Be Implemented Through a Series of Specifiable Steps*

False. The implementation of a change—such as increased worker participation—will inevitably create tension in other organizational variables, including the communication system, the design of work, and the reward system (Nadler & Tushman, 1977). To handle this interdependence of organizational variables, most QWL interventions deal with multiple system components. The simultaneous alteration of multiple QWL components, however, is an extremely complicated process that requires real-time monitoring and tinkering—hardly a predictable process.

QWL is essentially a philosophy—therefore, its implementation contains yet another level of complexity. Individuals must learn both the underlying world view and the implied behaviors. Design components that commonly occur in QWL projects work only when supported by the very values and behaviors they are intended to facilitate. Skill-based pay, for example, works effectively only when an organization values skill attainment enough to create opportunities for it to occur. Worker participation groups only succeed when workers have the necessary skills, knowledge, opportunity, and willingness to participate and when managers have the skills, knowledge, and willingness to respond.

QWL is a normative set of beliefs. It includes values, goals, decision criteria, and behaviors quite different from those commonly found in traditional American organizations and supported by our culture. We know very little about how to change the way people see and respond to their world or about the way they attach value to outcomes. We do know, however, that when managers hierarchically mandate QWL they do little more than reenact the status quo and reinforce the traditional world view. The implementation of QWL must be open-ended, flexible enough to respond to the unanticipated fallout, and creative enough to devise responses to the dilemmas of change at multiple levels of organization and psyche.

### Organizational Members Can Readily Gain the Necessary Knowledge and Skills To Sustain a QWL Program

False. Organizations tend to underestimate the amount of learning required to sustain a QWL program. The clichés that often mark the onset of a QWL program can mislead managers into thinking that for them the change will be simple or nonexistent. Most managers already conceive of themselves as "harnessing the energies of their people" or as promoting a work environment in which "we all work together." We often hear such statements as: "Our middle managers already act this way. We just need to get our supervisors to change." QWL often becomes something that upper management tells middle management to tell the supervisors to do for the workers.

The frequency with which people identify the need for change in others—while they see their own behavior as congruent with QWL—suggests that organizations' current theories-in-use probably differ from the espoused theories of their managers (Argyris & Schon, 1978). Paradoxically, we have found that the more paternalistic the organization has been in the past, the less aware the managers are of the extent to which their management style is incongruent with the goals of QWL.

Underneath the reflex denial of need to change lies considerable fear of the significance of the alterations in behavior implied by QWL concepts. This fear becomes most graphically evident among first-line supervisors. These persons will have to struggle with the day-to-day reality of such ambiguous guidelines as "Be responsive to the requests of subordinates" and "Let workers help decide how things should be done." This kind of system sounds to them like extra work and it also sounds like it might undermine the legitimate authority that often has been the major motivational tool of the first-line supervisor. Caught in a system that historically has rewarded predictability and tight control, the supervisor now is being asked to take a risk by responding to subordinates in a new way. The clichés that appeal to upper management hardly reduce the supervisors' ambiguity regarding the behaviors and skills managers expect from them.

Middle managers seldom realize that they create the context that requires the directive control orientation of first-line supervisors. Middle managers respond to contextual demands that do not match the changes in their own behavior, and this occurs on up the hierarchy. Each layer has generally developed elaborate strategies for responding to demands from above for certainty. Often these strategies prevent initiative at one's own level and stifles initiative from below. A middle-manager preparing to implement a QWL process would do well to ask "Can I make necessary changes in my own behavior that will allow those below me in the organization to change?"

## Implementing QWL Through Organizational Learning

QWL programs are organizational innovations that are not clearly defined, that must be implemented through an open-ended process, and that require alterations in both the assumptions and behaviors of organizational members at all levels. Success in implementing such fundamental and ambiguous innovations requires high amounts of employee involvement and learning. Organizational members themselves must develop a shared view of the kind of organization they desire. They must also develop the behaviors necessary to design, implement, and maintain the desired organization. This contrasts sharply with more traditional approaches to adopting innovations that emphasize external expertise and direction, compliance with a specified recipe or design, and programmed implementation. Although managers may and should get ideas from QWL processes in other organizations, internal "ownership" and direction play an integral part in the QWL philosophy.

Managers must do the following as part of this internally directed change process.

*Clarify the Values that the Organization*
*Will Promote Through the QWL Project*

The organization must determine the values it will promote through the QWL program so that all personnel will know the objectives. QWL processes are generally guided by simultaneous values of productivity and employee fulfillment. A failure to address this duality explicitly can cause frustration as different individuals work to maximize different outcomes. For example, worker problem-solving groups may work hard to improve such hygiene matters in the workplace as cleanliness or physical comfort. This will make supervisors frustrated because the problem-solving groups have neglected production issues.

Value clarification that leads to an image of a desired future state or an agreed-on set of principles—such as a philosophy statement—helps management guide a QWL process. The generation of such principles must involve members of the highest organizational level that requires behavioral change to support QWL in the operating units. A statement of principles allows individuals and groups to make sure their activities fit in with the intended direction of the organization.

### Diagnose the Current Situation To Decide
### Where the Major Changes Must Occur

Organizational learning requires the manager to identify gaps between the way the organization currently functions and the way it would in its desired state (Argyris & Schon, 1978). When managers skip this stage they fail to understand the dysfunctional aspects of the status quo. This diagnostic phase leads managers to realize that they are inadvertently stifling ideas from below. Without explicit change goals, people have little motivation to endure the difficult and challenging task of changing behavior. To formulate an accurate diagnosis, the members of the organization must generate accurate data about the current state of the organization. They can do this through a survey feedback process or through alternative techniques for promoting frank discussions within the organization.

### Generate Alternative Innovations Based
### On Available Knowledge and Research

People who design and guide a QWL program should generate a number of design alternatives from which to choose. All too frequently managers lock into one design—such as quality circles—without generating an array of potential innovations they can use to achieve their objectives. If the implementation of the first design yields disappointing results, the organization tends to allow the effort to atrophy rather than make modifications or implement alternate designs to try to reach organizational objectives. Thus, a general concept—such as employee involvement—becomes discredited, not just its narrow embodiment in quality circles.

An inability to specify the exact design and the steps of the implementation process makes on-site change agentry essential. QWL processes violate many of the organization's previous norms regarding openness and collaboration. They bring into question previous status definitions and disconfirm many individuals' self-images. Unlike other innovations, this basic upheaval is the *intent* of QWL and not an unfortunate side effect. A manager involved in such a change process requires the assistance of a trusted internal change agent who can provide feedback and guidance so that the manager's own behavior fits the goals of the process.

*Specify Minimally the Initial Design or Innovation and*
*Plan To Develop It More Fully During Implementation*

The manager's traditional need to know exactly what the change will look like and the steps necessary to get there can kill a QWL program. The manager should choose the initial changes with the full knowledge that the first steps of implementation will generate information helpful in modifying that design. The people who have on-line information about problems encountered can rework a minimally specified design during implementation. This approach builds the "ownership" and commitment necessary to sustain the difficult change process.

This approach flies in the face of the organizational tendency to reward certainty and efficiency. It is both suitable and necessary, however, for a system change that brings into question the philosophical underpinnings of traditional hierarchical structures. QWL requires profound alterations in the way members view their organizations, their roles, and their constraints.

*Implement the Innovation Using Data Feedback*
*To Modify and Adjust It to the Situation*

Data about the effectiveness of the implementation of the QWL design pinpoint whether the design or the manner of implementation is responsible for the outcomes experienced. We have witnessed several QWL projects in which management believed that design components had been implemented—without any confirmation that the components were in place and operating. The design actually implemented often differs greatly from what the managers intended. In one quality circle program, for example, employee-participation groups actually consisted of employees who were favored by their supervisors and who saw the meetings as time off work and a reward for good job performance.

The collection and discussion of data on the effectiveness of the implementations can provide a basis for modification in implementation procedures and/or the basic QWL design itself. A manager must handle the critical but difficult task of creating the budgetary and scheduling flexibility necessary for real-time responsiveness. If QWL programs become implemented with tightly constrained budgets and with rigid prescheduling demands, the learning group will have difficulty responding with the refinements and modifications necessary to keep the process alive and healthy.

*Evaluate the Overall Effectiveness of the QWL*
*Process and Decide on Resource Investment*

Evaluation of the effectiveness of the QWL effort takes a long time and cannot occur until the design becomes relatively stable—and the implementing organization understands it. A QWL process needs several years to stabilize, even in a relatively simple organization.

We question whether a "philosophy" can be evaluated. At some point, however, the organization must begin asking itself whether and in what form the resources allocated to the QWL program should continue. This involves a judgment about the current and expected contribution of the QWL process to the organization's effectiveness in its environment. The organization will find it difficult—if not impossible—to purposefully "discontinue" QWL if it has achieved any of the intended impact on people's expectations and behaviors. Managers who remove resources from the QWL effort must do so delicately because people's dreams, hopes, and self-concepts become wrapped up in the attempt of a social system to alter its philosophy.

## Conclusion

QWL demonstrates a conscious effort by American organizations to make the transition toward a new phase in management governed by a new set of assumptions. Managers cannot approach it as yet another innovation that they can try out and discard. The implementation of QWL programs has profound and sobering implications.

A QWL effort must attain three diverse qualities at the same time. It must be *systematic* and tenacious enough to overcome initial skepticism and long-standing habits. It must be *profound* enough to make people question basic assumptions and take personal risk. And it must be *flexible* enough to respond and adjust to unanticipated challenges and dilemmas.

The manager who treats QWL as a "quick fix" or feels pressure to "get on the bandwagon" has received poor advice. Individuals in units undertaking QWL efforts will simultaneously feel skeptical of the intentions of their organizational superiors, leery of personal risk, and intrigued by the question "What if this is a serious possibility?" Success requires that managers make a candid statement about their willingness to take such a risk and the commitment of visible and significant resources to the effort. Most important, it requires clear and consistent philosophical direction from respected leaders. This allows organizational members to develop a senses of purpose and the decision criteria to guide their efforts. Finally, QWL programs require competent and consistent facilitation from persons skilled in the process requirements of complex behavioral change.

## References

Argyris, C., & Schon, D. A. *Organizational Learning: A Theory of Action Perspective.* Reading, Mass.: Addison-Wesley, 1978.

Cummings, T. G., Molloy, E. S., & Glen, R. A Methodological Critique of Fifty-Eight Selected Work Experiments. *Human Relations, 30*(8), 1977.

Nadler, D. A., & Tushman, M. L. A Diagnostic Model for Organizational Behavior. In R. Hackman, E. Lawler, & L. Porter (Eds.), *Perspectives on Behavior in Organizations.* New York: McGraw-Hill, 1977.

The New Industrial Relations. *Business Weekly,* May 11, 1981, 84–98.

Working Smarter: What Happens When Workers Manage Themselves. *Fortune,* July 27, 1981, 62–69.

# Managing With Quality Circles

Roger A. Ritvo

*"Quality circles provide the opportunity and the needed process to tap the creativity of an organization's most important resource: its employees."*

Quality circles (QCs) have rapidly gained attention and widespread application in just a few years. A QC is a group of employees who do similar work and meet regularly to identify problems, investigate the causes and consequences of these problems, and make recommendations for change. It provides employees—whether in industry, government, human services, aerospace, or hi-tech settings—the opportunity to participate directly in decisions that will improve the quality, efficiency, and effectiveness of their work. If you are a manager, you may see a QC program on the horizon in your own organization. Behavioral scientists estimate that over 3,000 QC programs exist, a number that has multiplied ten-fold since 1979. This article describes the history of QC efforts and presents a series of recommendations for managers facing the challenge and opportunity of QCs.

## History

I am not surprised to report that QCs have their roots in Japan. Dr. W. Edwards Deming documented Japan's search for quality and excellence in the 1950s. Deming's efforts formed the basis of a national series of management seminars and training programs that reached over 7,500 middle and senior managers by 1980, forming a cadre of committed corporate leaders. These efforts stressed the need for "human relations" involvement—Japanese style, not American style (Tsurumi, 1981). They stressed leadership, commitment, and responsibility, not shared power and style. Charles Protjman became a leading proponent of the Japanese effort. By a strange coincidence, he was a young engineer at Western Electric's Hawthorne Works when the now-famous "Hawthorne Experiments" were conducted. Protjman urged organizations to emphasize productivity and output. Cooperative programs and discussion focused on the *production* and quality control elements. The payoff took a decade to refine and become recognized.

The first QCs began operating as early as 1962. Many Japanese firms used quality circles to enhance their production

© 1983 NTL Institute

departments. The Japanese have traditionally delegated much of the production planning and control to the production supervisor. The logic was clear: Those closest to the problem will likely have ideas on how to solve it. The actual success of QCs may help explain why only 20 years ago Americans viewed Japanese products as excellent imitations, but, as the 1960's ended, Japan's ability to provide products equal to those of the U. S. increased competition. Today, as the decade of the 1980s continues, many U. S. firms strive to achieve Japanese quality. The evidence shows that quality circles played a major part in Japan's 20-year turnaround. The successes of Sony, Toyota, Datsun, Seiko, and Mitsubishi illustrate this point clearly. IBM's zero defects program illustrates this concept in action in the United States.

At a Honeywell subsidiary, 94 employees held biweekly quality circle meetings. After nine months, the results included the solutions to 109 problems, which yielded $186,000 in savings. This included a 36% reduction in per-unit costs on the assembly line. Other qualitative indicators stressed increased cooperation, improved managerial response, and an opening of communication channels. When combined, these QC efforts have produced an effective program that ultimately improves productivity and product quality. Lincoln National Life Insurance Company achieved similar results. In 1975, it began a total improvement program. Not only has this effort led to dramatic savings, but it has altered attitudes, which allows supervisors to plan and manage, not just to control.

Quality circles have as their underlying premise the belief that employees *throughout* the organization possess both the information on ways to improve product quality and the motivation to share that information. This approach differs from management by objectives (MBO) efforts because the targets in MBO are end-points; the QC stresses the ongoing nature and production of a company's work. MBO focuses mainly on individual performance toward mutually agreed-upon goals; quality circle participants develop their own agenda for problem solving. While mangement retains the ultimate decision-making power, QC efforts stress that employees can potentially solve many of the problems in the workplace. In other words, they have a stake in their work.

## What Is a QC?

A quality circle consists of about 10 employees who volunteer to meet on a regular basis to discuss their work, its successes, problems, and constraints. They must be able to document the work through data collection, and make recommendations to management. Such efforts do not happen spontaneously. Employees and management often rely on a facilitator to aid the process of the QC group. These facilitators pay attention to avoiding the "bull session," assist the group in "brainstorming" creative solutions, and suggest effective methods for presenting its results to management. The weekly QC meeting should be scheduled for a minimum of 90 minutes during the normal workday. Participants should not treat the QC meeting as "time off" or as "extra work" to be done after everything else has been handled. To do so will effectively kill the QC work group before it even meets.

The QC effort may require the expertise of a facilitator, an expert in the process of developing a special program and in organizational change. This person can assist in the design and conduct the needed training, work with QC leaders, become a link with management, and be an advocate for QCs in the system. No manager should try to implement a quality circle program alone. This not only breeds possible suspicion and mistrust in subordinates, but will likely provoke questioning by the manager's superiors. The QC facilitator can provide the needed skills to overcome and manage these resistances and problems.

For employees to become members of a quality circle, they must be able to do the following:

• obtain the freedom to say what they think without fear of reprisal—either overt or subtle;
• discuss concerns with colleagues;
• meet and work with management;
• seek information about their jobs;
• influence decisions made about the quality and quantity of their work;
• see the results of their work; and
• receive appropriate recognition for successes.

The QC approach often requires new attitudes from a company's managers. Supervisors, middle managers, and CEOs must believe—or learn to believe—that employees have an interest in the quality of their work and have knowledge that can increase productivity, reduce errors, and increase profits. Will it work? QCs have already developed an enviable track record. One company used QCs to eliminate retooling time and saved $75,000. Another firm saved $9,000 by rescheduling certain planning meetings. A third industrial plant decreased inspection costs by $34,000 as a result of a QC effort, while an insurance company decreased its check processing costs by over $175,000. Organizations can expect a payback in the 6–1 range! Though they do not occur overnight, such results have been common in hospitals, financial institutions, government, airlines, trucking firms, and the computer industry.

Quality circles provide the opportunity and the needed process to tap the creativity of an organization's most important resource: its employees. Employees want to be treated as more than just "hired hands." They have a stake in their work. If so involved, people will take initiative, have pride in their work, and contribute to corporate goals. If managers assume that QCs cannot work with their employees to reach these goals, then QCs are not worth the effort. If, on the other hand, management believes that employees can offer more than just their eight hours of time, QCs provide a proven vehicle for them to do so.

## Myths about Quality Circles

In most new approaches to the management of work and workers, a mythology develops—and it often spreads faster than the facts! In this section, I will discuss the facts and fantasies of the QC approach.

### Myth 1: Quality Circles Are Gripe Sessions

A common misconception is that the QC exists to give the "rotten apple" an opportunity to vent feelings of frustration. The QC is not a coffee club; it is not a mutual gripe session. With the proper training and a strong commitment from top management, complaints can be converted into constructive recommendations. If the quality circle program only provides an opportunity to complain, then the concept behind it probably has not been explained or introduced properly. This problem becomes apparent when the QC focuses on individual performance, not on work, tasks, processes, and technologies.

### Myth 2: QCs Are Just Another Fad

I hope not. If the QC is a fad, organizations will find it difficult to sustain the needed interest and commitment to excellence. If employees or managers feel it will not work, perhaps *that* issue should be explored. While numerous efforts exist to improve the profitability of an enterprise, these fads come and go. From the available evidence of the last ten years, we can see that QC efforts become durable and self-perpetuating. Technology has changed the nature of management.

### Myth 3: We've Tried It Before—It Won't Work

This is one of the most common ways to resist any new idea. But QCs do not just provide an elaborate substitute for the suggestion box. They represent an opportunity for the company to open up *all* its lines of communication on issues central to its work and workers. If an organization's workers perceive a QC program as another way for the company to get their suggestions—or to "cool them out"—then QCs will surely fail.

## Myth 4: We Don't Need It Here

Such attitudes often arise from the feeling that if the organization adds a quality circle, something must be wrong. Managers can misinterpret an intense effort for excellence as a challenge to their competence. QCs go beyond what any manager can do in a boss-subordinate relationship.

## QCs For Middle Managers

The middle managers' and first line supervisors' attitudes determine whether QC programs succeed or fail. In fact, many companies' ability to grow, to change, to adapt lies with this key component. And, as with all change efforts, organizations should expect worker resistance. But they must deal with it directly and help managers overcome the following concerns:

*"QCs are a waste of time."* Organizations pressure employees to improve productivity and to push for better time-management techniques. Managers worry because QCs appear to move them in the opposite direction. Yes, QCs do—but only in the short run. The payoff exists, but managers may not see it in a two-month period.

*"QCs mean I lose control."* Since the quality circle is another work "group," managers worry that their staffs will develop divided loyalties. This does not happen, but it may appear plausible. Participation in a QC program creates another work responsibility that the manager must be aware of and schedule; it does not remove a supervisor's responsibility.

*"There is nothing in it for me."* Wrong. When the QC can improve the quality of work, reduce error rates, and decrease "down time," it reflects directly on you. As most managers move up the hierarchy, their technical skills receive fewer rewards than their "people" skills. And what better way to document effective communication than through quality improvement and increased productivity!

*"It's not my idea, so I won't get credit."* Also untrue. A QC can be implemented in any part of an organization. In fact, an organization may benefit from implementing QCs in one part of a plant and then building on its successes. A quality circle can begin in a department or with two groups whose work is

interdependent—e.g., sales and marketing, the admissions department and the emergency room, quality control and production, and recruitment and financial aid.

Well-implemented, successful QC programs exist in a wide variety of companies, including Babcock and Wilcox, Boeing, Honeywell, General Motors, Westinghouse, Chicago Title Company, and Champion Spark Plug. Besides the expected results, organizations seem to obtain other benefits from QCs. Some QC leaders have found that their own leadership potential becomes recognized, which leads to consideration for future promotions. In most cases, morale improves, reducing employee turnover. As operators develop a more intrinsic interest in their jobs, they may also begin to see how one job relates to the others in a department. This "big picture" often renews the employees' sense of importance. And, as managers begin to share information with workers and receive their ideas willingly, management becomes easier. I firmly believe that higher levels of management stress planning functions more than control functions. But organizations expect the first-line supervisor and the middle manager to "keep the troops in line." If quality circles can assist in this process, they offer both tangible and intangible benefits, thereby increasing the effectiveness of those who truly manage the employees.

Like all interventions, QC programs require management and organizational support. Since quality circle programs attempt to apply systematic problem solving to groups, experience dictates that the legitimacy of such groups must be unquestioned. The "what-right-do-they-have" attitude dooms a well-conceived program to failure. If an organization has a history of employee participation, then this norm should support the formation of such employee groups. If not, QC efforts will require greater, more visible management action to demonstrate commitment. I must restate that organizations must give QCs the needed data to do their work. Without timely information, QCs will quickly become mere artifacts. QCs are legitimate "company business." As such, they should be recognized as important meetings, warranting equal access to meeting rooms, scheduling, and the same staff support that any other task force or group in the organization receives.

## Conclusion

The quality circle implies a commitment to quality improvement. It is an ongoing process, a part of a company's work—not an ancillary set of meetings. For QCs to succeed, employees must feel that their participation can lead to meaningful change.

Management must be willing to listen, to respond, to act. And organizations must evaluate actions to see if they work. Do the results of a QC become part of the work? Did these changes create new problems? How can we learn from this experience? In the 1980s, increased productivity, decreased costs, reduced turnover, improved morale, and improved profits have become essential. With proper supports and preparation, quality circles provide a proven way to reach these goals.□

## Reference

Tsurumi, R. R. American Origins of Japanese Productivity: The Hawthorne Experiment Rejected. *The Pacific Report*, Summer 1981, 14–15.

## For Further Reading

Caution: Quality Circles Ahead. *Training and Development Journal*, August 1981.

Cole, R. E. Will Quality Circles Work in the U. S.? *Quality Progress*, July 1980.

Courtright, W. E. *Quality Circles at Hughes Aircraft*. Paper presented to the American Society of Quality Circles Conference, 1979.

Dewar, D. L. *Can Quality Circles Make It in the Western World?* Paper presented to the American Society of Quality Circles Conference, 1979.

Greenlaw, P., & Biggs, W. *Modern Personnel Management*. Hinsdale, Mich.: Dryden Press, 1979.

Hanley, J. Our Experience with Quality Circles. *Quality Progress*, February 1980.

Ishikowa, K. *Cause and Effect Diagram of a Quality Circle: Applications, Tools and Theory*. Paper presented to the American Society of Quality Circles Conference, 1976.

Juran, J. M. International Significance of the Quality Circle Movement. *Quality Progress*, November 1980.

Juran, J. M. The QC Phenomenon. *Industry Quality Control*, January 1967, 23(7), 329–336.

Lippitt, G. L. Quality of Work Life: Organizational Renewal in Action. *Training and Development Journal*, July 1978, 1–10.

Nichols, D. Can "Theory Z" Be Applied to Academic Management? *The Chronicle of Higher Education*, September 1981, 72.

Ouchi, W. G. *Theory Z*. New York: Avon Books, 1981.

Ouchi, W. G., & Joeger, A. M. Type Z Organization: A Corporate Alternative to Village Life. *Alumni Bulletin*, Fall 1977.

Pascale, R., & Athos, A. *The Art of Japanese Management.* New York: Warner Books, 1981.

Randall, E. Quality Circles—A "Third Wave" Intervention. *Training and Development Journal,* March 1981.

Yager, E. Examining the Quality Control Circle. *Personnel Journal,* October 1979, 682–708.

Zemke, R. Quality Circles: Can They Work in the United States? *Journal of Applied Management,* September–October, 1980.

# Stress Management in Organizations

Allen Hard

*"Our increasing knowledge of stress and its effects makes it likely that stress management will become part of many managers' jobs."*

Stress is part of daily life. It can be a positive factor or a destructive force. The ways people respond to and handle stress can determine their effectiveness as individuals, as employees, or as managers. Organizations need to be concerned with stress because it affects employee health and productivity. When handled appropriately, stress does not adversely affect productivity. Handled poorly, stress decreases effectiveness and productivity, eventually leading to psychological and physical illness. Therefore, organizations benefit from supporting stress management systems. To do this, however, those in organizations need to know what stress is, how to recognize its symptoms, how to manage it, and the effects living habits have on stress.

## What is Stress?

Interest in stress is relatively new. Hans Selye (1978) started substantial investigation into the nature of stress only 40 years ago. Interest has mushroomed in the past 10 years, as evidenced by the thousands of articles, workshops, and materials related to stress management. Individuals, businesses, and governments have become extremely concerned about the practical effects of stress.

A change in situation, an unpleasant or painful stimulation, or a loss of control of the environment can all cause stress. Selye defines stress as "the non-specific response of the body to any demand." A series of physiological reactions takes place in the individual regardless of the nature of the external stressor. Either a promotion or a firing produces stress, for example. Because of the similarity of reactions among individuals, Selye described the stress response as a "general adaptation syndrome."

Stress occurs not only as the result of what we do—or of what is done to us—but also of what we think. Biofeedback devices measure the physiological response to stress and show that both thoughts and external stimuli cause the stress response.

While researchers find these ideas exciting, they also have practical, everyday implications. Individuals tend to link concern

© 1983 NTL Institute

about stress to the "quality of life"—a term that suggests that life is to be enjoyed as well as endured. In many respects, we can control the quality of our lives by determining how we live and which parts are under control. Stress provides a general indicator of how we lead our lives and of useful changes. Pelletier suggests this approach in the subtitle of a book (1979), *Holistic Medicine: From Stress to Optimum Health*. If you concern yourself with your own good health, stress may have less to do with how soon you die.

Organizations have been motivated more by profits and by working effectively than by "quality of life" or stress. Organizations become more concerned with such issues when they see their connection to organizational effectiveness. Research documents increasingly link stress to worker satisfaction, attention span, energy, health, and longevity.

Stress, however, does not have only negative implications. Life can be pretty boring in the absence of stress. Stress often provides the spice of life, the thrills, the highs. In this case, stress is positive, or "eustress," according to Selye, as opposed to "distress," which can have destructive effects. Eustress occurs when someone wins a race, rides a roller coaster, gets an award, or completes a project. And even distress need not be damaging when promptly recognized and managed. It is not stress itself that is harmful, but chronic, prolonged stress. One seeks not to avoid stress, but to manage it.

Too little stress, as when challenge or even physical activity is minimal, can cause mental or physical "rusting out." Too much stress, whether positive or negative, results in "burn-out" and produces physical deterioration of the body. Between rustout and burnout lies an area unique to each individual in which he or she functions best in the long run, as indicated in Figure 1.

## How to Recognize Stress

People tend to think of stress in very gross terms, as when the front tire of a car blows out, or when one must make an unprepared speech before 300 people. People also see the absence of stress as being calm and able to think clearly. People usually do not recognize many potential signs of stress, like high blood pressure or dilation of the eye pupils. When people fail to recognize the physical indicators of stress, they often fall back on the subjective judgments or reports of other people who tell them they are calm.

These subjective reports do not indicate stress level well because people can tell themselves whatever they want to hear. We need new ways of recognizing physical signs that give direct information about the level of stress. Because we pay close

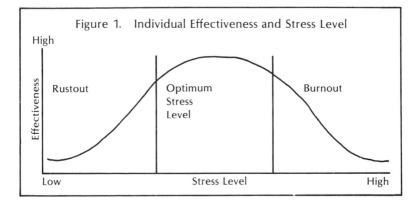

Figure 1.   Individual Effectiveness and Stress Level

High

Effectiveness

Rustout

Optimum
Stress
Level

Burnout

Low                          Stress Level                          High

attention to the important things going on in our lives, we don't usually pay attention to the minor changes in our bodies that provide us constant feedback. When body signals become so great they can't be ignored—headaches or stomach cramps, for example—we often interpret them as evidence of the need to take aspirin or Kaopectate rather than as signs of possible stress.

We can easily identify indicators of stress levels because the body's adaptation to stress follows a pattern. These indicators signal that a person needs to change thoughts or actions. Figure 2 shows stages of stress reactions developed in 1981 for a workshop by the Bureau of Land Management of the U.S. Department of the Interior.

In Stages II and III, symptoms signal that serious illness is imminent. People should regard these signs as warning signals for their bodies and take steps to manage their stress.

The psychological/behavioral styles of some people make them particularly prone to stress. Friedman and Rosenman (1974) have found a direct correlation between increased heart attacks and behavioral characteristics. This personality factor differs from the more traditionally studied factors, such as weight, smoking, and exercise.

In the behavioral description called Type A, or the "hurry sickness," a person consistently feels driven, anxious, competitive, and generally unable to relax. A Type B person has a more relaxed, controlled approach to problems and life's stress and strain. Type A personalities cannot turn dramatically into Type Bs by an act of conscious choice or will. They generally don't want or need to. Therefore, the Type A person needs to address the question: "How do I manage my personality to take advantage of its good points, like having a lot of energy, without burning out?" Everyone who experiences undue or prolonged stress needs to ask that question.

```
┌─────────────────────────────────────────────────────────────────┐
│              Figure 2.    Stages of Stress Response*              │
│                             STAGE I                               │
│                                                                   │
│  nervous sweat        headaches             worrying              │
│  smoking              feeling "on edge"     facial tension        │
│  sweaty palms         increased heart rate  feeling "uptight"     │
│  tense muscles        irritability          feeling short-        │
│  feeling anxious      overeating               tempered           │
│                                             crying                │
│                                                                   │
│                                                                   │
│                             STAGE II                              │
│                                                                   │
│  tight abdomen        hassles with supervisors/co-workers         │
│  quivering stomach    drinking alcohol to relax                   │
│  stomachache, cramps  feeling "not myself" at home                │
│  feeling "shaky"      backaches                                   │
│  intense anger        chronic tense neck and shoulders            │
│  insomnia             shortness of breath/hyperventilating        │
│  nervousness          cramps in legs or arms                      │
│  severe or chronic                                                │
│     headaches                                                     │
│                                                                   │
│                                                                   │
│                             STAGE III                             │
│                                                                   │
│  depression           lowered self-esteem   lack of interest in   │
│  frequent rage        diarrhea                 work               │
│  excessive weight gain migraine headaches   exhaustion            │
│  stomach tied in knots colitis              high blood pressure   │
│  loss of sexual desire skin eruptions       hypertension          │
│  heart pain                                 heart palpitations    │
│                                                                   │
│                             STAGE IV                              │
│                                                                   │
│  heart attack                                                     │
│  ulcers               frequent serious accidents                  │
│  cancer*              strokes                                     │
│  suicidal tendencies  ulcerative colitis                          │
│                                                                   │
│     * See Simonton, O. C., Mathews-Simonton, S.,                  │
│  & Creighton, J. (Eds.) Getting Well Again. Los An-               │
│  geles, Calif.: J. P. Tarcher, 1978.                             │
└─────────────────────────────────────────────────────────────────┘
```

## How to Manage Stress

To manage stress, individuals need to

• learn to recognize the physical signs that show their level of stress;
• learn the levels of stress and the lifestyles that work out well for them;

- learn to control their physical arousal; and
- identify and change the thought processes that create dysfunctional stress.

Managing stress allows us to live up to our full energy potential. Most stress programs emphasize self-management of stress. Some involve substantial organizational testing with implicit requirements for organizational change. Motivating an individual to manage stress is easier than mobilizing an organization with its plurality of interests. Nevertheless, some stress factors in the organizational climate or environment are dealt with best at the organizational level.

Most people go through a rethinking process in stress situations at work that allows them to lower their stress level and cope in useful ways. For most people, the question is simply how long it will take. Training in rethinking stress situations allows people to see how they can speed up the kind of useful thinking they already do. In some cases, it provides thoughts for coping if they don't already have them (Ellis, 1972; Meichenbaum, 1977). This involves writing out or mapping the thoughts that lead to overwhelming feelings of stress in a given situation. Then these thoughts are challenged and replaced by a set of ideas that change the person's perception of the situation and the choices it offers. People can practice mapping by rehearsing a mildly stressful situation. Figure 3, the "Stress Situation Analysis," provides road signs for the mapping exercise.

To do the analysis, take the situation in which you are asked to make a speech at the last minute. Your irrational beliefs about the situation might be, "I can't do it; everybody will think I'm a fool." This will lead to the undesirable behavior of trying to prepare a perfect speech while not getting anything ready adequately.

Rational beliefs about the situation might be, "Well, it will be hard, but I have enough time to put together an adequate speech." The desirable emotion would be self-confidence and calm. The desirable behavior would be putting together the main elements of the speech, without trying to nail down every detail about the subject.

In challenging the emotional beliefs, you might say to yourself, "Wait a minute. I know something about this topic. I can do it and people can probably learn something from me." This would lead to feelings of calmness and self-confidence, and to using the available time to plan the speech.

## Stress Management in Organizations

Stress management has become an important issue for organizations. A substantial amount of research shows that stress

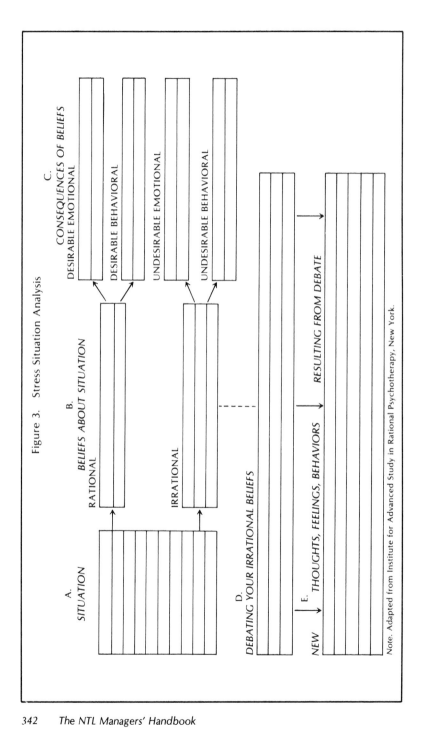

Figure 3.   Stress Situation Analysis

A.
SITUATION

B.
BELIEFS ABOUT SITUATION

RATIONAL

IRRATIONAL

C.
CONSEQUENCES OF BELIEFS

DESIRABLE EMOTIONAL

DESIRABLE BEHAVIORAL

UNDESIRABLE EMOTIONAL

UNDESIRABLE BEHAVIORAL

D.
DEBATING YOUR IRRATIONAL BELIEFS

E.
NEW   THOUGHTS, FEELINGS, BEHAVIORS

RESULTING FROM DEBATE

Note. Adapted from Institute for Advanced Study in Rational Psychotherapy, New York.

and the work environment go hand in hand. The stress may be psychosocial, as in the role ambiguity or participation level an employee faces, or physical due to inadequate lighting, noise, and other factors (Levi, 1981; NIOSH Conference Proceedings, 1980).

Managers have also started to sponsor stress workshops for employees and to talk about the potential impacts of stress on their organizations. Attempts have been made to assess the cost effectiveness of various approaches to stress management. It appears that self-hypnosis may be the most cost effective; physical exercise the most expensive (Shea, 1980).

Our increasing knowledge of stress and its effects makes it likely that stress management will become part of many managers' jobs. Managers can control many of the factors that affect stress. Albrecht (1979) makes a strong case for making top organizational managers stress program managers. These officials have the power and visibility to deal with the quality of the environment in which employees work.

When members of an organization team change from talking about what causes problems to what causes disease, they make a new metaphor—stress—available. The metaphor and language of stress provide new ways to diagnose what is problematic in organizations and make new solutions available.

The new questions for the manager become: "What are the most effective ways for necessary stress to be distributed in the organization? What are the best ways to manage that stress? How does the organization eliminate ineffective stress?" The answers to these questions come to those organizations that have defined stress management for their setting and have designed appropriate programs.□

## References

Albrecht, K. *Stress and The Manager: Making It Work for You.* Englewood Cliffs, N.J.: Prentice-Hall, 1979. Pp. 277–312.

Belloc, N. B. Relationship of Health Practices and Mortality. *Preventive Medicine*, 1973, *2*, 67–81.

Burns, D. D. The Perfectionist's Script for Self-Defeat. *Psychology Today*, 1980, *14*(11), 34–52.

Ellis, A. *Executive Leadership: A Rational Approach.* New York: Institute for Rational Living, Citadel Press, 1972.

Friedman, M., & Rosenman, R. H. *Type A Behavior and Your Heart.* Greenwich, Conn.: Fawcett, 1974.

Levi, L. *Preventing Work Stress.* Reading, Mass.: Addison-Wesley, 1981.

Meichenbaum, D. *Cognitive Behavior Modification: An Integrative Approach.* New York: Plenum Press, 1977. Pp. 143–182.

National Institute for Occupational Safety and Health (NIOSH). *New Developments in Occupational Stress: Conference Proceedings.* Washington, D.C.: U.S. Government Printing Office, 1980.

Pelletier, K. R. *Holistic Medicine: From Stress to Optimum Health.* New York: Delta, 1979.

Selye, H. *The Stress of Life.* New York: McGraw-Hill, 1978. Pp. 29–54.

Shea, G. F. Cost Effective Stress Management Training. *Training and Development Journal*, 1980, *34*(7), 25–33.

Smith, M. J. Recognition of Control of Psychosocial Job Stress. *Professional Safety*, 1981, *20*, 30–36.

# Effective Settings for Making Organizations Humane and Productive

R. Stephen Jenks

*"Just as a doctor must be a good diagnostician to devise an effective treatment plan, a manager must also make accurate diagnoses to build an effective setting."*

## What Is Organization Climate?

To understand organization climate, you must put it in context with other parts of organizational life. I will use Homans' (1961) valuable scheme here with some modification. Its three major parts—the *required system*, the *emergent system*, and the *outcomes*—are shown in Figure 1.

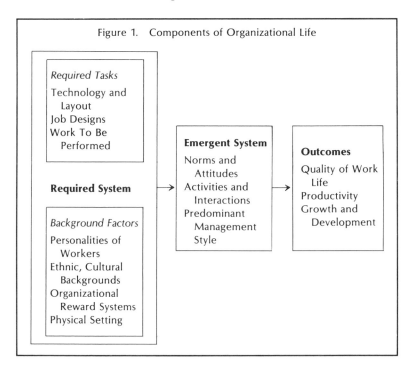

Figure 1. Components of Organizational Life

**Required System**

*Required Tasks*

Technology and
    Layout
Job Designs
Work To Be
    Performed

*Background Factors*

Personalities of
    Workers
Ethnic, Cultural
    Backgrounds
Organizational
    Reward Systems
Physical Setting

**Emergent System**

Norms and
    Attitudes
Activities and
    Interactions
Predominant
    Management
    Style

**Outcomes**

Quality of Work
    Life
Productivity
Growth and
    Development

Adapted from *Making Organizations Humane and Productive*, edited by H. Meltzer and Walter R. Nord, "Effective Settings for Making Organizations Humane and Productive," by R. Stephen Jenks, copyright © 1981 by John Wiley & Sons, Inc. Used with Permission.

The required system includes two primary parts: the required tasks and the background factors. The required tasks consist of the organization's *technology* (i.e., its product, such as clothes, cars, software, and so forth), the *layout* (i.e., plant size, production lines, functional departments, and so forth), the *job designs* (the structure of individual jobs) and the actual *work to be done*. The background factors consist of all the personal, cultural, and ethnic characteristics of the workers in the system and the characteristics of the physical setting in which the work takes place. The emergent system consists of those factors that emerge when the two aspects of the required system are brought together in any organization.

Organization climate is the major component of the emergent system, the characteristics that provide the day-to-day environment for those who work in the system. It is the social climate in which the work is embedded—what it *feels* like to be at work in the system—pleasures, demands, stresses, opportunities, constraints, and so on.

The organization climate has four dimensions. They help us understand the climate that exists in any organization and whether that climate enhances or inhibits productivity and the quality of work life. The dimensions are total amount of *energy* in the system, *distribution* of the available energy throughout the system, the amount of *pleasure* people experience in the system, and the amount of *growth* people in the system can experience (Steele & Jenks, 1977). I will explore each of these dimensions briefly.

### Energy

As in the physical weather system, some climates have high energy and others have low energy. Work environments can be described similarly. Some places are full of energy. People seem busy; lots of movement takes place; few people seem unoccupied. Other places have low energy. Things seem to move slowly; not much noise or enthusiasm exists. Think of places you are familiar with and the amount of energy you can sense there. For example, mentally compare banks, restaurants, factories, libraries, or offices with which you're familiar. Even places in the same category—e.g., restaurants—can differ greatly in the overall amount of energy in their systems.

### Distribution

Within any organization, the available energy is not spread evenly throughout the system. Some parts have high energy while other parts have low energy. This often occurs even with organizations as small as the family, in which children sometimes have much more energy than their parents. In work organizations, energy also tends to be distributed unevenly. Sometimes work flow cycles affect this distribution. Many manufacturing environments become very energetic at the end of the month, quarter, or fiscal year.

## Pleasure

Some organization climates are very serious. Others are more lighthearted and, in my opinion, are often as productive as they are pleasurable. One important contributor to experiencing pleasure in the work place is the nature of the work itself. Sometimes little can be done about work that is by nature dull, routine, and boring. Often, however, organizations can do a great deal to minimize the effects of such jobs. Therefore another important contributor to pleasure is the degree of flexibility in the job itself and the degree of influence a person has over such aspects of the job as work schedule, pace, scope, or hours. Cohen and Gadon (1978) have explored these notions thoroughly in their book *Alternative Work Schedules.*

## Growth

This dimension results from the other three dimensions cited above. If an organization has sufficient energy, a reasonably even distribution of energy throughout the system, and a fairly pleasurable climate, it will grow. It is hard in the abstract to define "sufficient energy," "reasonably even distribution," or "fairly pleasurable climate." In the physical environment tropical paradises enhance the growth of crops and deserts inhibit this— and the organizational environment can either enhance or inhibit the growth of people. The term "growth" includes increased awareness, knowledge, and skills. For this kind of growth to occur, the environment needs at least *some* of each of the three previously mentioned aspects of climate. In addition, growth requires a supportive reward system, one that encourages individuals to try new skills, stretch themselves, and take risks.

## Factors Determining Climate

Four key factors determine organization climate: physical settings, norms, communication patterns, and management style. I will explore each factor in detail in this section, since they are important to building humane and productive organizational

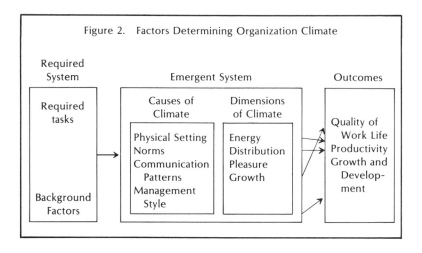

Figure 2.  Factors Determining Organization Climate

| Required System | Emergent System | | Outcomes |
|---|---|---|---|
| **Required tasks**<br><br><br><br>**Background Factors** | **Causes of Climate**<br><br>Physical Setting<br>Norms<br>Communication<br>Patterns<br>Management<br>Style | **Dimensions of Climate**<br><br>Energy<br>Distribution<br>Pleasure<br>Growth | Quality of<br>Work Life<br>Productivity<br>Growth and<br>Develop-<br>ment |

climates. Figure 2 shows the relationship of these four factors to the dimensions of climate discussed above.

*Physical Settings*

The physical setting in which work occurs has a major impact on the climate that develops in that work place. Of course, the kind of setting chosen or constructed in the first place may also reflect the organization's climate. In either case the physical appearance of the work place provides a source of information about what the system is like—it gives a person the first and most tangible "feel" for the place, and all kinds of inferences can be drawn from this. Fritz Steele and I wrote in *The Feel of the Work Place* that

The first piece of information we get about an organization is its geographic location. Being in midtown Manhattan (New York City) or in a posh, well-groomed industrial park communicates different messages about organization climate, values, and identity than does a location in an older, run-down part of a decaying urban area.

The next impression we receive about a system, after knowing its location, is prompted by the actual building, workshop, factory, [etc.] that defines and enclosed the organization's spaces. The features of external facade play a large role in shaping our initial impression. Many companies today strive to project an image of progressiveness, solidarity, and reliability by building up-to-date solid structures that look like other new office buildings.

For the richest visual picture of the climate of an organization, we must explore the interior spaces of the system. The way in which organization members shape and reshape their offices, production areas, and passageways provides us with most of our data about the social climate in which they operate. . . . An area that has all work benches fixed will encourage continuation of old activities, even when they are no longer particularly profitable or there is a better way to do the same tasks. A setting that allows noise or visual distractions can promote a climate of excitement and vitality but at the same time be negative for tasks that require concentration and uninterrupted sequences of activity.

On the causal side, settings operate as influences on climate through the activities they allow or inhibit, through the symbolic messages they contain, and through the memories and feelings they stimulate in users. (Steele & Jenks, 1977, pp. 106, 108, 115, 120)

Some characteristics of the physical setting that first appear rather trivial can significantly affect how humane a work place feels to those who work there. For example, most people find it hard to think carefully and analytically in a space that has little or no privacy, much noise, or many interruptions. Yet these are often the conditions under which people must do careful or exacting work. If a work place has no natural gathering spots where people can communicate informally, then less communication of any kind can occur and any social contact must take place at people's work stations and cause interruptions. A gathering spot where people can get coffee, messages, and perhaps copies permits informal communication to occur in a non-interruptive manner.

Many organizations have begun to use "open offices" consisting of moveable partitions that define each person's space. If these changes occur without the proper planning, they make the work place nearly intolerable because of the increase in noise and interruptions and the decrease in privacy. Open offices can and do work well if carefully planned. Noise can be reduced with a variety of sound-absorbing materials on floors, partitions, and ceilings and also by enclosing typewriters and other noise-generating office equipment. As building costs continue to increase—along with the need for flexibility in the use of work spaces—more organizations will use open offices. I have worked in both traditional closed office spaces and in a variety of open offices. The individual can control privacy, noise, and access much better in a traditional arrangement. Poorly planned open office space creates a sense of violation and unwanted intrusion that hinders work and decreases morale and productivity. Well-planned open office space, however, can actually constitute an improvement over closed offices in terms of communication, access, and the flexibility to rearrange work spaces when needed. When planning open offices, organizations should not only pay attention to noise factors but also to explicitly involving employees in these plans. Management at least needs to seek, hear, and respond to the employees' views before making these changes.

Some of what I have said about office space can also be applied to manufacturing space. Organizations obviously have less freedom to rearrange an individual's work space than they have in office arrangements, but they can still involve employees in planning and laying out their own work spaces. The more people feel they can affect or control the physical conditions in which they work, the better. Sometimes when organizations merely allow people to personalize their work space in some small way— e.g., through choosing the paint on the wall, having a plant, or hanging a picture—this provides enough employee satisfaction.


*Norms*

Norms are the unwritten rules of behavior for people in the organization. They are the "shoulds" and "shouldn'ts" organizations expect people to follow. When new employees are "shown the ropes," "taught the rules of the road," or told "how we do things around here," they are being told about the norms of the organization or work group they are joining. Some organizations have more elaborate initiation procedures.

> The primary function norms play is to lend some stability and predictability to the behavior of group members. Norms limit the range of possible things that can happen at any given instant, and so help provide identity and thrust to the group's actions. Every social system with any connection between members must have some norms to differentiate members from non-members. (Steele & Jenks, 1977, p. 41)

Norms can facilitate goals or inhibit them; they can be conscious and openly determined or unconscious and evolve over time.

Organizations reinforce some norms with statements of policy and procedures. Informal norms often become established and reinforced by the behavior of those at the top of the organization—i.e., those in power. If the president eats in expensive restaurants on a company expense account, others will likely do the same. Norms cover all aspects of behavior and set the tone of the organization. For example, few organizations have formal, written dress codes these days. Yet nearly every organization has some norms regarding dress, whether it expects everyone to wear ties or that no one should wear ties. Often an organization has norms regarding acceptable use of an employee's physical space. For example, though no policy may state that everyone must use the same type of desk and chair, nevertheless everyone does. The norms that operate in an organizational setting can often be inferred from observing people's behavior.

Organizations with many norms that constrain people's behavior tend to be less inviting places to work than those with norms that encourage individual expression, risk taking, and experimentation. Norms are the most important determinant of organization climate. At one end of a continuum is a climate of *fear* and at the other a climate of *excitement*. Managers can significantly affect the climate of their work groups by paying attention to the norms that exist and to the ones they reinforce or change through their own behavior. For example, a manager who genuinely seeks information from her or his subordinates and really listens to them—even when they have bad news— quickly sets a norm for open disclosure. Conversely, a manager who claims to want information but reacts angrily when the news isn't good sets a norm against open disclosure. Subordinates will tell the boss only what they think he or she wants to hear. Those in power create a climate of excitement when they are clear and open about their goals and encourage and reward individual initiative that serves those goals. Norms that support this behavior can most easily be established through the behavior of those at the top.

*Communication Patterns*

Communications patterns have several dimensions: the amount or volume, the quality, and the vehicle. In this section I will examine each dimension and discuss approaches to establishing effective patterns.

1. *Volume.* Organizations differ enormously in terms of the sheer volume of communication, just as individuals differ. Like people, some organizations are talkative and others are quiet. Some prefer written communication to oral communication and generate thousands of memos. No "right" amount of communications exists, and managers who search for it are bound to be frustrated. Some people will complain about communication overload, while others will complain about receiving too little information. The proper balance between too much communication and not enough depends upon the

individual manager's personality and style, the norms or policies of the organization, and the needs of the employees. Some organizations value a great deal of communication and invest heavily in new technology to aid in producing it (e.g., teleconferencing, facsimile transmission, computer networks for data exchange). Other organizations value sparse communication and train employees to write memoranda on single sheets of paper and to keep telephone calls to a minimum. No evidence has shown that mere volume of communication makes one approach better than any other.

2. *Quality.* Little argument exists about the benefits of quality communication. Organizations can measure quality by asking people who receive communications to report what they have heard from those sending it, and then checking with the senders to determine accuracy, intent, and emotional tone. I once did a research project on downward communication in a large organization, and found that only 10% of this communication was received accurately and as it was intended! The responsibility for quality lies with both the sender and the receiver, although the sender has the heavier burden of communicating clearly. The quality of communication generally increases when the sender carefully thinks out what must be communicated, the best way to communicate it, and the clearest and most concise way to say or write it. The receiver should check out with the sender any unclear parts of the message and provide the sender with feedback on what was actually received.

3. *Vehicle.* Communication often breaks down because the sender used the wrong method of sending the information. This occurs when something discussed over the telephone should have been done on a face-to-face basis so that people could communicate non-verbally through gestures and facial expressions. Other examples include writing a letter or a memo instead of talking on the phone or vice versa. I once managed a large group of people, most of them in remote locations. One technique that helped develop effective communications patterns was the creation of a list of the issues and topics that would warrant a trip to the remote location and face-to-face interchange, those that would warrant a telephone call, those that could be handled by telex, and those that required a letter or a memo. I sent the list to the people in the remote locations for their input and guidance. Mintzberg (1973) has noted that most managers prefer verbal vehicles of communication and short, concise interchanges. These preferences are fine if all communication can be accomplished by such means. One should examine the content of the intended message before choosing the method of sending it.

*Management Style*

Volumes have been written about management style since McGregor (1960) first wrote about Theory X and Theory Y. A growing consensus exists that no one management or leadership style is correct. In fact, the so-called contingency approach (Hunt & Larson, 1974) suggests that managers should consider a number of factors when determining an appropriate style. These include the nature of the task, the expertise of the manager, the attitudes and needs of subordinates, and time pressures. Many people believe that to create a humane work setting, the predominant management style should be highly participative. That conclusion is true when decisions are non-routine, when information is not standardized, when low time pressure exists, and when subordinates are independent and self-motivated. But how many situations meet those criteria? Some places like engineering design firms or law offices do, but automobile assembly plants certainly do not. An organization arrives at the appropriate management style by matching the situation to the leader and vice versa. In exploring the interactions of factors in the contingency approach, Cohen et. al (1980, p. 290) present a few highlights of effective style.

1. Nature of the task situation:
    If routine, [it] needs control, explicitness and standardization.
    Stressful tasks need high person-concern.
2. Expertise of the leader:
    The greater the expertise, the greater the appropriateness of control.
3. Attitudes and needs of subordinates:
    The greater the subordinate need for independence and ability, the less appropriate is tight control.
    If subordinates' survival is not threatened and work is not unusually challenging, high-task and people concern is appropriate.
4. Time pressure:
    The greater the time pressure, the less shared control is appropriate.

When the management style matches the needs of the situation, the organization climate is much better than when a mismatch occurs. Knowing how to create that match is more an art than a science and is usually accomplished by managers with a relatively wide repertoire of behavioral styles that they can draw upon when necessary. Therefore, the single-style manager is less likely to be effective in the complex work situation of today than a manager who can adapt her or his style to the factors discussed above.

## Building Effective Settings

From all that I have said, you should see that to build an effective work setting a manager must be good at balancing a dizzying array of variables, many of which he or she cannot control directly. Consequently, to succeed, managers need help from others, particularly in figuring out where things stand and where they ought to be headed. This task is relatively simple in the area of task requirements, but is very difficult in the area of organization climate.

Just as a doctor must be a good diagnostician to devise an effective treatment plan, a manager must also make accurate diagnoses to build an effective setting. Managers need to make thorough analyses of "what is" and devise clear visions of "what needs to be"—and then build bridges between the two. A thorough diagnosis of "what is" requires a degree of objectivity that most managers do not have because they have become completely involved in the situation. Occasionally a newly appointed manager has the necessary objectivity, but this person also suffers from needing to learn the details of operation as quickly as possible. Therefore, the diagnostic phase can often benefit from the help of an outsider, either an outside consultant or someone from another part of the organization who can bring a "fresh pair of eyes" and objectivity to the situation. Managers frequently become so bent on finding solutions that they do not spend enough time or energy on diagnosis. This produces a trial-and-error approach to improving organization climate.

Once a manager has completed a diagnosis of the present situation, he or she starts a process to define the desired situation. Information and suggestions from a wide sample of the organization's members are appropriate for arriving at a vision for the future. The process used must include mechanisms for evaluating and choosing among the alternatives suggested. The manager must put together a logical sequence of steps, and estimate the cost involved in each step. Finally, the manager must create a feedback mechanism to provide for midcourse corrections as the process moves forward.

### Physical Settings

Managers find it difficult to change physical settings for several reasons. First, the person(s) at the top of the organization holds the power to make decisions about the physical setting and how to use the spaces within it, because these decisions make such visible symbols of executive power. Second, many people do not attempt to influence decisions about physical settings because they treat them as "givens" in the environment—something that cannot be changed.

*Norms*

Managers may have less difficulty changing norms, but norms are much less visible than physical settings. Because norms are the unwritten rules for acceptable behavior, they seldom come under explicit scrutiny. When managers do scrutinize them, through a process called a "norm census," they can change or modify them fairly easily (Steele & Jenks, 1977). Norms also resist change because people see them as immutable, and because norms develop—and die—slowly over time instead of through conscious attention and explicit action.

*Communication Patterns*

Managers tend to tinker with communications patterns— particularly with vehicles of communications—more than most aspects of organization climate. Most positive changes move these patterns toward more open disclosure within the system. These kinds of changes require a change in philosophy toward an assumption that few official secrets should exist and that true facts are usually "friendly"—i.e., no one would be hurt by sharing them.

*Management Style*

Changes in management style result from education. First, a manager must learn that no single style is appropriate in all situations. Next, the manager must learn new behavioral skills to expand her or his repertoire. Finally, managers must balance the needs of the situation with their own experience, skills, and preferences to find an appropriate style for any given situation.

Conscious attention to these areas can enable the manager to make positive changes in the emergent system and thereby contribute directly to the building of more effective work settings as measured by the outcome measurements of quality of work life, productivity, growth, and development.

## Implications for Managers

Managers need to pay *explicit* attention to the kind of environment they create in the work place. Often, we think of

organization climate in the same way we think about the
weather—you can complain about it, but you can't do much to
change it. Managers *can* change the organization climate. This
requires awareness. Paying attention to norms, communication
patterns, and management style can provide a revelation in
understanding why a particular climate exists in an organization.
Once you understand the effects of these factors, you have
reached a starting point for making some positive changes.□

**References**

Cohen, A., Fink, S., Gadon, H., & Willis, R. *Effective Behavior in
Organizations (Revised Ed.)*. Homewood, Ill.: Richard D. Irwin,
1980.

Cohen, A., & Gadon, H. *Alternative Work Schedules*. Reading,
Mass.: Addison-Wesley, 1978.

Homans, G. C. *Social Behavior: Its Elementary Forms*. New York:
Harcourt, Brace and World, 1961.

Hunt, J., & Larson, L. *Contingency Approaches to Leadership*.
Carbondale, Ill.: Southern Illinois University Press, 1974.

McGregor, D. *The Human Side of Enterprise*. New York: McGraw-
Hill, 1960.

Steele, F., & Jenks, S. *The Feel of the Work Place*. Reading, Mass.:
Addison-Wesley, 1977.

# Overcoming Human and Organizational Barriers to Implementation of New Technology*

William A. Kraus
Nicholas W. Weiler

*"Implementors of new technology must view resistance as legitimate, appropriate, and something to be expected."*

## The Impact of New Technology on Work

Many people feel that the introduction of new technology will have a negative impact on the American workplace. Some managers resist technical changes because they fear that such "modernization" will add too many uncertainties and risks to their work. These managers feel safer using "tried-and-true" methods. When organizations implement new technology appropriately, however, this change can actually reduce risk by providing managers with a great deal more data and increased flexibility.

While some people believe that new technology will depersonalize the work place by fragmenting work, in fact, just the opposite can occur. Computer-based technology can make work become more interdependent and less fragmented. For example, when used properly, computers can help manufacturing and engineering departments work more closely together to produce a product design. The implementation of new technology can also encourage more collaborative organizational structures and processes because technology makes information available to a wide variety of individuals with different tasks.

## What Do We Mean by "New Technology"?

This paper defines new technology as information-based technology in which computers play an integral part. We refer specifically to robots; to computer-aided design, manufacturing, and testing (CAD, CAM, and CAT); to office automation; to teleconferencing; and to personal computers.

We can already see the impact of new technologies on our workplaces and homes in the following examples:

© 1983 William A. Kraus and Nicholas W. Weiler
  * The concepts in this paper were developed in a series of research projects conducted by General Electric Company in partnership with Block-Petrella-Weisbord of Plainfield, New Jersey, with McBer and Company of Boston, Massachusetts, and with Interaction Associates of San Francisco, California.

- computerized drafting;
- robots tied to personal computers;
- teleshopping—a catalog on a computer that can be used at home;
- telecommunication of information anywhere in the world;
- automated research labs;
- automated chemical analysis;
- direct numerical control for machines in factories;
- computer monitoring of dragline equipment;
- voice mail;
- computers replacing library card catalogs;
- computer simulations of map making; and
- video disc systems.

## Obstacles to Successful Introduction

Many organizations have already begun to introduce rapidly new technology to improve quality and productivity. Evidence shows, however, that technology often fails to provide the expected benefits because those introducing it have failed to identify and address obstacles in the organizational environment.

### Patterns for Addressing Obstacles

We have found that the behavior of managers and others who implement systems critically affects the successful adoption of new technology into their businesses. Over the past three years, we have examined the successes and failures of 70 organizations in the United States and Japan. We examined CAD/CAM, robots, inventory management, quality circle implementation, and productivity programs. Clear patterns of managerial behavior that affect the success of implementation emerged, and we found that

- by using a systematic, step-by-step diagnostic process, managers can identify and take specific actions to overcome predictable behavioral and organizational barriers to success; and
- when managers do take this systematic action, implementation is more likely to succeed (i.e., they meet objectives and significantly reduce time and cost of implementation).

### Key Variables

Technological knowledge and expertise were *not* the key factors that distinguished successful implementations from less successful ones in the organizations we studied. The *primary* barriers to success were human and organizational factors influencing the following variables:

- problem definition;
- organizational environment (e.g., work goals and measurements);
- implementation team selection;
- installation plan;
- end-user ownership; and
- vendor integration.

These variables affect success or failure in the following ways:

*Problem definition.* The higher the managerial level on which the problem is defined, the greater the chance of success in gaining support from top management. The closer the origin to the "end-users," however, the greater the chance of a successful implementation. Successful implementors find ways to get both top management *and* end-user support by defining the problem in words that clearly demonstrate that the solution will address both groups' unique needs.

*Organizational environment.* New systems that create an environment in which employees monitor their own achievements and accomplishment of goals succeed more often than systems designed to control people. Successful systems also tend to help the end-users accomplish the specific goals being measured. Less successful systems often attempt to advance the technology without a clear awareness of or a concern for the end-users' specific goals and measurements.

*Implementation team.* A team approach greatly enhances implementation. Six roles—which we will mention later in this paper—must exist on the team, and one person may play more than one role. The roles are tied to specific tasks, require specific competencies, and vary in significance depending on the stage of the implementation.

*Installation plan.* A successful implementation plan has the following characteristics:

- Managers plan implementations in a realistic fashion, building on previous successes and progressing at a rate the organization can absorb.
- Implementors recognize possible blocks to progress and take steps to overcome obstacles. For example, they make contingency plans, or they test equipment before it reaches the shop floor— where any breakdowns may cause harmful and demotivating lags in schedule.
- Implementors show a clear knowledge of the end-users and of the manufacturing process the users employ. The end-users participate at critical junctures throughout the system's design and implementation, and they help identify and prevent problems.

- Implementors use the knowledge of the end-users to build effective user-education programs.

## End-User Ownership

The end-user must become involved in the implementation process. Successful implementation

- reduces the risks for users,
- builds user ownership of the system early in the process, and
- results when implementors understand the users' learning style and adapt their training to it.

## Vendor Integration

Successful implementation teams work hard to make sure outside vendors understand the organization's problems. The teams *sell* their application needs to vendors, and work jointly with vendors to develop thorough system specifications. This significantly enhances the team's chances of getting products tailored to meet the organization's full needs—instead of getting slightly modified off-the-shelf products that will later cause problems by failing to address requirements that were communicated poorly.

## Key Variables to Success

Overall, our research surfaced five themes that influence the success or failure of the introduction of new technology. These themes are

- critical player ownership,
- education/communication,
- management commitment and support,
- organization dynamics, and
- critical change-team competencies.

## Critical Player Ownership

The people who have to use the new system, especially the end-users, must "own" the system before the organization can implement new technology successfully. Ownership is the feeling of control. When I own the system, I feel that it belongs to me, that it does something *for* me, not *to* me. The feeling comes from having some influence over the system design in all stages. It also develops when, for example, a new factory management system gives the operator some feedback about output or quality instead of trying to control her or his behavior. If management implements new technology primarily as a means to control behavior rather than as a feedback system, then the organization loses a powerful mechanism for user ownership and often simultaneously generates considerable user resistance.

## Education/Communication

Successful implementors of new technology work right from the start to educate those affected by the change. Education not only communicates information, but also prepares individuals and tasks for the implementation. When employees visit a robot vendor, for example, they not only begin to develop a new perspective on what robots can do, but they also develop an ownership of the new technology. An employee often reacts positively to this sort of education, believing, "They must really value my reactions since they are paying my expenses while I find out more about this." Send several people to the vendors' shop when you introduce a robot to the organization. Send several of the maintenance personnel, and send them early in the process rather than toward the end of it. Early education greatly enhances the end-users' feelings of ownership and improves the implementation's chances for success.

## Management Commitment and Support

Implementors almost always emphasize the need for management commitment and support, but they seldom understand the concrete behavior managers must employ to demonstrate this commitment. Managers cannot simply say that they are committed. People tend not to believe this unless the managers' behavior over time consistently reinforces their professed commitment. Examples of effective managerial behavior include the following:

- rewarding goal-directed behavior promptly;
- discouraging undermining and indifference;
- sustaining the commitment over an extended period of time;
- avoiding unnecessary conflict or blame by first trying to understand the bases for various resistors' concerns;
- checking periodically for goal clarity and key player agreement; and
- establishing specific, ongoing procedures to ensure that personnel discover and address emerging problems.

The successful introduction of new technology requires an influential sponsoring manager who clearly acts as an advocate. System implementors find it much easier to obtain this sponsorship if the technology they recommend solves a real problem for the business and if managers acknowledge this in the strategic plan.

*Organization Dynamics*

For a new manufacturing technology to succeed, implementors must examine the nature of the manufacturing process, the ways in which work gets done, the measurement system, the production control system, and a variety of other work-related systems, processes, and outputs—and they must examine them early and often throughout the implementation. Implementors must conduct a specific and systematic examination of the ways the new technology affects these dynamics at all levels in the organization. This examination should be made early in the implementation to generate ownership and reduce resistance.

*Critical Change-Team Competencies*

In successful implementations, six key ad hoc roles operate at various stages: the *catalyst*, the *entrepreneur*, the *sponsor*, the *technical gatekeeper*, the *integrator*, and the *manager*. These roles require specific competencies, and each one must be carried out at a specific stage of the implementation. A number of individuals may fulfill these roles, and one person may play more than one role. Organizations must carefully fill these roles with employees who have demonstrated the competency to do the work required. We have developed assessment tools to help organizations do this.

## Implementation Effort Trade-Off

Figure 1 shows the difference between the "traditional" and the "managed" ways in which organizations may implement new technology. In the traditional method, the organization expends little effort to build end-user understanding and commitment in the early phases of designing the system. The major communication and education effort comes after the design has been nearly completed and made ready for implementation. Serious problems then emerge as end-users see problems and try to adapt the design to meet their "real" needs. Managers generally label the users' efforts to introduce reality into the system as "resistance." In the managed—and more appropriate—way of introducing technology, the organization expends considerable effort to involve the end-users early in the process to test design realities and to build end-user ownership.

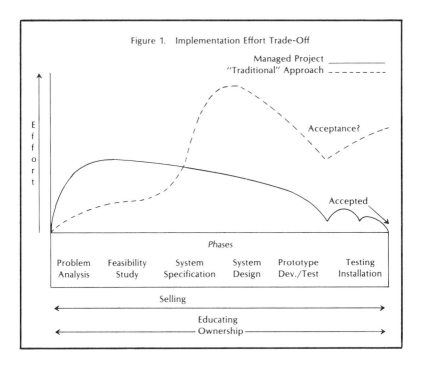

Figure 1.    Implementation Effort Trade-Off

Managed Project _____
"Traditional" Approach _ _ _ _ _ _ _ _

Effort

Acceptance?

Accepted

*Phases*

| Problem Analysis | Feasibility Study | System Specification | System Design | Prototype Dev./Test | Testing Installation |

Selling

Educating
Ownership

In the managed approach, the organization collects a great deal of information from end-users on what they need for the new technology to become useful to them. This approach employs an iterative process whereby all parties connected with the introduction of technology or affected by its use participate in defining the problem. To be effective at this juncture, the organization must identify the *stakeholders*—those who use the system—and help them to develop ownership. The end-users must have an early opportunity to become involved in the design.

Remember that education and ownership must occur during the entire implementation process. They do not act merely as discrete steps on a milestone chart. Education and ownership may appear on that chart several times as discrete entities, but they cannot be achieved once and then forgotten.

## Making the Research Useful

The results of our research can only help managers who use them to create specific guidelines for system implementation. We have developed a "road map" of the critical steps managers should take in each identified implementation phase. We have also developed a base line of practices that have proven successful in the introduction of new technology. Perhaps most important, we have developed a variety of diagnostic tools/techniques to do the following:

- test readiness for implementation;
- pinpoint problems and potential problems; and
- initiate corrective action in each phase of a system's installation.

Our consulting process includes the following steps:

- identifying the phase in which an ongoing or new project exists;
- pinpointing successes to date and problems that still must be corrected in phases already completed or underway;
- determining which of the available diagnostic tools should be used to identify and resolve important issues; and
- developing a roadmap for eliminating or minimizing problems predicted to occur in phases not yet completed.

The various diagnostic tools we use in this process include the following:

- managers' acceptance checklist;
- managers' action guide;
- implementation team assessment/selection guides;
- end-user acceptance checklist;
- work force acceptance checklist;
- potential pitfalls checklist;
- union involvement guidelines;
- vendor selection/management guidelines; and
- demonstrating management commitment checklist.

These diagnostic tools must always be used in cooperation with identified client stakeholder groups who learn the importance of key variables in the implementation process by participating in the diagnosis. This learning process also helps prepare the client group to continue this approach in future implementations.

## Summary

The following principles underlie a strategy implementors can use to overcome human and organizational barriers to the introduction of new technology.

1. Technology implementors must understand thoroughly the users' needs when they engage in problem definition and systems

design. The end-users of new technology must participate early in the design process, not just when the implementation system is "turned on."

2. Successful implementation requires the identification and the use of six behaviorally recognizable roles: the catalyst, the entrepreneur, the sponsor, the technical gatekeeper, the integrator, and the manager.

3. The introduction of new technology requires an iterative process, not a linear one. A great deal of cycling through issues with key constituencies and a continual fine tuning of the system based on stakeholder input occurs. By seeking and using this input, the implementors make the design more realistic and simultaneously develop stakeholder ownership.

4. The new technology must solve a business problem for the managers *and* it must solve a real problem for the end-user.

5. As the implementation proceeds, a continual examination of the emerging integration of the work and the technology must occur. This must include a continual examination of measurement systems, reward systems, production quotas, and the expectations and job descriptions of the various functions involved.

6. Implementors of new technology must view resistance as legitimate, appropriate, and something to be expected. Also, resistance often highlights real problems that must be corrected in the system design. Frequently, resistance stems from the resistor's experienced perception of overlooked issues, and implementors must address this perception for the system to meet business and end-user needs.

When organizations reduce the human and organizational barriers to new technology, then they can successfully adapt to the complex challenges of the future.☐

## Suggestions for Further Reading

Federico, P., Brun, K. E., & McCalla, D. B. *Management Information Systems and Organizational Behavior*. New York: Praeger Publishers, 1980.

Hapgood, F. Taming Your Computer. *Management*, Summer 1982, 10–13.

Reader, D. E. Human Factors in Automation. *Manufacturing Engineering*, October 1982, 43–45.

Whaley, G. The Impact of Robotics Technology upon Human Resource Management. *Personnel Administrator*, September 1982, 61–71.

Zmut, R. W., & Cos, J. F. The Implementation Process: A Change Approach. *MIS Quarterly*, 1979, *3*, 35–43.

# Managing the Computer Transition*

Saul Eisen
Ava Albert Schnidman

*"Despite all the opportunities and pressures, evidence indicates that most organizations are currently unprepared to implement new technology successfully."*

Computer technology is changing the way we produce goods and services, handle financial transactions, make business and personal decisions, and communicate with each other. It is also changing the way managers do their work. Word processing and spread-sheet software have entered the office and computer-aided design and manufacturing (CAD and CAM) have appeared in the factory. Electronic mail systems have made vast arrays of information available to anyone with access to a terminal, and personal computers have changed the executive suite.

Historians who look back on the 80s will probably identify this period as the decade of the "Great Computer Transition." This transition will have an impact comparable to those of other world-scale changes in modern history—such as the agricultural revolution caused by crop rotation, the industrial revolution fueled by petroleum-driven machines, and the mass media revolution produced by the invention of the vacuum tube and the transistor. We can more easily perceive and comprehend large-scale events after the main force of the shock wave has passed and some form of stability has emerged. When that happens, we can then discern the thematic and qualitative effects of the latest change in society, and even debate their value.

Organizations and managers are right in the thick of the computer transition. We can only guess at the eventual shape of the approaching cybernetic society. Naisbitt's research on this transition (1982) identifies "megatrends" that are moving our society from an industrial base to an information one and that generate a parallel increase in the value we place on "high tech" and "high touch." The systemic interaction between technology and human contact provides an important perspective on the difficult problems managers face during this transition period. This interaction also highlights possible strategies for dealing effectively with problems that occur in organizational settings.

© 1983 NTL Institute

* The authors wish to thank organization development and computer systems consultants Susan Colantuono (a partner of Deltech Consulting Group, Inc.) and Cyrus Gibson (vice-president of Index Systems, Inc.) for their assistance with this article.

Organizations are, of course, deeply affected by computerization. Firms use information to direct and control their marketing, production, and support functions. A new technology that makes this information more accessible, valid, and timely can give an organization a significant competitive advantage. After some organizations began to implement new technology, the results quickly showed us that any organization that fails to employ computers will find itself at a comparative disadvantage. So, for better or worse, the computerization rush is on.

Despite all the opportunities and pressures, evidence indicates that most organizations are currently unprepared to implement new technology successfully. In a recent survey of 18 significant new applications systems used by companies in the U. S., researchers found that only three companies had achieved all of the results management intended. These applications systems studied represented a sampling of the newest information technology, including office automation, computer-assisted design, on-line clerical processing, and "decision-support" systems for professionals and managers. The basic characteristic of failure was not inappropriate technology—the hardware or software—but the limited use and occasional rejections of those systems by both the work force and management. An analysis of the successes and failures revealed that the new systems required changes in work behavior, managerial control, and organization structure that the unsuccessful organizations had not anticipated or managed well.

If managers seek to benefit from automation during the next 20 years, then most organizations must understand and generalize the lessons obtained from the companies studied. Our thesis is that we can develop these lessons and research findings into effective management strategies for introducing automated systems to organizations.

## The Index Survey

Under the auspices of Index Systems, Inc., Ava Schnidman and Cyrus Gibson (1981) surveyed organizations that had implemented new computer systems. The researchers intended to determine the success or failure—in terms of business results—of major systems that applied the latest technology. The survey included 18 companies that used major application systems that ranged in cost from $250,000 to more than ten million dollars, and it asked organizations if their systems had achieved the desired business results—whether the firms sought hard cost benefits of such intangibles as improved decision making by executives or professionals.

The outcome of this survey was dramatic. Of the 18 cases studied, only three companies showed unqualified success. The main reasons that the other 15 firms failed have been placed in the following four categories:

## Changes in Needs

Four firms fully developed and implemented computer systems, but they did not displace the staff or increase the effectiveness of the system users. User managers made such comments as "We never anticipated that our needs would change after we approved the system design." In one case—a major insurance firm with a new on-line payments-support system—the organization runs the automated procedures parallel to the old labor-intensive manual process, which still remains largely unchanged.

## Data Base Problems

Five firms partially implemented computer systems, but each used less than 70% of the systems' technical or design capabilities. In the case of a savings bank system that employed a minicomputer, the organization never attained 75% of the intended information output. This happened because management failed to push for the development of a customer information file that would have provided the data base for new applications.

In both of the two categories discussed above, seven of the nine organizations reported that they still continued to work with the new technology—albeit far above and beyond their original budget and time estimates—in efforts to use the systems to some acceptable degree. Only two firms formally—and mercifully— killed their systems after implementation.

## User Resistance

Four firms partially or completely developed, tested, and debugged computer systems—but never implemented them. One senior manager commented, "We found that resistance to change by the users grew and grew as 'cutover' approached. We beat a tactical retreat."

## Lack of Information

In two cases, our contacts in the organization could not tell us whether the system had succeeded or failed. Neither firm had made a formal post-implementation audit. While few other firms actually made such an audit, these two respondents were unique in that they preferred not to make any sort of judgment regarding success or failure. Management had swept the results into a closet that no one wanted to open.

A computer system may simultaneously be both a technical success and a business failure. If organizations in general do no better than most of those surveyed, then the available technology will take a long time to yield the necessary business results. An analysis of these cases, however, suggests that managers can solve the underlying problems that inhibit full implementation and use.

The literature on the implementation of computer systems continues to grow in size and quality, and much of it concludes that user management involvement is one of the key factors to success (see, for example, Friedrich, 1981; Lucas, 1981; Margulies, 1982; and Mumford, 1975). At first blush, the survey results seemed to refute this. Two of the three successful firms mandated close, tight monitoring of users by their managers, not only in the system project, but also in the receiving organization. Nevertheless, the other successful organization had virtually no such involvement, while four of the failures did. A closer analysis revealed that success depended upon the appropriate kind of involvement by senior management, involvement that acknowledges the complex interaction of the technical, managerial, and social subsystems of the organization.

## A Sociotechnical Approach to Successful Implementation

To take the essential first step in the implementation process, managers should conduct a front-end assessment of the forces and conditions affected by the change. A careful look at both successful and unsuccessful new systems reveals that success requires an organization to manage sociotechnical change through tactics that assess these forces, while failure comes from inadequate or ill-advised assessment and action. We will present six important areas and some relevant actions that constitute part of our proposed implementation plan.

### Technology

For many organizations, the successful management of systems development remains an elusive achievement. The current situation leads either to no implementation or to systems that do not work. Attention paid to technology by technologists differs from the attention of a user or manager concerned with use and results. Managers must become involved in technology choices. The difference, to paraphrase Shel Davis, is between technology that does things right and technology that does the right things.

## Supervisory Behavior

In production and clerical automation, new systems invariably cause significant changes in the supervisor's job. The supervisor's commitment, like the manager's, can influence success if that person has the power to affect subordinates' attitudes.

## Organization Structure

In many truly revolutionary new systems, success depends on restructuring the reporting relationships of users and, often, of technologists needed to support the system. Consequently, many new systems implicitly require managers to change the organization's structure—and thus change an important anchor for identity, stability, and influence on work behavior. When management recognizes this, it strives to anticipate necessary organizational change and synchronize this change with the system implementation. In many cases, though, management has neither recognized the importance of structural change nor avoided it. Traditional systems developers themselves do not have the power to implement this kind of change—even when they see it coming—and line management may not want to tackle the tough political issues involved.

## Tasks and Work Flow

Tasks affected by major new systems may range from routine and repetitive clerical, data-entry, or machine operations tasks to highly variable, skilled, or judgment tasks. Like the technology of new systems, most standard approaches to implementation call for an analysis of the changes required in tasks and work flow. Indeed, the better-designed systems begin with an exhaustive documentation of current work and proceed with studies that create a blueprint of improved work flow..

## Policies, Procedures, and Planning

Most new systems require major changes in measuring work or productivity when, for example, organizations seek to encourage users to focus on certain tasks. When these measurements do not change, the system may become less useful.

## Work Culture and the Psychological Contract

The intangible nature of these forces may often cause the systems' designers and the users' line managers to overlook them—or to oversimplify them—when planning and implementing new automated systems. "Work culture" refers to the informal human relationships and the prevailing values that develop in any work setting. Everyone at work is subject to the informal rules and sanctions that peers and colleagues work by and apply. One's co-workers exert positive or negative pressure—however subtly—regarding the acceptance of new technology, change, and the achievement of positive results. The "psychological contract" refers to the unwritten agreement between an employee and the employer regarding what each person is expected to give and to receive in the work relationship. Here again the terms of the contract may include or exclude provisions requiring an employee to expect and support changes caused by new information technology.

These six areas hold the keys to determining the risk of information systems change and provide the road map for planned implementation. Organization managers must assess the organization's readiness for the new technology and the new technology's impact on the organization. If they seek to anticipate and manage organization change more adequately, managers must consider appropriate methodology.

The approach we propose originates with the development of an organizational assessment of how much the new system will affect and change the organization. Implementors must base this impact assessment upon the answers to questions about the state of each of the major organizational areas. These questions occur during structured interviews with those who "know" the organizations, and managers use information gained from these interviews to create a "gap" analysis. The gap analysis highlights areas of low, medium, or high risk in the user organization's ability to accept change.

During the time that implementors conduct a gap analysis in the user organization, they must also interview managers to ensure that these persons understand the concept of the system, its importance to achieving desired business results, and the organizational context required for successful implementation. Implementors consider the results of both the gap analysis and management reviews when developing an implementation strategy.

For areas of medium to high risk, implementors develop strategies for managing the change and for preparing the organization for the introduction of the system. In cases where the gap assessment finds major risks (large gaps) in most of the key organizational areas, the firm should strongly consider avoiding the project, should undertake a functionally less ambitious project, or should prepare to make changes over time.

## The Importance of a Comprehensive Perspective

This structured approach does not eliminate risk. It does, however, allow managers to develop implementation plans and strategies to reduce unintended consequences. By acknowledging the multifaceted impacts of new technology on the organization, managers can develop a comprehensive perspective of contingencies and possible resources. The following guidelines may help managers with this process.

1. *Acknowledge high stakes.* The potential benefits to the organization of installing and using new technology are as great as the possible calamities. Hence, management should invest the necessary time, human energy, and money to do the job well.

2. *Use an organization-wide framework.* Identify the key tasks performed by the organization as a whole, by its departments, by groups, and by individuals. Can these tasks be performed more effectively by automation or by other means?

3. *Take a design approach rather than a shopping approach.* Computer technology is inherently flexible, especially within a long-term perspective. You can design, configure, and program computers to fit your particular requirements. Use off-the-shelf hardware and software if it suits your needs—it will certainly cost less than specially designed systems. But don't limit your thinking to what's currently available. It makes more sense to design the right system than to purchase the wrong one.

4. *Acknowledge that implementation generates human stress and develop appropriate support and training activities.* Most people have mixed feelings about using a computer. We feel attracted and intrigued by its versatility, convenience, and power as a tool. But, we also feel put off by its encroachment into our lives—and by its apparent mechanization of our human faculties. Mature adults tend to experience some anxiety and resentment about their computer illiteracy and about having to "go back to school." Managers must use careful thought to design learning activities and formats that respond to adult learning needs and that include opportunities for social support among peers. Orientation and training sessions on the new technology must acknowledge and deal with the normal problems of computer stress and anxiety.

5. *Identify and support "bridging persons."* Although a boundary exists between the technical and non-technical parts of organizations, some people can function in either context—and these people are often interested in explaining and relating one world to the other. Management must identify the people who form these bridges and support them—both formally and

informally—for the valuable service they can render the organization as it experiences a computer transition.

## Conclusion

Managers no longer question that computers are changing the work place. Now they must ask how to manage the change so that they can maximize the benefits of the new technology and use it to improve the quality of life for the work force. This article presents a methodology for assessing the risks involved in a technological change and for choosing a strategy to manage that change. Managers have increasingly come to realize how crucial the "people element" is to a successful introduction of new technology. By focusing on both the human and technological aspects of change, managers will help ensure its success.□

## References

Friedrich, G. *Strategic Technical Planning: Shifting the Emphasis From Technological Imperative to Productivity Improvement.* Summary of a presentation made at the Conference on the New Communications Environment: Issues and Directions for Top Management, 1981. Available from the author at Digital Equipment Corporation, 555 Virginia Road, Concord, Massachusetts 01742.

Gibson, C. F., & Schnidman, A. *Information Technology and Organizational Change.* Paper done for Index Systems, Inc., Five Cambridge Center, Cambridge, Massachusetts 02142, 1981.

Lucas, H. C., Jr. *Implementation: The Key to Successful Information Systems.* New York: Columbia University Press, 1981.

Margulies, N., & Colflesh, L. A Socio-Technical Approach to Planning and Implementing New Technology. *Training and Development Journal,* December 1982.

Mumford, E., & Pettigrew, A. *Implementing Strategic Decisions.* New York: Longman, 1975.

Naisbitt, J. *Megatrends: Ten New Directions Transforming Our Lives.* New York: Warner Books, Inc., 1982.

# Future Before You Plan*          Ronald Lippitt

*". . . the future that we prefer . . . should not be limited
by presently perceived frontiers but triggered by the realities of the present and by emerging human technology."*

During the past five years, I have discovered that an activity called
"futuring" can provide an important prelude and adjunct to
strategic planning, to management by objectives (MBO), or to
other approaches to long- and short-range goal setting. In this
article, I will discuss the futuring designs that have emerged as
management strategies.

## Images of Potential *vs.* a Problem-Pain Focus

When graduate students in a social research methods course
recently analyzed 25 problem-solving groups, the students found
that these groups usually began their work by preparing an
inventory of problems or "problem census." Taped recordings
revealed that as the groups' meetings progressed, members
increasingly made statements attributing the causes of problems
to sources outside the group's control. The researchers
interpreted this data as evidence that the groups had developed a
rationale for rejecting problem-solving responsibility. The taped
recordings also revealed an increase in the frequency of words
and phrases that indicate feelings of impotence, futility, and
frustration. The decisions, goals, and plans of the groups seem to
indicate that these persons had devised short-term, symptom-
oriented goals to avoid pain rather than make positive goals for
the future.

These findings led three of us (Fox, Lippitt, & Schindler-
Rainman, 1973) to experiment with what we called "image of
potentiality" exercises. To quote from our work at that time,

> The motivations and perspectives generated by *getting away
> from pain* are not likely to contain the creativity or to
> generate the energy that derives from aspirations generated
> by images of concrete feasible steps toward desirable goals.
> *Images of potential* are not only strong initial sources of
> direction and motivation, but they also provide the basis for

---

© 1983 NTL Institute

* My colleague, Edward Lindaman, died in China in August 1982. A full-time
futurist, Ed was my mentor and inspiration. This chapter is derived from a book in
progress that we were writing together.

continuous feedback, motivation, and renewal. . . . The excitement and rationality of taking initiative toward the future must replace the anxiety associated with reactive coping with confrontation. (1973, p. 4)

## How to Obtain Data for Decisions about the Future

Fox, Schindler-Rainman, and I have found the following seven sources of data useful to our clients who seek to develop strategies for the future.

1. In our culture, we tend to avoid or to neglect *reflection on the past*—whether by countries, by communities, by organizations, or by individuals—as a source of perspectives for thinking about the future. We have had many of our clients participate in a "decades" exercise (Lindamann & Lippitt, 1979, p. 11), with revealing results. In this exercise, a group "brainstorms" on the themes of events they can recall from past decades and reflects on the meanings of those themes—as achievements, mistakes, important values, and methods for coping successfully.

2. A second neglected source of data for planning is a *review of policies and priorities* we have set but have not fully achieved.

3. A third, more familiar source can be found in our *assessments and surveys* of the needs, expectations, and desires of those we serve as clients, consumers, and markets.

4. We can obtain valuable data by reviewing *current operations and achievements*. Unfortunately, we tend to focus on problems and pains instead of on the accomplishments we are proud of. To balance this tendency, my colleagues and I use a "prouds-and-sorries" exercise (Lindamann & Lippitt, 1979, p. 17) in our work with clients.

5. The *policies and goals set by our superiors* provide important information. We must consider them as we set our own goals.

6. The *projections, trend analyses, and predictions* for the future made by "the extrapolators" provide a sixth, familiar source of data.

7. A seventh source of information that helps us to think creatively about the future is a scan of others' goals and successes that compare or relate to our own situations.

Data from all of these sources can trigger our imaginations to project scenarios for the future.

## Preferring *vs.* Predicting

In a presentation made during the NTL Laboratory on Futuring, which was held in Bethel, Maine in July 1982, Edward Lindaman remarked, "If we could only have used a small proportion of the millions of hours humankind has devoted to trying to predict the future to imagining preferred future options, we would be living in a different world today." Mere predictions have not been very valuable. Instead, they have led to a reactive psychology of adapting or fitting in rather than to an active posture of deciding "what we want." In his remarks, Lindaman quoted a leading futurist, John McHale, who has said, "The question is no longer 'Can we change the world?' but rather . . . 'What kind of world do we want?' " (Lindaman & Lippitt, 1979, p. 4).

The Pulitzer Prize-winning biologist Rene Dubos said the following in his last essay, "A Celebration of Life":

> Human beings inevitably alter the source of events and make mockery of any attempt to predict the future from an extrapolation of existing trends. In human affairs, the logical future, determined by past and present conditions, is less important than the *willed future*, which is largely brought about by deliberate choices—made by human free will. Our societies have a good chance of remaining prosperous because they are learning to anticipate, long in advance, the shortages and dangers they might experience in the future if they do not take technologically sound preventive measures. (Dubos, 1982, p. 1)

*Preferred futuring* requires us to examine the data of the past and the present—and the events, developments, and trends (EDTs) in our world, communities, organizations, and personal lives. We must use these data to imagine the *future that we prefer*, which should not be limited by presently perceived frontiers but triggered by the realities of the present and by emerging human technology.

We must then take that commitment to preferred images and implement a plan that makes best use of the human and technical resources of the organization.

## Differentiating Futuring and Planning

In my work with organization leaders and planning teams on futuring and planning, I have been impressed with the different psychological postures, group climates, and types of activity that produce the creativity of futuring and the discipline of planning. Quite a few managers who have worked with both processes have cited some of the distinctions between futuring and planning. Figure 1 shows an incomplete list of the distinctions these managers have noted.

| Futuring | Planning | Futuring | Planning |
|----------|----------|----------|----------|

**Figure 1.   Distinctions Between Futuring and Planning**

| Futuring | Planning | Futuring | Planning |
|----------|----------|----------|----------|
| Right brain | Left brain | Images | Goals |
| Daydream | Decision | Scenarios | Objectives |
| Predicting | Intending | Expansive | Limited |
| Wide-angle | Zoom | Prefer | Commit |
| Prefer | Design | Searching | Defining |
| Creative | Methodical | Hypothesis | Conclusion |
| Fluid | Disciplined | Surveying | Mapping |
| Free-wheeling | Focused | Abstract | Concrete |
| Visionary | Structured | Sensing | Risking |
| Unstructured | Structured | Mind | Brain |
| Field oriented | Linear | Mystic | Engineer |
| Conjecturing | Deriving | Spontaneity | Discipline |
| Guessing | Concluding | Explore | Map |
| Ambiguous | Certain | Direction | Path |
| Open | Committed | Stretching | Condensing |
| Non-judgmental | Evaluative | Inclusive | Selective |
| Qualitative | Quantitative | Forecast | Decide |
| Comprehensive | Bottom-line | Possible | Feasible |
| Rainbow | Black-white-gray | Alternatives | Consequence analysis |
| Intuitive | Systematic | | |

## A Case Example of the Flow of Work from Futuring to Planning

I have chosen to use a decentralized human service system as a model. The process I will describe here resembles what I have used in private-sector systems; in higher education; in communities; in local, state, and federal government units; in professional associations, and in action groups devoted to "causes."

1. *Creating a leadership nucleus.* A group of key persons (i.e., persons with influence and ability) from the horizontal and vertical structure of the human service system participated in a three-hour "what it might be like" session to explore the models of futuring and planning. The criteria for selecting participants included the age, gender, and racial mix of the resulting group, the participants' location in the system, and evidence of leadership initiative and respect.

The three-hour session included experiences in retrieving the past, ranking the "prouds and sorries" of present operations, and a review of a sample of current events, trends, and developments occurring in the society, the community, and the organization.

Then the group, in heterogeneous subgroups of six persons each, took a "future trip" to where they expected to be five years later. The participants observed the things that pleased them, including the behaviors, policies, attitudes, structures, and products that resulted from their five years of work. People used the present tense to describe all the preferred images they could imagine. Obs                            *ons or fantasies, b 

The 30 par 
of the desirec                                                    ɔped
at each table, 
ten priorities. 

We then st                                             ity of
the participar                                            tion
in futuring. V 
leadership gr                                                ıtion
of task forces                                              ı-
priority imag 

2. *Design 1* 
nucleus grou 

a. develop 
organizationa 
b. retrieve,                                                       d
trends mater 
c. prepare                                                       -are-
proud-of" statement from interviews with the historians and leaders of the organization; and
d. train pairs, including nucleus group members, to lead and document the subgroups' futuring sessions.

We prepared futuring kits and conducted sessions with organization staff units present throughout the geographically decentralized system. The board and the top corporate staff participated in futuring sessions.

3. *Creating integrated scenarios of preferred futures.* The nucleus group created a special team of five members and employed two editorial staff writers to read the ranked future images developed from the 40 future shop sessions. These images represented contributions from over 1,500 people. The team selected 25 top-priority images and wrote one-page descriptions of the images that had been achieved or were in the process of being achieved.

The planning staff, executive council, and board used these scenarios to begin work on goal formulation, feasibility analysis, priority sequencing, and potential implementation responsibilities.

4. *Decisions on major goals.* In a Board-staff two-day workshop, small-team task forces converted the preferred future scenarios into detailed goal statements. These statements included measurable criteria for achievement and identified the units in the system responsible for setting and implementing operational goals and designing the action steps and budget proposals. We presented the work of the task forces of the total Board as five-year goal and budget recommendations.

5. *Operational goal setting and implementation.* All the staff units now involved in designing implementation strategies had been involved in futuring sessions. The units had also done EDT analyses, examining trends in their own parts of the system and reviewing their own "prouds and sorries." Goals were not imposed from above; staff units made imaginative contributions.

6. *The continuous process of progress measurement, scanning, and re-futuring.* The planning staff of the organization worked on a pilot basis with several units to develop feasible procedures of "step-wise" progress analysis and reporting. These procedures would help each unit define its own progress toward achievement of the organization's goals. Organization goal monitors were selected for each goal. These persons received, reviewed, and reported on progress and identified outstanding successes that deserved recognition and celebration.

An EDT scanning task force identified the important trends in the environment or in the organization that should form the basis for generating new images of potential and ideas of re-futuring.

### Pitfalls in the Futuring-Planning Process

1. By limiting the futuring-planning process to a small team that attempts to "do all the planning," the organization not only limits its resources of experience and imagination for future imagery, but it also reduces tremendously the level of commitment and energy available to implement the goals.

2. We should not limit our scanning of the environment for trends and activities that potentially have major implications for the future. The futurist literature is exploding, and the current information revolution is generating—for most of us—an overload of data. We must organize our retrieval and analysis efforts and teams.

3. Predictions and preferences may be confusing. By clarifying our preferences, we must examine our values, which often causes us to confront and revise our organization mission statements.

4. Planners should not rush through a priority analysis of preferred images to convert images of potential into concrete, well-formulated goal statements.

5. Right-brain creativity enhances the disciplined process of implementation planning. The diagnostic analysis of alternatives for achieving accepted goals often restricts us to considering "how we have done it." Mind-stretching alternative ideas can free implementation planning to become a productive and creative process.

6. When good action plans have been made, the crucial step of rehearsal before planning may be neglected. In our work on "connecting images to action" (Fox, Lippitt, & Schindler-Rainman, 1973, p. 71; Lindaman & Lippitt, 1979, p. 35), we have tried to look at the large gap between goal plans and skillful action and to provide support for skill development and risk taking.

## Summary Comments

This article complements and supplements the more familiar notions of strategic and long-range planning. Managers can use futuring activities to enlighten and motivate their organizations toward setting positive goals for the future.□

## References

Dubos, R. A Celebration of Life. *Future Tense*, 1982, *4*, 1.

Fox, R., Lippitt, R., & Schindler-Rainman, E. *The Humanized Future: Some New Images.* La Jolla, Calif.: University Associates, 1973. (Out of print, but available from R. Lippitt, 1916 Cambridge Road, Ann Arbor, Michigan 48104.)

Lindaman, E., & Lippitt, R. *Choosing the Future You Prefer.* Washington, D. C.: Development Publications, 1979.

## For Further Reading

Barney, G. O. *The Global 2000 Report to the President of the U. S.,* *Vol. I.* Emsford, N. Y.: Pergamon Press, 1980.

Cornish, E. W. *The Study of the Future: An Introduction to the Art and Science of Understanding and Shaping Tomorrow's World.* Washington, D. C.: World Future Society, 1977.

Feather, F., Ed. *Through the 80's.* Washington, D. C.: World Future Society, 1980.

Harman, W. *An Incomplete Guide to the Future.* Stanford, Calif.: Stanford Portable Press, 1976.

Lindaman, E. B. *Thinking in the Future Tense.* Nashville, Tenn.: Broadman Press, 1978.

Polak, F. *The Image of the Future.* San Francisco: Jossey-Bass, 1972.

Schindler-Rainman, E., & Lippitt, R. *Building the Collaborative Community.* Washington, D. C.: Development Publications, 1980.

Ypsilanti Area Futures, Inc. *Building Together for the Ypsilanti Area's Future, Parts 1 and 2.* Ypsilanti, Mich.: Ypsilanti Area Futures, Inc., 1980.

## Important Futurist Periodicals

*Brain/Mind Bulletin.* Interface Press, P. O. Box 42211, Los Angeles, California 90042.

*Future Survey.* World Future Society, 4916 St. Elmo Avenue, Washington, D. C. 20014.

*The Futurist, a Journal of Forecasts, Trends, and Ideas about the Future.* World Future Society (address above).

*Technology Review.* Massachusetts Institute of Technology, Room 10-140, Cambridge, Massachusetts 02139.

*What's Next.* Congressional Clearinghouse on the Future, Room 3564, House Annex Number 2, Washington, D. C. 20515.

# About the Contributors

**John D. Adams** is a self-employed consultant to individuals, groups, and a wide variety of organizational clients. For the past several years his work has focused on the management of stress and life transitions. Adams is the author of *Transitions* and *Understanding and Managing Stress.*

**Kenneth H. Blanchard** is chairperson of the board of Blanchard Training and Development, Inc. This consulting firm specializes in leadership, management, productivity improvement, and health promotion and is the "home" of Blanchard's best-selling book, *The One-Minute Manager.*

**David L. Bradford** is a lecturer in organizational behavior at Stanford University and the editor of *Exchange: The O.B. Teaching Journal.*

**Nancy Brown** is an independent consultant to a variety of organizations in industry, education, health, government, and the ministry. Her areas of expertise include organization design, long-range planning, management development, and affirmative action.

**Richard E. Byrd** is president of his own organization development consulting firm in Minneapolis. During his career he has held a broad range of responsibilities, including executive, educator, consultant, writer, applied social scientist, and member of the clergy. He has written more than 40 articles and is currently an adjunct faculty member of the Union of Experimental Colleges in Cincinnati, Ohio.

**James R. Cleaveland** is president of Teleconomy, Inc., a management consulting firm in Washington, D.C. that specializes in planning and budgeting, management development, operations review, and organizational analysis.

**Allan R. Cohen** is a professor of management at Babson College in Wellesley, Massachusetts and senior vice-president of Goodmeasure, Inc., a consulting firm in Cambridge, Massachusetts.

**William J. Crockett** is a writer, lecturer, teacher, and consultant in the field of human relationships, organization development, and motivation. He has worked as a manager in both the public and the private sectors.

**Elsie Y. Cross** is an independent consultant and president of Elsie Y. Cross Associates, Inc. in Philadelphia. She has consulted with organizations in Europe and the Caribbean and has worked with major industrial corporations, government agencies, colleges, and universities in the United States on organizational change and development. Her interests include the management of diverse work groups; the elimination of racism, sexism, and other forms of discrimination; and the personal and organizational growth of individuals and teams. Cross served for three years as chairperson of the board for NTL Institute.

**Thomas G. Cummings** is an associate professor of organizational behavior in the graduate school of business administration at the University of Southern California. He is an associate editor of the *Journal of Occupational Behavior* and a former chairperson of the organization development division of the Academy of Management. Cummings has written several books and acted as a consultant in the field of productivity and the quality of work life.

**Rhetaugh Graves Dumas** is a nursing educator, researcher, and administrator. She has served as a faculty member at Yale University and as the deputy director of the National Institute of Mental Health, and is currently a professor in and dean of the school of nursing at the University of Michigan.

**Janice Eddy** is a consultant and entrepreneur specializing in the management of organizations and the diversity of the work force. She develops processes, structures, and leadership skills necessary to maintain an effective, pluralistic organization. Eddy co-founded and managed New Dynamics Associates, a consulting firm in Laconia, New Hampshire.

**Saul Eisen** is an associate professor in and the graduate coordinator of the master's degree program in management at Sonoma State University. He is also a consultant specializing in organization development and sociotechnical systems, and has introduced "computer conferencing" to educators, managers, and consultants.

**Caela Farren** is a management and organization development consultant with Farren and Associates, a firm in McLean, Virginia. She specializes in the field of career development systems.

**David L. Ford, Jr.** is president and founder of D. L. Ford & Associates, a management and organization development consulting firm that specializes in the design of organizational assessment, management development, affirmative action, project evaluation, and career management programs for a variety of public and private organizations. He is also an associate professor of organization behavior and management at the University of Texas at Dallas in Richardson, Texas, and a member of the NTL board of directors.

**Herman Gadon** is a professor of management in the college of business administration at San Diego State University. He has also taught as a visiting professor at the Indian Institute of Management in Calcutta, India, at IMEDE in Lausanne, Switzerland, and at the Institute of Social Studies in the Hague, Netherlands. Co-author of *Effective Behavior in Organizations* and of *Alternative Work Schedules: Integrating Individual and Organizational Needs*, Gadon has also written about flexible working hours, labor relations, decision making, and small-group dynamics. He has acted as a consultant to a variety of organizations, including industrial corporations, health care companies, universities, government agencies- and labor unions.

**Robert T. Golembiewski** is a research professor at the University of Georgia and a distinguished visiting scholar at the University of Calgary in Canada. He has authored or edited more than 40 books and has published approximately 175 scholarly articles. Golembiewski also works as a consultant to clients in business and government.

**Allen Hard** is a senior faculty member at the Federal Executive Institute, an organization that works primarily with career executives in the senior executive service of the federal government.

**Rita Hardiman** is a vice-president and co-founder of New Perspectives, Inc., a firm in Amherst, Massachusetts specializing in organization change programs in racism, sexism, and affirmative action. She has acted as a consultant to a variety of organizations, including unions, public education systems, and large corporations.

**Florence M. Hoylman** is a consultant in organizational planning and development for the Pacific Gas and Electric Company in San Francisco. She is also a partner in Organizational Consultants, Inc., a consulting firm with clients in both the public and private sectors, and a member of the NTL board of directors.

**Bailey W. Jackson** is a consultant on racism, black identity development, and organization change. He is the president and co-founder of New Perspectives, Inc., a firm in Amherst, Massachusetts that specializes in organization change programs in racism, sexism, and affirmative action.

**Kaleel Jamison**, of Kaleel Jamison Associates, is a consultant to a variety of industrial and financial corporations. She specializes in large system change efforts, and has extensive experience in developing high-performance teams that effectively use "self-empowerment" skills, conflict, and competition. Jamison assists organizations in becoming multicultural, using the valuing of differences as the foundation for her work.

**R. Stephen Jenks** is a founding partner of the Portsmouth Consulting Group in New Hampshire and an adjunct professor of organizational behavior at the University of New Hampshire. His consulting practice focuses primarily on high-technology firms. Jenks is co-author of *Designing and Managing Organizations*, and recently served as chairperson of the NTL board of directors.

**Natasha Josefowitz** is a professor of management in the college of business at San Diego State University. The author of *Paths to Power: A Woman's Guide from First Job to Top Executive* and of *Is This Where I Was Going?* (a book of verse about male/female relationships), she is also a consultant and lecturer who specializes in management. Josefowitz is a member of the NTL board of directors.

**Bonnie R. Kasten** is president of Kasten Associates in Newtown Square, Pennsylvania, a firm specializing in helping organizations and people reach agreements through conflict management negotiations and consensus team building. She has lectured throughout the United States on such topics as career management, organization politics, and personal power.

**Beverly L. Kaye** is an organization consultant specializing in career planning and development. She has worked with a variety of business, industrial, health care, educational, and government organizations. Her systems approach to career development is the subject of a film entitled "Career Development: A Plan for All Seasons" and her book, *Up Is Not the Only Way*.

**William A. Kraus** is a consultant for organization development and new technology implementation for General Electric's corporate engineering and manufacturing organization. He specializes in the organization issues involved in implementing such technological innovations as robots, CAD/CAM, and office automation. Kraus has worked with a variety of public- and private-sector organizations, and has published articles in many periodicals and books, including *Collaboration in Organizations: Alternatives to Hierarchy*. He is currently the consulting editor on technology for the *OD Practitioner*.

**Dale G. Lake** is president of the firm Human Systems Development and a part-time research investigator for the institute of social research at the University of Michigan. The author of *Measuring Human Behavior, Managing a State's Education*, and many articles, his expertise lies in organization development, evaluation, and personnel management.

**Zandy B. Leibowitz** is a counseling psychologist on the faculty at the University of Maryland. She has consulted many organizations in setting up career-development systems.

**Kathy M. Lippert** is an organization consultant in private practice in Cincinnati, Ohio. She also teaches many university courses in management and organization, in organization behavior, and in managerial psychology.

**Ronald Lippitt** is a consultant specializing in the field of futuring who has worked with more than 100 communities, churches, social systems, hospitals, human service agencies, and government organizations. He and his colleague Edward Lindaman co-authored the book *Choosing the Future You Prefer*, and Lippitt is completing work on their second book, *Future Before You Plan*. He is a member of the NTL board of directors.

**C. James Maselko** is a senior vice-president of the firm Block-Petrella-Weisbord in Ardmore, Pennsylvania, which specializes in the redesign of work in offices and factories through participative methods. He has consulted with a variety of organizations and currently focuses on the development of conflict resolution models and the transfer of skills in organizations.

**Susan A. Mohrman** is a research scientist at the center for effective organizations at the University of Southern California. She has written about and consulted on productivity and the quality of work life.

**Linda L. Moore** is a psychologist in private practice in Kansas City, Missouri. She is the director and founder of The Women's Institute, an organization in Kansas City that offers individual and group psychotherapy, consulting services, and education and training for individuals seeking to increase their skills in working with women.

**Carol Pierce** is a partner in New Dynamics Associates, a firm in Laconia, New Hampshire specializing in the issues of men and women working together as colleagues. She is a trainer, consultant, and futurist who deals with the processes of change and their effects on individuals, groups, and organizations.

**Larry Porter** is a consultant, trainer, author, and editor. He has specialized in team building, conflict management, management training, and the training of consultants and trainers. He lives in San Francisco and has worked with a variety of organizations in the United States, Canada, Australia, and England.

**W. Brendan Reddy** is a professor of psychology in and director of the community psychology institute at the University of Cincinnati. He specializes in organization development, training, staff development, and research.

**Roger A. Ritvo** is assistant dean of and an associate professor in the school of applied social sciences at Case Western Reserve University. He works as a consultant to human service and health systems, both in the United States and abroad. Ritvo has authored many books and articles on the management of health and social services, public policy analysis, hospital administration and governance, program evaluation, and organization development and behavior. He served as senior health policy analyst on the immediate staff of the Secretary of Health and Human Services in the Carter and Reagan administrations, and is a member of the NTL board of directors.

**Alice G. Sargent** is a consultant who currently works with E. I. Dupont de Nemours, the Federal Executive Institute, the Australian Institute of Management, and the Agency for International Development. She has consulted with the Overseas Private Investment Corporation and with a variety of governmental agencies and large corporations. Sargent teaches in several educational institutions and was previously director of the master's degree program in business administration at Trinity College. She has authored two books, *Beyond Sex Roles* and *The Androgynous Manager*, and serves on the board of the Organizational Development Network.

**Edgar H. Schein** is the Sloan Fellows professor of organizational psychology and management in the Sloan school of management at the Massachusetts Institute of Technology. He has taught, done research, and worked as a consultant for more than 25 years.

**Nancy Schlossberg** is a professor in the counseling and personnel services department at the University of Maryland. She has written extensively about adult and career development.

**Craig Eric Schneier** is an organization consultant based in Washington, D.C. and a professor of personnel/human resource management and organization behavior in the college of business and management at the University of Maryland.

**Ava Albert Schnidman** is a partner of Deltech Consulting Group, Inc., a firm in Simsbury, Connecticut, and an independent consultant specializing in organization development and sociotechnical systems. She obtained her experience in implementing new technology from both her work as a consultant and as a line manager for one of the largest financial institutions in the world.

**Charles Seashore** is a consulting social psychologist based in Washington, D.C. and chairperson of the group psychotherapy training program at the Washington School of Psychiatry. His professional practice concentrates on adult education, life transitions, organization development, and applied social research.

**Morley Segal** is a professor of public administration at the American University in Washington, D.C. He is also a partner in

Berkeley Developmental Resources, Inc., a management consulting firm in Annapolis, Maryland.

**John J. Sherwood** is president of Organizational Consultants, Inc., a San Francisco-based firm of management consultants who specialize in increasing the effectiveness of the "people side" of organizations. He has consulted with a variety of clients from every sector and was for 17 years a professor in the Krannert graduate school of management at Purdue University.

**Gail Silverman** is a consultant who has worked with a variety of public- and private-sector organizations and educational and health-care systems for 15 years. She has taught courses and conducted workshops in human relations and management, and also counsels individuals and families.

**Peter B. Vaill** is a professor of human systems in the school of government and business administration at The George Washington University. He has also consulted and trained with a variety of organizations in both the public and private sectors. His work includes such areas as strategic planning, organization development, and the philosophy of social science, and he created the theory of high-performing systems. Vaill has authored many articles that have made new concepts of management, leadership, and human systems relevant to practitioners.

**David Wagner** is an independent organization development consultant affiliated with the firm New Dynamics Associates and with the Vermont Consulting Network. He has worked extensively with the issues of men and women working in large corporations. His consulting practice deals mainly with small and medium-sized business and health organizations.

**Nicholas W. Weiler** is manager of consulting practices and manpower for General Electric's (GE) corporate engineering and manufacturing organization. He has authored the book *Reality and Career Planning* and has spent 20 years doing human resources work with GE in such areas as executive assessment, succession planning, career strategies counselling, and organization development regarding the introduction of new technology.

**Marvin R. Weisbord** is a senior vice-president with Block-Petrella-Weisbord in Ardmore, Pennsylvania, a firm that specializes in the redesign of work in offices and factories through participative methods. He has consulted with a variety of businesses, medical schools, and hospitals, and is the author of *Organization Diagnosis: A Workbook of Theory and Practice.*